THE IDEAS INDUSTRY

THE IDEAS

INDUSTRY

DANIEL W. DREZNER

OXFORD
UNIVERSITY PRESS

OXFORD
UNIVERSITY PRESS

Oxford University Press is a department of the University of Oxford. It furthers
the University's objective of excellence in research, scholarship, and education
by publishing worldwide. Oxford is a registered trade mark of Oxford University
Press in the UK and certain other countries.

Published in the United States of America by Oxford University Press
198 Madison Avenue, New York, NY 10016, United States of America.

CIP data is on file at the Library of Congress
ISBN 978–0–19–026460–4

1 3 5 7 9 8 6 4 2
Printed by Edwards Brothers Malloy, United States of America

This book is dedicated to the teachers at Avon High School and Williams College who nudged me into something resembling a writer:

Evelyn Blitzer, Robert Buckley, Roger Dennis, Renata Kadden, Ken Lukasiewicz, Janet Schwartz, Alicia Willet, Sam Crane, Robert Whitesell, and especially Jim Shepard.

The idea is not a substitute for work; and work, in turn, cannot substitute for or compel an idea, just as little as enthusiasm can. Both, enthusiasm and work, and above all both of them jointly, *can entice the idea.*

— Max Weber, "Science as a Vocation"

CONTENTS

—◆—

ACKNOWLEDGMENTS

—◆—

This was a fast, nerve-wracking book to write. It was fast because soon after starting I realized that I had been mulling over *The Ideas Industry*'s core themes for well over a decade. The arguments, evidence, and anecdotes contained in these pages emerged from over two decades of experience navigating the modern marketplace of ideas. It was nerve-wracking because, halfway through *The Ideas Industry*'s first draft, I recognized that this was only nominally a book about international relations. Although the subject of this book has been the marketplace of foreign policy ideas, the arguments made herein are really about changes in American politics. Like a traditional public intellectual, I am making arguments a bit afield from my principal area of expertise.

This new terrain leaves me even more grateful than usual to the many people who have assisted me during the writing of this book. I first must thank David McBride and Niko Pfund at Oxford University Press for their early encouragement and enthusiastic support when I had merely a vague proposal. I am also grateful to Kathleen Weaver, Cat Boyd, Rob Wilkinson, Mary Harper, and the copy editor Heather Hambleton for shepherding this book from computer files to print.

I have been the beneficiary of considerable institutional support while writing this book. At the Fletcher School, Dean James Stavridis and Academic Dean Steven Block have created a vibrant space for me to think about intellectual affairs. I am also grateful to my Fletcher colleagues Zeynep Bulutgil, Nancy Hite-Rubin, Kelly Sims Gallagher, Sulmaan Khan, Michael Klein, Eileen Babbitt, Ian Johnstone, Bhaskar Chakravorti, and Jette Knudsen for their feedback and insights. Rachel Brown, Sheri Callender, Paulette Folkins, Meg Guliford, Aaron Melaas, Estefania Marchan, Emily Morgenstern, Melanie Reed, and Mohannad Al-Suwaidan all provided invaluable administrative and research support. As a nonresident senior fellow at the Brookings Institution, I profited greatly from the feedback of Bruce Jones, Tom Wright, and Tamara Cofman Wittes. At the Chicago Council on Global Affairs, Dina Smeltz held my hand through some of the public opinion discussions.

Foundation support, a key driver behind the Ideas Industry, was also a key driver behind the writing of *The Ideas Industry*. The Michael and Andrea Leven Foundation provided crucial financial support during the research and drafting of this book. The Carnegie Corporation's Rigor and Relevance Initiative provided a grant to the Fletcher School and helped inform my thinking as I was revising the manuscript. The Rockefeller Foundation provided me a residency at their Bellagio Center to put the finishing touches on the book.

Between 2014 and 2016 I organized a series of four Ideas Industry conferences at Fletcher on various dimensions of the marketplace of ideas. The conferences themselves, as well as the informal conversations surrounding the panels, were invaluable to me as I was getting a grip on what made the modern Ideas Industry tick. I am grateful to everyone who participated and assisted in those conferences. I also inflicted an embryonic version of the book manuscript on my Spring 2016 Politics of Statecraft students. I am grateful for their feedback, particularly the trenchant points made by Denise Baltuskonis, Jon Cheatwood, Kate Jordan, Ian Kapuza, Matt Keller, Kerney Perlik, Seth Turner, and Mike Wackenreuter.

Many of the ideas, notions, and actual paragraphs in the text had their origins in blog posts and essays for other outlets. I thank Benjamin Pauker at *Foreign Policy*, Susan Glasser and Blake Hounshell at *Politico*, Evan Goldstein at the *Chronicle of Higher Education*, and Mike Madden and Adam B. Kushner at the *Washington Post* for their editorial guidance. They all made me look like a better writer than I actually am. A nascent and condensed version of Chapter 5 appeared in the December 2015 issue of *International Journal*. I am grateful to the editors of that journal for releasing their copyright.

I talked, in formal and not-so-formal interviews, with a variety of participants in the Ideas Industry to get a better grasp on my subject matter. I am indebted to Gideon Rose, Fareed Zakaria, Niall Ferguson, and Joseph Nye in particular for setting aside time to answer my many queries. I appreciate the correspondence and conversations I had with Franklin Foer, Nicholas Kristof, Jeffrey Sachs, and Nassim Taleb. The 209 respondents to my elite survey also made this project much, *much* easier, and I thank those very busy people for taking the time to answer my questionnaire.

I am far from the only person interested in this subject. In the process of writing this book I received extraordinarily useful feedback from a variety of close readers. Bethany Albertson, Deborah Avant, Nada Bakos, Bear Braumoeller, Josh Busby, Kristin Butcher, Stephanie Carvin, Charli Carpenter, Brad DeLong, Steve Del Rosso, Michael Desch, Rob Farley, Henry Farrell, Justin Fox, Suzanne Fry, David Gordon, Heather Hurlburt, Leslie Johns, Sulmaan Khan, Ron Krebs, Michael Horowitz, Michael Levi, Jacob Levy, Jonathan Kirshner, Kate McNamara, Jeffrey Isaac, Jonathan Monten, Daniel Nexon, Milena Rodban, Mary Sarotte, Elizabeth Saunders, Laura Seay, Randy Schweller, Erin Simpson, Dina Smeltz, Mike Tierney, Jill Ultan, Lynn Vavreck, and Diana Wueger provided comments that made this book much better. Any remaining faults are strictly my own.

Finally, I must thank my family. Being a participant and an observer of the Ideas Industry often meant being away from home at this conference or that symposium or another workshop. Figuring out the equilibrium between attending such functions and attending to my family was learned through the painful process of trial and error. I will never be able to thank Erika, Sam, and Lauren fully for the patience and kindness that they showed me every time I left on a trip or holed myself up to revise. They have taught me what is obvious to most people but is fuzzy to most academics: there is far more to life than ideas.

PART I

Introduction: The Transmogrification

Nothing, in my opinion, is more deserving of our attention than the intellectual and moral associations of America.

— Alexis de Tocqueville

THE MARKETPLACE FOR FOREIGN policy ideas in the United States has changed. Foreign affairs intellectuals are constantly trying to insert new notions about American power and purpose into public debates. The best recipe for propagating new ideas, however, is evolving in ways that can affect even the most powerful people in the world.

To get a sense of these changes, consider the foreign policy musings of presidents Barack Obama and Donald Trump. It would be safe to say that these two people treat ideas *very* differently. What is interesting is how similarly the marketplace of ideas has treated both of them.

When Obama was elected, the first African-American president was heralded as the rare politician who was also a true intellectual.[1] He was a law professor and respected author before running for national office. A cornerstone of his first presidential campaign was a powerful critique of existing foreign policy. He called for "a new vision of leadership" in foreign affairs, "a vision that draws from the past but is not bound by outdated thinking."[2] He was nonetheless receptive enough to opposing points of view to espouse a "team of rivals" approach to his administration. He retained Robert Gates, George W. Bush's last secretary of

defense, to serve in his cabinet. He appointed Hillary Clinton, his fierc-
est party rival, to be his secretary of state. Beyond his cabinet, Obama
made a concerted effort to reach out to opinion columnists and foreign
policy experts—including those who were not ideological soulmates.[3]
As an incoming president, Obama wanted to engage with the marketplace of foreign policy ideas.

During his time in office, however, the president grew increasingly
frustrated with his attempts to affect the dominant foreign policy narrative. The phrase that seemed to encapsulate his first term's foreign policy
was "leading from behind," used by an unnamed Obama advisor to describe America's role in the 2011 Libya intervention.[4] It invited considerable scorn within the foreign policy community. The foreign policy
phrase that went viral during his second term was Obama's own: "Don't
do stupid shit."[5] Critics derided the slogan as offering a blinkered message about American grand strategy.[6] Even Hillary Clinton criticized
that mantra, saying in an interview, "Great nations need organizing
principles, and 'Don't do stupid stuff' is not an organizing principle."[7]
The president's continued wariness of military intervention—which
the Libya aftermath only intensified—led him to spurn calls for a more
robust military response to myriad crises in the Middle East. Obama's
repeated assurances that all was well on the foreign policy front clashed
with the rise of the Islamic State, a revanchist Russia, and a broken
Middle East. Many critics responded to Obama's calm by loudly insist-
ing that the world was on fire.[8]

The rising tide of criticism from the foreign policy community
rankled the president and his national security staff. Throughout his
time in office, Obama was a voracious reader of opinion journalism
even if he disagreed with much of it.[9] This was particularly true in
the area of foreign policy. And as one of his former National Security
Council staffers observed, "whenever there is a wise man consensus in
Washington, [Obama's] first instinct is to defy it."[10] His staff grew increasingly irritated with the animating ideas of Washington's foreign
policy establishment. Obama's deputy national security advisor and
foreign policy amanuensis, Ben Rhodes, vented, "The discourse in
Washington just becomes like a self-licking ice cream cone of maximal-
ist foreign policy. . . . That's what gets your think-tank paper read."[11] In

another interview, Rhodes referred derisively to the DC foreign policy community as "The Blob."[12]

By the end of his second term, Obama's frustrations with the marketplace of foreign policy ideas had boiled over. This was reflected in his comments to *The Atlantic*'s Jeffrey Goldberg on various aspects of American foreign affairs. What stood out in the president's statements were the frustrations he felt when he dissented from the foreign policy community. In August 2013, as his administration edged closer to launching military strikes on Syria, Obama felt trapped by the foreign policy consensus that presidents must demonstrate resolve. His refusal to use force vexed many foreign policy observers—including some within his own administration. Goldberg concluded that "Obama generally believes that the Washington foreign-policy establishment, which he secretly disdains, makes a fetish of 'credibility'—particularly the sort of credibility purchased with force."[13] Obama was also candid about how he felt the foreign policy community's dominant set of ideas constrained him as president:

> There's a playbook in Washington that presidents are supposed to follow. It's a playbook that comes out of the foreign-policy establishment. And the playbook prescribes responses to different events, and these responses tend to be militarized responses. Where America is directly threatened, the playbook works. But the playbook can also be a trap that can lead to bad decisions. In the midst of an international challenge . . . you get judged harshly if you don't follow the playbook, even if there are good reasons why it does not apply. [14]

In the end, Obama took great pride in ignoring the conventional wisdom on using force in Syria. But what is interesting is Obama's acknowledgment to Goldberg that his defiance of foreign policy intellectuals cost him politically. Indeed, his Syria decisions revived an intense debate about the importance of credibility and reputation in international affairs that remains unsettled.[15] This might explain why moments like Syria were the exception rather than the rule during Obama's presidency. More often than not, Obama followed the playbook when it came to the American use of force.[16] As president, he tried to shape the marketplace of foreign policy ideas—but he also found his policies constrained by that market in ways he did not like.

Obama articulated his discontents at the same time that Donald Trump was bucking prognostications that he would fade away as a presidential candidate. In marked contrast to Obama, Trump reveled in running one of the most heterodox foreign policy campaigns in the last half-century. While the New York real estate mogul lacked command of foreign policy detail, he had forged a consistent zero-sum worldview on how international relations worked.[17] He adopted a slogan of "America First" to explain his foreign policy beliefs, despite its association with 1930s isolationism. Trump disparaged numerous US-created multilateral regimes as antithetical to the national interest, including NATO, the World Trade Organization, and the United Nations.[18] He argued that America's allies needed to pay the United States more for security provision. He speculated that South Korea, Saudi Arabia, and Japan should develop nuclear weapons to combat their security threats—even as he decried nuclear proliferation as the world's greatest threat. And he believed that the liberal international economic order needed to be radically revised in America's favor.[19]

Trump engendered considerable blowback from a wide array of elites. In his initial interviews with the *Washington Post* and *New York Times*, Trump displayed little understanding of world politics; follow-up interviews on the topic suggested little in the way of learning.[20] His stumblings and fumblings on questions of foreign policy during the campaign were legion and fostered a narrative of incompetence that he had to battle throughout the campaign.[21] Economists, political scientists, and historians spurned Trump en masse.[22] Foreign affairs analysts spanning the ideological spectrum panned his pronouncements.[23] Realists, the foreign policy experts who should have been the most sympatico with Trump's worldview, shunned him.[24] The Economist Intelligence Unit went so far as to label Trump one of the top ten geopolitical risks for 2016.[25]

Liberals within the foreign policy establishment were unanimous in their condemnation of Trump's rhetoric. Conservative intellectuals, however, were equally vehement in their critiques.[26] Leading conservative outlets such as the *National Review* published issues dedicated to opposing Trump. Republican columnists such as David Brooks, Robert

Kagan, Charles Krauthammer, Max Boot, and George Will stated that they would never support Trump. Most conservative think tanks distanced themselves from his policies.[27] In March 2016 more than 120 GOP foreign policy professionals signed an open letter declaring unequivocally that they would not support Trump in the general election.[28] Similar GOP petitions followed over the next seven months. Even as the GOP's congressional leadership acquiesced to Trump, its foreign policy community remained implacably opposed to his campaign.[29] As Ross Douthat noted, "the conservative intelligentsia—journalists, think-tankers, and academics—has been conspicuous in its resistance."[30]

If America's foreign policy community judged Trump harshly, he judged them right back. During the Republican primary, his campaign rejected most outreach efforts by GOP-friendly think tanks to help tutor him on questions of world politics. In his own rhetoric, Trump explicitly disavowed the value of existing foreign policy expertise. In an April 2016 foreign policy speech, Trump argued, "It's time to shake the rust off America's foreign policy. It's time to invite new voices and new visions into the fold." He went on to state that his foreign policy advisors would not be "those who have perfect résumés but very little to brag about except responsibility for a long history of failed policies and continued losses at war."[31] By the end of the general election campaign, Trump had framed the foreign policy debate as one between populist nationalists and elite globalists, warning about "a small handful of special global interests rigging the system."[32]

In making these arguments, Trump openly questioned mainstream narratives about American foreign policy—with some measure of success. A few conservative commentators welcomed Trump's questioning of GOP foreign policy orthodoxy.[33] Senator Bob Corker, the chair of the Senate Foreign Relations Committee, praised Trump for "challenging the foreign policy establishment that has been here for so long." The *New York Times*' Maggie Haberman and David Sanger noted that "what made Mr. Trump's statements most remarkable was that the bedrock principles of American security were being debated at all."[34] Henry Kissinger concluded, "The Trump phenomenon is in large part a reaction of Middle America to attacks on its values by intellectual and academic communities."[35]

Politico's Michael Grunwald concluded, "When a major-party nominee calls Mexicans rapists, suggests a global trade war would be no big deal and argues that vaccines harm children, he's shorting the entire marketplace of ideas."[36] But Trump's rhetoric was more complicated than that. Zeynep Tufekci, a scholar studying social movements, argued that Trump's populist campaign had profoundly affected the contours of public debate. She concluded, "Mr. Trump doesn't only speak outrageous falsehoods; he also voices truths . . . that have been largely ignored, especially by Republican elites." Indeed, Trump's successful campaign led some to conclude that the dominance of neoconservative thought in Republican foreign policy discourse was coming to an end.[37] Many conservatives worried that the entire intellectual edifice of their party had collapsed.[38] While Obama keenly felt the constraints of the marketplace of ideas, Trump delighted in disrupting every norm and custom in the foreign policy playbook. Whether this will persist throughout the Trump administration remains a very open question.

The tales of Obama and Trump suggest two things. First, the marketplace of ideas can impose constraints on even the most powerful actors. Second, the marketplace of ideas for foreign policy might not be working perfectly.

We are at a curious moment in the marketplace of foreign policy ideas. It is the best of times for thought leaders. It is the worst of times for public intellectuals. It is the most disorienting of times for everyone else.

These terms need to be unpacked. By "marketplace of ideas," I mean the array of intellectual outputs and opinions about foreign affairs, and the extent to which policymakers and publics embrace those ideas. When a scholar publishes a book explaining why American foreign policy needs a rethink, that book contributes to the marketplace of ideas. When a think tank issues a report evaluating some aspect of statecraft, that report adds to the marketplace of ideas.[39] When a global brand strategist gives a TED talk about how the country's climate change policy should be managed like a hedge fund, that argument will probably find its way into the marketplace of ideas.

For the purposes of this book, when I refer to "public intellectuals," I mean experts who are versed and trained enough to be able to comment on a wide range of public policy issues. As Friedrich von Hayek put it, public intellectuals are "professional secondhand dealers in ideas."[40] The public intellectual serves a vital purpose in democratic discourse: exposing shibboleths masquerading as accepted wisdom. Public intellectuals are critics, and critiquing those who hawk bad policy wares is a necessary function in a democracy. A public intellectual's greatest contribution to the marketplace of ideas is to point out when an emperor has no clothes. When public intellectuals lose their prestige, it becomes that much easier for politicians or charlatans to advance an idea into the public consciousness, regardless of its intrinsic merits, through sheer, unflagging will.

The provenance of the term "thought leader" is far more recent than "public intellectual." Nevertheless, a quick glance at Google Trends reveals that by 2012, the former term had eclipsed the latter in terms of usage.[41] How is a thought leader distinct from a public intellectual? *New York Times* columnist David Brooks—a man thoroughly steeped in this milieu—archly defined one as a "sort of a highflying, good-doing yacht-to-yacht concept peddler."[42] Brooks's wry description might be entertaining, but it is insufficient for our purposes. The private sector talks a lot about "thought leadership," without ever being precise in its meaning.

For the purposes of this book, a thought leader is an intellectual evangelist. Thought leaders develop their own singular lens to explain the world, and then proselytize that worldview to anyone within earshot. Both public intellectuals and thought leaders engage in acts of intellectual creation, but their style and purpose are different. Public intellectuals know enough about many things to be able to point out intellectual charlatans. Thought leaders know one big thing and believe that their important idea will change the world.

Table 1 illustrates the differences between the two archetypes. To adopt the language of Isaiah Berlin, public intellectuals are foxes and thought leaders are hedgehogs. The former are skeptics; the latter are true believers. The former is a critic; the latter is a creator. A public intellectual is ready, willing, and able to tell you everything that is wrong with everyone else's worldview. A thought leader is desperate to tell you everything that is right about his own creed. To the extent that they are intellectuals, Barack Obama functions as a public intellectual and Donald Trump is the brassiest thought leader in existence.

TABLE 0.1 Public Intellectuals vs. Thought Leaders

Public Intellectuals	Thought Leaders
Critics	Creators
Foxes	Hedgehogs
Skeptics	Evangelists
Deductive	Inductive
Prioritizes expertise	Prioritizes experience
Pessimists	Optimists

Public intellectuals and thought leaders are not completely different animals; both sets of intellectuals truck, barter, and exchange in the world of ideas. The dichotomy between the two categories is as much one of style as substance. Indeed, at different times and in different moments, the same person can function as a public intellectual and then a thought leader.[43] As Berlin acknowledged in his famous essay on foxes and hedgehogs, pushing a binary distinction too hard is unwise. But he also noted that, if true, it offers "a starting point for genuine investigation."[44] Dividing people into public intellectuals and thought leaders clarifies our understanding of the modern marketplace of ideas. And this book will argue that the modern marketplace of ideas benefits all intellectuals, but it benefits thought leaders far more than others.

Why is this happening? What does it mean?

What is happening is that the marketplace of ideas has turned into the Ideas Industry. The twenty-first-century public sphere is bigger, louder, and more lucrative than ever before. This industrial revolution in the public sphere has been going on for some time now. David Brooks argued fifteen years ago that the intellectual class no longer stays aloof from the market, society, or the state, as the contributors to *Partisan Review* did in the 1950s.[45] *Foreign Policy* annually publishes a list of the top hundred global thinkers, sometimes throwing gala events to roll it out. A surge of high-level panels, conference circuits, and speaker confabs allows intellectuals to mix with other members of the political, economic, and cultural elite in a way that would have been inconceivable a half century ago. There has been an explosion of American "Big Idea" events—TED, South by Southwest, the Aspen Ideas Festival, the Milken Institute's Global Conference, anything sponsored by *The Atlantic*—that tap "provocative" thinkers to sate the curiosity of attendees. This parallels a global surge in big think confabs, ranging from the World Economic Forum at Davos to the Boao Forum for Asia to the Valdai Discussion Club. The number of platforms, forums, and outlets eager to broadcast provocative ideas has also exploded.

Obviously, the dizzying array of new outlets has played a role in turning the marketplace of ideas into the Ideas Industry. This surge in demand has benefited the entire intellectual class, but there has been another interesting effect. The Ideas Industry now rewards thought leaders far more than public intellectuals. This is due to three interlocking trends that configure the modern marketplace of ideas: the erosion of trust in authority, the polarization of American politics, and the dramatic increase in economic inequality.

There has been a slow-motion *erosion of trust in prestigious institutions* and professions for the past half century. The litany of fiascoes stretch back as far as the Vietnam War and continue through Operation Iraqi Freedom into the present day. After a post-9/11 spike in trust, the rest of the twenty-first century has witnessed a steady decline of trust in authority—and authority figures. This is particularly true in foreign affairs. This degradation of trust makes the Ideas Industry a more competitive environment. In a world in which authority figures are respected, the gatekeepers of intellectual guilds can restrict entry with prerequisites like degrees or books or relevant experience. As the power of those gatekeepers has declined, the ability of thought leaders to bypass traditional sources of authority has risen. The democratization of the marketplace of ideas has made it much harder for traditional public intellectuals to argue from authority. This allows for new concepts to emerge but also makes it more difficult to expose bad ideas.

The *polarization of American society*—and American political institutions—is another phenomenon affecting the marketplace of ideas. The creation of parallel, segmented audiences that will support ideologically pure intellectuals has led to the emergence of new kinds of thought leaders. It is now possible for conservative intellectuals to attend Hillsdale College, intern at The Heritage Foundation, work at

Breitbart, win a Koch grant, author a book for Regnery Publishing, secure a contract from a conservative speakers bureau, and then talk about it on Fox News. They can thrive in an information ecosystem devoid of contrary points of view. Replace the names—say, Soros for Koch—and liberals can do much the same. As more money gets funneled into advancing polarizing political agendas, the opportunities for partisans on both sides to profit from this part of the Ideas Industry will continue to grow.

The most important trend, however, has been *the growth in economic inequality* and the increasing importance of wealthy benefactors as a force in the marketplace of ideas. The massive accumulation of wealth at the top end of the income spectrum has created a new source of funding for the generation and promotion of new ideas. As America's elite has gotten richer and richer, they can afford to do anything they want. It turns out a surprising number of them want to go back to school—or, rather, make school go to them. A century ago, America's plutocrats converted their wealth into university endowments, think tanks, or philanthropic foundations. Today's wealthy set up their own intellectual salons and publishing platforms—and they are not hands-off about the intellectual output of their namesakes. They also attend high-profile Big Idea get-togethers. Intellectuals will fiercely compete to get on the radar of a wealthy benefactor, because of the financial resources potential patrons can bring to the table. Thought leaders will have an advantage over public intellectuals in pushing ideas that resonate with plutocrats.

These three factors have made it increasingly profitable for thought leaders to hawk their wares to both billionaires and a broader public. Successful intellectuals are superstars with their own brands, sharing a space previously reserved for moguls, celebrities, and athletes. Such a claim sounds like hyperbole—until one sees prize-winning authors Niall Ferguson and Ayaan Hirsi Ali supplanting celebrities on the cover of tabloids, Nobel Prize-winning economist Paul Krugman cameoing in big budget films, and political scientist Melissa Harris-Perry making headlines for leaving MSNBC.[46]

These forces help to explain how thought leaders are extolled at the same time that public intellectuals can be disparaged. In many ways, this shift has been a long time coming. The rise of thought leaders plays into how human beings are hard-wired to process ideas. A stylistic element that matters greatly for success in the modern Ideas Industry is confidence. Cognitive psychology shows that human beings prefer confident predictions over probabilistic ones, even though all of the empirical evidence says that the latter approach yields better predictions and more resilient ideas. As Philip Tetlock and Dan Gardner, the authors of *Superforecasting*, note, "continuous self-scrutiny is exhausting, and the *feeling* of knowing is seductive."[47] Thought leaders excel and public intellectuals suffer in projecting the supreme confidence that their ideas are absolutely correct. This confidence is cognitively satisfying to audiences; even critics of thought leaders acknowledge the seductiveness of their confident sales pitch.

What does all of this mean for the public sphere? Since none of these tectonic forces show any signs of abating, neither will the incentives of the new Ideas Industry. This does not thrill everyone. Many have decried the "corporatization" of intellectuals. In the intellectual argot of today, "marketplace of ideas" sounds better than "Ideas Industry."[48] The former term evokes a skilled artisan, the latter a factory filled with mindless toil. Craftsmanship sounds better than industrialization. Thought leaders are mocked far more widely than public intellectuals.[49] It would be easy to infer that this transformation is a bad thing.

But to extend the metaphor, it is worth remembering that the real Industrial Revolution led to an explosion of mass affluence as well as Dickensian horror stories.[50] In the world of ideas, reality is far more complicated than "It was better before." The notion that thought leaders cheapen public discourse is an odd critique. They are responding to a genuine thirst for new ideas—and valid reasons for the decline of trust in the foreign policy establishment. It is churlish for critics to complain for decades about the coarsening of American culture and then act all snippy when a subculture emerges that yearns for something more. Anyone who cares about the world of ideas should never be upset that interest is on the upswing.

There is a great deal of good that can come from the twenty-first-century Ideas Industry. It is surely noteworthy that a strong demand has emerged for new ideas and vibrant ways of thinking about the world. But like any revolution, there are winners and there are losers. These trends also handicap more traditional purveyors of ideas housed in universities or think tanks. Public intellectuals rely more on sources of funding that have either plateaued or abated. Some of these institutions have not adapted as quickly to the new ecosystem of ideas, even though some individuals housed within these institutions have. The result—like previous revolutions in agriculture and manufacturing—is a massive churn in the intellectual class.

It is not surprising that some who suffer from this intellectual creative destruction lament the current state of affairs—but it doesn't mean that their criticisms are entirely wrong. There are some vaguely troublesome rumblings buried within this phenomenon. The most obvious issue is whether the Ideas Industry generates anything in the way of a critical rebuttal to the ideas being propagated. When one watches a TED video, for example, all one sees is the sales pitch. More than half the TED lectures end with a standing ovation; the reactions are all affirmation without any constructive criticism.[51] Yet it is how ideas survive the gauntlet of criticism that really matters. For foreign policy ideas in particular, it would be better to have a public sphere that pokes, prods, and generally stress-tests each New New Thing.

What is needed is a symbiosis—not just TED talks, but TED talks with discussants. The cure for what ails the Ideas Industry is not a return to more powerful gatekeepers—it is more discord and more debate. Indeed, public intellectuals are now needed more than ever. They serve a new and vital purpose. They need to analyze and criticize popular thought leaders. Public intellectuals are necessary to filter the quality thinkers from the charlatans.

The marketplace of ideas affects far more people than just intellectuals. Despite loud laments about the anti-intellectualism of American society, ideas matter a great deal to US policy and politics. As *Washington Post* columnist George Will noted once, "although many intellectuals consider American political theory unsophisticated, it is more central to political practices than theory is in other countries."[52] One could argue that foreign policy is where ideas have mattered the most. From the Cold War doctrine of containment, to the constant tug of war between liberals and realists, to the rise and fall of neoconservatism, to the effect of neoclassical economics on foreign economic policy, ideas have profoundly affected the conduct of foreign affairs. One recent academic assessment concluded, "From the beginning of the twentieth century to the beginning of the twenty-first, the United States has had the most intellectual foreign policy in the world."[53]

Intellectuals have played a vital role in the development of American foreign policy, and will continue to do so into the future. Even the most erudite officials are hard-pressed to think deep thoughts; the daily grind crowds everything else out. Sandy Berger, Bill Clinton's last national security advisor, noted, "Washington is a town in which the urgent always overtakes the important."[54] Berger's successor at the job, Condoleezza Rice, once told me that a policymaker's intellectual capital stock starts depreciating the moment after taking office. As a candidate, Barack Obama was able to challenge dominant foreign policy narratives; as president, Obama was more constrained. For good or for ill, policymakers need the marketplace of ideas to replenish, articulate, and challenge the reasons why they do what they do in world politics.[55]

Big ideas and the intellectuals who articulate them are especially worthy of scrutiny as they get closer to those who wield power. The possibility of officials using or abusing the marketplace of ideas is very real. George W. Bush's administration became such a forceful promoter of the democratic peace that one of the theory's leading scholars admitted, "Many advocates of the democratic peace may now feel rather like many atomic scientists did in 1945. . . . Our creation has been perverted."[56] Realists expressed similar dismay at the Bush administration's appropriation of realpolitik rhetoric.[57]

When those in power are not exploiting ideas to justify their actions, some intellectuals are eager to do so in the service of power. Some have defended the intellectuals' alliance with the powerful. These arguments range from the utility of offering expert counsel on thorny policy questions to the more critical task of speaking truth to power.[58] These are powerful arguments, but history offers a sobering rejoinder. As Richard Hofstadter acknowledged in *Anti-Intellectualism in American Life*, "there is no way of guaranteeing that an intellectual class will be discreet and restrained in the use of its influence."[59] There is an entire genre of work consisting of intellectuals bashing other intellectuals for a catalog of political sins.[60] In the twentieth century, intellectuals justified the most heinous actions imaginable when they got close to power.[61] This century is little better. In the wake of the September 11 terrorist attacks, many conservative intellectuals resuscitated arguments in favor of American empire. Intellectuals can cause just as much harm as good in the world of foreign policy; the closer one is to power, the more tempting it is to justify or excuse immoral actions. As Janice Gross Stein has warned her fellow international relations scholars, "we will be seduced by the proximity to power and shade what we say in order to retain access."[62] It is precisely because the Ideas Industry is intermixed with the rich and the powerful that it merits explication.

One of the difficulties with dissecting the marketplace of ideas is that our analytical tools are limited. Even in a world of big data, assessing trends in the public sphere remains a rudimentary and impressionistic endeavor. I will focus on the areas that I know best—the world of American economic and foreign policy discourse. To describe the evolution and effects of the Ideas Industry, I will rely on extant commentary about the state of the public sphere, peer-reviewed research into the drivers behind the modern Ideas Industry, public opinion data, and accounts of particular public intellectuals and thought leaders. I also surveyed more than four hundred participants in the Ideas Industry on a welter of issues and interviewed a variety of participants in the modern marketplace of ideas.[63]

My empirical support will also include one other source of data—my own experiences. The changes wrought by the modern Ideas Industry—the academic search for "impact," the mushrooming of "Big Idea" conferences, the development of online platforms, the rise of billionaire benefactors, the growth of the for-profit sector of the foreign policy community—are all phenomena I have witnessed firsthand. I have taught at universities for twenty years, but I've also developed my own online course.[64] I have published more than fifty peer-reviewed journal articles and book chapters, but I have also blogged for more than a decade, half of that time at *Foreign Policy* and the *Washington Post*. I've presented at numerous academic conferences and published many university press books, but I've also given TEDx talks and participated in Comic-Con panels. I've drifted away from a more conservative worldview, but also received grants from conservative foundations. When it comes to the Ideas Industry, I know something of what I write.

My own experiences are not a substitute for actual ethnographic research. The danger of drawing upon one's own background is that personal experience might not be generalizable to the rest of the phenomena being described. Indeed, this is a common flaw among thought leaders. A caveat comes with that acknowledgment, however. There are certain kinds of inside information that Michael Polanyi labeled as "tacit knowledge."[65] This is knowledge that can be best gained through experience. In writing about the transformation of the marketplace of ideas, I will be informed by the tacit knowledge that comes with participating in the public sphere.

One last point: although I will be concentrating on the marketplace of foreign policy ideas in the United States, I would suggest that the forces shaping that particular Ideas Industry also exist in other policy arenas and in other countries. This book focuses on American foreign policy because it is the arena I know best and it is intrinsically important. But public intellectuals and thought leaders exist in the world of domestic policy as well. Similarly, the erosion of trust, increase in polarization, and rise of economic inequality are not limited to the United States. Other countries' marketplaces of ideas are not carbon copies of the United States. Nonetheless, these structural forces are powerful enough to suggest that what I am describing here might also be taking place across the globe.

The rest of the book is organized as follows. Part I sets the table. Chapter 1 makes the case for why we should care about the marketplace of ideas. It is convenient for cynics and social scientists to assume away intellectual affairs as exercises in sophistry. While easy, such an assumption is also silly and self-defeating. *Of course* ideas matter; otherwise pundits and social scientists would not be writing in the first place.[66] A functioning marketplace of ideas is necessary for a dynamic democracy. Chapter 2 takes a closer look at the three systemic forces that have shaped the new Ideas Industry: the erosion of trust in established authorities, the political polarization of the audience, and most important, the rise of economic inequality that empowers plutocrats. Combined, these three trends have increased demand for all intellectuals—but it has been particularly good for thought leaders.

Part II of the book considers how the emergence of the modern Ideas Industry has affected some of the marketplace's key suppliers. Chapter 3 looks at the oldest source: the academy. Universities find themselves accused of myriad sins, including obscurantism, irrelevance, and political homogeneity. The truth is more complex. Many professors within the ivory tower have managed to survive and thrive in the Ideas Industry. The forces that have shaped the modern marketplace of ideas have nevertheless made the intellectual climate for higher education more challenging. Chapter 4 compares and contrasts the fortunes of two social science disciplines. Economics has thrived in the modern marketplace of ideas, whereas political science has only survived. This is not due to the superiority of economic models or methods. Rather, it is because the intellectual style and substance of economists sync up better with the new drivers of the Ideas Industry. Chapter 5 moves from the detachment of the ivory tower to the fevered Foggy Bottom swamp of think tanks. Developments within the Ideas Industry have created new pressures on think tanks to maintain their status as a bridge between abstract theory and concrete policy. While think tanks are quickly adapting to the changes wrought by the Ideas Industry, they are doing so in ways that compromise the practices that gave them legitimacy and autonomy in the first place. Chapter 6 looks at the private market for public ideas. Whether based in corporate think tanks like the McKinsey Global Institute, political risk consultancies like the Eurasia Group, or hybrid structures like Jigsaw, the private sector has inculcated thought leadership as a business strategy. The Ideas Industry has made that strategy a potent option.

Part III of the book examines how well the Ideas Industry functions as a market, and whether that market can be improved. Chapter 7 considers the "superstar" intellectual. The modern marketplace of ideas rewards intellectuals who are able to brand themselves. The Ideas Industry has turned a lot of idea entrepreneurs into titans. That said, in the world of ideas and criticism, becoming a brand leaves one vulnerable to overexposure. How well have superstars like Fareed Zakaria or Niall Ferguson survived their stumbles in this world? In part, it depends on whether they self-identify as thought leaders or public intellectuals. Chapter 8 argues that the modern marketplace of ideas is just as prone to bubbles as is the financial sector. The waning influence of public intellectuals enables thought leaders to expand the influence of their ideas far beyond what would be appropriate. Like asset bubbles, intellectual fads will bloom from the germ of an interesting idea, expand rapidly, and then crash. Chapter 9 considers the relationship between the Ideas Industry and the online world. In the twenty-first century, all intellectuals have to engage with social media to promote their policy ideas. The toxic aspects of the digital landscape, however, have made it easier for intellectuals to reject online criticism. Regrettably, this creates a slippery slope where it becomes easier to reject more substantive critiques as well. The final chapter is more personal, reflecting on my own experiences as I've navigated through the world I describe. It also proffers some advice for individuals interested in navigating the Ideas Industry, and considers whether the modern marketplace of ideas can be improved.

Before considering what makes the modern Ideas Industry tick, however, it is worth asking a simple question: does any of this really matter?

I

Do Ideas Even Matter?

Experts in international relations, one of the fungible intellectual industries credentialed during the cold war, inhabit by professional necessity a cloud-cuckoo land of fantasy and speculation.

— Pankaj Mishra

JEFFREY SACHS IS A brilliant economist, a fact that he is happy to tell you himself. Anyone who writes, "As a young faculty member, I lectured widely to high acclaim, published broadly, and was on a rapid pace for tenure, which I received in 1983 when I was twenty-eight," does not suffer the curse of modesty.[1]

That boast was not the most audacious thing he wrote in *The End of Poverty*, however. Sachs's faith in his own analytical abilities enabled him, a relative newcomer to development economics, to declare that he had unearthed the formula for ending extreme global poverty. He proposed that the wealthy countries of the world increase their combined foreign aid budgets to $150 billion annually for the next two decades. Sachs argued that a properly allocated surge in development aid would eliminate extreme global poverty—people living on less than one dollar a day—by 2025.

That Sachs suggested such an audacious plan is hardly out of the ordinary. Plenty of academics, think tank fellows, and policy entrepreneurs propose ambitious programs for making the world a better place. A few things made Sachs stand out, however. First, he offered the possibility that development aid could make a difference. This contrasted with the consensus view in the mid-2000s: government corruption was the primary roadblock to development and so boosting aid was a futile move. This view was "a deeply pessimistic mindset that also stymied fresh thinking on the matter," in the words of *Foreign Policy*.[2] Hope is a powerful elixir in the world of development economics.

Second, Sachs had the intellectual cachet and political capital to force people to listen. When he published his anti-poverty manifesto, Sachs was working as an advisor to the United Nations Secretary-General, tasked with devising an international response to poverty. Furthermore, Columbia University had recently poached Sachs from Harvard. The university gave Sachs four different titles, including director of the university's Earth Institute, with an operating budget in excess of $10 million.[3] The good professor went on to serve as an advisor to multiple countries in sub-Saharan Africa, including Ethiopia, Kenya, Nigeria, and Uganda.[4]

Third, Sachs possessed the self-confidence and sheer unflagging will necessary to proselytize his ideas to anyone and everyone who would listen. Nina Munk ably chronicled Sachs's campaign to implement his policy ideas in *The Idealist*:

> Day after day, without pausing for air, it seemed, Sachs was making one speech after another, as many as three in one day. At the same time he lobbied heads of state, testified before Congress, held press conferences, attended symposiums, advised government officials and legislators, participated in panel discussions, gave interviews, published papers in academic journals, wrote opinion pieces for newspapers and magazines, and sought out anyone, anyone at all, who might help him spread the word. The only time he seemed to slow down was when he was sleeping, never more than four or five hours a night.[5]

His publicity and marketing efforts bore considerable fruit. For example, *The End of Poverty* made the cover of *Time*. This was an unusual occurrence for books about development economics, or even books in general.

Fourth, Sachs was adroit at collecting allies, particularly celebrities and philanthropists. U2's frontman Bono wrote the foreword to *The End of Poverty*, characterizing Sachs as "my professor." On an MTV documentary, Angelina Jolie described him as "one of the smart-est people in the world."[6] He befriended and secured funding from George Soros and Tommy Hilfiger to attempt to put his development theories into practice with the Millennium Villages Project (MVP).[7] Indeed, Soros was so convinced by Sachs that the billionaire overruled his extremely skeptical board of philanthropic advisors. Sachs attracted hundreds of millions of dollars in funding from a variety of interna-tional organizations and private foundations. His Earth Institute then attempted to implement his plan in a series of villages in east Africa.

As Sachs pursued his quest, he faced tremendous pushback from a welter of sources. The development aid community, used to its standard operating procedures, thought Sachs's messianic goal was at best naïve and at worst counterproductive.[8] He proved able to bulldoze through those bureaucratic impediments. The criticism from development economists was more severe. William Easterly made his name with a series of books arguing that development aid suffered from a "techno-cratic illusion" that poverty was a purely technocratic problem ame-nable to purely technocratic solutions such as fertilizers, antibiotics, or nutritional supplements.[9] Easterly argued that Sachs's aid proposal was worse than useless without institutions of good governance. Esther Duflo, the head of the MIT Poverty Lab and the co-author of *Poor Economics*, worried that Sachs's arguments were simply the latest fad to pervade development economics. She warned that without comparing Sachs's interventions with a control group of villages that would not receive any interventions, there was no way to determine if his efforts would be the cause of any improvement.[10] Nancy Birdsall, the head of the Center for Global Development, concurred with Duflo's critique and urged Sachs to use a control group.

Sachs dismissed these objections as effortlessly as those from the de-velopment bureaucracy. He explicitly rejected the idea of measuring progress in comparison villages.[11] He and the Earth Institute plowed ahead, and the initial results seemed promising. Sachs has argued that the MVP program inspired the widespread adoption of free antima-larial bed nets, which in turn reduced the spread of that disease.[12] In a 2012 paper published in *The Lancet*, Sachs and his coauthors claimed that his villages were reducing the child mortality rate three times faster than the overall rate in sub-Saharan Africa.[13] Sachs hailed the "scientific results" in an editorial for CNN, proclaiming, "We can end the deaths of millions of young children and mothers each year by building on recent innovations."[14]

By 2013, however, the luster had worn off the project. Sachs and the Earth Institute tried to manage the project from New York. This left key decision makers uninformed about conditions on the ground when they proffered their advice to the villages. Inevitably, this management style frustrated local representatives.[15] Sachs ignored his own board of advisors, improvising responses to adverse outcomes or negative publicity, at times contradicting previous plans. External assessments concluded that there was no way to determine if the MVP villages were any better off than other villages, because Sachs's team never compared their villages to ones that had received no aid. Sub-Saharan African economic development was robust during this period, and infant mortality rates across the continent had fallen dramatically.[16] There was simply no way to determine if the positive effect in the MVP villages was due to Sachs's interventions or to strong economic growth. Indeed, according to one measure, the drop in the MVP infant mortality rate was less than the national average in the host countries.[17] This problem, as well as other methodological errors, forced the lead author of Sachs's paper to acknowledge in a letter to *The Lancet* that the "three times faster" claim on child mortality was "unwarranted and misleading."[18]

Sachs responded by trying to retroactively demonstrate such a significant effect from his villages, and he brought in outside experts to assist him. Still, the effort was unlikely to restore credibility to the project. One of Sachs's researchers told *Nature*, "I expect that the authors will conclude that, although we cannot prove that MVP works, we also cannot rule out that it works."[19] Compared to Sachs's soaring rhetoric a decade prior, this was quite a scaling back of ambition. A health expert brought in by Sachs acknowledged that it would be impossible to assess any past effect from the Millennium Village Project. One of Sachs's former research assistants, now an economist at Berkeley, told *Foreign Policy*, "No one takes the Millennium Villages seriously as a research project—no one in development economics."[20] Bill Gates, who resisted funding Sachs's project, concluded that, "Sachs seems to be wearing blinders."[21] When I asked Sachs what he thought the Earth Institute's greatest accomplishments were, he did not mention the Millennium Village Project in his response.[22]

Sachs's later books did not sell as well as *An End to Poverty*, and his subsequent quest to become president of the World Bank failed to get any traction. Sachs himself seems to have moved on somewhat. When asked by Munk about all of this, Sachs replied, "It is what it is . . . You can have a firm conviction even in an uncertain world—it's the best you can do, actually—and that is the nature of my conviction."[23] His post-2014 syndicated columns focus less on development economics than they used to. Instead, he has written more about macroeconomics, foreign policy, and theories to explain the Kennedy assassination.[24] It would seem that he has transitioned back from thought leader to public intellectual. Sachs might have been the most successful thought leader in the history of development economics. A decade after he started, however, the real-world results appear to be disputed at best.

The rise and fall of Jeffrey Sachs raises a troubling question for intellectuals: Does any of it matter? There are four ways to argue that intellectual debates in the United States right now are irrelevant. The first argument is materialist: ideas are meaningless in a world in which deeper material forces rule the roost. It was therefore silly of Sachs to push against the powerful inertia of the status quo. The second argument is defeatist: the proliferation of media platforms renders it impossible for any intellectual to be heard. Even if the MVPs yielded successes, that news would be drowned out by an avalanche of uninformed criticism—as has been the case with contrived controversies about vaccines, climate change, or genetically modified foods. The third argument is populist: big, abstract ideas are doomed to failure. The failure of Sachs's project demonstrates the ways in which intellectuals can only make things worse. The final argument is nostalgic: compared to the past, the current crop of superstar intellectuals is so depraved that ideas have lost their meaning as anything other than the rationalizations of the rich or the reactionary. According to this argument, there simply are no great intellectuals any more. Sachs achieved his celebrity in part by consorting with musicians and starlets. Surely this is something that the heralded New York intellectuals of the mid-twentieth century would have disdained.

This chapter outlines and then weighs each of these four arguments. Spoiler alert: ideas still matter very much, and analyzing what makes the marketplace of ideas tick is more vital than ever. But fair is fair—let us give these critiques a full hearing.

The materialist argument is familiar to social scientists, because so many of them use some variant of it when talking about the role of ideas. Economists and political scientists begin with the premise that power and interest are what make the world go around. Almost all economic theory revolves around the question of constrained optimization: How can individuals maximize their utility in a world of hard resource constraints? This kind of modeling is not terribly hospitable to the prospect of ideas mattering. Political science is little different: the assumption driving the entire discipline is that all politicians are interested in attaining and holding power, a scarce zero-sum commodity. Ideas are not an important part of that assumption. To use the language of social science, ideas matter by altering actor preferences; to use ordinary English, ideas matter by changing people's minds. Most social scientists, however, assume that individual and institutional preferences remain fixed and frozen. In other words, they believe that most people do not change their minds unless their material incentives have changed. On their own, ideas do not persuade.

The materialist argument holds particular sway over America's foreign policy community. For example, why did President George W. Bush's post-2001 rhetoric stress unilateralism and democracy promotion so much? According to some scholars and pundits, the increase in US hegemonic power explains the willingness to act unilaterally.[25] According to some *realpolitik* scholars, a powerful, well-funded pro-Israel lobby explains American foreign policy miscues in the Middle East.[26] The notion that neoconservativism had any independent effect on American foreign policy in the Middle East is often rejected out of hand by American foreign policy scholars. This is true even though any fair reading of the Bush administration's rhetoric makes it hard to ignore how neoconservative ideas trumped *realipolitik*.[27] Ideas are treated by most foreign policy analysts as "hooks"—arguments that powerful interests will promote to pursue their materialist ends.

The materialists look at the Sachs parable and think of it as an object lesson for intellectuals trying to make a difference. They would note three salient facts that doomed Sachs's chances before he started. First, he thought he could simply steamroll the complex web of political compacts that represented the development status quo. It is not surprising that this generated blowback. Second, he was playing with other people's money—money that would be difficult to obtain. Since foreign and development aid is a politically unpopular budget item, it was always going to be impossible to generate the necessary political will to do what he wanted. Finally, that lack of political support guaranteed that even small flaws in the Millennium Villages would be enough to torpedo Sachs's agenda.

The defeatist argument begins by noting that any idea requires an audience to make any difference. And we live in a world where the explosion of media platforms has fragmented the audience. In the old marketplace of foreign policy ideas, it was easy to write something that commanded attention. An op-ed in the *New York Times* or *Financial Times* was guaranteed to spark conversations, an essay in *Foreign Affairs* even more so. The narrow number of platforms meant that the value of each platform was very high. The gatekeepers of those platforms exercised vast influence over the marketplace of ideas.

The proliferation of cable news, talk radio, and online content has changed all of that. Nowadays, posts on Medium can command as much attention as a *New York Times* column. The surge of content providers also means the fracturing of the American audience into a hundred different subcultures. To counteract this fragmentation, individual intellectuals have an incentive to engage in more extreme modes of argumentation to attract attention. David Frum has complained about the nasty discourse of the blogosphere, noting, "such criticisms—so personal, so rude, and so imperfectly grammatical—elicit only countervailing scorn from their targets." Jacob Heilbrunn has lamented, "In a prior time, [public] intellectuals could be judged by their output; today it is by the noise they make and the comments they generate."[28] Both those complaints were lodged nearly a decade ago, *before* the explosion of social media. Now, some commentators think of blogs as "simply constituting more noise in an already cacophonous marketplace of ideas."[29] The defeatist argument concludes that when town criers dominate the public square, there is simply no way for a sober intellectual to break through.

The defeatist argument affects the marketplace of foreign policy ideas primarily by expanding the public sphere that covers everything else. In the three-network era of the mid-twentieth century, traditional media outlets felt compelled to focus somewhat on international affairs, educating disinterested citizens. The explosion of new media largely follows public interest. And the public does not care too much about world politics. For example, when the Chicago Council on Global Affairs prods Americans about their foreign policy worldviews, the results are crystal clear: the majority of Americans want the US government to focus less on the rest of the world and more at home.[30] This has forced traditional world politics venues to shift their focus as well. *Foreign Affairs* editor Gideon Rose told me explicitly, "There's no such thing anymore as a foreign policy journal. The foreign policy journal is a function of the twentieth century."[31] Under Rose's tenure, *Foreign Affairs* has branched out beyond traditional areas of international relations. Because the public is largely disinterested in foreign affairs, more media outlets can elide world politics.

In this disinterested public sphere, the only foreign policy arguments that will resonate are the extreme ones. Proposals to use military force to kill the families of terrorists or to build a wall along the Mexican border will get heard. Nuanced takes on how to reconfigure international peacekeeping forces or enhance the multilateral trade regime will be ignored. After the Iranian nuclear deal was negotiated during the summer of 2015, for example, interest groups like the American Israel Public Affairs Committee and think tanks like the Foundation for the Defense of Democracies coordinated a massive effort to criticize the deal. By all reports, the deal's skeptics easily outspent supporters in advertising.[32] This blitz had an effect; in subsequent polling, the Pew Research Center found that there was an appreciable increase in opposition to the deal. But Pew also found something else: despite the blizzard of advertising and media coverage surrounding the Iran deal, respondents stated that they knew *less* about the contours of the deal two months after the debate started. The issue "had not resonated widely with the public."[33] The defeatist argument therefore concludes that the explosion of media platforms leads to a cacophony of voices. And these voices cancel each other out, diminishing anything written about foreign policy. When the only option intellectuals have is hyperbole, the marketplace for ideas becomes a race to the bottom.

Defeatists look at the Sachs parable and conclude that he never had a chance. If the public does not care about foreign policy all that much, it cares about foreign aid and economic development even less. Indeed, it is a staple of public opinion research that a strong majority of Americans want to scale back foreign aid. At the same time, an even stronger majority of Americans radically overestimate how much the United States spends on foreign economic assistance. When asked how much wealthy countries should give, Americans always respond with an answer that would increase US foreign aid tenfold.[34] This paradox in public attitudes has persisted for decades, yet no one has ever been able to exploit it. Sachs was simply another casualty. The only way he could change the dynamic was to use his celebrity power to evoke sympathy for his cause—and even that strategy was bound to run into compassion fatigue.[35]

The populist argument asks a simple question: Who died and put intellectuals in charge of the world? The United States in the twenty-first century has witnessed endless wars, financial crises, and stagnant economic growth; elites themselves have belatedly noticed the rising anger against them.[36] According to populists, this is because our meritocratic society rewards a very narrow set of academic skills.[37] Elites rely on unrealistic ways of thinking. Ideas—particularly grandiose ideas about foreign policy—are abstractions that dissolve into nothingness when examined closely. The elites who talk about foreign policy doctrines are disconnected from the real-world consequences of those ideas. Unsurprisingly, public policy debates are rarefied and remote. The grander the idea, the more likely it is detached from reality and therefore worse than useless. As the humorist P. J. O'Rourke once noted, "I don't like big ideas. And I'm not alone. Distaste for grandiose notions is embedded in our language: 'What's the big idea?' "[38]

Populists would posit that the intellectual history of post-Cold War American foreign policy demonstrates the negative value of big ideas. Administrations without big ideas have muddled through;

administrations with grand ideas have done poorly on questions of war and peace. The Clinton administration, for example, was remarkably devoid of big ideas about how to conduct foreign policy. Indeed, Clinton's national security advisor Sandy Berger bragged to the press about his lack of grand strategy and the virtues of an ad hoc approach to foreign policy.[39] During his tenure, the United States managed to avoid any protracted, violent conflicts.

In contrast, the Bush administration articulated an ambitious, far-reaching national security strategy after the September 11 terrorist attacks. John Lewis Gaddis, the dean of Cold War history, praised the Bush strategy as "more forceful, more carefully crafted, and . . . in tune with serious academic thinking." He concluded that it was, "the most important reformulation of U.S. grand strategy in over half a century."[40] Similarly, Bush's second inaugural address, dedicated to the proposition of democracy promotion, was highly aspirational and filled with big ideas. Bush articulated a clear, coherent, and ambitious grand strategy about how to remake the world in the twenty-first century. In trying to implement those ideas, of course, the United States became bogged down in two costly and disastrous wars. Compared to the high and mighty ideas of the Bush administration, Clinton's ad hoc approach, or Obama's "Don't do stupid shit" mantra, seem more appealing.

Populists conclude that the influence of intellectuals on public policy has been mostly malign—and should therefore be rejected entirely in favor of common sense principles divined from public opinion. They would also argue that the American public agrees with them. A 2014 Chicago Council of Global Affairs survey suggests that Americans believe their voice should carry more weight in foreign affairs, while universities and think tanks should play a lesser role.[41] As noted in the introduction, a core appeal of Donald Trump's 2016 campaign was the notion that he is not beholden to consensus ideas—or any ideas for that matter. Trump steamrolled the entire Republican field despite the strident opposition of the GOP's intellectual elites. Similarly, despite Hillary Clinton's near-monopoly of the Democratic Party's policymaking elites, Bernie Sanders mounted a serious challenge. Sanders and Trump succeeded despite their lack of foreign policy experience or advisors; indeed, both candidates played up their lack of expert advice as a strength during their campaigns.[42]

The populist resurgence demonstrates the extent to which the American people have rejected the intellectual establishment. Populism corrects the tendency of elites to adopt a cosmopolitan worldview at odds with the views of fellow citizens. As the American Enterprise Institute's Charles Murray has argued, current elites are too detached from the rest of the United States to understand it: "The members of the New Elite may love America, but, increasingly, they are not of it."[43] The single best way to be identified as a part of the cosmopolitan establishment is to be called an intellectual.

To the extent that populists would care about Jeffrey Sachs's crusade to end poverty, they would point to it as emblematic of everything wrong with grandiose intellectual projects. In the end, more robust economic growth proved to be a much greater palliative for the poorest of the poor in sub-Saharan Africa. Sachs asked for and received enormous sums of money to try to eradicate extreme poverty. Unsurprisingly, public opinion polls have historically demonstrated that Americans think the federal government spends too much on foreign aid and that it should be cut.[44] Sachs's failures do not merely represent the failure of his ideas; they represent the failure of *all* big ideas.

The most commonly articulated critique is *the nostalgic argument*. Skepticism about the notion that the ideas used to be better in the past permeates public debate. But such assertions are not exactly new. Intellectual elites have been decrying the decaying state of intellectual life since the invention of elites.[45] This has been a common trope in American discourse for a century. From Thorstein Veblen's *Theory of the Leisure Class* to Richard Hofstadter's *Anti-Intellectualism in American Life*, from Allan Bloom's *Closing of the American Mind* to Thomas Sowell's *Intellectuals and Society*, it would seem that anyone writing on this subject does little but bemoan the declining quality and diminishing prestige of intellectual elites. Various subgroups rue the loss of "their" public intellectuals to advance their causes.[46] Dyspeptic discussions about the state of American letters, such as Susan Jacoby's *The Age of American Unreason* or William Deresiewicz's *Excellent Sheep*, usually conclude that the current intellectual landscape is a barren wasteland.

The nostalgic argument makes it easy to interpret the fall of public intellectuals and the rise of thought leaders as emblematic of everything that is wrong with the state of debate in this country—and worse, conclude that nothing can be done about it. Indeed, the main point of contention among these intellectual pessimists is carbon-dating the beginning of this decline and fall. For some, it started with the birth of the Internet; for others, the dawn of the Cold War. More curmudgeonly writers place the date even earlier, ranging from the heyday of John Stuart Mill to the death of Socrates.

The passing of myriad twentieth-century public intellectuals has bolstered the nostalgic argument in public discourse. Milton Friedman, David Halberstam, John Kenneth Galbraith, Susan Sontag, William F. Buckley Jr., and Gore Vidal have all left the stage since the dawn of this century, leading those still alive to argue that no one will be able to replace them. Former *New York Times Book Review* editor Sam Tanenhaus wrote that "Mr. Buckley and Mr. Mailer represented something different. More than public intellectuals, they were citizen intellectuals, active participants in the great dramas of their time, and eager at times to pursue their ideas in democracy's more bruising arenas." *Vox* co-founder Ezra Klein lamented, "They would write serious books of political analysis and sell millions of copies—they were the writers you had to read to call yourself an actual political junkie. Now, the space they inhabited in the discourse is held by the [Ann] Coulters and [Bill] O'Reilly's of the world."[47] In his eulogy for Milton Friedman, *New York Times* columnist David Brooks observed: "From the 1940s to the mid-1990s, American political life was shaped by a series of landmark books: *Witness, The Vital Center, Capitalism and Freedom, The Death and Life of American Cities, The Closing of the American Mind*. Then in the 1990s, those big books stopped coming."[48]

A parallel conversation has taken place in the world of foreign policy. The death of George Kennan a decade ago triggered a paroxysm of laments that they don't make foreign policy thinkers like him anymore.[49] Kennan was the first director of policy planning at the State Department. His doctrine of containment was a useful framework to guide American foreign policy during the Cold War. Kennan was a true public intellectual, crafting elegant prose about American foreign policy and many other subjects long after he left the State Department to reside at the Institute for Advanced Study at Princeton. He achieved something rare in the world of ideas—at a crucial moment in history, he came up with a big idea that was both influential and correct. Various administrations committed various blunders in the name of containment, but a lot more good than harm was done to honor Kennan's idea.

A recurring theme in current international relations debates is that today's foreign policy community lacks the sagacity of George Kennan and his peers.[50] In retrospect, the architects of containment managed to craft a coherent strategy that was tactically flexible. As an idea, containment was powerful enough to produce a strong, bipartisan Cold War consensus.[51] American foreign policy during the post-Cold War era, however, has generated bipartisan scorn. Both liberals and conservatives argue that the United States frittered away its inestimable advantages in the generation after the Berlin Wall fell.[52] This would seem to be as much of an indictment of foreign policy thinkers as it is for successive US administrations. Radical critics like Glenn Greenwald stress this point, railing against the "orthodoxies [that] are ossified 50-year-old relics from the Cold War" dominating twenty-first-century foreign affairs debates.[53]

As a data point to support that thesis, consider the Princeton Project on National Security—a multi-year, multi-pronged effort to develop a twenty-first-century doctrine that could achieve what containment accomplished during the Cold War. The effort to create a "Kennan by committee" involved hundreds of foreign policy analysts—myself included. After dozens of meetings, the final report concluded that "such an organizing principle—such as containment, enlargement, balancing or democracy promotion—would not be forthcoming."[54] It turned out that Kennan by committee produces something far more forgettable than Kennan writing alone.

The nostalgic argument applies to Sachs's story as well. For all of his claims of originality, the arguments he presented in *The End of Poverty* strongly echoed the "Big Push" theory of economic development articulated during the Cold War. Indeed, much of Sachs's argument can be summed up in this passage from Walt Rostow's 1960 book, *The Stages of Economic Growth*: "The central fact about the traditional society was that a ceiling existed on the level of attainable output per head. This ceiling resulted from the fact that that the potentialities which flow from modern science and technology were either not available or not regularly and systemically applied."[55] Sachs's failure to acknowledge that he was making a retread argument was unfortunate, because it might have led him to avoid the pitfalls of Rostow's approach. The waste and corruption of that era fattened up UN agencies and recipient governments at the expense of the poor.

So, stepping back, there are four ways to argue that the marketplace of ideas is irrelevant to the way we live now. First, ideas are simply irrelevant. Second, the proliferation of platforms means that it is impossible for new ideas to break through. Third, the populist rejection of intellectual elites has discredited the utility of big ideas. Finally, the current marketplace of ideas is but a shadow of what the marketplace of ideas used to be.

Elegies like these are not hard to find. They are just not terribly persuasive.

The materialist argument is the easiest to refute, because it is so extreme. Intellectual historians and social scientists have carefully documented the myriad ways in which ideas have real effects in the policy world.[56] Powerful ideas can legitimize new policies or discredit existing ones. During times of uncertainty, ideas can function as road maps to guide grand strategy—or to reach agreement among different international actors.[57] During periods of crisis, foreign policy leaders will often look to new ideas to help explain the causes and point toward possible solutions.[58] If communities of experts reach a consensus on a set of ideas, that consensus acts as a powerful constraint on policymakers.[59]

To conclude that ideas matter is not to say that power is irrelevant. Rather, it is to suggest that power and ideas cannot be separated as neatly as materialists would like. One of the most significant dimensions of power is the ability to "define the given," to develop a concept that simply becomes accepted as true by everyone.[60] When actors define their interests, their goals, or their strategies, they are resting on a foundation of given ideas.

When intellectuals insert new ideas into the body politic, those concepts have the potential to bubble up into real change. For example, the notion that the countries benefit from freer trade is non-obvious. Generations of economists developed these ideas to the point where they are politically palatable. Economic historians have demonstrated that truly revolutionary ideas—like free trade—can be just as significant as radical technological innovations.[61] Similarly, any proper history of the legalization of same-sex marriage must include Andrew Sullivan's provocative 1989 cover essay in *The New Republic*.[62] Any honest accounting of the surge in Iraq acknowledges the crucial role that defense policy intellectuals played in formulating the strategy before the Bush administration even realized it was needed.[63]

In the end, the materialist argument against the marketplace of ideas rests on a narrow vision, one not shared by a long line of observers who have pointed out the independent political power of ideas. These observers are no intellectual slouches. Abraham Lincoln posited that "he who molds public sentiment goes deeper than he who enacts statutes or pronounces decisions."[64] Nearly four score years later, John Maynard Keynes echoed those sentiments:

> The ideas of economists and political philosophers, both when they are right and when they are wrong, are more powerful than is commonly understood. Indeed the world is ruled by little else. Practical men, who believe themselves to be quite exempt from any intellectual influence, are usually the slaves of some defunct economist. Madmen in authority, who hear voices in the air, are distilling their frenzy from some academic scribbler of a few years back.[65]

Businessmen devoted to the bottom line, or cynics who believe that material interest drives everything, might scoff at Keynes's sentiment. The revealed preferences of scholars and statesmen, however, suggest that Keynes's assertion about the power of ideas holds with even greater force in this century than the last one. Consider that at the beginning of 2012, Nobel Prize-winning economist Paul Krugman took to his *New York Times* blog to squelch online enthusiasm for him to become the next secretary of the treasury. Speaking candidly, Krugman observed, "Those who hold the position [of a columnist], if they know how to use it effectively, have a lot more influence on national debate than, say, most senators. Does anyone doubt that the White House pays attention to what I write?"[66]

Even some former senators agreed with Krugman. At the end of 2012, Senator Jim DeMint of South Carolina, ensconced in a perfectly safe seat, resigned to become the new president of the Heritage

Foundation, a conservative think tank. The greater financial rewards of moving to Heritage appeared to play only a small role in his decision.[67] What played a bigger role was DeMint's belief that he could exercise more political power running a think tank than serving in Congress. Less than a year into his tenure at Heritage, DeMint told NPR, "There's no question in my mind that I have more influence now on public policy than I did as an individual senator."[68] His efforts at Heritage have been mixed, as we see in Chapter 4. But the fact that Krugman and DeMint agree on the importance of their intellectual output is the best contradiction of the materialist argument. When given a choice between political power and intellectual power, both of them preferred the latter.

Clearly, at least some elites are acting as though the marketplace of ideas is still relevant. When Sachs was able to secure hundreds of millions of dollars to pursue his vision, he succeeded against entrenched interests. Even if his policies did not turn out as he expected, his success in trying it rebuts the materialist argument.

The defeatist argument is also easy to refute, because it rests on a faulty premise. Defeatists believe that the growth of media platforms dilutes the power of each individual platform, thereby making it difficult for public intellectuals and thought leaders to reach an audience. But all of the evidence suggests the opposite. The proliferation of content providers has given intellectuals new platforms to make their arguments. As the rest of this book demonstrates, every segment of the Ideas Industry—universities and think tanks, nonprofit and for-profit organizations—has doubled down on exploiting every publishing platform available.

More outlets for informed opinion enhance rather than diminish the marketplace of ideas. As financial commentator Felix Salmon noted, "Wonkery is like the diamond stores on New York's 47th Street: Each one makes money not *despite* the nearby competition, but *because* of it. . . . In the era of the social web, the potential audience for such material has grown by orders of magnitude—and, what's more, it's exactly the highly educated, affluent audience that advertisers crave."[69] Rather than drowning each other out, social media sites like Twitter, Facebook, and Reddit amplify arguments that break through the background chatter. As former Carnegie Endowment for International Peace president Jessica Tuchman Matthews notes, "against all expectations, the massive proliferation of largely unedited new media has made it easier to locate top-quality work and to identify the individuals and institutions that are consistently producing it."[70] Social media has its drawbacks, as Chapter 9 will discuss. But contrary to defeatist fears, the most extreme ideas do not necessarily rise to the top of online discourse. Instead, a virtuous circle exists in which social media elevates interesting arguments rather than crowding them out.

The amplification effect matters because the marketplace of ideas is not strictly about the new. Eliot Cohen, an academic-turned-policymaker-turned-academic again, has written about the utility of outside ideas in foreign policymaking. Cohen argues that outsiders have impact less through the articulation of new ideas than the re-framing of existing ones:

> The best commentary has an impact, less because it offers new ideas (most ideas have been considered, however incompletely, on the inside) than because it clarifies problems or solutions that the insiders have only vaguely or incompletely considered. A tight, well-written, and carefully reasoned examination of a policy problem will bring into focus an issue that the officials have not had the time, or often the literary skill, to capture precisely. That kind of analysis is very much worth reading. [71]

The best ideas have "heuristic punch"—clear enough to comprehend and potent enough to persuade. Ideas with heuristic punch cause even those in power who have thought about a problem long and hard to think about it in a different way. Similarly, ideas can guide previously indifferent publics into caring about an existing policy problem. Ideas with heuristic punch can motivate even disinterested citizens into re-thinking their position on an issue.

In the modern Ideas Industry, supply creates its own demand. This has certainly applied to the publishing ecosystem of international relations. Over the past decade, the number of possible outlets for serious foreign policy writing has exploded. *Foreign Policy*'s big 2009 push into the online world was hugely successful in generating traffic and triggered a copycat phenomenon among other outlets. Soon other journals such as *Foreign Affairs* and *The National Interest* bolstered their online content. A host of online-only publications devoted to international relations also emerged, including *The Diplomat, Open Democracy, War on the Rocks*, and *World Politics Review*.[72] Other political outlets such as *Politico*, the *Huffington Post*, and *Pacific Standard* expanded their international relations-related sections, increasing the number of online outlets even more.

Sachs succeeded in setting the development economics agenda precisely by exploiting so many of these platforms. There are many problems facing the modern Ideas Industry, but a lack of publishing venues is not one of them. Claiming that the number of platforms makes it difficult for intellectuals is akin to arguing that the proliferation of television channels makes it more difficult for actors.

The populist critique suffers from a flaw common to populists: an exaggeration of the populist outrage against intellectuals. For example, for all of the talk of rising resentment against free trade and immigration, the polling data suggest no such resurgence. Both Gallup and Pew polling data show that since the 2008 financial crisis, Americans have become more receptive to free trade, not less.[73] Chicago Council on Global Affairs polling demonstrates that concerns about illegal immigration were much greater in the 1990s than in the run-up to the 2016 campaign.[74] Despite the protectionist positions of both major party candidates in the 2016 election, there was no increase in protectionist sentiment in the public opinion data. It is easy for populists to claim that they have inherited the mantle of mass anger; it is somewhat more difficult to demonstrate genuine populist resentment of particular ideas.

This is not to deny periodic bouts of anti-intellectualism in America. But it would be more accurate to say that American attitudes toward intellectual elites have been cyclical, waxing and waning over time. As Richard Hofstadter and other intellectual historians have chronicled, the United States has had a long history of attachment to and then rejection of intellectuals.[75] The marketplace of ideas, like other economies, experiences business cycles.

Populists are correct to notice the current wave of anti-intellectualism, a phenomenon that Chapter 2 discusses in greater detail. If anything, however, the populist resentment of intellectuals illuminates their importance. The blowback against big ideas presumes that these concepts actually affected real-world outcomes. To be sure, it is possible that the members of the Ideas Industry are simply convenient scape-goats for populists, much like foreigners or government bureaucrats. In a sphere of life where perception can create its own reality, however, populist outrage at intellectuals can actually magnify their perceived influence.

The populist critique also labors under a false premise: that a world of no ideas and no intellectuals is even possible. All individuals, and es-pecially all policymakers, traffic in ideas—it is merely a question of how conscious they are of the ideas that animate their behavior. Those who pride themselves on pragmatic or ad hoc approaches to problem solv-ing will reject explicit articulations of abstract ideas. They will be eager, however, to advance narratives, analogies, or metaphors as if these con-cepts are completely different from abstract ideas. Populists hold strong ideas about how foreign policy should work; they just do not like to call them ideas. As Hofstadter put it, "the leading anti-intellectuals are usually men deeply engaged with ideas, often obsessively engaged with this or that outworn or rejected idea."[76] Populists are mistaken when they claim to rely on common sense rather than ideas. Indeed, the un-conscious advocacy of analogies or rules of thumb as a means of making policy merely highlights the importance of a functioning marketplace of ideas. Foreign policy intellectuals can highlight the hidden theoreti-cal assumptions that guide populist policymakers—assumptions that can lead them into making mistakes.

A thriving public sphere should not only reward new and worthy notions but also discredit bad ones. As Chaim Kaufmann has argued with respect to international affairs, "the marketplace of ideas helps to weed out unfounded, mendacious, or self-serving foreign policy arguments because their proponents cannot avoid wide-ranging debate in which their reasoning and evidence are subject to public scrutiny."[77] In the absence of such a debate, policymakers and pub-lics can fall victim to myths and misperceptions, which in turn con-tribute to catastrophic decision making.[78] An unheralded virtue of foreign policy intellectuals is to vigorously push back on stupid or inane ideas.[79] A functioning marketplace of ideas is both necessary and significant.

Finally, public opinion alone functions as a poor guide to policymakers, in no small part because the public often does not care about world politics. Most Americans are "rationally ignorant" about foreign affairs—as busy people, it is simply not worth their while to learn much about world politics. As a result, relying on public attitudes in areas requiring specialized expertise can be problematic. For example, while Americans believe that the federal government spends too much on development aid, they also dramatically overestimate how much the government actually spends. Recent polls show that Americans believe on average that 28 percent of federal spending goes to foreign aid; in actuality it is less than 1 percent.[80] Indeed, when told of the actual spending figures, most Americans support an *increase* in the foreign aid budget.[81] The public might conclude that Jeffrey Sachs's ideas about promoting economic development have not worked—but when informed about the actual size of the foreign aid budget, a majority of Americans would not want to abandon the effort.

The nostalgic argument rests on the misperception that nostalgia usually generates. Over time, lesser intellectual lights fade from view—only the canon remains. Intellectuals like Sontag or Friedman occupy their exalted status in the present because they survived the crucible of history. As Richard Posner acknowledges, "one of the chief sources of cultural pessimism is the tendency to compare the best of the past with the average of the present, because the passage of time filters out the worst of the past."[82] It is therefore natural to presume that all of the writers from a bygone era are great. For every Walter Lippmann who stands the test of time, there are ten Walter Winchells who do not.

Even when focusing on the intellectual giants of the past, current public commentary is more likely to gloss over notable errors and instead focus on their greatest moments. The obituaries for William F. Buckley Jr. largely glossed over his favorable comments about racial segregation during the early days of *The National Review*. Praise for John Kenneth Galbraith's intellectual legacy tended to obscure the ways in which his socioeconomic predictions proved to be wildly off-base. If populists exaggerate the degree of antipathy that Americans hold toward elites, nostalgists exaggerate the virtues of past intellectuals. No matter what intellectual misanthropes suggest, slow national descents into illiteracy or madness are rare.

This is true in foreign policy as well. The hagiography of George Kennan's foreign policy acumen omits some blemishes on his record.[83] For all of his conceptual clarity, Kennan erred in many of his predictions. He opposed the creation of NATO, the most successful alliance in world history. By the early 1990s, when he wrote *Around the Cragged Hill*, he clearly believed the United States was doomed to decline. Asserting that the United States was devoid of "any sort of discriminating administration," he proposed several democracy-restricting measures.[84] And the less said about Kennan's view of non-WASPs, the better. While Kennan was a brilliant analyst of the Soviet Union, he evinced little understanding of his own country.

The last redoubt of those who believe in the nostalgic argument is to ask, "Who are the intellectual lions right now?" But it is not hard to list current foreign policy thinkers who could have held their own with Kennan. The problem is not naming one; it is naming too many. I would not agree with everything that Anne Applebaum, Rosa Brooks, Eliot Cohen, Ross Douthat, James Fallows, Niall Ferguson, Francis Fukuyama, John Lewis Gaddis, James Goldgeier, Richard Haass, Julia Ioffe, John Ikenberry, Robert Kagan, Robert D. Kaplan, Paul Krugman, Melvyn Leffler, Walter Russell Mead, John Mearsheimer, Peggy Noonan, Joseph Nye, Samantha Power, Barry Posen, Robert Putnam, David Remnick, Dani Rodrik, Nouriel Roubini, Anne-Marie Slaughter, Lawrence Summers, Cass Sunstein, or Fareed Zakaria write about American foreign policy. But they could have sparred with Kennan and lived to tell the tale. As will be discussed in Chapter 7, the difference between Kennan's heyday and the current moment isn't the lack of leading lights; it is the surfeit of them.

As with public intellectuals more generally, the nostalgia filter helps to explain the conviction that the current foreign policy community is a pale reflection of the best and the brightest. It is worth remembering the source of that phrase; the best of the Eastern Establishment were responsible for prosecuting the Vietnam War, a conflict that tore America apart far more than any twenty-first-century war. Consistent with the effects of nostalgia, it should not be surprising that less than fifteen years after David Halberstam's *The Best and the Brightest*, Evan Thomas and Walter Isaacson's *The Wise Men* offered a more favorable view of Cold War policymakers. To put it another way, Francis Fukuyama's *The End of History and the Last Man* might look wrong in retrospect, but it is not *more* wrong than, say, Daniel Bell's *The End of Ideology*. Similarly, Sachs's failure at solving the problem of extreme poverty looks no worse than some of the Cold War-era fiascos of economic development.[85]

For good or for ill, ideas still clearly matter in the public sphere. Jeffrey Sachs's ability to inject his controversial ideas about economic development into real-world public policy debates shows the power of ideas. The failure of his ideas to produce the outcomes he and his backers expected is simply evidence that not all ideas pan out. It is not, in and of itself, an indictment of the entire Ideas Industry.

Four standard arguments are commonly trotted out to explain why everything in the marketplace of ideas is meaningless or horrible. None of them are persuasive. The materialist argument is correct to point out the importance of power and interest in affecting affairs of state. But most scholars who study the importance of ideas do not dispute that point. Even if power and preferences matter, ideas still have important and independent effects on the world. The defeatist argument is correct to observe the proliferation of platforms for people to opine, which in turn can lead to raucous disagreements. But this is a feature and not a bug of the new Ideas Industry. The demand for new content has been one of the drivers of growth for the marketplace of ideas. The populist argument is correct to point out the current disdain for intellectual elites. But this does not mean that ideas themselves are unimportant, merely that populists dislike the leading lights of the modern Ideas Industry. The nostalgic argument simply asserts that everything was better when the New York intellectuals or the transcendentalists were America's intellectual elite. This argument has the problems that all nostalgic arguments have: a warped sense of history combined with an overly cynical view of the present day.

Disdain for public discourse has swelled at the same time that there has been a massive surge in both the supply and demand for thought leaders. Analyzing how the Ideas Industry has evolved is a task worth doing. What are the key drivers fueling the modern Ideas Industry? Why are thought leaders displacing public intellectuals? What does this mean for the marketplace of ideas? What does it mean for the United States?

2

How Pessimists, Partisans, and Plutocrats Are Changing the Marketplace of Ideas

Intellectuals have come to see their careers in capitalist terms. They seek out market niches. They compete for attention. They used to regard ideas as weapons but are now more inclined to regard their ideas as property.

— David Brooks

DAVID ROTHKOPF HAS A near-perfect resume to play the part of a foreign policy pundit. A former Commerce Department official in the Clinton administration, Rothkopf subsequently worked at all the right consulting firms and affiliated himself with all of the right think tanks. He has written a mix of serious tomes about foreign policymaking and somewhat lighter fare like *Superclass* and *Power, Inc.* He is currently the president and CEO of the consulting firm Garten Rothkopf, as well as the FP Group, which publishes *Foreign Policy*, one of the premiere outlets for world affairs. He writes weekly columns with portentous titles like "American Power at a Crossroads." He takes foreign policy and the ideas animating foreign policy seriously. If anyone should be attuned to the subtle shifts in the intellectual eddies and currents of the Beltway foreign policy community, it is Rothkopf.

In the fall of 2014, Rothkopf unleashed a jeremiad against Washington's stale intellectual climate. He argued that in the nation's capital, "originality is not only frowned upon, but it is actually institutionally quashed."[1]

He offered multiple explanations for this sin, but zeroed in on one recent phenomenon:

> One particularly odious element of it is what might be called pop intel-
> lectualism. Big, buzzy ideas are boiled down into short books that provide
> more cocktail-party conversation than significant concepts that require
> a little work to grasp. Think *The Tipping Point* and *The Black Swan*. . . .
>
>   Worse still is the whole TED talks phenomenon, which offers the
> intellectual equivalent of diets in which someone can lose 10 pounds
> in two weeks without giving up ice cream sundaes or pizza. In just 18
> minutes, a person can be exposed to breathlessly earnest genius—a
> slickly marketed brand of chicken nuggets for the brain.[2]

Rothkopf's critique was not exactly original. Intellectual broadsides against the entire TED phenomenon had long predated that column, and the ubiquity of TED's brand had made it vulnerable to satire for years.[3] What *was* unusual was that after penning that column, Rothkopf was invited to speak at TED2015. He accepted and delivered a talk about the poverty of foreign policy ideas in Washington.[4]

Soon afterwards, Rothkopf wrote a follow-up column signaling a full-blown conversion to the TED phenomenon. Like most converts, he was zealous about his newfound belief system:

> I find TED to be an exceptional event attended by remarkable
> people and far and away the best-run, best-conceived program of its
> kind I have ever had the privilege to participate in, but it actually af-
> fected me far more deeply than that. On several occasions, listening
> to some of the scientists and technologists who were presenting talks
> about their work, I was actually moved to near tears. Actually it was
> more like an existential gut punch. I felt like I was wasting my life
> in the bullshit factory of Washington while these people were really
> working at changing the world. . . .
>
>   The attendees were as much a part of the event's appeal as the
> speakers. Accomplished in their own right, they ensured that the
> sidebar discussions and discussions over meals were as energized and
> enlightening as the panels. I think it was because for all who came,
> the trip to TED was at least in part a search for new ideas and an

antidote to the kind of rote thinking that is a pitfall of going to work in the same place in the same industry day in and day out.[5]

Rothkopf insisted that his change of heart had nothing to do with TED's speaking invitation. To be fair, it is possible that this is true. Rothkopf's enduring complaint has been that Washington fails to appreciate the importance of technological change in world politics. If there is one thing that TED specializes in, it is fostering the notion that technology disrupts every status quo and can solve every policy problem. Little wonder, then, that Rothkopf concluded, "The real people reshaping global affairs . . . are the kind of folks who were in Vancouver this week and not the ones with the flags in their offices or the ones being covered by the Washington press corps."[6] In making this assertion, Rothkopf was echoing Oprah Winfrey, who said, "TED is where brilliant people go to hear other brilliant people share their ideas."[7]

The validity of Rothkopf's more grandiose claim about disruption will be addressed in Chapter 8. What is equally interesting is the effect that the TED experience had on Rothkopf's intellectual mien. In the span of six short months, a DC cynic's mind was changed; he became an enthusiastic proselytizer for the new Ideas Industry. By 2016 he was writing columns defending the World Economic Forum in similar ways.[8] Rothkopf's conversion experience demonstrates one way that thought leaders are supplanting more traditional public intellectuals. But TED is simply a conduit to get ideas out into the public sphere. What are the drivers behind TED and like-minded formats? Why are thought leaders suddenly so chic?

This chapter will trace out the three underlying forces driving the new Ideas Industry: the erosion of trust in established authorities, the growth in political polarization, and the increase in economic inequality. It should be stressed that none of these forces are historically unique. Even a passing familiarity with American history reveals that there have been prior waves of institutional pessimism, political partisanship, and plutocratic opulence. Indeed, there is at least some evidence suggesting that partisanship and inequality are correlated.[9] What is new, however, is all three of these factors cresting at the same time.[10]

Combined, these trends have affected the marketplace of ideas in two ways. First, they have paradoxically bolstered the demand for all intellectuals. Each of these forces increases the size of the audience willing to listen to ideas that diverge from accepted wisdom. This provides aspiring foreign policy intellectuals a proliferating number of pathways to carve out a sustainable niche in the marketplace of ideas. Second, the nature of these tectonic shifts has created an environment far more hospitable for thought leaders than for more traditional public intellectuals. Public intellectuals delight in taking issue with various parts of the conventional wisdom. By their very nature, however, they will be reluctant to proffer alternative ideas that appeal to any mass audience. Thought leaders will have no such difficulty promising that their ideas will disrupt or transform the status quo. And the shifts discussed in this chapter only increase the craving for clear, appealing answers.

Eroding confidence in authority and expertise is the most obvious trend behind the new Ideas Industry. The public opinion data showing rising levels of pessimism toward major institutions and professions is incontrovertible. Over the past half century public trust in almost every major public institution has fallen. In the aggregate, faith in the federal government has plummeted, as the data show in Figure 2.1. According to Pew, 1964 was the apex of public trust in government in the postwar era, at 77 percent. The expansion of the war in Vietnam and the Watergate scandal cut that number by half over the next decade. The

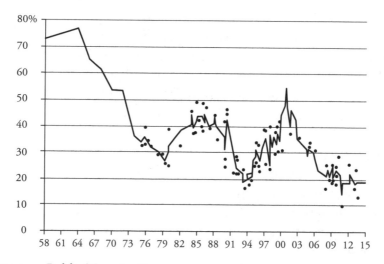

FIGURE 2.1 Public Trust in Government: 1958–2015
Source: Pew Research Center.

trust number bounced around for the next few decades, peaking in this century at 54 percent immediately after the September 11 attacks. For the rest of this century, however, it has moved steadily downward, reaching a low of 19 percent in November 2013 in the aftermath of the government shutdown.[11] A Gallup survey conducted at the same time found that a record-high 79 percent of Americans believed that corruption was widespread in the government.[12] Pew concludes, unsurprisingly, that "trust in government remains mired near record lows."[13]

This erosion of faith in the authorities is not limited to the federal government as a single entity. Gallup has repeatedly polled Americans about their trust in specific public institutions. As Figure 2.2 demonstrates, the results are not pretty; almost all of them show eroding trust levels between 1991 and 2014. Gallup's data show that trust in Congress has sunk the fastest and the farthest, from 42 percent in 1973 to a low of 7 percent in the middle of 2014.[14] Trust in the executive and judicial branches has fallen as well, however. Faith in the Supreme Court peaked at 56 percent in 1988; by 2015 it had fallen to 32 percent, a record low according to Gallup. Trust in the president was at 72 percent in 1991; by 2014, that number had fallen to 29 percent.[15] Overall trust in the government to handle international problems fell from 83 percent in September 2001 to 43 percent in September 2014.[16] When

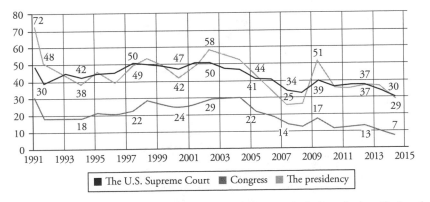

FIGURE 2.2 Americans' Trust in the Three Branches of the Federal Government: 1997–2015

Notes: Figures are percentages expressing "a great deal" or "a fair amount" of trust.

Source: Gallup.

Gallup reframed the question to ask more generally about the executive, legislative, and judicial branches, the results were the same: a slow decline in trust levels throughout this century.[17] Other public opinion polling, like the General Social Survey, confirms this trend.[18] The only federal government institution that has seen its trustworthiness rise in recent decades is the military. Even this institution faces waning levels of trust among the millennial generation, however. Indeed, the eighteen to twenty-four age cohort is the most pessimistic about all public institutions, including democracy as a form of government.[19]

The erosion of trust is not limited to the federal government either. Gallup also polls Americans about their belief in other institutions: local police, unions, public schools, organized religion, business, and the healthcare system. As Figure 2.3 demonstrates, the results for all of them are the same: a trend of increasing distrust. Indeed, according to Gallup, at no time in the past decade has the bulk of the institutions polled yielded trust levels higher than the historical average. Similarly,

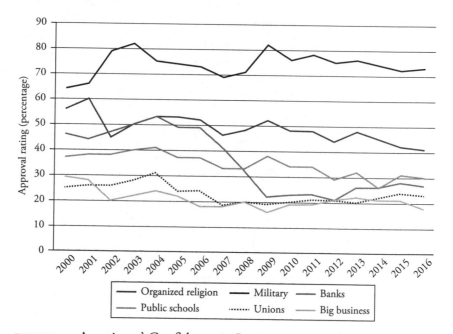

FIGURE 2.3 Americans' Confidence in Institutions: 2000–2016

Source: Gallup, "Confidence in Institutions," http://www.gallup.com/poll/1597/confidence-institutions.aspx.

trust in most major sources of information—including television news and newspapers—is also at an all-time low.[20] Trust in journalists declined over the past decade, falling well below chiropractors.[21] The General Social Survey data shows a similar across-the-board loss of confidence.[22] In essence, with the exception of the military, every institution in the United States has been viewed with rising suspicion over this century.

Survey data on public confidence in social science does not exist, but it is easy to infer from other polls that distrust in social science expertise has likely increased. The General Social Survey has polled Americans for confidence in institutions associated with learning and knowledge: the scientific, medical, educational, and organized religion communities. In 1974, the average confidence level for these institutions peaked at approximately 50 percent. By 2012, confidence in these institutions had dropped to an average of 31 percent.[23] This decline has not been as acute as the erosion of public trust toward government.[24] That said, opinion surveys also show rising levels of distrust of science.[25] Americans are also more open to alternative belief systems that experts had previously discredited. For example, in 2012 more Americans believed that astrology had some scientific basis than at any time in the previous thirty years.[26] On a host of scientific issues, ranging from climate change to childhood vaccines, public skepticism has persisted.[27] And the public holds views about how politics works that are significantly different from the consensus of political scientists.[28]

My own 2016 survey of opinion leaders suggests an erosion of confidence in social science over the past decade. In January 2016 I polled more than 440 academics, think tank fellows, newspaper reporters, opinion columnists, and corporate officials in foreign policy on their attitudes toward the marketplace of ideas.[29] Asked whether, compared to ten years ago, they had more or less confidence in social science research, 48 percent of respondents said their confidence was unchanged (see Figure 2.4). But 33 percent of the respondents said they were less confident now than a decade ago—decidedly more than the 19 percent who expressed greater confidence.

It should be stressed that increasing pessimism toward authority is not simply an American phenomenon. Within the advanced industrialized economies, trust in government fell by roughly ten percentage points between 2007 and 2012.[30] Trust in government traditionally falls

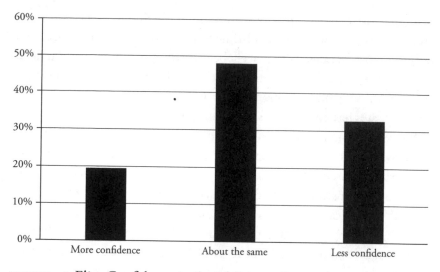

FIGURE 2.4 Elite Confidence in Social Science Research

Notes: Ideas Industry elite survey response: "Compared to ten years ago, do you have more or less confidence in social science research?" (Number of respondents = 196). *Source*: Author survey.

during periods of economic downturn, but this wave of distrust transcends that explanation. Faith in democracy as a form of government is also eroding across the advanced, industrialized world.[31] Edelman produces an annual trust barometer across a wide array of countries about peoples' attitudes toward government, business, the media, and nongovernmental organizations. Their 2015 survey revealed that "the number of countries with trusted institutions has fallen to an all-time low among the informed public."[32]

Perhaps the best example that the erosion of trust in authority is not simply an American phenomenon can be seen in the June 2016 Brexit referendum and the debate that preceded it. In the run-up to the vote, a plethora of prestigious economic organizations published analyses of what would happen if the United Kingdom exited the European Union. The IMF, OECD, Bank of England, Federal Reserve, Price Waterhouse Coopers, Barclays, Moody's, and Economist Intelligence Unit all warned that the costs of Brexit would be significant. When asked about these analyses, Michael Gove, a leader of the Leave campaign, responded confidently, "I'm glad these organizations aren't on my side." He continued: "I think people in this country have had enough of experts."[33] A Conservative MP told the *Financial Times* that "there is a fundamental breakdown in trust not just between voters and politicians but also with the BBC, the Bank of England, the City of London, and so on."[34] On the strength of the distrust of experts, a majority of British voters supported the Leave campaign.

The loss of public confidence in authority has not gone unnoticed by observers across the political spectrum. Steven Teles, Heather Hurlburt, and Mark Schmitt write: "The authority of scientific, journalistic, and other establishment institutions took crushing blows from left-leaning forces in the 1960s and from right-leaning forces in the 1970s. The country lost the mediating power that these institutions had over public discourse, and in particular their ability to certify basic claims of fact."[35] As MSNBC commentator Chris Hayes argued in *The Twilight of the Elites*, this distrust is a damning indictment of the system. And to be fair, a whole rash of scandals affecting respected institutions ranging from the Catholic Church to Harvard University to the US Secret Service has justified heightened levels of skepticism. But as Hayes notes, that skepticism comes with a significant price: "We now operate in a world in which we can assume neither competence nor good faith from the authorities, and the consequences of this simple, devastating realization is the defining feature of life at the end of this low, dishonest decade." He warned that "if the experts as a whole are discredited, we are faced with an inexhaustible supply of quackery."[36]

Hayes is to the left of center, but concern about the eroding faith in authority is bipartisan in nature. Yuval Levin has fretted in the *Wall Street Journal* about the "loss of faith in institutions" over the past few decades.[37] Tom Nichols, a Naval War College professor writing in the conservative outlet *The Federalist*, lodged a very similar complaint:

I fear we are witnessing the "death of expertise": a Google-fueled, Wikipedia-based, blog-sodden collapse of any division between professionals and laymen, students and teachers, knowers and wonderers—in other words, between those of any achievement in an area and those with none at all. By this, I do not mean the death of actual expertise, the knowledge of specific things that sets some people apart from others in various areas. There will always be doctors, lawyers, engineers, and other specialists in various fields. Rather, what I fear has died is any acknowledgement of expertise as anything that should alter our thoughts or change the way we live.[38]

The growing distrust and rejection of professional expertise has a profound impact on the marketplace for foreign policy ideas. The combination of popular distrust of elites combined with a perception of public powerlessness can be toxic. The gap between mass public attitudes and elite public attitudes over questions of American foreign policy has grown over the past three decades.[39] Lawrence Jacobs and Benjamin Page argue that the preferences of key elite groups have a much stronger effect on policymakers than the broad public.[40] This correlation of preferences is so strong that Jacobs and Page contend that a "foreign policy establishment" still exists and matters in the United States.[41]

The general public's lack of influence can be alienating. This alienation deepens with a public that is suspicious about the competence of foreign policy elites. And it is not as though America's foreign policy elites have done much to distinguish themselves during this century. Whether it was the Best and the Brightest in charge of the Vietnam War, or the Vulcans in charge of the Second Gulf War, or the Team of Rivals in charge of post-2008 foreign policy, the results have been depressingly similar: an esteemed group of policymakers come to power and make a hash of things. None of the post-Cold War presidents have demonstrated any consistent competency in their use of force. Their only difference has been in the magnitude of the mistakes. Neoconservatives fell into disrepute after the fiasco of the Iraq War.[42] Other foreign policy thinkers have done little better. According to the publisher and chairman of *The National Interest*'s advisory group, "the quality of America's foreign-policy discussion has demonstrably deteriorated over the last thirty years."[43]

The growing pessimism of public authorities has also, paradoxically, been a boon for the Ideas Industry. In some ways, the erosion of trust energizes the American marketplace of ideas. When authoritative institutions are no longer trusted, debates about first principles re-emerge. For thinkers like John Stuart Mill, the rejection of expert consensus makes it possible to question "dead dogma," revivifying public debate.[44]

In the case of American foreign policy, for example, the cacophony of the 2016 presidential campaign reignited previously settled debates about the continuation of birthright citizenship, trade liberalization, and utility of alliances in international affairs. For anyone critical of the status quo, distrust in consensus is a very healthy thing.

The erosion of trust nevertheless benefits thought leaders more than public intellectuals, for a few reasons. A comparative advantage of traditional public intellectuals in the marketplace of ideas is their ability to argue from authority—that is, they possess endowed chairs, MacArthur genius grants, Pulitzer prizes, and the like. In the past, earning these achievements empowered public intellectuals to "offer distant responses and to weigh in on diverse matters," in the words of Christopher Hitchens.[45] Public intellectuals benefit when they can argue from authority, particularly if they are venturing beyond the penumbras of their own expertise. This is how Fareed Zakaria could write a wine column, or Gregg Easterbrook could blog about professional football, or Cass Sunstein could author a book on *Star Wars*.

Arguing from authority only works if the authority is recognized and legitimized by others. In a world in which traditional titles, awards, and accreditations do not carry the same prestige they once did, public intellectuals must work harder to make their voices heard above the din. The erosion of trust levels the playing field in the marketplace of ideas. It also permits thought leaders to make their case. Even if thought leaders lack traditional credentials, they can argue from personal experience. In any age when authenticity is a prized commodity, that gambit can work more effectively for thought leaders (who often derive their arguments inductively from experience) than for public intellectuals (who often work out their arguments using deductive analysis).

While a general distrust of scholarly expertise is on the rise, many analysts point out that it is particularly concentrated among conservatives.[46] Indeed, in my survey of opinion leaders, there was a significant difference in the confidence that conservatives and libertarians had about social science compared to everyone else. As Figure 2.5 shows, a plurality of these respondents had less faith in social science research

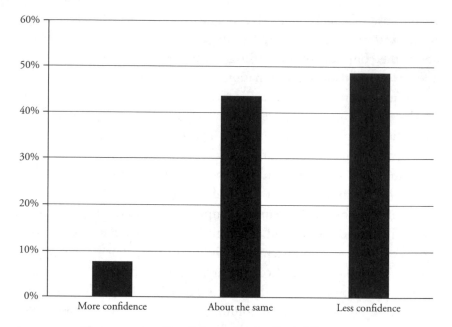

FIGURE 2.5 Conservative Confidence in the Social Sciences

Notes: See Figure 2.4, responses filtered by those self-reporting as "conservative" or "libertarian." (Number of respondents = 39).

Source: Author survey.

than they did a decade ago. This reflects the second trend that is animating the new Ideas Industry: the polarization of the American body politic.

Rising levels of partisanship are not new in the United States. Polarization has waxed and waned over the decades. There are plenty of qualitative accounts and centrist laments about the recent rise in political polarization.[47] But an orgy of evidence demonstrates that we are currently living in an era of peak polarization. The most iron-clad evidence comes from measures of congressional voting. From the mid-1970s onward, partisan splits can explain an increasing fraction of roll-call votes in Congress. Political science measures of ideology show that over the past four decades the average Democrat has moved leftward, and the average Republican has moved further to the right. As Figure 2.6 demonstrates, Congress is more polarized now than at any time in the past 125 years.

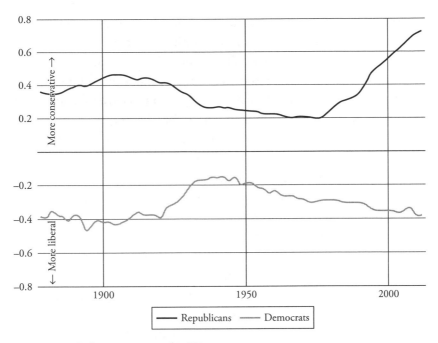

FIGURE 2.6 Polarization in the House

Notes: Party and regional mean DW-NOMINATE scores on the first dimension.

Source: VoteView.com.

The evidence for rising levels of partisanship goes well beyond Congress. Other measures of partisan conflict show a similar increase in political polarization.[48] According to a 2014 Pew survey, the number of citizens who demonstrate consistently liberal or conservative viewpoints has doubled in the past generation.[49] For both Democrats and Republicans, party elites have become more ideologically extreme than the broader party membership.[50] Political elites are now more ideologically extreme than at any time in postwar history. As one Pew survey concludes, "divisions are greatest among those who are the most engaged and active in the political process."[51] The ideological composition of both political parties has also become much more homogenous in recent decades. Democratic voters are more likely to identify with the Democratic Party's positions on different policies, and Republican voters feel similarly about the GOP's party platform. Political scientists label this phenomenon "partisan sorting."

Some political scientists argue that increased partisan sorting does not mean that the public is more polarized. But even the data produced by polarization skeptics show that political polarization among the mass public has been on the increase since the turn of this century.[52] Furthermore, even partisan sorting alone generates psychological effects that impinge on the marketplace of ideas.[53] By having one's identity defined by ideology, it becomes much easier to stigmatize those who hold contrary views. One recent public opinion analysis concluded, "The sense of partisan identity is increasingly associated with a Manichean, 'us against them' view of the political world."[54] Simply put, identification with one partisan group makes it easier for individuals to demonize members of the other partisan group.

There is an abundance of evidence showing that partisans on one side increasingly dislike and distrust partisans on the other side. Party activists now report that they dislike the other party's activists more than they did a generation ago.[55] Between 1994 and 2014, the percentage of Republicans and Democrats who believe that the other party is "a threat to the nation's well-being" has more than doubled.[56] Compared to thirty years ago, they also believe that the other party's members are less intelligent. One recent experimental study concluded that Americans discriminated more based on political partisanship than on either race or gender.[57] Or, as David Brooks put it, "becoming a Republican or becoming a Democrat has become an ethnic category."[58]

The growth of polarization has also segmented informational sources for political partisans. While the range of media outlets have grown dramatically, the audience for many of these platforms has fragmented far beyond the traditional three-television-network world of the mid-twentieth century. The explosion of cable news, talk radio, speakers bureaus, and online content allows individuals to select their own media diet. The result is a world of balkanized media, in which people can "cocoon" themselves with news and information that reinforces their pre-existing interests and beliefs.[59] Conservatives can watch Fox News, listen to Rush Limbaugh or Hugh Hewitt, read Breitbart or the *National Review*, and purchase books from Regnery and Free Press exclusively. Liberals can watch MSNBC, listen to Bill Press or Ed Schultz, read *Salon* or *The Nation*, and read books published by Zed or Verso. Pew found that conservatives were more likely to distrust almost every mainstream media outlet in existence; liberals felt the same way about Fox News.

There is a feedback effect between rising levels of partisanship and media cocooning. The former phenomenon exacerbates the latter, which in turn reinforces the former. Carried to its extreme, the result is a phenomenon that the Cato Institute's Julian Sanchez labeled "epistemic closure":

> One of the more striking features of the contemporary conservative movement is the extent to which it has been moving toward epistemic closure. Reality is defined by a multimedia array of interconnected and cross promoting conservative blogs, radio programs, magazines, and of course, Fox News. Whatever conflicts with that reality can be dismissed out of hand because it comes from the liberal media, and is therefore ipso facto not to be trusted. [60]

Of course, this works in reverse as well. It is easier for leading liberals to dismiss stories that originate in the conservative press, regardless of whether they are grounded in fact. In 2011, *New York Times* columnist Paul Krugman blogged the following about his information diet:

> Some have asked if there aren't conservative sites I read regularly. Well, no. I will read anything I've been informed about that's either interesting or revealing; but I don't know of any economics or politics sites on that side that regularly provide analysis or information I need to take seriously. I know we're supposed to pretend that both sides always have a point; but the truth is that most of the time they don't.[61]

It should be noted that the rise of political polarization also goes beyond the United States. To be sure, for much of the post-Cold War era, the evidence suggests that European political parties actually depolarized.[62] As the rise of UKIP and the Brexit referendum result suggest, however, political extremism has increased across Europe as well. Since the 2008 financial crisis, incumbent governments in the advanced industrialized economies have faced ever-higher levels of instability.[63] All of the large European economies are experiencing a rise in nativist parties: the

National Front in France, UKIP in the United Kingdom, Law and Justice in Poland, and AfD in Germany. Many of the economies stagnating from the Eurozone crisis have seen the rise of radical left parties: Podemos in Spain, Syriza in Greece, and the Five-Star Movement in Italy. On a variety of global issues, both reactionary and radical movements have gone global. The post-2008 Occupy movement has crossed borders to protest globalization and global elites. Conservatives have fostered populist "Baptist-Burqua" networks on various cultural and regulatory issues.[64] Anti-American movements in Russia and Iran have also engaged in efforts to increase polarization in the advanced industrialized states around contentious issues.[65]

Rising levels of partisanship have two pronounced effects on the marketplace of ideas. On the one hand, they expand the overall demand for intellectuals. The reason is simple: each ideological grouping wants its own in-house intellectuals. Conservatives are interested in conservative policy ideas, and liberals want to know about liberal solutions. People from each group are far more likely to trust intellectuals who share their ideological affinity and background than someone with more heterodox views.[66] For any given policy arena, there are intellectuals who can speak to the left, those who can speak to the right, and even those who will attempt to engage moderates. So rather than a supply of centrist thinkers, there is now a wider ideological menu.

On the other hand, polarization disproportionately benefits ideologically homogenous thought leaders. The strong demand for ideas within each ideological group is specific: it is strictly for *their* intellectuals. It becomes cognitively easy for partisans of one side to reject the criticisms lobbed from someone affiliated with the other political party. They can be dismissed away as partisans rather than thinkers. This makes it extremely difficult for heterodox public intellectuals to effectively critique cherished beliefs. Partisans possess an array of psychological defense mechanisms to resist such criticisms—indeed, such efforts will often reinforce existing misperceptions.[67] Thought leaders willing to reinforce pre-existing partisan beliefs will be hailed as original thinkers, however, regardless of how their views are perceived by the broader marketplace of ideas.

Dinesh D'Souza is the modern exemplar of a successful partisan intellectual. D'Souza started his career as a conservative firebrand at Dartmouth.

He moved on to be an editor at *Policy Review*, a domestic policy advisor for the Reagan administration, and then a fellow at the American Enterprise Institute. His first successful book, *Illiberal Education*, was excerpted in *The Atlantic*, a magazine not commonly thought of as conservative.[68] The book earned critical raves in outlets not sympathetic to his conservative worldview, such as the *New Republic* and *New York Review of Books*. D'Souza credited the success of the book to his editor, who urged him to "write for the critics" in the room, to "hew to a high standard of argumentation" intended "to persuade an intelligent and open-minded adversary."[69] In the early 1990s, D'Souza was severely conservative but able to command attention from all parts of the political spectrum.

A generation later, D'Souza's intellectual reputation looks somewhat different. The polite word to describe his books published between 1995 and 2016 is "controversial." The more accurate term would be "hysterical." In these tomes, he argues that racism no longer exists in the United States; that a breakdown of traditional family values in the United States enabled the September 11 terrorist attacks; that Obama's governing philosophy was grounded in "Kenyan anti-colonialism"; and that America is besieged from within by a fifth column of Hollywood, academia, and the mainstream media.[70]

These books were not nearly as well received among intellectuals; *The New Republic* withdrew its offer to publish an excerpt of *The End of Racism* because TNR editor Andrew Sullivan considered it subpar.[71] In a review of his book on Obama's governing philosophy, *The Weekly Standard* castigated D'Souza for "misstatements of fact, leaps in logic, and pointlessly elaborate argumentation."[72] D'Souza's later books received praise from some politicians, such as Newt Gingrich. Conservative intellectuals, however, largely disowned or ignored D'Souza's theses. In recent interviews even D'Souza acknowledged going overboard with some of his rhetoric.[73]

What is interesting is how little any of this criticism mattered to D'Souza's professional success. D'Souza explained in one interview, "The book industry was changing after *Illiberal Education*, and I found out you could make money by not writing for the critics, that book reviews didn't matter."[74] In another interview, he elaborated further:

> I picked up that there are two ways to sell books that were much better than book reviews: speaking and media. After *Illiberal Education*,

I just got an avalanche of speaking invitations. For a while, I felt like I was a political candidate. I was speaking every day. . . .

Then I realized that there's radio and television, too. People are interviewing you about your book directly. There's no intermediary telling the audience whether they like the book or not . . .

One of the things I discovered in the late '90s is there is a large populist conservative audience of people who want to learn. And yet, don't know. A typical Tea Party member isn't an intellectual. But he or she has a real affinity with the American founding, a belief that a return to our original principles can save us, and wants to know what those principles are. Not just in crayon outline, but in fleshed-out detail. And I say to myself, I can help that guy, and make a much more valuable contribution than by operating in what I now saw as the very small world of the ambivalent liberal.[75]

The rise of partisan speakers bureaus made it intellectually easier and more lucrative for D'Souza to address movement conservatives rather than go through the trouble of engaging the wider marketplace of ideas.[76]

D'Souza has endured a raft of personal scandals in recent years. He resigned from the presidency of King's College due to sexual misconduct. He pleaded guilty to one criminal count of making illegal campaign contributions.[77] He has also suffered an undeniable loss of prestige from his partisan thought leadership. Most observers now share reporter David Weigel's intellectual epitaph of D'Souza as "just a right-wing pundit, regressing to the mean."[78] Other conservatives feel free to disparage the intellectual quality of his writing.[79] Nevertheless, his latest books have been *New York Times* bestsellers, and two documentaries based on those books have been quite profitable. Even while incarcerated, he delighted in giving interviews, catering to the conservative base, and having fringe conservatives defend him as a political martyr.[80]

The effect of polarization on the marketplace of foreign policy ideas is similar. One could argue that for decades, the mainstream consensus within the US foreign policy community has been liberal internationalism. This doctrine marries the conservative preference for power projection with the liberal preference for exercising influence with partners, allies, and multilateral support. The liberal internationalist consensus has frayed badly, however.[81] Charles Kupchan and Peter Trubowitz write, "The polarization of the United States has dealt a severe blow to the bipartisan compact between power and cooperation. Instead of adhering to the vital center, the country's elected officials, along with the public, are backing away from the liberal internationalist compact, supporting either U.S. power or international cooperation, but rarely both."[82] A decade after they made that claim, Donald Trump was sworn in as president of the United States. Consistent with that conclusion, it easy to find polling support for the bifurcation of American foreign policy. Across a wide array of foreign policy questions—climate change, counterterrorism, immigration, the Middle East, Russia, and the use of force—US public attitudes are polarized.[83]

This has made it difficult for public intellectuals to affect public attitudes. Political scientists Alexandra Guisinger and Elizabeth Saunders ran survey experiments to see how the public responded to views from elites on an array of foreign policy questions.[84] They found that an expert consensus could alter public attitudes on issues where the public was not already polarized. When the public was already split along partisan lines, as with climate change, polarization rendered elite cues worse than useless. Indeed, expert opinions from out-of-party sources simply made respondents double down on their pre-existing positions. Greater polarization imposes a powerful constraint on the ability of public intellectuals to influence public attitudes. That same polarization opens doors for new thought leaders to propose ideologically reliable foreign policy doctrines.

The most important driver behind the transformation of the Ideas Industry, however, is the spike in economic inequality. Whether one looks at wages, income, or wealth, the data in the United States is clear cut: over the past thirty to forty years, the wealthiest Americans have done much better than everyone else. Indeed, economic inequality in the United States is the highest it has been since before the Second World War.

Figure 2.7 charts the increase in income inequality in recent decades. In 1975, the top 10 percent of Americans earned less than 30 percent of national income; by 2010, that figure had climbed to over 45 percent.[85] The top 1 percent has done particularly well for itself during this period.

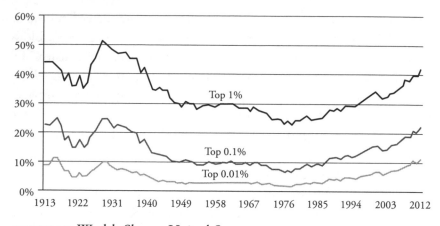

FIGURE 2.7 Wealth Shares, United States, 1913–2012

Source: Emmanuel Saez and Gabriel Zucman, "Wealth Inequality in the United States since 1913: Evidence from Capitalized Income Tax Data," August 2015.

It has more than doubled its share of national income over the past forty years, from less than 10 percent to more than 20 percent.[86] Indeed, the 1 percent captured 52 percent of the gains in national income between 1993 and 2008; between 2009 and 2012, that share climbed to 95 percent.[87] And just as the top 1 percent has done better than the top 10 percent, the top 0.1 percent has done even better than that. Over the same time period, the richest of the rich have more than quintupled their share of national income, from approximately 2 percent to 11 percent.[88] Similarly, between 1974 and 2014, the top 0.01 percent has increased its share of national income sixfold, to approximately 5 percent. The current distribution of wealth in the United States has returned to the Gilded Age levels of 1910.[89]

Nor is this phenomenon restricted to the United States. Between 1980 and 2005, the Gini coefficient—the most widespread measure of income inequality—increased in 80 percent of the advanced industrialized economies. According to Credit Suisse, the number of billionaires more than doubled between 2008 and 2014.[90] While the rise in inequality has been concentrated in the United States, it also reflects a more widespread, global phenomenon.[91] Whether the cause has been globalization, the rise of finance, the economics of superstars, or the ineluctable laws of capitalism is irrelevant for our concerns. What does matter is that both wealth and income inequality are on the rise, and there are excellent reasons to believe that the concentration of wealth at the top could increase further over time.[92]

As the inequality of wealth has increased in the United States, so has the inequality of contributions to political life. Survey data show that the wealthy are far more politically informed and active than the rest of the public. Political scientists Fay Lomax Cook, Benjamin Page, and Rachel Moskowitz concluded that "[it is] the wealthy who are the real Über-citizens of the American polity. Their participation levels far exceed any others that scholars have found."[93] A parallel study by Page, Larry Bartels, and Jason Seawright polled very affluent Americans and found that 84 percent paid attention to politics most of the time, 99 percent of them had voted in the previous presidential election, and 40 percent of them had been in personal contact with a US senator.[94] All of these percentages are significantly higher than for the American public as a whole. This reflects gaps in contributing to political campaigns. According to the *New York Times*, fewer than 160 families were responsible for close to half the campaign contributions made during the first phase of the 2016 election cycle, "a concentration of political donors that is unprecedented in the modern era."[95] According to the *Washington Post*, just fifty families were responsible for more than 40 percent of all super-PAC funding in the primary phase of the campaign.[96]

The effect of economic and political inequality on the Ideas Industry is profound. On the one hand, rising income inequality and declining income mobility have bred dissatisfaction with the state of the American Dream. Since the start of the twenty-first century, poll after poll has shown that Americans believe their country is headed in the wrong direction. Since January 2004, Gallup's monthly poll about America's direction shows that a majority of citizens are dissatisfied with the way things are going in the United States.[97] This discontent has fueled movements as diverse as Occupy Wall Street and the alt right. It has also led to a thirst for ideas to diagnose and treat the problems that seem to plague the United States. Ideas as extreme as the US withdrawal from the World Trade Organization are now discussed in intellectual confabs.

The most profound impact of rising economic inequality is on the supply side of the Ideas Industry. The massive accumulation of wealth at the top has created a new class of benefactors to fund the generation and promotion of new ideas.[98] Indeed, one is hard-pressed to find a profile of a billionaire that does not also reference an interest in ideas. Bill Gates takes great pride in listening to the Teaching Company's Great Courses series. Inspired by one of them, he sponsored a revamp of high school history classes with his Big History Project. Gates also played a key role in financing and promoting the Common Core curriculum movement.[99] One of Mark Zuckerberg's first notable acts of philanthropy was to donate $100 million to the Newark, New Jersey, school system. He later started a monthly book club on Facebook.[100] Charles Koch bragged to the *Financial Times* about instructing his children in the ideas of Aristotle, Milton Friedman, and Friedrich von Hayek every Sunday evening.[101] A wave of wealthy patrons have revitalized traditional newspapers like the *Washington Post* or *Boston Globe*, or set up new journalism ventures such as *The Intercept*.

Twenty-first-century benefactors are proudly distinct from their twentieth-century predecessors. The big benefactors of the previous century set up foundations that would endure long after they died. While many of these plutocrats had ideas about the purpose of their foundations, most were willing to trust the boards they appointed.[102] John D. MacArthur, for example, gave his board no instruction at all: "I'll do what I do best—make the money. After I die, you guys will have to learn how to spend it."[103] Foundations set up by J. Howard Pew and Henry Ford also wound up promoting ideas at odds with the political philosophies of their benefactors.[104]

This century's patrons adopt a more hands-on role in their engagement with ideas. Echoing billionaire Sean Parker, they largely reject "traditional philanthropy—a strange and alien world made up of largely antiquated institutions."[105] To twenty-first-century plutocrats, the mistake of past benefactors was to delegate too much autonomy to posthumous trustees. A new set of "venture philanthropists" or "philanthrocapitalists" has emerged to stimulate new thinking about a host of public policy issues.[106] In contrast to the older foundations, these new entities are designed to articulate a coherent philosophy consistent with a living donor's intent. Organizations like the Gates Foundation and Omidyar Network have developed a large footprint in significant areas of public policy.

Most of these new philanthropic foundations are obsessed with the "three Ms"—money, markets, and measurement.[107] Potentially game-changing ideas are like catnip to plutocrats. The head of the Silicon Valley Community Foundation, one of the wealthiest philanthropies in the country, told the *New York Times* that "West Coast philanthropy is marked by innovation, it's about disruption, it's about change."[108] One wealthy benefactor explained to me, "Money flows to the right ideas." Each of these venues and organizations tap bold thinkers to sate the curiosity of attendees. Remember, what dazzled David Rothkopf about TED was not just the conference itself—it was the accomplished attendees as well.

The eagerness to please benefactors affects both the content and the suppliers of the ideas. As Harvard Business School professor Gautam Mukunda notes, the outsized influence of a small group of plutocrats can have a pronounced effect on the public sphere:

> The ability of a powerful group to reward those who agree with it and punish those who don't also distorts the marketplace of ideas. This isn't about corruption—beliefs naturally shift in accord with interests. As Upton Sinclair said, "It is difficult to get a man to understand something when his salary depends on not understanding it." The result can be an entire society twisted to serve the interests of its most powerful group, further increasing that group's power in a vicious cycle.[109]

In the Ideas Industry, thought leaders fiercely compete to get on the radar screen of wealthy benefactors. The heads of intellectual organizations—universities, think tanks, and like-minded structures—will voluntarily reshape themselves to "become highly attuned to the needs, preferences, and idiosyncrasies of major institutional donors," as one scholarly analysis put it.[110] And many new philanthropies are leery of traditional social science in favor of other sources of ideas. As one Ford Foundation official notes, "I am struck by how few social scientists are employed at the new 'mega-philanthropies.' Instead, the people most sought after are management consultants, business people, former industry leaders or lobbyists, and scientists."[111]

Another concern arises if this new benefactor class shares similar ideas to promote. As Darrell West notes, "the super rich, as a group, hold policy views that are significantly different from those of ordinary citizens."[112] While the rise of the plutocratic class is a boom for intellectuals, that boom tilts in a more libertarian direction. This comes through in both surveys of wealthy Americans and impressionistic accounts of their worldviews. According to Page, Bartels, and Seawright, wealthy Americans favor cutting government spending on Social Security, Medicaid, and national defense. Only 35 percent of wealthy Americans support spending what is necessary to ensure good public schools, a sharp contrast to 87-percent support from the general public. To be sure, compared to the general public, wealthy Americans more strongly favor public spending on infrastructure and scientific research. The caricature of plutocrats as pure Randians is flatly false. Nevertheless, on average, wealthy Americans are far less supportive than the general public of unemployment insurance, worker retraining, economic regulation, or government redistribution of income.[113]

The lived experiences of global plutocrats further alters their perspective on public policy. Today's philanthropists attend glamorous intellectual gatherings, set up their own intellectual salons or foundations, and sponsor other high-profile confabs. Many of them participate in the same circuit of events, mingling with each other to the exclusion of anyone from different economic strata.[114] As a result, the number of "Big Idea" events has mushroomed, from PopTech to the Aspen Ideas Festival to TED to the World Economic Forum. As Chrystia Freeland notes, "the real community life of the twenty-first century plutocracy occurs on the international conference circuit."[115]

After a steady diet of global confabs, a certain mindset begins to calcify. Freeland observes: "For the super-elite, a sense of meritocratic achievement can inspire self-regard, and that self-regard—especially when compounded by their isolation among like-minded peers—can lead to obliviousness and indifference to the suffering of others."[116] Psychology studies confirm that wealthy people, because they are surrounded primarily by other wealthy people, overestimate the wealth of others and undervalue the benefits of social insurance policies.[117] This problem becomes even more acute as inequality increases.[118] Such insulation can lead to an atrophying of political antennae. Entrepreneur Elon Musk telling dinner companions that poverty is not that big of a problem in South Africa would be one example.[119] Billionaires writing letters to the *Wall Street Journal* comparing progressive concerns about inequality to the first days of *Kristallnacht* provide another example.[120]

The rise of philanthrocapitalism poses some interesting opportunities and challenges for the marketplace of foreign policy ideas. Compared to the mass public, most plutocrats are far more interested in global issues. This presents an opening for foreign affairs intellectuals to capture their attention and motivate them to fund research or action about the *problematique du jour*.

On the other hand, many plutocrats also share an aversion to the intractable policy problems that plague world politics. Author Greg Ferenstein surveyed more than a hundred Silicon Valley founders to determine the gap between their political attitudes and those of the mass public.[121] Silicon Valley elites were less likely to view political conflict as an entrenched problem so much as a piece of faulty code that needed to be hacked. Compared to the public, more than three times as many founders believed that "there's no inherent conflict between major groups in society (workers vs. corporations, citizens vs. government, or America vs. other nations)." Many plutocrats will prefer policy solutions that simply bypass the state completely rather than try to reform existing policies. The ability of nonstate actors to implement policy solutions has a decidedly mixed record, however.[122] And the plutocratic theory of frictionless politics is somewhat problematic. As *New Yorker* journalist George Packer noted, "the ideal of a frictionless world, in which technology is a force for progress as well as a source of wealth, leaves out the fact that politics inevitably means clashing interests, with winners and losers."[123] Even if plutocrats and intellectuals share common ends, they might disagree about the best means to achieve those ends.

Intellectuals who wish to cater to this crowd will find it difficult to contradict the narrative of meritocratic achievement. Or, to put it more bluntly, they cannot speak truth to money. David Frum noted about the GOP's donor class: "One of the more dangerous pleasures of great wealth is that you never have to hear anyone tell you that you are completely wrong."[124] Understandably, the intellectuals that will thrive in this milieu are those that stress disruption, self-empowerment, and entrepreneurial ability—the values that are a core part of the identity of philanthrocapitalists.

Not surprisingly, the increase in economic inequality favors thought leaders far more than public intellectuals. Thought leaders specialize in promoting new ideas through uplifting narratives. As Chapter 8 discusses further, thought leaders will push ideas or policies that promote disruptive innovation. These concepts appeal to those who have managed to stay on top in the global economy. Public intellectuals, in contrast, will tend to be more critical of the structures that enabled the wealthy to get to their station in life. Worse, public intellectuals are more likely to challenge the notion that plutocrats achieved their status entirely through merit. Between thinkers who can push a positive agenda for change and thinkers who will complain about everything, the new class of benefactors will be far more interested in the first group.

Three tectonic forces drive the modern Ideas Industry. Pessimism toward traditional sources of authority has made Americans more suspicious of intellectuals who argue from authority. This has widened the field of thinkers who can argue their way into developing an audience. Rising levels of political polarization have made it harder for partisans on one side to persuade members of the opposing party of their arguments. Increasingly, party stalwarts need their own house intellectuals, expanding the demand for ideologically trustworthy thinkers. Finally, the growth of economic inequality has created a class of patrons hungry for new and interesting ideas. As plutocrats have gotten richer and richer, they can afford to do anything they want, and they want to hear from interesting thinkers. Intellectuals are earning an increasing share of their income by catering to these audiences.

Again, it should be stressed that, in isolation, none of these trends are new. As Richard Hofstadter and other intellectual historians have chronicled, previous waves of creedal passion in the United States also emerged from distrust in established institutions.[125] The phenomenon is hardly unique to the current moment in America. The subfield of American politics is replete with studies showing the past strength of political polarization in the United States. Similarly, the history of intellectual titans earning their keep through the patronage of wealthy benefactors stretches back further than American history.[126] What is more novel is the combination of these three forces in a world of proliferating media platforms.

For reasons outlined in this chapter, all three trends have increased the demand for thinkers. The distrust of traditional experts has created an avenue for nontraditional thinkers to enter the public sphere. The growth of political polarization has offered opportunities for more ideologically radical intellectuals to find their audience. And the rise of the benefactor class has been a boon not only to libertarian thinkers but to those willing to jet to Davos or Aspen to engage with plutocrats. The result is a marketplace of ideas that looks far more heterogeneous than what existed a few decades ago. This is particularly true in foreign policy.

Each of these drivers also favors thought leaders far more than public intellectuals. In many ways, the problem with the more radical public intellectuals of the past is that they have won a Pyrrhic victory. Their criticism of hegemonic ideas has gone mainstream, but not in the way that they intended. Distrust of traditional sources of expertise has gone up. Conservatives no longer trust liberals and vice versa. Wealthy patrons are interested in new ideas for how to solve global problems. Each of these trends rewards thinkers who exude optimism, self-confidence, and appealing solutions to hard problems. Traditional public intellectuals possess, at best, one of these three criteria. Each of these drivers rewards both the style and substance of thought leaders, regardless of their ideological leanings.

Another effect of the new Ideas Industry on the public sphere is the need to debate first principles again and again. Daniel Patrick Moynihan famously said, "You are entitled to your opinion. But you are not entitled to your own facts." For Moynihan, public policy debates occur in areas where facts are not in dispute but explanations for how to change those facts remain unsettled. Moynihan might have been right when he said those words, but he was wrong about the twenty-first century. The erosion of trust in experts and the rise of political polarization means that not everyone will accept a common set of stylized facts even if there is a consensus among intellectuals. Some thought leaders will have an obvious incentive to craft arguments around facts not in evidence to hawk their policy ideas. As a result, in many areas of foreign policy, there is no consensus about the "stylized facts" that ordinarily frame a debate.[127] This means, in turn, that first principles underlying these debates are also litigated by intellectuals. The result is more debate but not necessarily more productive debate.

The combined effect of these tectonic forces also creates an interesting bifurcation among foreign policy thought leaders. On the one hand, they incentivize excessive pessimism from some quarters. The loss of confidence in public institutions, demonization of ideological adversaries, and stagnation of the middle class makes it easy for thought leaders to assert that the world is on fire. In the ecosystem of foreign affairs punditry, pessimism sells.[128] The great thing about the three drivers discussed in this chapter is that they provide ready-made bogeymen for explaining why international relations are getting worse. Aspiring thought leaders can blame a corrupt and discredited system, or the other party, or the rise of plutocrats. Any or all of these villains will resonate more effectively with a twenty-first-century audience than will astringent claims that the current situation is not so bad.

On the other hand, these drivers also help to explain the rise of TED talks as a phenomenon. TED talks are designed for thought leaders to appeal to plutocrats. At less than twenty minutes, they are mercifully short—a perfect format for potential patrons. The working rich are busy people operating on a compressed schedule. Time is their scarcest resource, and they have limited attention spans. Talks pitched at the TED length have a far better chance of resonating with them than a more nuanced, in-depth take. The format itself also rewards more utopian thinking. There are no discussants for TED talks, no critical feedback. As Nathan Heller observed in the *New Yorker*, if TED has a political worldview, it is "framed in terms of broad and undeniable goods: education, environmental sustainability, equal rights."[129] This is perfectly consistent with the Silicon Valley theory of conflict-free politics in which technological solutions can triumph above all. As a medium that rewards emotional appeals and personal authenticity, TED benefits thought leaders far more than public intellectuals.

The rest of this book explores how these tectonic forces have affected the more established and emerging parts of the current marketplace of ideas. Going forward, the overwhelming focus will be on the state of the American marketplace of ideas, particularly with respect to foreign policy. But it is worth noting that each of the three drivers identified here have also been observed beyond the United States. It will be easy for non-Americans to identify the modern Ideas Industry as a peculiarly American invention. That is certainly a possibility. It is equally possible, however, that the United States is more harbinger than outlier for the future of the global marketplace of ideas.

PART II

3

The Standard Indictment Against the Academy

The recondite element in learning is still, as it has been in all ages, a very attractive and effective element for the purpose of impressing, or even imposing upon, the unlearned.

— Thorstein Veblen

AN OP-ED COLUMNIST FOR the *New York Times* might have the best possible perch to observe and expound upon the American marketplace of ideas. Even with the fragmentation of the media, the rest of the intellectual class listens when a *Times* columnist weighs in. So when Nicholas Kristof wrote in a February 2014 column that "some of the smartest thinkers on problems at home and around the world are university professors, but most of them just don't matter in today's great debates," the Ideas Industry noticed.[1]

According to Kristof, academics suffer from a multitude of sins. Academic orthodoxy has caused professors to reject newfangled technologies like social media. Just as well, since Kristof also asserted that the trend toward quantitative methods and "turgid prose" has rendered social scientists incapable of communicating with civilians. The academy "fostered a culture that glorifies arcane unintelligibility while disdaining impact and audience." The rigors of "publish-or-perish" in peer-reviewed scholarly journals extinguished any drive to write for a broader audience. Despite coming in at less than eight hundred words, Kristof's bill of indictment was thorough and detailed.

Kristof was hardly the first person to make this argument against the academy. Indeed, it has been made so frequently that I will label Kristof's bundle of arguments as the "Standard Indictment." Eighteen months before Kristof's op-ed, the head of the MacArthur Foundation also offered his own version of the Standard Indictment: "The theoretical turn across the social sciences and humanities that has cut off academic discourse from the way ordinary people and working professionals speak and think." A half-decade before Kristof's column, Joseph Nye argued in the *Washington Post*, "Scholars are paying less attention to questions about how their work relates to the policy world, and in many departments a focus on policy can hurt one's career. Advancement comes faster for those who develop mathematical models, new methodologies or theories expressed in jargon that is unintelligible to policymakers."[2] Even earlier than that, one public commentator concluded that "academic political scientists and economists have largely joined the Swiss guards, and abdicated the high prerogative of speculative thought." That last quote is from 1930, which suggests that the Standard Indictment has been around for a while.[3]

Many prominent commentators in the foreign policy community endorsed Kristof's thesis in the days after it appeared. Josh Marshall, the founder of Talking Points Memo, wrote, "Every incentive in academic life is geared against engagement with the world outside of academics. There's no other way to put it."[4] Richard Haass, president of the Council on Foreign Relations, tweeted that the academic social sciences focus on what is quantifiable rather than what is important. David Rothkopf, the CEO of *Foreign Policy* magazine went even further. He wholeheartedly endorsed Kristof's message, noting that "Kristof gets why we at FP are dialing back academic contributions—too many are opaque, abstract, incremental, dull."[5]

Still, something else happened after Kristof's op-ed appeared—a bevy of social scientists pushed back hard across a variety of media. This pushback did not appear in abstruse scholarly journals, but in the pages of the *Washington Post, Foreign Policy, Politico*, and elsewhere. Scholars as ideologically diverse as Corey Robin and Samuel Goldman rebutted the Standard Indictment, listing numerous concrete counterexamples of social scientists contributing to the public sphere. Georgetown

University professor Erik Voeten, writing in the *Washington Post*, con-cluded, "[Kristof's] piece is just a merciless exercise in stereotyping. It's like saying that op-ed writers just get their stories from cab drivers and pay little or no attention to facts. There are hundreds of academic political scientists whose research is far from irrelevant and who seek to communicate their insights to the general public via blogs, social media, op-eds, online lectures and so on."[6]

Voeten's argument was simply one of many that emerged to chal-lenge Kristof and his supporters.[7] The most obvious criticism was that Kristof's criteria for what qualified as "relevant" was extremely narrow. There are more ways for professors to matter than huddling with top policymakers. Indeed, that rarely happens for any group of individuals outside the government. Academics can influence the marketplace of ideas through a number of pathways.[8] Erica Chenoweth, a pioneer in research on nonviolent moments, noted, "This is the part that surprised me the most about Kristof's article: the supposition that our work is only relevant if it directly influences 'important people.' But what if one's work speaks to people outside of these traditional halls of power? Is such impact irrelevant?"[9]

As the pushback continued, Kristof acknowledged that the acad-emy had "erupted in outrage," but he mostly held his ground. The *New Yorker*'s Joshua Rothman surveyed the debate and concluded, "The response from the professoriate was swift, severe, accurate, and thoughtful. . . . if they didn't win with a knock-out blow, the professors won on points." When I asked Kristof a year after his column appeared whether he had changed his mind on the question, he said that he hadn't, but allowed that there were "some hopeful signs of progress, particularly in political science."[10]

At a minimum, academics had debated Kristof and his supporters to a draw. But this raises the question of why the Standard Indictment continues to be made again and again and again. Is this simply a case of "truthiness" dominating the actual truth, or are Kristof and his sup-porters right to conclude that "over all, there are . . . fewer public intel-lectuals on American university campuses today than a generation ago"?

I am an academic, so my short answer is the same frustrating one that all academics offer: it's complicated. The longer answer constitutes the rest of this chapter. Many academics have exploited the changes in the modern marketplace of ideas. For many more ensconced in the ivory tower, however, the current state of the Ideas Industry creates new and significant barriers to any effort to become a public intellectual. To put it another way, the Standard Indictment is not true of many individual academics, but parts of it are true about the academy writ large. And compared to other components of the Ideas Industry, the academy has lagged in adapting to the underlying changes discussed in the previous chapter.

Ironically, a generation ago social commentators were bemoaning the fact that academics were the *only* intellectuals left to supply the marketplace of ideas. In 1987, Russell Jacoby argued in *The Last Intellectuals* that the academy had crowded out all other thinkers. According to Jacoby, socioeconomic changes had rendered the bohemian life of an unaffiliated intellectual to be fiscally impossible. Beginning in the 1960s, the restructuring of cities triggered a migration to the suburbs, endangering any autonomous urban intellectual subculture.[11] Once-independent intellectuals naturally migrated toward the academy—which was expanding in the 1960s to accommodate the surge of baby boomers attending college. The New York intellectuals of the 1950s were not sustainable in this kind of ecosystem. Academia, on the other hand, was thriving. The ivory tower was the last refuge for aspiring intellectuals. As Jacoby lamented, "to be an intellectual requires a campus address."[12]

The academy's importance was even more pronounced in foreign affairs. The growth of American power in the first half of the twentieth century generated a demand for intellectuals to make sense of America's role in the world.[13] The onset of the Cold War meant that the federal government needed experts who could proffer advice on the Soviet Union, grand strategy, nuclear deterrence, and international economics. After the launch of Sputnik, the National Education Act of 1958 significantly boosted federal funding of university education. The Higher Education Act of 1965 and subsequent programs boosted it even further.[14] Universities raked in millions of research dollars to train graduate students in all the social science fields. In *The Power Elite*, C. Wright Mills asserted that "some universities, in fact, are financial branches of the military establishment, receiving three or four times as much money from the military as from all other sources combined."[15]

Mills exaggerated, but more recent accounts confirm the tight relationship between the academy and the federal government during the Cold War.[16] Professors played an outsized role in the discourse on national security and foreign policy.

The financial and personal ties between the ivory tower and the state had a profound effect on the academic contribution to the marketplace of ideas. Prominent scholars characterized it as a "golden age" in which "scholarship influenced American behavior, especially in the areas of nuclear strategy and arms control."[17] Writing about the Cold War era recently, the chairman of Georgetown University's department of government noted with a tinge of nostalgia, "Where the country was truly hegemonic was in its unmatched knowledge of the hidden interior of other nations: their language and cultures, their histories and political systems, their local economies and human geographies."[18] The 1950s and 1960s also saw the birth of the behavioral revolution—the belief that the aggregate collection of data would allow social scientists to derive general rules of the social world. Rational choice theory grew out of academic efforts to create scientific theories of decision making. A small coterie of game theorists and other social scientists helped to puzzle out theories of nuclear deterrence.[19] John Kennedy's best and brightest included a large helping of Harvard faculty. The national security advisors who dominated the 1960s and 1970s—Walt Rostow, Henry Kissinger, and Zbigniew Brzezinski—all began their careers as academics. Theodore White gushed about "action intellectuals" in *Life*, arguing that "this brotherhood of scholars has become the most provocative and propelling influence on all American government and politics."[20]

Not everyone viewed these trends as an unalloyed good. Many of the New York intellectuals scorned the migration of their fellow bohemians into the academy. In his essay "The Age of Conformity," Irving Howe lamented:

> Whenever they become absorbed into the accredited institutions of society they not only lose their traditional rebelliousness but to one extent or another *they cease to function as intellectuals.* The institutional world needs intellectuals *because* they are intellectuals but it does not want them *as* intellectuals. . . .

Here, in conversation with the depressed classes of the academy, one sees how the Ph.D. system—more powerful today than it has been for decades, since so few other choices are open to young literary men—grinds and batters personality into a mold of cautious routine.[21]

Howe exaggerated. As the Vietnam War progressed, it was the academy, not unaffiliated intellectuals, who led the opposition to the conflict.[22] But scholars and students embraced Howe's critique and rebelled against the cozy Cold War relationship between the academy and the state. Noam Chomsky's initial rise to public prominence came after he published "The Responsibility of Intellectuals" in the *New York Review of Books*. Chomsky's broadside against academic involvement in support of the Vietnam War echoed Howe's argument from a decade earlier. He scorned "the scholar-experts who are replacing the free-floating intellectuals of the past" and who "construct a 'value-free technology' for the solution of technical problems that arise in contemporary society."[23]

The widening of political tumult on campus and the narrow focus of professionalization caused academic intellectuals to retreat from the public sphere to the more removed landscape of academic debates.[24] After Vietnam, the number of concrete policy recommendations that appeared in *American Political Science Review* articles plummeted.[25] Thomas Schelling noted after the conflict in Southeast Asia ended, "I lost the access, I lost the audience, and I lost the motivation" to influence policymakers.[26] Academia turned inward. A generation later, Jacoby wrote, "The academic enterprise simultaneously expands and contracts; it steadily intrudes upon the larger culture, setting up private clubs for accredited members. That it is difficult for an educated adult American to name a single political scientist or sociologist or philosopher is not wholly his or her fault; the professionals have abandoned the public arena."[27]

These critiques raised an important point about precisely how academics could contribute to the marketplace of foreign policy ideas. One possibility is to advise the state—indeed, as many intellectual historians have observed, intellectuals and government can be closely intertwined.[28] Another option, however, is to critique state actions. Throughout the Vietnam era, the number of academic critiques of

American foreign policy increased, leading to the creation of a Caucus for a New Political Science within the discipline. During the Cold War, even radical academic critiques garnered official attention.[29] In 1957, Bertrand Russell wrote an open letter to the leaders of both superpowers calling for a summit to discuss "the conditions of co-existence." Nikita Khrushchev responded for the Soviet Union and John Foster Dulles for the United States. The exchange of letters did not change any policy, but the fact that both governments felt compelled to respond to Russell suggests the outsized influence of academic intellectuals during this period.

The end of the Cold War had a mixed effect on academia. Without question, one legacy of the Vietnam War and the Reagan Revolution was a distancing of the academy from the government. As Jacoby noted, professors became more and more wary of entering the political sphere. With their retreat, other non-academic generators of ideas made up for the shortfall. As Chapter 5 discusses, think tanks emerged as an alternative source of expertise and analysis for the government.[30]

At the same time, one could make a case that this was the heyday of academic influence on American foreign policy thinking. The Soviet collapse rendered the grand strategy of containment obsolete. US officials looked to the academy for ideas.[31] This sparked serious intellectual efforts to describe the post-Cold War world—and to devise strategies for American foreign policy. A number of academic thought leaders stepped forward to offer new ways of thinking about world politics. Francis Fukuyama argued that it was the end of history. John Mearsheimer postulated that the end of the Cold War would reintroduce instability into Europe. Joseph Nye put forward the first of several articulations of his concept of "soft power"—getting others to want what we want. Samuel Huntington warned about a coming clash of civilizations. An entire literature articulated the emergence of a democratic peace that could slowly expand as more countries democratized. Another debate raged over the durability and stability of American hegemony on world politics.[32] Even skeptics of academic influence over American foreign policy acknowledged that these debates framed how policymakers thought about the post-Cold War world.[33]

There are a few noteworthy aspects about this raft of arguments. First, they transcended scholarly journals. Many of the ideas in the preceding paragraph appeared in scholarly venues, but all of them also appeared in more accessible outlets like *The Atlantic* or *Foreign Affairs*. They were provocative enough to generate a penumbra of media coverage and commentary about each idea. Each of them had sufficient impact to be debated well beyond policy and academic circles. Catchphrases like "end of history," "clash of civilizations," and "soft power" wormed their way into the public sphere. Indeed, their legacies are so powerful that the authors of these ideas revisited them for a generation.[34] Like other foreign policy thought leaders, they have continued to market their arguments.

Second, many of these arguments proved to be either partly or wholly incorrect. Realists like Mearsheimer made overly pessimistic predictions about how the immediate post-Cold War order would affect NATO, nuclear proliferation, violent conflict, and balancing against the United States.[35] In actuality, the twenty years after the breakup of the Soviet Union saw dramatic declines in almost every category of political violence, particularly interstate wars.[36] Huntington's predictions were even more problematic. Even though they grabbed more headlines, clashes between civilizations proved far less prevalent than intracivilizational conflicts. For every civilizational conflict in the Balkans, there were bloodier wars between Sunni and Shia, or Tutsi and Hutu. One historian argued that Huntington's thesis was "proof as to why politicians should never listen to political scientists."[37] Fukuyama's optimism about the end of history was perhaps misplaced; he has focused more recently on the concept of "political decay," acknowledging that even successful and stable liberal democracies do not necessarily remain so in perpetuity.[38] Even more widely accepted concepts like soft power or the democratic peace have proven difficult to convert into practicable foreign policies.

While academics debated post-Cold War grand strategy, however, the collapse of the Soviet Union also meant a collapse of government support for international relations scholarship. The end of the Cold War happened during a period of record-setting federal budget deficits. In a climate of fiscal probity, the easiest programs to cut were those related to international affairs, such as foreign aid, information services, and diplomacy.[39] Programs like the National Security Education Program and the Foreign Language Assistance Program atrophied.[40]

These cutbacks resonated with an American public that became disinterested in the outside world. In 1986, 26 percent of Americans cited international issues as a problem for the United States; by 1998, only 7 percent made the same assertion.[41] As the American public turned inward, philanthropic funding for international affairs also plummeted. Foundation grants for most causes more than doubled in the 1990s, but in security studies, philanthropic support declined by 7 percent. University courses in security studies fell even further, by 30 percent.[42] It might not be a coincidence that, in contrast to the end of the Cold War, the September 11 terrorist attacks did not inspire a similar profusion of grand strategy musings from the academy.

The terrorist attacks and the US government's response had ambiguous effects on the academy's role in the public sphere. On the one hand, the academy's collective efforts to revive the critical intellectual activism of the Vietnam era proved to be awkward. The foreign policy contretemps during the George W. Bush years highlight this point. Political scientists abjectly failed to influence the marketplace of ideas in the run-up to the Second Gulf War. This was not due to a lack of effort. In the fall of 2002 a prominent group of international relations scholars took out an ad on the *New York Times* op-ed page warning against an invasion of Iraq. Many of these scholars published op-eds and essays arguing against going to war. These sentiments reflected the majority sentiment among international relations scholars. Nevertheless, their efforts generated little news coverage and even less acknowledgment in the corridors of power: as Chaim Kaufman concluded, "few [academic experts] presented comprehensive critiques, and fewer of those received wide media attention."[43]

On the other hand, the federal government did recognize anew the need for academic advice. The emergence of a new counterinsurgency doctrine came in no small part from the exposure of military officers to the social sciences.[44] In 2009, the Department of Defense started its Minerva program, awarding multimillion-dollar grants to political scientists to better understand areas of "strategic importance to U.S. national security policy."[45] When he announced the initiative, Secretary of Defense Robert Gates explicitly evoked the Cold War era when the federal government embraced "eggheads and ideas."[46] In 2011 the State Department formed a Foreign Affairs Policy Board to provide outside input to senior officials; the board was a mix of academics and former diplomats. An array of institutionalized and informal channels emerged through which academics could proffer their opinions to policymakers and the interested public.

Academics have played an important part in affecting the marketplace of foreign policy ideas in the past. There is at least some evidence that they can continue to play a role in the present. But it is also clear that the academy still wrestles with a long-simmering tension about consulting with the state. Some social scientists aspire to this role. Others are repulsed by it. By and large, political scientists proved amenable. The American Anthropological Association, however, explicitly rejected the Human Terrain System, an Army initiative for developing scholarly understanding of indigenous ethnic groups in places rife with terrorism. As a result, that program was discontinued in 2015.[47]

For all of the casual claims that the academy does not affect the marketplace of foreign policy ideas, in actuality its relevance has been robust in most decades.[48] Will the academy's relevance persist? To understand the academy's dilemma over its role in the modern marketplace of ideas, it is worth reviewing the particulars of the Standard Indictment to see if any of it is actually true.

The most accurate part of the Standard Indictment is that the professional incentives of scholars are not aligned perfectly with engaging the wider marketplace of ideas. For an academic, the most important audience remains other academics. As numerous critics beyond Kristof have observed, the professionalization of the academy prioritizes peer-reviewed publications over other forms of writing. Professors allocate the bulk of their efforts to researching, writing, and publishing in their field journals. The first task of any professor—particularly junior professors—is to publish in prestigious peer-reviewed outlets. Even scholars who have some facility with engaging a wider audience have warned that it takes time away from research.[49] It is great when academics also express their ideas to a wider audience. Professional incentives dictate, however, that this will always be the hobby and not the job.[50]

In this century, most scholarly papers are literally inaccessible to the lay public. Strict paywalls guarantee that those without a university email address cannot access most journal articles most of the time.[51]

Working papers are often available. Excerpts and summaries of high-profile papers will appear in popular newspapers and magazines. Some publishers now make some of their articles accessible to the interested public at propitious moments. The economics of publishing in the Internet age, however, guarantees that these will be rare occurrences. If academic publishers made all of their journals accessible to everyone all of the time, they would quickly go bankrupt.

Even if the paywalls fell, peer-reviewed journal articles would remain figuratively inaccessible to most of the lay public. The simple fact is that most academics either do not or cannot write for a public audience.[52] The reasons for this are disputed. Numerous critics have blasted the academy for "turgid, soggy, wooden, bloated, clumsy, obscure, unpleasant to read, and impossible to understand" prose.[53] Every few years a tale makes the rounds of an academic who got an article accepted despite churning out nothing but postmodern gobbledygook.[54]

To reiterate a theme, however, academics write scholarly articles for their most important audience: other academics in their specialty. Those readers are pivotal to tenure, promotion, awards, honors, and grants. And it is simply easier for professors to rely on jargon when crafting prose for that audience. All disciplines, professions, and careers develop their own specialized argot to economize on communication.[55] UCLA political scientist Lynn Vavreck notes that "jargon exists within disciplines to facilitate the fast and efficient exchange of knowledge or information among experts."[56] In other words, a layperson's unnecessary jargon is an expert's convenient shorthand.

For example, if I were to write that a new US alliance with Vietnam might trigger a "security dilemma" with China, every international relations expert would immediately understand my meaning. If I use that term in an essay designed to reach a wider audience, however, it requires multiple sentences to explain what I mean. A security dilemma occurs when:

1) One country, perceiving a threat to its security, bolsters its defense capabilities.
2) That action in turn makes rival actors nervous, because they see such measures as threatening to them.

3) These other countries respond with arms buildups and alliances of their own.

4) One's own efforts to enhance its security paradoxically increase one's insecurity.

Among my colleagues, all I have to say is "security dilemma" and they know precisely what I mean. By using professional argot, social scientists—and academics in general—are able to write and communicate with each other more quickly than by using plain language.

Many of the tropes that non-academics don't like about academic prose also reflect a scholarly inclination toward hedging. For example, one of my principle areas of research is economic sanctions. I have researched and written peer-reviewed articles and books about when economic coercion will be used, the conditions under which they will yield political concessions, the negative side effects of sanctions, and how they have evolved over time. But when I have been asked to write on this subject for a more popular audience, an editor has inevitably asked me to distill my argument to answer a simple question: "Do sanctions work?" The result is an inevitable negotiation between an editor who wants a simple thesis and my desire for a more nuanced take that reflects my actual research findings.

The classic academic answer to almost any question is "it depends." In academic journals, social scientists can articulate all of the qualifications, exceptions, and emendations that come with their central argument. This hedging instinct makes it tricky, however, to convert a scholarly article into something more accessible to the general-interest reader. Editors and readers want a writer to get to the point with clear, forceful prose. One political scientist, in recommending how to communicate through the mainstream media, advises "clear, clean language using colorful metaphors" and the use of "emotional connotations" in arguments.[57] Academics are preternaturally leery of these tropes, because the messages they convey will be far more sweeping in scope than the academic's original argument. This is an inherent tension between scholarship and communication, one that breeds resentment for academics trying to engage a wider audience as well as readers who have to wade through complex, cautious prose.

How should academics respond to the accusation of jargon-y, hedge-filled prose? To start, by pointing out that it is rather rich of pundits, policymakers, and politicians to complain about the inelegant language of academics. I heard far more jargon used in my time in government than as an academic. Criticism of political rhetoric long predates any criticism of academic discourse, and rightly so. At least academic jargon is designed to make it easier for scholars to communicate with each other; much political jargon exists to obfuscate the plain meaning of words from the public. As George Orwell noted in 1946: "Political language—and with variations this is true of all political parties, from Conservatives to Anarchists—is designed to make lies sound truthful and murder respectable, and to give an appearance of solidity to pure wind."[58] Modern political argot is far more likely to obfuscate than to inspire. The ways that twenty-first-century American politicians have used phrases like "existential threat," "kinetic action," "abundance of caution," and "politically incorrect" suggest that academics are far from the worst abusers of the English language.[59]

A less *tu quoque* response is that it is possible for academics to write different versions of the same argument for different audiences. A welter of publications ranging from the *Washington Post* to *FiveThirtyEight* to *Vox* crave social science research to translate for the masses. As academics expand their public outreach, they have made serious inroads into mainstream media outlets. In recent years, the *Washington Post* subsumed several multi-author blogs run by social science academics—The Monkey Cage and Volokh Conspiracy—under its umbrella.[60] In the same week that Kristof's op-ed ran, the *New York Times* hired two political scientists and an economist to aid in creating the Upshot, its project in analytical journalism. These new outlets have had a salutary effect on academic contributions to the marketplace of foreign policy ideas.

The Standard Indictment's claim that professors disdain the mainstream media and social media is particularly off-base. Indeed, academics have embraced new online platforms with gusto, welcoming the growth of venues beyond peer-reviewed publications to hawk their wares to the general public. A profusion of outlets ranging from *The Diplomat* to *Defense One* to *War on the Rocks* have expanded the reach of international relations scholars. Blogs have been around so long that they are now accepted as something that professors do on the side. Political scientists are happy to contribute to the Monkey Cage, Mischiefs of Faction, or Political Violence at a Glance. Other disciplines such as sociology and economics have done the same.[61] Academics are also embracing other social media to communicate with policymakers and the public, ranging from Twitter to TEDx. Kristof's contention that academics were ignoring new media outlets was simply wrong, as he found out in numerous Twitter responses after his column ran.

But even if one can engage a public audience, is it in that academic's career interest to do so? This is another part of the Standard Indictment. As Stephen Walt notes, "the academic field of [international relations] is a self-regulating enterprise, and success in the profession depends almost entirely on one's reputation among one's peers. There is therefore a large incentive to conform to the norms of the discipline and write primarily for other academics."[62] Walt's description of international relations applies to the entire academy.

To understand the fear of this part of the Standard Indictment within the ivory tower, consider two personal anecdotes from the last decade. In 2004, a combination of good luck and good timing meant that I had submitted an essay to *Foreign Affairs* about offshore outsourcing just when that issue blew up in the national media. As a result, my first-ever essay in that august journal would be the lead article. This was heady news for an untenured academic. Later that day, I bumped into a senior colleague in my department at the University of Chicago. Naturally, I told him about having the lead article in *Foreign Affairs*. In response, this senior scholar cocked his head, looked at me, and asked, "Why?"[63] I had no answer to the question; to me it was obvious that publishing in the most widely read international relations publication was a good thing. In retrospect, I should have recognized then that my future prospects at Chicago were precarious. After they denied me tenure, I became a cautionary tale for junior scholars who wanted to write for a public audience.[64]

A few years later, as a full professor, I attended a small conference devoted to the idea of getting scholars and policymakers in the same room to talk about US policy toward another great power that shall not be named. The idea was that government officials could highlight issues that professors might have overlooked, and vice versa. Everything was going along swimmingly until one of the policymakers in the room complained about one of the academic memos being a little too long.

In response, an eminent international relations scholar—someone who is very well known inside the academy and decidedly not well known outside of it—went off on a righteous rant. She asked why people in Washington don't actually read what experts think about a particular issue. It isn't just that political scientists are being marginalized, she vented—they have good insights and yet are being completely ignored.

This provoked a rollicking good debate, and afterward, many of the academics in attendance gathered around the eminent political scientist to laud those remarks. We then chatted about how political scientists could enter the public sphere with a bit more vim and vigor. Someone suggested that this might be easier if younger scholars felt that they could engage in public debate without the fear of disapproval from the profession. At which point she frowned and said something to the effect of, "Oh, no. Once someone has tenure, and a full publishing pedigree, then they can start making public pronouncements. But not until then."

These parables were not outliers. Last decade the *Chronicle of Higher Education* was replete with essays warning scholars against the hazards of engaging the wider public.[65] In an article encouraging junior scholars to engage with a wider audience, political scientist Cheryl Boudreau noted, "It is not uncommon for junior scholars to believe that they should be read but not heard."[66] Lynn Vavreck has published widely in scholarly journals and is a regular contributor to the *New York Times*. But she warned junior colleagues:

> Obviously, the time that I spend writing for the *New York Times* is time that I'm not spending writing articles for peer review, so that's a cost. You have to be ready to make that tradeoff. Because of this, I would not recommend that assistant professors engage in this work. It takes time away from doing research, and we need our young scholars doing science.[67]

Now there are a few things wrong with Vavreck's advice. First, junior scholars are usually on the cutting edge of social science research; in political science, for example, junior scholars author or co-author two-thirds of all articles in top-tier journals.[68] It is precisely because junior scholars are publishing new and innovative work that they should also try to make that work more accessible to the rest of the world. Second, senior scholars too often assume that it takes the same length of time to craft a paragraph of text for an op-ed or a blog post as it does to create a paragraph of scholarly text. Speaking from my own experience, this is simply not true. A scholarly article of ten thousand words takes me months if not years to research, write, and revise. A *Foreign Affairs* essay of four thousand words takes me less than two weeks. A column for the *Washington Post* takes me anywhere from thirty to ninety minutes. Not all prose takes equal effort. This misperception contributes to a massive overestimation of the effort devoted to public engagement, and a subsequent exaggeration of the opportunity costs in the form of lost scholarship.

Even more problematic is the notion that engaging the public sphere is a pure substitute for scholarship. The proliferation of media platforms has helped the discipline in numerous ways. Part of the reason the academy has adapted so quickly to social media and online publication is that these platforms also facilitate traditional academic research programs.[69] Blog posts or tweets can substitute for the traditional practice of exchanges of letters in journals. For political scientists in particular, engaging with the public or policymakers permits them to discover issue areas where the public viewpoint or the policy consensus is at variance with accepted political science. That creates opportunities for further engagement.

Even if this attitude is changing—and it is—these parables reveal the depths of the problem. Vavreck's flawed advice has consequences. Most people who want to earn a Ph.D. in the social sciences have some desire to influence public debate when they enter graduate school. But academics are also creatures of habit. During their formative years in the profession, they are socialized to focus exclusively on peer-reviewed publications and write only for fellow academics. All it takes is a few cautionary notes from senior academics to encourage junior scholars to self-censor. If they are both lucky and good, it will take most social scientists anywhere from ten to fifteen years to earn a Ph.D., a tenure-track job, and then tenure. It is unrealistic to expect them to suddenly exercise communication muscles that have atrophied for decades. It would be like asking a world-class basketball player to excel at baseball because he loved the sport as a kid.

A related problem is that the Ideas Industry's hierarchy of prestige does not perfectly match the hierarchy that exists strictly within the academy. The skills needed to survive and thrive in the public sphere are not the skills needed in traditional academic scholarship. The latter rests on a bedrock of original research, careful fact checking, rigorous peer review, and citations to authoritative and relevant academic literatures. Writers who excel at public engagement possess different comparative advantages: speed, clarity, wit, and the ability to provide self-assured, real-time analysis. This skill set is unevenly distributed across the academic hierarchy. An adjunct professor, graduate student, or lay person might be marginalized within the traditional confines of the academy; in the wider marketplace of ideas, their power could be much greater.

The modern Ideas Industry rewards intellectuals who are willing to engage a wider audience. Academics reward scholarship and care less about accessibility to outsiders. While some scholars might excel at both tasks, it is more likely that some professors will be better at public outreach than others. These skills create new pathways to public recognition beyond the control of traditional academic gatekeepers. And any usurpation of scholarly authority breeds resentment and discontent among those who benefit the most from the scholarly status quo. Exposure to norms or hierarchies at variance with pre-existing academic structures will naturally trigger suspicion and resentment. Senior scholars who join social media to advertise their scholarly work must confront the reality that despite their hard-earned academic prestige, there will be graduate students with more Twitter followers.

There is also the guilt that some academics feel if they do break through to a wider audience. My academic colleagues occasionally tell me that I am a good writer. To normal people this sounds like praise; because of my socialization as an academic, however, I will always interpret it as a backhanded compliment. If one is known for being a good writer, the subtle signal is that the presentation is better than the ideas—and it is the ideas that animate the professoriate. Many scholars conflate clarity with simple-mindedness. Long ago John Kenneth Galbraith warned economists, "Any specialist who ventures to write on money with a view to making himself intelligible works under a grave moral hazard. He will be accused of oversimplification."[70] Boudreau echoed this problem when noting that "some junior scholars are concerned that their research will not be perceived as 'real' political science if it is written or presented in lay terms."[71] I was once told that some colleagues believed my writing ability had enabled me to get middling articles published in superior journals.

It will always be amusing to imagine my prose being so mellifluous that it bamboozled peer reviewers into abandoning their critical faculties. In actuality, this charge is absurd. Galbraith observed that "in the social sciences, much unclear writing is based on unclear or incomplete thought. It is possible with safety to be technically obscure about something you haven't thought out. It is impossible to be wholly clear on something you do not understand. Clarity thus exposes flaws in the thought."[72] Bad writers can more easily truck bad ideas through the peer-review process unless referees admit that some model, estimation technique, or critical analysis fails to make sense.[73] Nevertheless, when I am told that I am a good writer, my inner academic feels a twinge of insecurity.

If the professional incentives of academics are stacked against public engagement, then why did so many academics push back against the Standard Indictment when Kristof repeated it? The first reason is that the norms have changed considerably even in the past decade. University administrators and academic chairs have grown more appreciative of professors capable of writing for a general audience. There have also been a series of initiatives to ensure that junior scholars translate their academic research into more accessible forms, particularly in the social sciences. The Tobin Project, for example, sponsors academic research that is pertinent to policy debates. They also arrange meetings between policymakers and academics to enable the exchange of ideas. Similarly, the Carnegie Corporation funded the Bridging the Gap Initiative, a consortium of three universities that tutor junior scholars and connect them with policymakers from the diplomatic, defense, and intelligence communities. The Scholars Strategy Network, an association of academics and researchers directed by noted sociologist and political scientist Theda Skocpol, pursued a similar strategy toward national, state, and local issues.[74] The Op-Ed Project focuses on training women academics to write essays for a wider audience.

A lot has changed in the past decade. Many of the trends toward pure scholasticism seem to have peaked around the turn of the century. Even critics acknowledge that these trends have reversed somewhat.[75] Survey after survey of international relations scholars shows a widespread acceptance of engaging with the public sphere. A majority of international relations scholars stated that they had consulted with other political actors, engaged in advocacy to advance their expert opinions, and shifted their research agenda in response to real-world events.[76] According to a 2012 survey of international relations professors, more than 51 percent believed that blogs had improved the state of the scholarly field. Fully 90 percent of respondents thought blogs had improved foreign-policy formulation.[77] Retrograde efforts to block such outlets have been beaten back with little difficulty. Many scholars have advanced their professional careers by developing well-respected blogs. No one will get tenure solely for being good at social media, but that aspect of public outreach is no longer viewed as a negative inside the academy.

As previously noted, the larger media landscape has also changed. In direct response to Kristof's op-ed, Stanford University political scientist James Fearon demonstrated that political scientists had actually increased their visibility in the press at the same time Kristof claimed the opposite had occurred.[78] In 2010, Ezra Klein noted the marginalization of political science in the *Washington Post*; four years later, Klein argued in *Vox* that "perhaps the single best thing that's happened to political journalism in the time I've been doing it is the rise of political science."[79] Ironically, claims that academics rely too much on quantitative techniques reached a crescendo just as that work began to gain mainstream acceptance.

Even if parts of the Standard Indictment have mattered in the past, its effect on the academy has waned. The ivory tower is trending in the right direction. But if bad writing and specialization are not the primary source for the academy's woes, what is? The changes that have created the modern Ideas Industry have also affected the academy's ability to influence the marketplace of ideas—and mostly not in a good way.

The erosion of trust in heretofore respected institutions is a problem for the ivory tower. Academics attempting to weigh in on public affairs confront a delegitimizing assault on the academy—call it the "War on College." As college tuition prices continue to outpace inflation and wage growth, economics writers have decried the explosion of student debt and declared the existence of a higher-ed "bubble." An ever-more heterogeneous array of critics continues to pick at the myriad flaws of the academy. The War on College has been a staple of the political right for some time. Conservatives have been blasting the ivory tower as godless, leftist, and insular from the days of William F. Buckley's *God and Man at Yale.* The conservative broadside against the academy is a generational rite, passing down from Buckley to Allan Bloom's *The Closing of the American Mind,* then to Ross Douthat's *Privilege,* and Naomi Schaefer Riley's *The Faculty Lounges.*

The more recent conservative criticism of the academy focuses on speech restrictions. Greg Lukianoff and Jonathan Haidt have decried the growing problem of mollycoddling students because of political correctness, "to scrub campuses clean of words, ideas, and subjects that might cause discomfort or give offense."[80] Lukianoff heads the Foundation for Individual Rights in Education (FIRE), which has been quite busy documenting instances of political correctness run amok. Lukianoff and Haidt are hardly the only observers to make this point.[81] Nor is there a shortage of appalling anecdotes. These range from a Northwestern University professor who faced a Title IX inquisition for publicly criticizing the sexual harassment process at her university to a Wesleyan University student movement to defund a school newspaper for publishing a controversial op-ed.[82] Each case bolsters the supposition that the spirit of intellectual inquiry is being stifled on campus.

Conservative criticisms of the academy are not new. What is new is the vocal criticism coming from the left. Feminists have attacked universities for being havens of rampant sexual assault. Minority groups have critiqued the structural privilege that allegedly exists in campuses inhabited mostly by white and Asian students. Professors themselves have bemoaned the misplaced priorities within the university, as tenured professor lines decline and staff and administrative positions explode.[83] Leftist critics deplore universities as bastions of elitism, neoliberalism, and corporatism, sublimating the goal of higher education in favor of appeasing corporate donors.

The core of William Deresiewicz's *Excellent Sheep*, for example, is a critique of the university's surrender to neoliberal principles.[84] He deplores preparing students for the market economy at the expense of higher learning. In a follow-up essay in *Harper's*, Deresiewicz doubled down on his criticisms, accusing universities of sacrificing the aims of intellectual and moral inquiry to the altar of market principles: "This is education in the age of neoliberalism . . . an ideology that reduces all values to money values. The worth of a thing is the price of the thing. The worth of a person is the wealth of the person. Neoliberalism tells you that you are valuable exclusively in terms of your activity in the marketplace—in Wordsworth's phrase, your getting and spending."[85] Deresiewicz is hardly alone in this critique. Others have bemoaned the "creeping corporatism of the American university."[86]

These critiques are in fundamental tension. As Lukianoff and Haidt observe, political correctness "teaches students to think in a very different way. It prepares them poorly for professional life, which often demands intellectual engagement with people and ideas one might find uncongenial or wrong."[87] If this is true, then Deresiewicz is wrong to accuse universities of being neoliberal incubators. If Deresiewicz is correct, then Lukianoff and Haidt's hypothesis is exaggerated. Still, the fact that both critiques are flourishing at the same time demonstrates the bipartisan support for a War on College, and the growing disdain for the professors housed in those ivory towers. It makes it easier for policymakers and citizens to dismiss academic interventions in the public sphere. It is little wonder that the Standard Indictment continues to find a sympathetic audience.

Even if one thinks of academic research as independent from the general ills of higher education, there has been an erosion of trust. Many top-tier professors have had their reputations tarnished with plagiarism scandals. In this century, high-flying academics such as Stephen Ambrose, Doris Kearns Goodwin, Charles Ogletree, Laurence Tribe, and Matthew Whitaker were caught plagiarizing material from lesser-known scholars. Financial economists have been accused of significant conflicts of interest between their scholarly work and their consulting work.[88] Other academic frauds have been unearthed in recent years as well. In 2011, famed social psychologist Diederik Stapel admitted to outright fabrication of data. In 2015, after a political science paper published in *Science* was retracted, the *New York Times* reported that "the case has shaken not only the community of political scientists but also public trust in the way the scientific establishment vets new findings."[89] The editors of a blog called "Retraction Watch," devoted to cases of academic fraud, observed that such cases are more likely to occur at more prestigious journals.[90]

Even in instances when no academic fraud has been committed, the robustness of social science research is increasingly under question. Two Federal Reserve economists surveyed the state of replicable findings in top-tier economics journals, and found that, on their own, they were only able to reproduce a third of the surveyed findings. They concluded: "Because we successfully replicate less than half of the papers in our sample even with assistance from the authors, we conclude that economics research is usually not replicable."[91] One recent study of psychology journals made headlines after concluding that only a third of the findings were robust to replication. Naturally, that study has itself been challenged on methodological grounds.[92] To any lay reader, such back-and-forth further discredits the discipline's authority. Numerous social science disciplines are attempting to ratchet up the ability to replicate findings, but these initiatives are also encountering significant blowback about misapplied standards.[93] With these kind of scandals, revelations, and controversies, it is extremely easy for outside observers to doubt the value of the academy.

The other changes in the marketplace of ideas—rising levels of political polarization and economic inequality—also impair the ability of academics to thrive in the modern Ideas Industry. Indeed, Kristof's accusation of political homogeneity in the academy cannot be refuted, and it is unsurprising that this is the area he followed up on in subsequent columns.[94] The problem with political polarization is that academics are almost universally on one side of the political spectrum. Whether one looks at public opinion surveys or the flows of campaign contributions, the data is incontrovertible: as a group, American academics are far more liberal than the rest of the country.[95] Past surveys of academics suggest that professors have always been more liberal than the American public. That divergence has increased over the past twenty-five years, however. According to UCLA's Higher Education Research Institute, which polls academics every three years, the number of self-identified liberals and leftists in 1990 was roughly equal to the number of moderates in the ivory tower. As Figure 3.1 demonstrates, by 2010 there were twice as many liberals as moderates, and almost six times as many liberals as conservatives. If one looks only at the social sciences and the humanities faculties, these ratios are even more stacked in the favor of liberals and leftists.[96]

To be clear, this leftward drift of the academy does not necessarily have to lead to politically biased scholarship, any more than a rightward drift in the officer corps of the armed forces imperils civil-military relations. Both the military and the professoriate are *professions*. Regardless of political or personal proclivities, professionals do their job based on their training, which in turn is determined by the codes and standards of the discipline. This is an idea that academics have embraced since the days of Max Weber.[97] In the military, this means that soldiers respect the chain of command and adhere to their honor codes. In the academy, this means a divorce between one's political views, one's research findings, and what one teaches in the classroom. Corey Robin, for

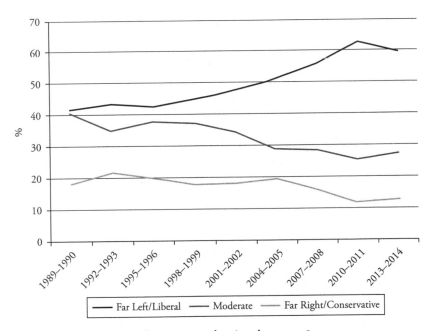

FIGURE 3.1 Political Preferences in the Academy, 1989–2014
Source: http://heterodoxacademy.org/problems.

example, is well to the left of the American body politic, and engages in political activism outside the classroom. He nonetheless is quite severe in segmenting that activism from his professional duties of teaching and research.[98]

While professionalism can ensure that left-leaning academics can still do good research, the lack of political heterogeneity poses deeper problems. One examination of social psychology concluded that liberal political bias did not invalidate existing research but did bias the direction of future research. Most significantly, "researchers may concentrate on topics that validate the liberal progress narrative and avoid topics that contest that narrative."[99] Sociology suffers from a similar problem. One article concluded that the leftward tilt of public sociology "compresses the range of acceptable scholarship, and constrains sociological insight."[100] These problems are hardly unique to these subfields; other research has demonstrated a link between a scholar's political tilt and their research trajectory in international relations research and legal scholarship.[101] The leftward drift of the academy makes it easy for conservatives to ignore or deride the public interventions of academics.

The leftist tilt on campus has had a deleterious effect on alumni donations,[102] but there is an even bigger problem with universities seeking financial assistance from the modern Ideas Industry. The academy's relationship with philanthrocapitalists has soured compared to other institutions. In the past, America's plutocrats were some of the biggest boosters of the ivory tower. During the last Gilded Age, titans such as John Rockefeller, J.P. Morgan, Henry Ford, and Andrew Carnegie founded or funded some of America's greatest universities. To be sure, universities still receive a great deal of money from extremely wealthy alums, but the current crop of plutocrats are interested in "impact investments," even in their philanthropy.[103] Benefactors want their giving to have direct impact on both the real world and the marketplace of ideas. But as the Brookings Institution's Darrell West notes, the academy is an imperfect vessel for this kind of advocacy:

> With colleges and universities increasingly drawn into divisive policy controversies, it is becoming harder to separate academic philanthropy from advocacy. Many donors who have a strong point of view want educational institutions to hold events, publish reports, or

even offer courses that address the subjects of interest to them. Such demands can put the academy, which tries to be non-partisan as an institution, in a difficult position.[104]

Another, more vocal group of billionaires suggests that the merits of universities have been vastly overrated. Part of this comes through example: Bill Gates, Steve Jobs, and Mark Zuckerberg never graduated from college, and yet they thrived in Silicon Valley. Commentators like Instapundit's Glenn Reynolds have gone so far as to argue that this should be evidence that college is a vastly overrated enterprise, despite overwhelming data to the contrary.[105]

Some billionaires go further and argue that the current incarnation of the ivory tower actually retards the marketplace of ideas. According to this line of thinking, universities exist merely as credential factories. PayPal founder Peter Thiel has gone the furthest down this road. He has set up Thiel fellowships, which reward winners with $100,000 provided they "skip or stop out of college" for the two years of the program.[106] Thiel argues that "college can be good for learning about what's been done before, but it can also discourage young people from doing something new—especially when it leaves them in debt." He has doubled and tripled down on this thesis in myriad interviews and op-eds. In an interview with *Weekly Standard* editor William Kristol, Thiel said:

> The university system in 2014, it's like the Catholic Church circa 1514. . . . you have this priestly class of professors that doesn't do very much work, people are buying indulgences in the form of amassing enormous debt for the sort of the secular salvation that a diploma represents. And what I think is very similar to the 16th century is that the Reformation will come largely from outside.[107]

In other interviews and writings, Thiel has used different analogies, comparing elite universities to zero-sum tournaments or trendy nightclubs.[108]

Why is there hostility between the academy and an industry whose geographic epicenter is Stanford University? To be fair, part of it is that the credential of a college degree is far less necessary in the tech sector than in other parts of the economy. But I would argue that much of the hostility plutocrats feel toward academics comes from two other sources. The first is the tendency of most social science research to dismiss the "Great Man" theory of events. The next chapter covers this more thoroughly, but what matters here is that most academics tend to think that most plutocrats succeed because they are standing on the shoulders of giants. Their own abilities matter, but those abilities are not a sufficient explanation for their success. This contradicts the standard plutocratic narrative of the self-made men, and as such can be intellectually or even existentially discomfiting.

The final clash between the academy and the plutocratic class is cultural. Both groups are very curious about ideas, but their intellectual mien could not be more different. Twenty-first-century philanthropists are interested in action; professors are interested in analysis. This gap goes back to Max Weber's "Science as a Vocation," in which he implored professors to keep their academic tasks separate from other spheres of life, especially politics. This was not to say that academics could not engage the public sphere; Weber noted that the primary task of a professor was to "teach his students to recognize 'inconvenient' facts." Weber further argued, however, that political action was a different activity altogether: "The qualities that make a man an excellent scholar and academic teacher are not the qualities that make him a leader to give direction in practical life, or, more specifically, in politics."[109] An academic acting as a public intellectual is trying to straddle both of these roles, and risks doing both poorly.[110]

The professoriate has largely adhered to the Weberian notion of being removed from politics. Academics look at the social world as something to be studied, to be researched, to be analyzed, even to be opined—but not to be acted upon. What has changed is the way that others view the academic approach. It is now viewed with disdain rather than respect in some quarters. Tom Wolfe, for example, concluded a scabrous essay on academic intellectuals with the following: "All the intellectual wants, in his heart of hearts, is to hold on to what was magically given to him one shining moment a century ago. He asks for nothing more than to remain aloof, removed, as Revel once put it, from the mob, the philistines . . . 'the middle class.'"[111] To critics, the academic perch of seeming above it all is elitist. To potential benefactors, it is seen as a surrender to inaction.

The Standard Indictment against the ivory tower is both right and wrong. No doubt, the academy has many quirks and foibles, such as the jargon-filled prose and the career incentives. But Kristof and his supporters are wrong to argue that these idiosyncrasies are what keeps the academy from influencing the marketplace of ideas. Many individual academics have exploited the new Ideas Industry to the fullest. Some have taken advantage of the proliferation of media platforms to engage with a wider audience. Some social scientists have entered the partisan fray and managed to survive, moving on to serve in government and maintaining their reputation across the political spectrum. And some academics have managed to curry favor with wealthy benefactors interested in funding their research.

One problem is that the academics most likely to thrive in the Ideas Industry are those who adopt the tropes of thought leaders. The degree of relative self-confidence a scholar projects has an undeniable effect on how others perceive the argument. As much as published scholarship is supposed to count *über alles*, there is no denying that confident scholars can sway opinion. I know colleagues who make fantastically dubious but bold predictions, and I envy their serene certitude.

While individual academics have learned how to survive and thrive in the Ideas Industry, it would be harder to say that the academy has done the same. Part of it is the academic norms that are part of the Standard Indictment. Part of it is that the academy is vulnerable to partisan attack. And a big part of it is that many of conclusions of academic researchers do not jibe with the worldview of policymakers, media outlets, and potential funders. Academics frequently intervene in the marketplace of ideas as traditional public intellectuals, ready to explain why some new policy idea is unlikely to work. Patrons would much rather bankroll thought leaders. Thought leaders have two qualities that benefactors like: a positive idea for change and the conviction that they can make a difference.

Of course, the term "academy" masks a number of different disciplines. Some of these disciplines, such as economics, have done better in the Ideas Industry than others, political science being one example. Why?

4

The Disciplines: Why Economics Thrives While Political Science Survives

Imagine that the job market was better for sociologists or political scientists than for economists. This would unnerve economists no end.

— Richard Freeman

WHEN I WAS IN GRADUATE school studying economics and political science, I heard the same joke over and over: an economist who switches to political science raises the average intelligence of both departments. It's a clever joke that happens to be false. The problem is, a lot of otherwise smart people believe it to be true.

While Nicholas Kristof's broadside against the academy was aimed at the ivory tower writ large, he concentrated most of his fire on political science. Kristof lamented that his "onetime love, political science, is a particular offender and seems to be trying, in terms of practical impact, to commit suicide."[1] He has hardly been alone in levying that accusation. Indeed, little more than six months after Kristof's commentary, Tom Ricks made nearly identical complaints about "the extraordinary irrelevance of political science" in *Foreign Policy*.[2]

Political scientists have routinely engaged in self-flagellation over the alleged sins of the discipline. Robert Putnam, in his 2002 presidential address to the American Political Science Association, noted that "serving the public (and the public interest) has become an afterthought to our other professional rights and duties."[3] A few years later Alan Wolfe wrote in the *Chronicle of Higher Education* that "one can only hope that political scientists will decide to . . . go back to an era in which understanding reality was more important than advancing one's pet methodology." More recently, noted international security scholar Steven Van Evera blogged that "U.S. social sciences are frozen in poisoned amber. . . . The disciplinary silos of this structure foster blinkered, sterile academic monocultures." Michael Desch concluded, "The problem, in a nutshell, is that scholars increasingly equate rigor with particular techniques (mathematics and models) and ignore broader criteria of relevance."[4] All of this would seem to be grist for Kristof's mill.

There are two problems with this argument, however. The first is that complaints about the irrelevance of political science date back decades before Kristof's op-ed. In 1927, American Political Science Association president Charles Beard despaired over how "minute and unimportant academic study" was leading to "the peril of narrowing the vision while accumulating information." In 1939, Robert S. Lynd observed that the problem with political science was that it did not move fast enough to keep pace with policymakers. He concluded that "academic political scientists lived in a genteel world apart from the rough-and-ready ward-politician." In 1951, David Easton wrote in the *Journal of Politics* that "the task of the social scientist has been too sharply and artificially divorced from that of the politician."[5] Political scientists have complained about the perceived irrelevance of political science since long before tools like formal modeling or Bayesian statistics were widespread in the discipline. The notion that recent methodological fads alone are responsible for the perceived marginalization of political science relies on some convenient amnesia.

The bigger problem is that all of the alleged sins of political science exist in even more concentrated form in the field of economics. Economics has gone the furthest down the road in the social sciences in the use of game theory, advanced econometrics, randomized control trials, and more arcane methodologies. The significant complaints levied against the social sciences—the confusing techniques, the complex equations, the turgid prose—pervade economics. As for economists writing accessibly for a public audience, good luck with that. Paul Krugman is a lucid wordsmith, but as he once confessed to his readers: "I hope you think that I am an acceptable writer, but when it comes to economics I speak English as a second language: I think in equations and diagrams, then translate."[6] Krugman is among the more

self-aware of economists; most others could care less about the quality
of their prose. If Kristof's accusations against the academy were caus-
ally correct, then economics should be the *least* influential of the social
sciences. And yet, as we shall see, the opposite is true. Indeed, the influence and prestige gap has been so great that political scientists stretch-
ing back to Beard have yearned for closer ties to economics. Economists
as variegated as John Kenneth Galbraith and Gordon Tullock share one
commonality, however: rubbishing political science.[7]

Kristof's characterization of political science is not necessarily wrong,
but it is irrelevant. Even though the academy as a whole has improved
its accessibility to the outside world, economics is the social science
discipline that best fits Kristof's caricature, and it is the most influential
in the marketplace of ideas. Why has economics thrived while political
science has merely survived? The answer points to how and why the
modern Ideas Industry rewards and punishes different social science
disciplines.

Any assessment of the relative influence of economics and political science concludes that economists have an outsized voice inside and outside the academy. According to sociologist Marion Fourcade, economists are at the apex of the social sciences' pecking order.[8] Economists
earn the highest average salaries of the social sciences. They excel at
populating themselves across the academy. Economists do not merely
inhabit their own department. The discipline has colonized faculty slots
in most business and public policy schools, and they are encroaching
on law schools as well. Other academic disciplines cite economists frequently, but economists do not return the favor nearly as often. Noted
economist Dani Rodrik explains, "Because economists share a language
and a method, they are prone to disregard, or deprecate, nonecono-
mists' point of view."[9] Fourcade and her colleagues conclude:

> Most economists feel quite secure about their value-added. They are
> comforted in this feeling by the fairly unified disciplinary frame-
> work behind them, higher salaries that many of them believe reflect
> some true fundamental value, and a whole institutional structure—
> from newspapers to congressional committees to international policy
> circles—looking up to them for answers, especially in hard times. [10]

The influence of economics extends well beyond the academy. As noted in the previous chapter, the visibility of political scientists has increased, but the discipline's influence pales next to the dismal science. Policymakers, media outlets, and the wider public seem to value what economists have to say more than other social science disciplines. When Treasury or Federal Reserve officials testify before Congress, they often refer to the scholarly economic literature to justify their thinking; neither State Department nor Pentagon officials cite international relations scholarship. Political scientist Jacob Hacker notes, "When you go talk to policymakers, if there's someone else in the room who is a social scientist, 90 percent of the time she is an economist."[11]

When economists develop an overwhelming consensus on an emergent policy issue—say, the need for Keynesian stimulus in the fall of 2008—their advice can have an appreciable policy effect.[12] When political scientists form a consensus, their effect on public policy remains negligible. For example, in the fall of 2004 a larger group of international relations theorists formed "Security Scholars for a Sensible Foreign Policy." The group drafted and signed a petition demanding a change of course in US foreign policy, and commissioned a public relations firm to help with media outreach. The effort was clearly designed to influence the 2004 presidential election. This form of what its organizers labeled "Weberian activism" was notable mostly because of its lack of success. The petition generated minimal media coverage. The chief architects of Security Scholars for a Sensible Foreign Policy later concluded, "In its larger purpose of public education the effort was a miserable failure ... the contribution the letter made to the national marketplace of ideas was vanishingly small."[13]

Surveys of current and former foreign affairs policymakers show that they place a far greater value on economic research than political science research—flummoxing researchers who believe that economic techniques are off-putting.[14] In a survey of senior policymakers, political scientists Michael Desch and Paul Avey found that political science theories and methods were frequently categorized as "not very useful" or "not useful at all."[15] These same policymakers found economics to be of value, however. My own survey of public policy opinion leaders confirms this finding, as Figure 4.1 shows. When asked how much impact different social science disciplines have on public policy and

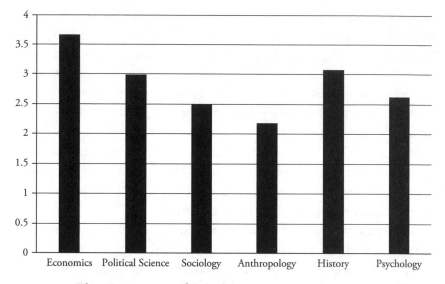

FIGURE 4.1 Elite Perception of Social Science Impact on Foreign Policy

Notes: Ideas Industry elite survey response to: "In your opinion, how much impact do these social science disciplines have on public policy and foreign policy?" (Number of respondents = 196, possible confidence ranking from 1–4).

Source: Author survey.

foreign policy, economics easily outpaced political science, history, sociology, and the rest. Political science was the third most relevant, behind both economics and history.

Bruce Jentleson and Ely Ratner run the Bridging the Gap Initiative, designed to improve connections between academic political science and the policy community. They nonetheless admit that "there remains limited interest on the part of the policy community in reaching beyond the Beltway to connect with scholars and consume academic research."[16]

Media outlets feel similarly about economists and political scientists. Melissa Harris-Perry—a professor of political science at Wake Forest and a former MSNBC commentator—explained, "The media thinks differently about various experts. Economists carry great and inherent weight. There is a presumption that economists simply know what they what they are talking about."[17] Unsurprisingly, in the decade after 2006, the *New York Times* referenced "economist" 7.5 times more frequently than "political scientist"; since 2008, the gap in mentions has become a chasm.[18]

From at least the beginning of this century, prominent intellectuals are more likely to possess backgrounds in economics than in the humanities. In Richard Posner's list of the top one hundred intellectuals from the turn of the century, economists outnumbered every other academic discipline.[19] A more recent analysis of the online influence of thought leaders also showed that economists easily dominate all other academic disciplines.[20] Last decade, Steven Leavitt's *Freakonomics* was a publishing sensation. This decade, Thomas Piketty's eight-hundred-plus-page treatise on inequality, *Capital in the Twenty-First Century*, translated from French, rose to the number one sales rank on Amazon.[21] Economics appears to have supplanted literary criticism as the "universal methodology" of superstar intellectuals. The dismal science dominates the marketplace of ideas.

The perception problem extends beyond policymakers and the mainstream media. The broader public appears to share policymakers' disdain for political science. In 2014, the American Political Science Association commissioned a task force to report on the public's perception of the discipline. The task force's glum conclusion: "The wider public does not seem to view political science as a useful resource for a better understanding of politics or as an aid to solving public problems. . . . To the extent that the American knows what political science is, they know it more as something that is taught at universities rather than something that has more widespread use."[22]

Political scientists have deeply internalized the irrelevance of the discipline in public policy debates. Most essays by political scientists on this topic offer up Eeyore-like laments about their own ineffectiveness. Stephen Walt is one of the most widely known international relations theorists, a coauthor of the controversial book *The Israel Lobby*, and a regular contributor to *Foreign Policy*. He nevertheless wrote in 2012 that "academic theory—including my own work—has had relatively little direct or indirect impact on actual state behavior. Scholars may tell themselves that they are 'speaking truth to power,' but most of the time the powerful don't listen."[23] Stephen D. Krasner, a prominent international relations theorist who served as Condoleezza Rice's director of policy planning at the State Department, has offered a similar assessment.[24] Multiple studies and surveys conclude that international relations scholars believe that the discipline has drifted away from policy-relevant scholarship toward more basic research—even though most scholars also believe that their own research *is* policy relevant.[25] The American Political Science Association acknowledges that "there is a strong consensus . . . that scholars are unnecessarily detached from many audiences that want to know more about political science."[26] Even as blogs like The Monkey Cage have expanded the means through which political scientists can influence the marketplace of ideas, economist Tyler Cowen concludes that "political science still lags far behind economics."[27]

To sum up: all of the evidence shows that economics sits at the top of the social science pyramid; it is the most significant discipline in the marketplace of ideas. Political science is less significant, even in the sphere of international affairs.

What is particularly impressive about economics' pre-eminence in the marketplace of ideas is just how badly the profession has screwed up over the past decade. Prior to 2008, numerous economists had claimed that the state of macroeconomic theory was excellent and that a broad intellectual consensus had been achieved. Nobel Prize-winner Robert Lucas crystallized this consensus when he wrote, "Macroeconomics in this original sense has succeeded: Its central problem of depression prevention has been solved, for all practical purposes, and has in fact been solved for many decades."[28] International Monetary Fund (IMF) chief economist Olivier Blanchard opened a spectacularly ill-timed August 2008 paper by asserting, "The state of macro is good."[29] Very few finance economists accurately warned about the dangers of the housing bubble prior to the 2008 financial crisis.[30] Indeed, when economist Raghuram Rajan raised concerns about excessive financial engineering in 2005, Larry Summers accused him of being a "Luddite." Ideas like the efficient markets hypothesis helped to spur the policy conditions that created the bubble in the first place.[31]

The years since the 2008 financial crisis have also not been kind to economic contributors to the marketplace of ideas. Forecasters of all stripes have failed badly. Behavioral economist Richard Thaler concluded, "Economic models make a lot of bad predictions."[32] He was not exaggerating. Economists at the Federal Reserve have persistently overestimated projected growth since the collapse of Lehman

Brothers. The IMF's forecasters have had to continually revise downward their short-term projections for global economic growth. The failure rate was so bad that the IMF devoted research to why so many revisions have been necessary.[33] The trouble is that the incentives of the economics profession do not place a high value on predictive accuracy. As economist Noah Smith noted in Bloomberg, "the kind of theories that are held in the highest regard are usually not empirically successful ones, but new ones—theories that use new kinds of math, for instance."[34] The field of macroeconomics has committed particularly egregious errors, with its primary model a "rhetorical swindle on the lay public," as one economist phrased it.[35] After a brief consensus around Keynesianism that emerged after the collapse of Lehman Brothers, a group of more conservative economists began to dissent. Two key economic papers offered intellectual succor to pro-austerity policies. In October 2009, Alberto Alesina and Silvia Ardagna published a National Bureau of Economic Research (NBER) paper that made multiple pro-austerity arguments.[36] In January 2010, Carmen Reinhart and Kenneth Rogoff also published an NBER paper buttressing the argument for fiscal austerity by arguing that countries with a debt-to-GDP ratio higher than 90 percent would experience severe growth slowdowns. Paul Krugman asserted that Reinhart and Rogoff's paper "may have had more immediate influence on public debate than any previous paper in the history of economics."[37] Acting as thought leaders, these economists went beyond their findings in delivering policy recommendations. The effects of these austerity policies ranged from contractionary to devastating.[38] Subsequent research challenged the findings of both papers, but only after austerity wreaked economic and political havoc across Europe.[39] Little wonder that World Bank chief economist Paul Romer concluded, "For more than three decades, macroeconomics has gone backwards."[40]

As for financial economics, University of Chicago economist Luigi Zingales has lambasted his own subfield, acknowledging that "our view of the benefits of finance is inflated."[41] Stanford University professor Paul Pfleiderer accuses finance scholars of using models as chameleons, engaging in "theoretical cherry-picking" to advance ideas that are not necessarily grounded in reality.[42] Investment adviser Barry Ritholz has repeatedly blasted the "zombie ideas" that economists have put forward before and after the 2008 crisis.[43] Other economists acknowledged that a narrow focus on financial variables caused them to miss political sources of the crisis and its aftermath.[44] These failures buttress Alan Blinder's decades-old maxim that economists are listened to the most when they agree with each other the least.[45]

Even in areas where the consensus of economists has been particularly strong, such as free trade, mistakes have been made. Survey after survey of economists show widespread support for trade liberalization. Economists overwhelmingly concur that free trade increases productivity and consumer choice, and in the long run these gains are much larger than any effects on employment.[46] Nonetheless, economists have frequently oversold the benefits of free trade in policy debates.[47] There is strong evidence, for example, that China's admission to the World Trade Organization had severe distributional effects on the US economy. Wages stayed stagnant and unemployment rates remained high for a decade in many sectors after China trade shock commenced. Furthermore, workers who lost jobs due to Chinese imports experienced greater job churn and a permanent reduction in their lifetime income.[48] Several economists have bemoaned the fact that economists make such simplistic arguments for free trade to the public, even though they debate the precise benefits among themselves.[49] The *New York Times*' economics correspondent Binyamin Appelbaum concluded that "economists have oversold their case" when it comes to free trade.[50]

Such high-profile errors are legion and increasingly recognized within the profession.[51] Barry Eichengreen acknowledged that "[the 2008 financial crisis] has cast into doubt much of what we thought we knew about economics. . . . We now know that much of what we thought was true was not." Paul Krugman wrote, "As I see it, the economics profession went astray because economists, as a group, mistook beauty, clad in impressive-looking mathematics, for truth."[52] Romer has expressed concern with the "mathiness" of debates in academic economics.[53] Even sympathetic pundits are writing about the field's internal flaws.[54] And yet little has changed in terms of the discipline itself. The economists that made the most errant statements about the 2008 financial crisis have actually seen their citations increase. Economics "looks like a closed, inefficient market with high barriers to entry."[55]

To be clear, it is not as though political science has a sterling record either. Major shocks like the peaceful end of the Cold War, the 2011 Arab Spring, and the 2016 GOP presidential primary have surprised political scientists.[56] Even on smaller predictions, the discipline has gotten things wrong.[57] Still, political science has also gotten some big things very, very right. Political scientists took the lead in beating back arguments that civilian casualties in violent conflict were all about "ancient hatreds."[58] Most international relations scholars opposed the 2003 invasion of Iraq and resisted the "rally round the flag" that occurred in the run-up to the invasion.[59] The 2016 election forecasting models of political scientists, which rely on factors like economic conditions and incumbency, significantly outperformed forecasts that relied exclusively on polls.[60] There are areas where political science has developed a strong consensus at variance with the Beltway consensus: the exaggerated importance that policymakers place on reputation in world politics, or the limited influence foreign ownership of US debt has on American foreign policy. Nonetheless, policymakers have pretty much ignored political scientists on these issues.

There is a vague recognition among foreign policy elites that maybe economics has some issues. My survey of opinion elites showed that they believed economics was the most influential discipline, as Figure 4.1 showed. However, in terms of which discipline they found to be personally the most useful, Figure 4.2 shows that economics lagged behind history. Despite all of this, economists are still the cock of the walk among the social sciences, crowding out other disciplines that could proffer policy advice.[61] As Thaler noted, "of all the social scientists, economists carry the most sway when it comes to influencing public policy. In fact, they hold a virtual monopoly on giving policy advice. Until very recently, other social scientists were rarely invited to the table."[62] Or, as Harris-Perry explains, the mainstream media perception is that "there's no presumption that political scientists have unique information that can't be garnered by economists."[63]

What is particularly striking is the contrast between how economics responded to its intellectual crises in the 1970s versus how it has responded over the past decade. In the 1970s, the failure of economics led to a sea change in the discipline. Keynesian theories, which had dominated the discipline in the postwar era, were cast aside in the wake

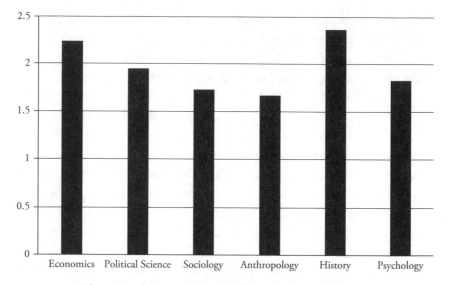

FIGURE 4.2 Elite Confidence in Social Science Disciplines

Notes: Ideas Industry elite survey response to: "How much confidence do YOU currently have in the research generated from the following social science disciplines?" (Number of respondents = 198).

Source: Author survey.

of stagflation.[64] Approaches grounded in individual choice, rational expectations, and the power of markets quickly took hold. These theories failed to cope with the vicissitudes of the 2008 financial crisis and its aftermath. And yet this failure has not led to any ideational shifts in the discipline. Indeed, according to one analysis, economics is the social science with the greatest degree of paradigmatic rigidity.[65]

Economists have committed every possible sin that Kristof accused the academy of as a whole. The discipline has not changed much at all in the wake of discomfiting real-world events that call some core assumptions into question. Nevertheless, economists continue to thrive in the Ideas Industry. Why?

As Fourcade and others have observed, one source of economists' influence over the marketplace of ideas has been their supreme confidence in the rightness of their core principles.[66] Economists believe that, compared to their kindred social scientists, they possess a superior analytical toolkit. Indeed, this confidence breeds a casual arrogance. Economists treat other branches of the social sciences with condescension that borders on contempt.[67] Consider Dani Rodrik. He has demonstrated an appreciation for the value of other social science disciplines in much of his work. Nevertheless, in *Economics Rules* he offers up numerous asides about how economics is more rigorous than the rest of the social sciences: "Economics is by and large the only social science that remains almost entirely impenetrable to those who have not undertaken the requisite apprenticeship in graduate school."[68] Even when economists acknowledge that non-economic factors are important, their descriptions of those factors are derogatory. In their book *This Time Is Different*, Carmen Reinhart and Kenneth Rogoff acknowledge that "institutions, corruption, and governance" matter far more than capital/labor ratios in determining relative national affluence, but they describe these as "'soft' factors."[69] If there is one word that social scientists do not want associated with their research, it is "soft."

In a society in which economic literacy is low and innumeracy is high, this kind of confidence is in and of itself a form of intellectual power. The self-confidence of economists becomes self-reinforcing; since they are given the most respect, it stands to reason that they must have earned it.

Economists also out-earn mathematicians despite not being as well trained in mathematics.[70] This suggests that the higher status of economists is not really a function of better analytical tools. Nevertheless, other social sciences, particularly political science, have tried to ape economic methods, techniques, and style. Quantitative articles went from making up less than 40 percent of *American Political Science Review* articles in 1968 to more than 60 percent by 1998.[71] Economists embraced game theory in the 1970s; political scientists embraced it soon after. As economists shifted into experimental methods and randomized controlled trials in the 1990s, political scientists embraced this technique in the 2000s.

At a minimum, this scientific turn has caused fellow scientists to treat political science with more respect. When Congress cut National Science Foundation funding for political science, the National Academy of Science held an event outside Capitol Hill to protest the attack on the social sciences.[72] Both *Science* and *Nature*—the leading journals in all of the sciences—ran editorials condemning these efforts.[73] Numerous scientific associations ranging from the American Physical Society to the Union of Concerned Scientists also released statements blasting the move.[74]

As political scientists adopt the methodologies of economics, they have also tried to ape their self-confidence. Political scientists increasingly cast themselves as scientific experts when engaging the public, policymakers, and each other. Some have labeled this as a "resurgent neo-positivism."[75] This had some interesting effects on how political scientists talk to each other. Within international relations scholarship, there has been a concerted effort by some scholars to argue that paradigmatic debates are a thing of the past. According to this logic, "isms" like realism, feminism, or constructivism do not matter as much as scientific scholarship.[76] This has been reflected in prominent textbooks about international relations, which do not talk about paradigmatic approaches but instead emphasize interests and institutions.[77] Lawrence Mead notes about political science discourse:

> Formerly, giving a paper at a seminar or conference would lead to questions about the argument and then a wide-ranging discussion of the issues raised. Today, the questions are much more about methodology, and there is little interest in the argument otherwise. Compared to their predecessors, today's political scientists are more skilled technically but less knowledgeable about politics and government and less intellectual.[78]

These tropes are entirely consistent with how economists talk to each other. This mindset affects how political scientists engage with the public—or refrain from doing so. Vavreck, for example, argues that scholarly political scientists do not need to present their work in an accessible fashion because "it is not any scientist's job to make the results of their scientific work accessible to a layperson."[79] At this point, the fundamental difference between the two disciplines is that economic policymakers and business leaders accept the idea that economic methodologies and theory-building enterprises have value and are worth using as a guide to policymaking. Policymakers view economists as experts, but political scientists as charlatans. Many members of the foreign policy community explicitly reject the notion that political science methodologies and techniques can explain much in world politics. Political scientists who have served in government have confirmed this claim.[80] Economic policymakers have imbibed the methodology and jargon of economists in a way that foreign affairs officials have not with international relations. Indeed, foreign policy leaders clearly possess their own implicit theories of how international relations works, and those theories are often at variance with scholarly approaches.[81] Even other intellectuals look down on political scientists. In *The Age of American Unreason*, Susan Jacoby blasted public officials for embracing "junk thought" at the expense of the natural sciences. Nevertheless, she also blasted political scientists because: "When they draw conclusions about the future behavior of the human species on past behavior, their reasoning is often highly unscientific."[82]

Political scientists therefore appear to have the worst of both worlds. They are trying to copy the insularity that makes economists successful within the academy, but they have not earned the same professional cachet. And political scientists confront public audiences that do not view them with the same confidence as they view economists. Maybe, just maybe, political scientists have misinterpreted the reason that economists have thrived in the marketplace of ideas.

Economists have stayed at the top of the social science pyramid because when they engage the public sphere, they do not act like public intellectuals; they act like thought leaders. Economists share a strong consensus about the virtues of free markets, free trade, capital mobility, and entrepreneurialism. From Adam Smith onward, economics has been able to preach a "win-win" doctrine. If individuals pursue their self-interest, society as a whole will benefit, as if guided by an invisible hand. The liberating power of markets was emphasized even more in the wake of Keynesianism's decline in the 1970s. Free market critics like Joseph Stiglitz or Paul Krugman nonetheless favor having the state use market forces to cure market ills, and even liberal economics textbooks talk about the inefficiencies of regulation.[83] Dani Rodrik notes in *Economics Rules*, "Promoting markets in public debates has today become almost a professional obligation. . . . In public, the tendency is to close ranks and support free markets and free trade."[84]

Economists are able to proselytize ideas that are music to the ears of those plumping for the modern Ideas Industry. Conservatives suspicious of state intervention in the economy wholeheartedly embrace a laissez-faire message. Liberals suspicious of free markets will nonetheless accept advice on how to use market methods to tweak regulations and incentivize behavior. Plutocrats who believe in the power of economic dynamism and technological innovation embrace the ideas put forth by neoclassical economics.

The growth of the modern Ideas Industry has provided powerful support to the economics profession. As Thomas Piketty noted in his tome on inequality, "among the members of these upper income groups are US academic economists, many of whom believe that the economy of the United States is working fairly well and, in particular, that it rewards talent and merit accurately and precisely."[85] And as Chrystia Freeland observed, "academics in fields the plutocracy values can multiply their salaries by working as consultants and speakers to super-elite audiences. . . . Even as they cash their speaking fees from the super-elite, these academics shape the way all of us think about the economy."[86] A Stanford professor of finance acknowledged to a reporter: "In economics and finance, if I'm trying to decide whether I'm going to write something favorable or unfavorable to bankers, well, if it's favorable that might get me a dinner in Manhattan with movers and shakers."[87]

In contrast, critics accuse political science of ignoring "the real world" and not being a true science.[88] The discipline's doubling down on positivism is problematic for two reasons. First, political scientists lack the strong normative consensus of economics. Regardless of ideology or method, almost all economists share the core normative emphasis on Pareto optimization. In economics, a Pareto-improving move is one that makes at least one person better off without making anyone else worse off. If an economic policy meets these criteria, then every economist in the world would laud such a move. This principle of allocative efficiency is at the root of all mainstream economics. Such a principle narrows the range of debate but it also makes it easier for economists to debate policy among themselves.

Political science lacks a common normative core—and for good reasons. There are different political values that are considered worthwhile beyond "efficient" institutions. Concepts like democracy, sovereignty, equality, order, security, justice, and liberty are all valued but can conflict with each other. There is no consensus within the political science discipline about which values should be prioritized. And without that basic normative consensus, political scientists will disagree about first principles. This renders the discipline less appealing to laymen.

The erosion of trust, combined with political science's insistence on its scientific status, further hampers the discipline's ability to influence the broader public. For example, when Congress forced the National Science Foundation to cut funding for political science, the *Nature* editorial that criticized the action stated, "The idea that politicians should decide what is worthy of research is perilous. The proper function of democracy is to establish impartial bodies of experts and leave it to them."[89] This theory of government might sit well with some progressives, but for many citizens, it sounds elitist, condescending, and anti-democratic. Not surprisingly, the *National Review* responded to the editorial by pointing out, "*Nature's* blatant advocacy of technocracy stands in direct contradiction to the text of and principles embodied by the U.S. Constitution."[90] Political scientists want to argue that they offer expertise. But in the political sphere, the assertion of expertise can imply that citizens either should not or do not have a right to decide. That can be somewhat off-putting in a democracy.

Political science is also more vulnerable than economics to the charge of partisan bias. To be sure, academic economists are less conservative than the American public. Many of the most prominent economists, such as Paul Krugman and Joseph Stiglitz, are liberals. Still, the survey data clearly demonstrate that compared to political scientists, economists hold relatively conservative policy views.[91] Whether one looks at party affiliation, voting patterns, or policy preferences, the results are the same. Compared to the rest of the social sciences, the economics profession is more conservative and demonstrates a greater heterogeneity of views. Furthermore, as Daniel Klein and Charlotta Stern conclude, "in nearly every case, academic economists of both parties are less supportive of economic intervention than their counterparts in the other disciplines."[92] Intriguingly, conservatives are more likely to go into macroeconomics or finance—two of the fields in which economics exercises the most outsized influence on public policy.[93]

In contrast, political scientists are more liberal and more homogenous in their liberalism. Their policy advice is therefore easier to caricature as partisan. Political scientist Rogers Smith noted, "If political scientists pay special attention to the poor and to marginalized communities, they are likely to be accused of . . . doing nothing beyond spouting liberal biases."[94] Fellow political scientist Ronald Rogowski concurs, noting that "contemporary political science suffers from too much policy relevance, not too little. Politicians simply do not like the policies that scholarly research supports, prefer policies (often put forward by charlatans) that better suit their . . . ideologies."[95] Robert Jervis, one of the most erudite international relations scholars in the field, admits, "It makes a difference to our research that most of us are liberals."[96]

Conservatives take great glee in highlighting the ways in which academic political science is out of touch with the rest of the country.[97] It is unsurprising that the latest congressional push to limit National Science Foundation funding of political science originated with conservative Republicans.[98] In the present day, the easiest way for a conservative to discredit any political science intervention in the marketplace of ideas is to describe it as academic—and therefore left of center. An American Political Science Association task force report concluded, "Political science often occupies an uncomfortable place in the public sphere. As recent events in Washington remind us, partisan participants in policy and government are not obligated to give political science much deference, even if political scientists have valuable expertise and seek to convey it in a non-partisan manner."[99]

The accusation of partisan bias particularly affects areas where political science scholars have a collective and informed opinion that is at variance with the majority of the American electorate. There are several issues, for example, on which international relations scholars collectively hold different attitudes than either policymakers or the public. Academic political scientists are far more skeptical about the use of force than the public. Comparison polling of political scientists and the general public in 2015 showed that the American public was far more optimistic about using force to handle problems in Ukraine, Sudan, Myanmar, and the Middle East more generally. The gap was widest on Iran: 63 percent of Americans supported using military force against a near-nuclear Iran. By contrast, the use of force earned only 22 percent support from international relations scholars.[100] Disagreements like these are precisely the arena where the weight of academic expertise would hopefully have an impact on public opinion. Because of rising political polarization, however, it is difficult for partisans to treat political science as an objective body of knowledge.[101]

The greatest culture clash between political science and the Ideas Industry, however, comes with the rise a new class of plutocrats. The problem goes to the nature of so many of the discipline's conclusions. Ezra Klein ably observed:

> Political scientists traffic in structural explanations for American politics. They can't tell you what an individual senator thinks, or what message the president's campaign will try out next. But they can tell you, in general, how polarized the Senate is by party, and whether independent voters are just partisans in disguise, and how predictable elections generally are. [102]

This is true, and mirrors the gap between political scientists and the American public on policy outcomes. Ordinary Americans consistently emphasize the influence of individual politicians on policy; political scientists are more inclined to emphasize structures.[103] Former American Political Science Association president Jennifer Hochschild thinks that political scientists have gone too far in the direction of structuralist arguments: "the loss of human agency as a driving force in explaining political phenomena—that's the core transformation [in political science] from 1960 to 2000."[104] As a result, the discipline has been hampered in its ability to explain when human agency can change the course of politics.

International relations scholars also stress structural factors. Very little international relations research focuses on individual-level variables like leadership—much less focuses on individual leaders.[105] The major international relations paradigms in recent decades have been systemic in nature. They mostly argue that the international system imposes powerful structural constraints on state behavior. The bible of academic realists is Kenneth Waltz's *Theory of International Politics*, which explicitly states, "The texture of international politics remains highly constant, patterns recur, and events repeat themselves endlessly.

The relations that prevail internationally seldom shift rapidly in type or in quality. They are marked instead by a dismaying persistence." Waltz adds, "Over the centuries states have changed in many ways, but the quality of international life has remained much the same."[106] For realists, little has changed in international relations since the days of Thucydides. Similarly, the dominant approach to international political economy is "open economy politics." This paradigm stresses the myriad ways in which domestic interests and institutions constrain the ability of even powerful decision makers to deviate from status-quo policies in the absence of exogenous shocks. It is not systemic in the same way as realism, but it nevertheless posits a world in which structures and institutions impose powerful constraints on individual actors. Decision makers have limited autonomy in the open economy politics paradigm.[107]

Structural explanations of politics do not go over well with either policymakers or plutocrats. The essence of structuralist narratives is that individuals have little agency in the here and now. Policymakers, in contrast, are biased toward trying to do something. They are therefore interested in the best course of positive action, not all of the reasons for doing nothing. As Stephen Walt notes, "policymakers are often less interested in explaining a general tendency than in figuring out how to overcome it."[108] International relations scholarship focuses on aggregate data; both entrepreneurs and policymakers are notorious for overemphasizing the particular pieces of firsthand information they possess.[109] Indeed, the problem is more existential than that; most international relations scholarship does not think that any particular policy principal is terribly important. This is a worldview that no policymaker wants to hear. When former secretary of state Dean Acheson found out that he was being treated as a dependent variable in one study, he strenuously objected, feeling that he was an independent variable.[110] Media outlets are also uninterested in this kind of deterministic worldview. Political scientists make boring pundits, because their standard response to most headlines is "It's not that important."

As much as policymakers and the mainstream media might not like to hear political scientists sound structuralist, potential patrons like hearing it even less. Plutocrats hold a worldview of politics that is somewhat at variance with how actual politics works; they believe that policy problems consist mostly of either engineering problems that can be fixed quickly, or of situations ripe for the disruptive culture of Silicon Valley. Most philanthrocapitalists simply fail to appreciate the notion of clashing interests. For plutocrats to change their minds about how politics work, they would have to want to listen to political scientists. Which they largely do not.

Successful entrepreneurs believe that they got to their current station due to effort, creativity, and risk taking.[112] In other words, plutocrats very much believe in their own agency. They have little patience for less wealthy academics who would suggest anything different. Furthermore, many philanthropists are interested in spending their money to influence the marketplace of ideas. If they are honest, political scientists are likely to tell them that the influence of their super PACs or their activist foundations will be vastly overstated. When political science does this, however, it is essentially telling plutocrats that they do not matter as much as they think they do. This is the one thing that billionaires do not want to hear.

Some economists recognize that although they are powerful brokers within the Ideas Industry, this may not be such a good thing. Rodrik acknowledges that "when it comes to the issues of the day, [economists'] views often converge in ways that cannot be justified by the strength of the available evidence."[113] He goes on to note those economists who engage with the public—whom he labels "hedgehogs"—are different from the "foxes" that comprise the rest of the discipline:

> The hedgehogs take on a problem that can always be predicted: the solution lies in freer markets, regardless of the exact nature of and context for the economic problem. Foxes will answer "it depends"; sometimes they recommend more markets, sometimes more government.
>
> Economics needs fewer hedgehogs and more foxes engaged in public debate.[114]

Rodrik might be correct that more foxes would lead to more nuanced economic advice, but he misunderstands the source of his discipline's influence. Economists believe that their power is due to the inherent superiority of their discipline. The truth is somewhat less savory; they succeed precisely because they act as confident thought leaders. What other social sciences lack is a message that resonates with the patrons of the new Ideas Industry. As a result, disciplines like political science have taken as many steps backwards as forwards in engaging the public sphere. Many political scientists have gotten better at adapting to the modern Ideas Industry. The discipline writ large, however, has imbibed the wrong lessons from the success of economics.

The shift in academic political science rhetoric to a more scientific cast has, if anything, exacerbated the problem. It affects how many political scientists think about engaging the rest of the public. Trying to talk about politics to a general audience using only the language of science has consequences. The use of scientific argot to discuss political phenomena makes sense when political scientists talk to each other, but not to the wider public. When political scientists use the neutral language of science to discuss genocide or police brutality, the public views them as talking about terrible things matter-of-factly.[115] More generally, when debates about policy pivot over methodological disputes, the public tunes out completely.

Economists have done well in the new marketplace of ideas. Collectively, the rest of the social sciences have not done as well. They possess all of the insularity and inaccessibility of economics and none of the public cachet. So it would seem that the rest of the social sciences have big problems.

It could be worse, however; they could be working at a think tank. The next chapter discusses how and why think tanks have it even worse than political scientists.

5

This Is Not Your Father's Think Tank

Travel down Massachusetts Avenue in Northwest DC and you'll find yourself in the heart of an industry that was, when it began, unique to the nation's capital.

— Peter Singer

WHEN JIM DEMINT SUCCEEDED founder Edwin Feulner as president of The Heritage Foundation in early 2013, he took the reins of the conservative movement's premiere think tank. Since its inception in 1973, Heritage had pushed aggressively and successfully to capture the ear of Congress. The think tank was known for producing short policy briefs with analytical bite. In the fall of 2012, the Cato Institute's Ed Crane described Heritage as "the leading conservative organization in the country." Even liberals like the Progressive Policy Institute's Will Marshall acknowledged that under Feulner, Heritage "wrote the book on how to market and popularize political ideas."[1] It is impossible to read press accounts of Heritage without seeing statements like "de facto policy arm of the congressional conservative caucus" or "the gold standard of conservative, forward-looking thought" or "provided the blueprint for the Republican Party's ideas in Washington" shot through them.[2]

The evidence to back up those assertions was compelling. Heritage's Index of Economic Freedom has been an important gauge of the market-friendliness of national policies around the world; it is also a component of the US Millennium Challenge Corporation's criteria for dispensing American foreign aid. The foundation's Center for Data

Analysis had the necessary intellectual firepower to compete with the Office of Management and Budget and the Congressional Budget Office in modeling the economic impact of proposed legislation. On issues ranging from health care to missile defense, The Heritage Foundation reports had been influential over Republican and Democratic administrations alike. Regardless of whether politicians liked or disliked the content of Heritage's ideas, they could not ignore them.

There was some trepidation among conservative intellectuals when the DeMint announcement was made.[3] Feulner was known as a full-blown policy wonk; DeMint was known to be many things, but an intellectual was not one of them. Upon hearing the news of DeMint's appointment, *Commentary* editor John Podhoretz warned, "If ideas do not play the central role, Heritage will hollow itself out, and that would be a great shame." *Weekly Standard* editor William Kristol was equally wary: "My concern is perhaps too much activism (which of course I have nothing against) and too little thinking."[4] Liberals were more blunt. Ezra Klein noted, "You don't name Jim DeMint head of your think tank because you're trying to improve the quality of your scholarship."[5]

Both Heritage and DeMint portrayed it as a perfect pairing, however. One of Heritage's senior fellows viewed DeMint's presidency as a natural extension of Heritage's traditional strengths: "What this means is that the intellectual rigor and innovative ideas of our scholars and researchers, as well as our strong membership base, will now be united with the most effective, principled political leader on Capitol Hill."[6] DeMint echoed these sentiments. He said in his announcement that "the conservative movement needs strong leadership in the battle of ideas" and pledged to the *Wall Street Journal* that he would "protect the integrity of Heritage's research and not politicize the policy component. Heritage is not just another grassroots political group."[7] He told the *Washington Post*, "The key for me is to make sure that the Heritage Foundation is not politicized in any way. There is never going to be any policy issued by the Heritage Foundation directed for the benefit of some political goal."[8] A year later, DeMint was still sticking to that message, telling the *New York Times*, "I had no intention to get more political. The whole conservative movement counts on Heritage for its intellectual integrity."[9]

After DeMint took office, however, there was something of a shift in Heritage's corporate culture.[10] DeMint invested more heavily into marketing Heritage research across different platforms. The think tank launched The Daily Signal, a digital news site that drew on Heritage analysis and catered to younger conservatives.[11] Policy briefs were designed and promoted for social media. DeMint explained that "conservative ideas are invigorating. We had allowed them to become too serious."[12] Heritage's resources were also brought to bear to promote DeMint's own brand; in 2013 he traveled across the country with Senator Ted Cruz to rally opposition to Obamacare. In 2014 DeMint went on tour to promote his new book.[13]

The changes went far beyond marketing, however. Under the old regime, Heritage was organized into a number of decentralized policy concentrations, such as education, health care, and national security. Under DeMint, the think tank created temporary teams devoted to whichever issue he wanted to push that day. DeMint's staff reviewed all Heritage papers to ensure that they conformed to the official policy of the think tank. He also boosted the profile of Heritage Action, the think tank's 501(c)(4) political action arm.[14] Heritage Action was the brainchild of the chairman of Heritage's board, private equity millionaire George Saunders III. According to a Wall Street Journal op-ed announcing its creation, Heritage Action was to be the "new fangs" to Heritage's "beast."[15] Under DeMint, Heritage Action created a scorecard to grade members of Congress on their ideological fealty. The head of Heritage Action had a background in political campaigns but not policy. One veteran Heritage staffer described Heritage Action's leadership as follows: "I was always struck at how they felt absolutely no intellectual modesty. They felt totally on par with people who had spent thirty years in the field and had Ph.D.s."[16]

Even the most generous assessment of DeMint's record at Heritage would conclude that he has produced mixed results. Within the first year of DeMint's tenure, several respected senior researchers left the policy shop, including the heads of its Center for Data Analysis, Center for Policy Innovation, and senior national security scholars. More problematic, however, was Heritage's missteps in its research. The think tank released a study claiming that comprehensive immigration reform would cost more than $6 trillion.[17] It quickly became clear that the number was based on ludicrous assumptions; a Congressional Budget Office analysis of the same bill concluded that it would actually cut the deficit by $200 billion over ten years. *Business Insider* labeled the Heritage report as "diametrically incorrect."[18] Conservative economists were even more critical of it. Keith Hennessy, a research fellow at the Hoover Institution, said that the Heritage study was "useless for making policy decisions."[19] Former Heritage staffers were just as skeptical. The former head of Heritage's Center for Data Analysis described the report as one-sided. Tim Kane, a former Heritage staffer who had also written on immigration, blogged that he was "disappointed in its poor quality" and that "the pileup of outlandish Heritage estimates presents a credibility hurdle."[20] Eventually one of the co-authors of the report resigned from Heritage when it was revealed that his dissertation had focused on the alleged genetic inferiority of Hispanic immigrants.[21]

Immigration was hardly the only issue area where Heritage stumbled. The think tank commissioned former Bush administration Office of Legal Counsel head Steven Bradbury to write two papers on the role of the National Security Administration's controversial surveillance programs. Bradbury concluded that the surveillance programs were in fact legal. According to multiple reports, however, DeMint did not like the paper's conclusions and therefore scotched its publication at Heritage.[22] The Brookings Institution eventually published one of Bradbury's papers—providing a marked contrast with Heritage's ideological rigidity.

As Heritage's advocacy for DeMint's positions mounted, so did the political and intellectual blowback. Heritage Action ran afoul of conservative members of Congress in 2013 on how it scored votes on the farm bill. Both Heritage and DeMint found themselves on the receiving end of criticism from numerous conservative politicians, including Senators Tom Coburn, Marco Rubio, and Orrin Hatch.[23] Less than a year into DeMint's tenure, Heritage staffers were banned from the weekly lunches of the Republican Study Committee, one of the linchpins of the conservative caucus. Congressional staffers reported that they relied less on Heritage Foundation analyses for their information. By 2016, the think tank was in the peculiar situation of hosting a reception to honor House Speaker Paul Ryan's chief of staff at the same time that Heritage Action was lobbying to derail Ryan's proposed budget plan.[24]

Many liberal intellectuals had derided Heritage's intellectual quality in the past.[25] What changed under DeMint was that conservatives began doing so as well. They griped to *The New Republic, The Atlantic*, and the *New York Times* about the eroding quality of Heritage's research.[26] One GOP communications expert noted ruefully, "The Heritage Foundation used to be a place where you had a debate of ideas. Now it's much more tactical, how to raise money." He warned, "I guarantee they won't be [pro] free trade when DeMint is done with them."[27] Sure enough, in June 2015, DeMint wrote an essay for *The National Interest* opposing trade promotion authority for president Obama, claiming that the legislation had, "turned into a special interest boondoggle."[28] Heritage's outreach to Donald Trump was greater than any other right-leaning think tank.[29]

The effect of Heritage's new style on its influence was uneven. Among foreign and public policy intellectuals, the think tank's standing plummeted. In my 2016 survey of opinion leaders, an overwhelming 79 percent of respondents said they had little confidence in Heritage reports, more than double the percentage of any other think tank in the survey. This is not merely a liberal bias against a conservative think tank; among opinion leaders who explicitly identified as conservative, 74 percent expressed little confidence in Heritage reports. Its low standing can be traced directly to the recent transfer of power. In Feulner's last year as Heritage's president, the University of Pennsylvania's Global Go To Think Tank Index ranked it among the top fifteen think tanks in security, foreign affairs, and international economic relations. Three years into DeMint's tenure, Heritage had fallen out of the top twenty in all three categories.[30] On foreign policy questions, smaller right-wing think tanks like the Foundation for the Defense of Democracies supplanted Heritage's influence.[31] Whatever sway Heritage ever had over moderate or liberal politicians dissipated.

Nonetheless, the new regime at Heritage persisted in its new tactics, arguing that backbiting from Republican politicians is "the eternal price of disruptive thinking."[32] The head of Heritage Action argued that their ability to leverage grassroots support through improved communications technology gave the think tank greater political clout. Heritage's chief operating officer pointed out that policy reports were meaningless unless politicians felt political pressure to read them, and that activities like Heritage Action's scorecards created that pressure: "Our role is not to make politicians happy or angry. Our goal is to get the best policy adopted that we can for the country."[33] Heritage senior vice president James Jay Carafano argued that Heritage was actually a template to be copied by other think tanks: "In the future, highly competitive and effective think tanks are more likely to be paired with sister organizations . . . that perform lobbying and grassroots organizing activities."[34]

DeMint and Carafano have a case to make. Even if Heritage's intellectual reputation is not what it once was, its influence remains. The two areas where Heritage improved its Global Go To Think Tank Index ranking dramatically after DeMint's first three years were in "best advocacy campaign" and "most significant impact on public policy."[35] Dick Durbin, the number two Democrat in the Senate, said that during DeMint's tenure at Heritage, "the money that he's been able to generate there has created a political force." Furthermore, for reasons explained later in this chapter, Heritage managed to avoid the rash of conflict-of-interest allegations that plagued more mainstream think tanks like Brookings or the Center for Strategic and International Studies. The decline of Heritage's intellectual quality has come as its political grip over the GOP has increased. Despite backbiting about Heritage Action, its influence was large enough to entice most of the 2016 GOP presidential candidates to attend their September 2015 Take Back America candidate forum. It is the Washington think tank most closely associated with the Trump administration.[36]

In recent years no other think tank has experienced the kind of disruption that DeMint has encouraged at The Heritage Foundation. Does this mean that Heritage is an outlier or a harbinger for these kinds of organizations?

American intellectuals have a love-hate relationship with the concept of think tanks. On the one hand, by definition, these organizations are supposed to participate in the public sphere. Indeed, in contrast to universities, the primary purpose of think tanks is to make a difference in the real world of public policy. A senior vice president of the Center for Strategic and International Studies told the *Washington*

Post, "Our number one goal is to have impact on policy."[37] On the other hand, a fair number of intellectuals look down upon the think tank world. In his 2012 book *Think Tanks in America*, sociologist Tom Medvetz argued that "think tanks must carry out a delicate balancing act that involves signaling their cognitive autonomy to a general audience while at the same time signaling their heteronomy—or willingness to subordinate their production to the demands of clients—to a more restricted audience."[38] In essence, Medvetz suggested that the comparative advantage of think tanks has been their ability and willingness to kowtow to rich and powerful patrons. In doing so, they monopolize what Medvetz labels the "interstitial field" between the world of academic ideas and public policy. This is not a terribly flattering portrayal of the only industry that is indigenous to Washington, DC.

I know something about think tanks. I currently serve as a nonresident senior fellow at the Brookings Institution and the Chicago Council on Global Affairs. In the past I worked at two other think tanks—RAND and the Council on Foreign Relations. I have written commissioned papers, delivered talks, and participated in roundtables at numerous others. From my firsthand observations, I would suggest that the reality is more nuanced than Medvetz suggests. The think tanks I worked with felt like a hybrid between an academic department and a law firm. The substantive discussions were just as serious and analytical as those I would have encountered at the University of Chicago or the Fletcher School. But there were some uneasy moments as well. On at least one occasion, I felt like my think tank boss was trying to reverse-engineer a report I was writing. He knew the conclusions he wanted the report to draw and just wanted to make sure that my analysis was consistent with that conclusion. There were also additional discussions about the presentation and marketing of ideas that simply did not occur in the academy. My first exposure to PowerPoint was at RAND; by the mid-1990s they had already developed detailed guidelines about how to optimize its use. A generation later, most of the academy has yet to catch up.

A more charitable interpretation of the hundred-year history of think tanks is that they have always steered between two shores. They have strived for rigorous, policy-relevant scholarship consistent with the highest academic research standards.[39] As former American Enterprise Institute president Christopher DeMuth put it, "think tanks serve as storehouses of ideas, patiently developed and nurtured, waiting for the crisis when practical men are desperately seeking a new approach."[40] Think tanks believe that policymakers will listen to them because of the quality of their ideas, and rigorous analytical work is one way to maintain that quality. At their best, think tanks inform, frame, and elevate policy debates, leveraging their intellectual capital into affecting policy outputs. They exist as crucial reservoirs of expertise and incubators of talent that governments can tap when they face an acute policy challenge. A heterogeneous array of think tanks can offer the contrarian voice to a policy community that might be beset with groupthink. In 2006, a Mackinac Center intern coined the term "Overton window" to refer to the politically acceptable range of policy options at any given moment. He argued that one purpose of a think tank was to forcefully articulate ideas consistent with its political philosophy, even if those policy ideas are outside that window: "Think tanks can shape public opinion and shift the Overton window by educating legislators and the public about sound public policy."[41] In this way, a think tank can nurture ideas that disrupt the status quo and eventually become politically palatable.

These are some lofty aims. However, both think tanks as institutions and individual analysts in the employ of think tanks must also cater to client demands more than even the most conciliatory of academics. Universities have larger endowments and an additional revenue stream from tuition; think tanks are much more reliant upon benefactors, donors, and grants to finance themselves. Individual researchers at these institutions are also more interested in serving the government, causing them to be more solicitous of the needs of the bureaucracy.[42] This incentive structure suggests that think tanks pushing for a seat at the policymaking table will be less critical of powerful organizations than academics.[43] Furthermore, think tanks measure their self-worth expressly on their public visibility in important debates and private influence over key policymakers. Top-tier academic departments and public policy schools want to influence the marketplace of ideas; think tanks *need* to do so. In the competition for public attention, needing it more matters.

Since their inception, think tanks have struggled to navigate the cross-pressures that are now buffeting the rest of the Ideas Industry. During some periods they have managed this tension well. Recently, however, there is a growing lament inside Washington that American think tanks are not what they used to be. Bipartisan nostalgia about previous eras when think tanks mattered more in foreign policy debates suggests that maybe they are currently not living up to their potential.[44] David Rothkopf declares that "far too little bold thinking goes on in the country's think tanks."[45] Senior Obama administration officials view much of the think tank community as in the pocket of either Arab or Israeli funders.[46] The Trump administration has, at best, a strained relationship with conservative think tanks.[47] The disconnect between what think tanks used to be and what they are now may be a function of nostalgia bias. It is easy, through the sands of time, to elide the numerous issues on which think tanks had no discernable impact on policy outcomes. Nevertheless, academics, journalists, policymakers, and think-tankers themselves share the perception that the think tank ecosystem has changed in the United States.

If the academy is finding the new Ideas Industry to be choppy waters, think tanks are confronting a full-blown tsunami. James McGann, who directs the University of Pennsylvania's think tanks and civil society program, has flatly stated that "think tanks face extinction unless they learn how to innovate and adapt to a rapidly changing political economy."[48] The shifts discussed in Chapter 2 have had profound effects on how think tanks fund and commission research. These tectonic shifts have also triggered a raft of allegations about the relative autonomy of these organizations from their donors. Many US-based think tanks have received funding from sources that could implicitly or explicitly constrain their intellectual autonomy. Recent reporting alleges that these donations have affected the research aims of several prominent think tanks.[49] Whether American think tanks can maintain their collective relevancy going forward—and whether that is a good thing—depends on how they adapt to the new Ideas Industry. The Heritage Foundation's evolution under DeMint highlights one problematic path, but the collective travails of "nonpartisan" think tanks highlight another one. Clearly, the Ideas Industry has changed the intellectual and economic climate for think tanks.

The history of think tanks in the United States is conventionally divided into three stages.[50] The first wave of these organizations emerged during the Progressive Era. Leading reformers believed that technical expertise should supplant partisanship and patronage as the best way to assist government policymakers. An alliance emerged between progressives eager to inject expertise into government and businesses frustrated with capricious government meddling.[51] The beginnings of the regulatory state triggered a concomitant need for outside experts to consult the government on the best ways to craft policy. Think tanks were thus born with seed funding from the Rockefeller, Ford, and Russell Sage Foundations. In 1910, the Carnegie Endowment for International Peace was founded. Six years later, the Institute for Government Research—an entity that later became the Brookings Institution—was created. In the aftermath of the First World War, when most of the country was clamoring for economic isolation, American financiers helped set up the Council on Foreign Relations (CFR) as a way of advocating for a more internationalist posture.[52] CFR started publishing *Foreign Affairs* in 1922.

The next generation of think tanks emerged because of the Second World War. The war vastly expanded the size of the foreign policy apparatus, creating additional demand for foreign policy expertise. According to one count, 350 institutes were set up to engage in military research in the war years after Pearl Harbor, including the American Enterprise Institute (AEI).[53] But the primary distinction between this generation of think tanks and the previous one was the sources of funding. The pre-eminent think tank born in this era was the RAND Corporation. Originally a Douglas Aircraft creation for the Air Force, RAND was eventually hived off to be a federally funded research and development center. In contrast to Brookings or Carnegie, RAND secured funding primarily through government contracts. It made significant contributions to the articulation of Defense Department policy for the next several decades. A coterie of RAND experts were extremely influential in the formation of US nuclear doctrine during the Cold War. RAND also developed the "systems analysis" approach to decision-making under uncertainty.[54] Other think tanks also played a prominent role in the articulation of early Cold War foreign policy. Much of what became the Marshall Plan was hammered out at Brookings, for example.[55]

The first two generations of think tank creation shared many common traits. Both waves were demand driven. First progressives and then government technocrats needed analytical support beyond the official bureaucracy, thereby opening up a niche for think tanks. Both waves shared the belief that social science expertise was the key to solving policy problems. In his history of think tanks, Andrew Rich observed that "the business leaders and individuals who provided the financial support to the early think tanks were the strongest advocates for their pursuing reform through objective, scientific research."[56] As a result, the linkages between the first two waves of think tanks and the academy was relatively strong. Most of the individuals affiliated with Brookings and Carnegie in their first decades had full-time academic appointments at prestigious universities. A glance at the RAND group that focused on nuclear deterrence shows that most of these think tank denizens moved in and out of the academy at will. At midcentury, it was accurate to describe think tanks as "universities without students."

The third generation of think tanks began in the 1960s and 1970s, and the motivation for their creation differed from the technocratic impulses of the first two waves. Led by Heritage, these think tanks diverged in key ways from their predecessors—and these differences are emblematic of the forces shaping the modern Ideas Industry. The most obvious difference was ideology. Whereas Brookings, RAND, Carnegie, CFR, and AEI all proclaimed themselves to be nonpartisan, the newer think tanks were overtly ideological in orientation. Heritage was expressly designed to be conservative in approach. The Cato Institute, created in 1977, was libertarian in thought and creed. It took another generation for liberals to create their own overtly partisan think tanks, but they eventually did with the Center for American Progress (CAP) in 2003.

Three other distinctions separated the new generation of think tanks from their predecessors. First, consistent with the role of plutocrats in the modern Ideas Industry, they secured their funding through individual philanthropists. In the case of Heritage, the brewer Joseph Coors provided the bulk of the start-up funds. Charles Koch provided the first three years of operational funding for the Cato Institute.[57] Second, in contrast to previous generations of think tanks, the new wave concentrated more on political advocacy than scholarship. Even before Jim

DeMint became president of Heritage, the think tank's intellectual output was designed to be accessible to congressional staff. In essence, Heritage preferred briefings over books. And when the CAP was created, so was the Center for American Progress Action Fund, a 501(c)(4) advocacy group. That was the inspiration for the 2010 creation of Heritage Action.[58]

The final difference was that the latest generation of think tanks placed less weight on academic credentials. According to the Hudson Institute's Tevi Troy,

> Think tanks that were founded earlier tend to have significantly more scholars with Ph.D.s today than do younger institutions. Among a representative group of think tanks founded before 1960, for instance, 53% of scholars hold Ph.D.s. Among a similarly representative group of think tanks founded between 1960 and 1980, 23% of scholars have such advanced degrees. And among those founded after 1980, only 13% of scholars are as highly educated.
>
> Granted, the Ph.D. is an imperfect measure, and it is certainly possible to do high-level policy work without an advanced degree. But the decline in the percentage of Ph.D.s does signal that the more recently created Washington-based think tanks are no longer adhering to the "university without students" model.[59]

What mattered more to this new wave of think tanks was ideological consistency. The head of the Competitive Enterprise Institute told one interviewer, "Groups like ours, how do we earn our credibility? Well, we have very strong bright-line standards. We have a very strong point of view and we've never deviated from that point of view."[60]

The effects of the third generation on the entire think tank ecosystem have been mixed. On the one hand, the increase in competition among different think tanks probably helped all of them improve their political advocacy and effectiveness. Donald Abelson, an academic who studies think tanks, observes, "What has changed over the past few decades is how deeply invested think tanks have become in the marketplace of ideas. They are more politically savvy, more technologically sophisticated, and better equipped to compete."[61]

Indeed, American think tanks have played a critical role in the formulation of US foreign policy in recent history. The playbook for the first year of Ronald Reagan's presidency was The Heritage Foundation's *Mandate for Leadership*. The Reagan administration implemented roughly 60 percent of Heritage's more than two thousand suggestions. After the collapse of the Soviet Union, a bipartisan collection of think tanks did the first serious work on how to expand NATO into Eastern Europe. AEI and the Institute for the Study of War were crucial to the formulation of President Bush's surge strategy in Iraq in 2007.[62]

It would be a gross exaggeration to claim that think tanks were the tail wagging the dog of the US foreign policy establishment. They did, however, affect critical junctures in American foreign policy. More generally, the foreign policy community within think tanks functioned as a useful sounding board for government officials interested in floating new ideas. Most policy principals engage with think-tankers as a way of "working the refs"—but the dialogue cuts both ways.[63] If a bipartisan collection of think tank experts formed a consensus about a particular course of action, policymakers had no choice but to acknowledge and respond to it. Right or wrong, that consensus was a political fact of life that altered the calculus of policymakers. This constraint of this consensus is what frustrated Obama while he was in office, and angered Trump while he was running for it.

At the same time, rising levels of think tank competition mixed with rising levels of polarization has lowered the probability of such consensus. Conservatives undoubtedly profited from the flowering of partisan think tanks, but some participants also signaled their unease. AEI's Karlyn Bowman told one researcher, "I wonder what is happening sometimes to the think tank currency, whether it's becoming a bit like paper money in Weimar—currency without a lot of value because of the proliferation and because of the open advocacy of some of the think tanks."[64] Similarly, the Hudson Institute's Tevi Troy wrote, "New think tanks must distinguish themselves from the others. And as such distinctions become increasingly narrow, institutions have found that they can stand out by adopting a more strident ideological bent—a practice that led to think tanks' increasing politicization."[65]

Despite the rising levels of polarization, twentieth-century think tanks were still able to fulfill their potential because of the tightly networked foreign policy community in the United States. US-based think tanks traditionally catered to a primarily elite audience of insiders. As Anne-Marie Slaughter, the head of the New America Foundation, noted, "in our traditional business model, we publicized specialized reports aimed at decision makers. They either take it or leave it."[66] Senior fellows at think tanks tended to be former cabinet and subcabinet officials seeking a temporary perch until their return to the official corridors of power. These "formers" had built-in networks with government officials, giving think tanks the ability to access information and to transmit their own policy ideas to the right officials. Indeed, the comparative advantage of think-tankers has historically been the informal scuttlebutt they glean from being based in Washington, DC. Compared to academics, policy analysts based at think tanks tend to know much more about the bureaucratic or legislative state of play surrounding a particular policy arena. I cannot recall an instance in which I knew more about the policy arcana of a particular issue than my colleagues based at think tanks.

Think tanks were less concerned with public engagement for a very simple reason: the American public was either disinterested or disempowered on questions of foreign policy.[67] This was particularly true as the Cold War faded from memory. Two events in this century, however, had transformative effects on the role of think tanks in the marketplace of ideas. September 11, 2001, was the first inflection point. Public interest in foreign affairs spiked after the al-Qaeda attacks. Think tanks soon found themselves pushed into a new role of public outreach. This was the moment when think tanks stopped speaking only to policy elites and started addressing a wider audience that was newly interested in international affairs. These kinds of public engagement required significant investments beyond foreign policy experts. Such outlays included new facilities, interactive websites, public relations materials, and strategic communications staff.

The post-9/11 demand for international affairs research meant flush times for foreign affairs think tanks. This was reflected in increases in staff and facilities. The terrorist attacks led to a bumper crop of well-trained experts in counterterrorism, military statecraft, and Middle East politics who could staff policy shops. The United States government concomitantly increased spending to fight the global war on terror—as well as ground wars in Iraq and Afghanistan. The geyser of defense dollars went to the uniformed services, defense contractors—and, inevitably, to the think tanks geared to research the myriad dimensions of the global war on terror. International affairs think tanks continued to add staff and overhead. Salary inflation took off among think tanks fellows.[68]

The sustained demand, combined with the pre-2008 boom in asset markets, triggered a surge in think tank budgets. At the Brookings Institution, for example, annual revenues nearly tripled between 2003 and 2007 from $32 million to $92 million.[69] The endowments of these institutions also swelled during the pre-2008 asset boom. AEI's assets more than tripled in the years after 2002, as did those of the Center for Strategic and International Studies. CAP's assets quintupled.[70] In the five years after the September 11, 2001, terrorist attacks, one was hard-pressed to walk down Massachusetts Avenue in northwest Washington without seeing ground being broken for a new think tank building. Both the CFR and the Peterson Institute for International Economics erected posh new DC headquarters. The Carnegie Endowment for International Peace expanded its global presence, establishing centers in Beirut and Brussels during this period. New think tanks like the Foreign Policy Initiative and Center for New American Security geared up quickly, influencing policymakers almost immediately after their creation.

Then the second inflection point arrived: the 2008 financial crisis. The Great Recession forced some wrenching changes in the economics of think tanks. The most direct effect was the dramatic contraction in their traditional sources of financing. Endowments naturally shrunk in the wake of the 2008 financial crisis, as did the income earned from them. Two other primary funding sources were equally affected. Longstanding philanthropic groups like the Carnegie Corporation and the MacArthur Foundation were forced to reduce their grant giving because their own endowments contracted during the Great Recession. At the same time, the yawning federal budget deficit, combined with the drawdowns from Afghanistan and Iraq, dried up government support. As Secretary of Defense Robert Gates said in 2010 about national security budgets, "spending on things large and small can and should expect closer, harsher scrutiny. The gusher has been turned off, and will stay off for a good period of time."[71] The ensuing defense sequester further reduced funding for think tanks that had grown fat on government contracts. For example, the Center for Strategic and Budgetary Assessments, the premier think tank on defense spending, saw its contributions and grants fall by more than 40 percent between 2011 and 2013. The bulk of that decline was due to a drying up of funds from the Defense Department's Office of Net Assessment.[72]

For all of Heritage's intellectual missteps, the think tank persevered because it was far less reliant upon these conventional sources of funding. Its primary source of revenue comes from individual contributors. According to its 2014 annual report, its individual donor base is responsible for close to 85 percent of its revenue.[73] This has made it easier for Heritage to not seek out new funders. Indeed, Heritage's James Jay Carafano argues that the best business model is one in which "the think tank taps a large number of private funding sources, eschewing government support entirely and having only minimal reliance on corporate giving and grant-making institutions."[74] Not surprisingly, this resembles Heritage's financing model but is a relative rarity among these organizations.[75] Heritage is clearly a partisan policy shop but it is a fiscally solvent one.

The contraction of traditional revenue streams forced most think tanks to tap more unconventional sources. In some cases, this has meant more partnerships with multinational corporations. At the same time that the Center for Strategic and Budgetary Assessments' government funding shrank, its private consulting revenue increased nearly tenfold.[76] A welter of think tanks, including CFR, Center for Strategic and International Studies (CSIS), and Brookings, developed corporate sponsorship programs to offer these companies select privileged access to their experts. According to the Council on Foreign Relations, a six-figure corporate contribution carries with it an extra perquisite: "three CFR fellow briefings tailored to the company's interests."[77] This matches the privileges bestowed to members of the Brookings Institution's Corporate Council. The Center for New American Security offers four briefings for a similar level of funding.[78] This outreach effort has paid off. Brookings offers a good example. Between 2003 and 2013,

corporations went from being responsible for 7 percent of large donations to being responsible for 25 percent.[79]

For the corporations, this kind of partnership can be as valuable
as spending on lobbyists. Think tank funding is less heavily regulated
than more traditional forms of political spending, such as campaign
contributions and lobbying members of Congress. It is therefore unsurprising that more corporate money began flowing their way. It is a
form of influence arbitrage. Even short of direct influence, corporate
sponsorship of think tanks offers greater access to policy analysts as they
develop new positions and proposals. And even think tank officials acknowledge the influence. Bill Goodfellow, the executive director of the
Center for International Policy, said, "It's absurd to suggest that donors
don't have influence. The danger is we in the think tank world are being
corrupted in the same way as the political world."[80] *New York Times*
reporters have documented the ways that corporations like JPMorgan
Chase and FedEx partnered with prestigious think tanks like Brookings
and the Atlantic Council. The journalists concluded that "in the chase
for funds, think tanks are pushing agendas important to corporate
donors, at times blurring the line between researchers and lobbyists."[81]

Corporate support can affect research at think tanks when individual fellows directly receive funding due to consultant work or similar
activities. Defense contractors have a long track record of aiding hawk-
ish analysts at think tanks by placing them on their corporate boards.
Jack Keane's primary affiliation in his writings is as chairman of the
board of the Institute for the Study of War; his presence on the board
of General Dynamics comes up less frequently.[82] Roger Zakheim used
his visiting fellowship at AEI to push for greater military spending
at the same time that he worked as a lobbyist for the defense firm
BAE Systems. CSIS has approximately seventy affiliated experts who
also do private-sector consulting. When asked by the *New York Times*
about some of these arrangements, CSIS responded by acknowledging
"a lapse in oversight."[83]

The financial sector has been equally active in leveraging support
of think tank research. Hedge funds have used intermediaries to fund
think tank analysts that advocate for their policy preferences.[84] Senator
Elizabeth Warren pressured the Brookings Institution to force economist Robert Litan to resign as a nonresident senior fellow. Litan had

testified to Congress on regulating individual retirement accounts without disclosing that a financial firm had funded Litan's research. In a letter to the president of Brookings, Senator Warren warned that "the funding sources of some Brookings-affiliated researchers call into question the independence of their research and its conclusions." Outside observers were less circumspect: Helaine Olen noted that "companies looking to get the government to set rules that just happen to benefit their bottom lines often seek out wonks looking to supplement their pay who will make arguments on their behalf in a dispassionate way."[85]

Another new source of think tank funding came from foreign governments. In 2014 alone the Atlantic Council disclosed receiving financial support from twenty-five different foreign governments. The government of Qatar was the principal backer of the Brookings Institution's Saban Center for Middle East Policy. Even think tanks that expressly forbid receiving funds from foreign governments, such as CFR, do accept funds from foreign state-owned enterprises and foundations. A Chinese construction firm with close ties to the Chinese government sponsored a new institute at CSIS for "geostrategy."[86] Other small oil exporting nations, such as Kazakhstan, Norway, and the United Arab Emirates, have been equally active in funding a welter of foreign policy think tanks. An internal Norwegian government report justified the funding by explaining that "in Washington, it is difficult for a small country to gain access to powerful politicians, bureaucrats and experts. Funding powerful think tanks is one way to gain such access, and some think tanks in Washington are openly conveying that they can service only those foreign governments that provide funding."[87] The percentage of cash donations from foreign governments to Brookings nearly doubled between 2005 and 2014.

The final new source of funding has come from wealthy individual benefactors. These donors comes with their own complications. Many of these individual patrons bring a more overt partisan agenda with their funds. Conservative funders like Sheldon Adelson, Paul Singer, and Bernard Marcus have plowed significant sums into conservative think tanks like the Manhattan Institute or the Foundation for the Defense of Democracies.[88] At the same time, more liberal institutions, such as the Truman National Security Project, have sought the support of funders like George Soros or Tom Steyer. Think tanks have sought out money from Wall Street and Silicon Valley benefactors to bolster their coffers.

As think tanks confront the changes in the Ideas Industry, they face some intellectual tradeoffs. Relying on more partisan sources of funding comes with costs and risks. A comparative advantage of think tanks is their ability to convene more bipartisan events and initiatives than would otherwise occur in Washington. AEI and Brookings, for example, sponsor a number of joint projects. On foreign policy questions, different parts of the American political spectrum can find common cause on a specific policy initiative, such as trade policy, counterterrorism, or promoting religious freedom abroad. This approach is anathema to partisans, however. As Anne-Marie Slaughter and Ben Scott note, "expert positions in many debates are alien to the mobilized bases of both parties."[89] Donors that are more accustomed to funding political campaigns can see such initiatives through a zero-sum lens. They will ask who stands to benefit politically, rather than consider the effects of policy implementation. As a result, these funders have voiced qualms about funding think tank initiatives that have bipartisan support. Partisan donors are simply warier of partnering with ideologically distinct patrons on a particular project.

If think tanks choose to cater to partisan donors, they face severe risks if they display any sign of intellectual heterodoxy. As Jane Harman, director of the Wilson Center, explained, "for many think tanks, open discussions are just bad business. How can you afford to challenge members of your audience if they might take their ears and eyeballs elsewhere?"[90] In an age of partisan donors, this concern covers pocketbooks as well.[91]

A more direct concern is that this funding translates into the exercising of greater control over the think tank. In September 2015 a cache of emails revealed the degree to which Heritage was walking a tightrope between the more extreme views of some of its wealthy patrons and a desire to maintain a modicum of intellectual independence. The emails showed Heritage donors expressing doubts about President Obama's US citizenship, or suggesting specific anti-Islamic speakers that Heritage should invite. In response to the latter, a Heritage development officer coddled the donor, "We are asking the questions that other think tanks simply are not asking. And, part of that is inviting speakers to Heritage that will forthrightly confront the problem that you highlight." He later asked the individual for an additional six-figure contribution to the think tank.[92]

Another example happened in 2011 when the Koch brothers, who helped found the Cato Institute, began making moves to pack its board of directors. Their aim was to dislodge Ed Crane, Cato's president, and install a new president that would defer more to the Kochs' political agenda. According to the chairman of Cato's board, David Koch explained that he wanted Cato "to provide intellectual ammunition that we can then use at Americans for Prosperity and our allied organizations."[93] Crane resisted, arguing, "Who the hell is going to take a think tank seriously that's controlled by billionaire oil guys?"[94] The Kochs eventually succeeded in forcing out Crane, although they also took a step back from direct control over Cato's research.[95]

New philanthrocapitalist vehicles pose an additional challenge for traditional think tanks. These benefactors primarily earned their billions in the finance or tech worlds. They are used to competitive, results-oriented return on investment. They are not at all used to arenas where government policies significantly affect policy outcomes. Consistent with their business practices, donors are more likely to provide project-specific funding rather than more general financial support. They are less interested in funding think tanks than "do tanks." This is a sharp contrast from the old days when, according to McGann, "donors gave unrestricted money to think tanks, and said, 'You guys know what you're doing. Think the big ideas.'" Now, despairs a former head of the Stimson Center, "think tanks are struggling to adjust to an environment that no longer seems to value knowledge for knowledge's sake." The environment has changed so much that Brookings' managing director told the *New York Times*, "Wouldn't it be nice to go back to the greatest generation, in the post-World War II era of philanthropy, where they said, gosh, 'Here is $1 million; spend it how you wish'?"[96]

As these donors have migrated toward the policy world, they have favored allocating resources to operational organizations rather than think tanks. McGann recently noted that "think tanks are competing with consulting firms, law firms, SuperPACS, lobbyists and advocacy groups. That puts pressure on think tanks to be more responsive to donors."[97] In my discussions with think-tankers, the one common thread across the ideological spectrum was the recognition that they were competing with other entities to provide policy advice. As the Brookings Institution's Ted Piccone put it to me: "We're all think tanks now." A plethora of old and new institutions are now competing in the same space as stand-alone think tanks, as the next chapter examines. This wider universe creates a fiercer competitive environment.

It will be difficult for think tanks to please every master while fulfilling their original purpose. The Carnegie Endowment for International Peace offers one cautionary warning. Carnegie prides itself on the global nature of its brand; by 2006 the think tank had opened up offices in Beijing, Beirut, Brussels, and Moscow, as well as Washington. In theory, Carnegie is well positioned to act as a convener for Track II events. In practice, questions have been raised about the intellectual independence of its leaders. Several policy analysts for Carnegie also work for lucrative consulting partnerships. Russian dissidents, as well as multiple think-tank analysts based in the United States, accused Carnegie of sacrificing its intellectual autonomy and analytical rigor to maintain its Moscow headquarters.[98] The validity of these accusations has been hotly disputed by others[99]—but in an arena where the appearance of impropriety is a problem, nonpartisan think tanks will face challenges similar to Carnegie.

The CAP example suggests the risks of yielding to partisanship. CAP experienced an internal revolt in late 2015 when its leadership invited Israeli prime minister Benjamin Netanyahu to speak. This was part of an Israeli effort at fence mending with liberals after years of bellicosity toward both the Obama administration and the Palestinian Authority. While CAP leadership assented, left-leaning CAP staffers were furious. In a contentious open staff meeting, they asked the leadership: "How do we engage in conversation with world leaders whose views and actions undermine our core principles, while maintaining the integrity of those principles?"[100] Other think tanks, including Demos on the left and the Center for the National Interest on the right, have fired individuals who made public statements contrary to institutional preferences.[101]

Think tanks face significant challenges in coping with the modern Ideas Industry, but it would be premature to sound their epitaph. Some have done so, arguing that think tanks simply cannot compete in the twenty-first century. Intelligence analyst Michael Tanji declared that "virtual think tanks" could eventually supplant their brick-and-mortar forefathers. He founded the online-only Center for Threat Awareness, convinced that "think tank 2.0" would prove to be leaner and meaner than organizations with such high payrolls, physical plant, and over-head.[102] Tanji made this prediction in August 2010; his Center for Threat Awareness lasted only a year.[103] The brick-and-mortar versions of these organizations are not going extinct.

In the post-Great Recession world, think tanks confront more strin-gent funding constraints. They face ethical dilemmas and tradeoffs in mining new sources of revenue. Most seriously, they now face a more competitive world. They are no longer just vying for policy influence among themselves, but with an array of other organizations, including university-based research institutes, law partnerships, consulting and lobbying firms, and operational philanthropic agencies.

Think tanks reacted to previous shocks with entrepreneurial adapt-ability and have responded to their current predicament in a similar fashion. They are already practicing greater transparency in revealing their sources of revenue. Some organizations, like the Peterson Institute for International Economics, CFR, and Brookings are also dedicated to making the diversification of funding sources an express goal so as to minimize dependency on any singular source of funds. Finally, the more activist philanthropists are likely to recognize the limits of their activism—particularly if their goal is to influence government actions. These entrepreneurs are accustomed to simply bypassing politics in achieving their goals. For the policies they now want to promote, how-ever, political support is a necessary condition for action. As these new philanthropists learn about how policy impact works in Washington, they will likely channel their funds toward more traditional pathways of influence—such as think tanks.

Heritage Action has certainly made its presence felt in Congress under DeMint's tenure. This has come at the expense of The Heritage Foundation itself, however. Some think tank directors, like Slaughter, suggest more strenuous "pre-partisan" efforts at civic engagement.[104] In essence, think tanks would engage in the political outreach and ad-vocacy more traditionally associated with activists or lobbying groups. But taking on such activities runs the risk of diluting the core function of these organizations. At a minimum, their monopoly over the "interstitial field" between the academy and policy has quickly eroded. Even more than the academy, think tanks face profound challenges in adapting to the new marketplace of ideas.

Of course, this raises an interesting question. How have for-profit actors sidestepped the conflict-of-interest accusations that have enmeshed think tanks?

6

The Booming Private Market for Public Ideas

Thought leadership has come to dominate the marketing activities of consulting firms, and with good cause.

— Advertisement for a firm analyzing management consulting

ONLY A FOOL GOES into foreign affairs for the money. In this century, tech or finance or myriad other areas offer more lucrative careers than foreign policy. This poses an existential problem for my arguments about the Ideas Industry. If no one can make money from big ideas, then any discussion of a real marketplace of ideas seems fanciful. For markets in anything—even ideas—to exist, there have to be profits. If universities and think tanks are in turmoil, so what? They are non-profit ventures. If the stakes are this small, then does the disruption of the traditional sources of ideas really matter?

In his book on the subject, Richard Posner assumed that there was no private-sector supply or demand for the work of public intellectuals.[1] This was inaccurate when he wrote *Public Intellectuals*, and it is wildly inaccurate fifteen years later. To be fair, Posner was simply following the lead of political scientists, who think of the private sector affecting foreign policy primarily through interest group lobbying. This overlooks the crucial role that the private sector can play in supplying the public sphere with new ideas.[2] Increasingly, the power of the private sector in foreign policy comes from their ideas as well as their interests.

Chapter 2 discussed the surging demand that has created the new Ideas Industry. This chapter describes the surging private-sector supply of thought leaders. It turns out that people with money also like to go into international relations thought leadership. And to truly appreciate the magnitude of Posner's error, you have to appreciate the phenomenon of the BRICS.

BRICS is an acronym for Brazil, Russia, India, China, and South Africa. The leaders of these emerging markets have held regular summit meetings of their leaders from the start of the 2008 financial crisis.[3] Between 2009 and 2016, the BRICS heads of state held fourteen summit meetings.[4] Initial evidence suggests that the five member states have honored most of the pledges made in their communiqués.[5] As the grouping has strengthened, ministerial summits have also been organized in agriculture, education, environment, finance, health, and trade. Beyond the summit communiqués, the grouping has been institutionalized in other ways. An entire Track II process has emerged around the BRICS summits, including forums for business leaders, mayors, and members of parliament from each of the member states. A cottage industry of think tanks, research centers, and academic forums has emerged to analyze the BRICS.

The most significant BRICS initiatives have been in the area of finance. All of the member countries have taken steps to invoice trade in their own national currencies, to suggest independence from the dollar as the world's reserve currency.[6] In 2014, the grouping launched a $100 billion New Development Bank to disperse loans to the developing world. The BRICS also announced the creation of a $100 billion Contingent Reserve Arrangement designed to ensure liquidity in case any member faced acute financial volatility. They have continued to demand a greater voice in traditional Bretton Woods institutions like the IMF or World Bank.[7] This has been a recurring theme of the BRICS members since 2008, when they called for "reform of international financial institutions and global governance."[8]

Both the rising power and the revisionist purposes of the grouping have been a source of considerable debate.[9] While the influence of these BRICS structures at the present moment is small, a battalion of commentators has argued that they can serve as a down payment for more revisionist global governance structures in the future.[10] Even skeptics would have to acknowledge that it is one of the more influential groupings of its kind. With the exception of OPEC in its heyday, the most important club of developing countries in history is the BRICS.

What is extraordinary about the BRICS grouping is its origin story. As its official website acknowledges,[11] the initial idea did not emerge from the chancellery of any of these countries. Nor did it come from any university or think tank headquartered in those nations. Rather, it was the brainchild of a Goldman Sachs employee: Jim O'Neill, then the head of Goldman Sachs's global economic research department. In a November 2001 paper, O'Neill trumpeted the BRICs (minus South Africa) as the major growth centers for the global economy. His growth projections for the BRICs turned out to have been conservative. O'Neill concluded: "In view of the expected continued relative growth of the BRICs, the opportunity should be taken to incorporate China and probably Brazil and Russia and possibly India, [into] the key body of global economic policy coordination."[12] Within seven years, O'Neill's speculation had come true as the G-20 supplanted the G-7 as the world's premier economic forum. A follow-up paper by two of O'Neill's Goldman Sachs colleagues asserted that by 2050, the BRICs would be almost as large as the G-7 grouping.[13]

It bears repeating: the BRICS grouping originated as a marketing idea from Goldman Sachs.

It could be argued that O'Neill simply saw the handwriting on the wall and that the BRICS grouping was inexorable. This claim does not hold up, however. The heterogeneous nature of the BRICS made their formation far from obvious. Most international bodies have some geographical, security, or economic rationale for their existence. The BRICS possessed none of these commonalities. Indeed, a recurring criticism of the BRICS idea is that the dynamics of world politics are driven as much by rivalries within the developing world as by their relationship with the West.[14] The member countries are scattered across three continents, and trade consider changing to "among" them remains limited. Unlike the OECD, the BRICS have heterogeneous political and security profiles. The group consists of two autocracies and three democracies. On security issues, India, China, and Russia have diverse and sometimes conflicting interests. Beyond a feeling of resentment at being underrepresented in traditional global governance structures, there is little that the BRICS members have in common.[15]

It could also be argued that O'Neill invented the BRICs term solely as a means to attract more customers to Goldman Sachs. O'Neill has explicitly denied this in interviews—but there is no denying that this was one outcome of his idea. The BRICs concept generated considerable interest among Goldman Sachs's corporate clientele, particularly consumer products firms interested in cracking those markets.[16] To exploit the concept to its utmost, in 2006 Goldman Sachs created a BRICs fund that invested in all of those countries, attracting more than $800 million at its peak.[17] Other investment banks and hedge funds paid O'Neill the greatest compliment—they too began developing financial products specifically for the BRICs. Geopolitical analysts ran with the concept as well, arguing that there would soon be a "world without the West" in which developing economies would be "decoupled" from the advanced industrialized states due to the BRICS' superior "connectivity."[18]

Neither Goldman Sachs's economic projections nor the concomitant enthusiasm about BRICS proved to be sustainable. China's growth rate has fallen by half since O'Neill wrote his paper. The country faces a serious demographic crunch, high levels of debt, and financial instability. Each of these trends poses problems for its medium-run growth trajectory and political stability.[19] Comparatively speaking, China is the healthiest BRICS state. While China has risen to be an economic power of the first rank, the rest of the BRICS have largely stagnated since 2008. Indeed, contrary to pre-2008 predictions, the BRICS have neither accelerated their economic growth nor decoupled from the OECD economies.[20] Morgan Stanley's Ruchir Sharma concluded that "no idea has done more to muddle thinking about the global economy than that of the BRICs."[21] Most geopolitical analysts concur that the BRICS grouping has generated fuzzy understandings about their actual power.[22] By 2013, even O'Neill had admitted that the phenomenon he had named was wildly overhyped.[23] His employers at Goldman Sachs agreed; in August 2015, after hemorrhaging losses for five straight years, Goldman Sachs quietly merged its BRIC fund with a broader emerging market fund.[24] This came on the heels of additional investment analyses concluding that the BRICS in particular and "acronym funds" in general were poor investment vehicles.[25]

The irony is that the BRICS grouping took political life just as the progenitor of the idea discarded it. While the BRICS might not be economically thriving at the moment, the *idea* of the BRICS remains powerful to policymakers and intellectuals. In the fifteen years since O'Neill's idea, other investment bankers and geopolitical analysts have tried their hand at coining a new term of emerging markets. Groupings such as MIKTA, BRICSAM, and MINT have bandied about to describe other emerging economies, though none have been as successful.[26] As Gillian Tett noted in the *Financial Times*,

> Even if Brics is self-interested spin, such spin—an idea in itself, really—can sometimes take on a life of its own, beyond what its creators expect or even hope for. By creating the word Brics, O'Neill has redrawn powerbrokers' cognitive map, helping them to articulate a fundamental shift of influence away from the western world. And if you believe that the way humans think and speak not only reflects reality, but can shape its future path too, then this Brics tag has itself come both to reflect and drive the change. . . .
>
> Or as Felipe Góes, the Brazilian official in Rio charged with setting up the world's first Brics think-tank, says: "It is somewhat ironic [that we use the word Brics] . . . but that reflects the fact that *in the modern world it is people like Goldman Sachs and McKinsey who have the resources and minds to develop ideas.*" Indeed, what makes a large institution such as Goldman so influential these days is not simply its trading acumen and political connections, but also its ability to invest heavily in what bankers sometimes call "thought-leadership," by funding analysis and ensuring it is read around the world.[27]

The persistence of the BRICS is a testament to the growing power of private sector thought leaders. Whether based in investment banks like Goldman Sachs, management consultancies like McKinsey, political risk firms like the Eurasia Group, or tech firms like Google, new private-sector institutions have cropped up to act as the new knowledge brokers.

As with think tanks, the private sector of the Ideas Industry has encountered significant criticism from traditional public intellectuals. In many ways, these firms are particularly vulnerable to criticism, because of the explicitly for-profit nature of their activities. If universities and think tanks have to worry about funding, these firms, by definition, have to worry about profits. Because much of their information comes from their proprietary work, the transparency of their intellectual products is opaque at best. Compared to academics, their presentational style can be dazzling—and to most scholars, this is a bad thing. For many critics, these reasons alone discredit their intellectual output.

Over the past decade, however, I have found myself increasingly interacting and participating with this sector. I have spoken at conferences run by financial firms and participated at McKinsey confabs. I have consulted for some political risk firms. And I have even offered some pro-bono advice to Google. More importantly, however, I have observed thought leaders from these sectors interact with more traditional members of the foreign policy community. And they cannot be dismissed so easily. They have an obvious comparative advantage in style, but they also possess it in some areas of process and substance. The forces shaping the modern Ideas Industry have also aided and abetted the relative rise of for-profit thought leaders.

Research universities, the oldest part of the Ideas Industry, emerged in the United States in the late nineteenth century. Think tanks started to form a generation later. The private-sector portions of the Ideas Industry are the newest actors, emerging soon after the first think tanks. They can largely credit their existence to the Great Depression.

As business historian Christopher McKenna explains in *The World's Newest Profession*, although the first management consultancies were created earlier, the profession's rise is a direct outgrowth of the 1933 Glass-Steagall Act.[28] Glass-Steagall is primarily known for separating investment banks from commercial banks. Firms such as Goldman Sachs and Morgan Stanley owed their existence and corporate identity to Glass-Steagall. That law, however, also restricted banks from engaging in the consulting and reorganization activities that they had traditionally shouldered in the 1920s. The Securities Act of 1933 placed similar limits on accounting firms like Arthur Andersen from expanding into non-accounting activities, so as to preclude conflicts of interest with their primary task of financial audits. With the Depression-era financial laws in place, nascent first-generation firms like McKinsey, A. D. Little, and Booz Allen were able to expand.[29]

It would be natural to assume that management consultants did not concern themselves with intellectuals or abstract ideas. Indeed, as Walter Kiechel notes in his history of business strategy, "if you want to make a management consultant squirmingly uncomfortable, even one who churns out articles and books, just ask whether he or she thinks of himself or herself as an intellectual."[30] In actuality, however, management consultants take ideas very seriously, and have done so throughout most of their history. Just as the first generation of think tanks maintained close ties with the academy, so did the founders of the first management consultants. A. D. Little was a former president of the American Chemicals Society and headquartered his firm in Cambridge, Massachusetts, to build strong connections with MIT. James McKinsey was a former president of the American Association of University Instructors in Accounting, and founded his eponymous firm while an accounting professor at the University of Chicago. He maintained his ties to the university well after founding McKinsey. Edwin Booz had a similar relationship with the psychology department at Northwestern University.[31]

Soon after founding their separate firms, Booz and McKinsey co-founded the Association of Consulting Management Engineers (ACME) to establish professional codes and standards for the emergent field. McKinsey quickly became the industry leader, a template for later generations of management consulting firms like A. T. Kearney.[32] That was largely due to Marvin Bower, James McKinsey's successor as head of the firm. Bower advocated a strategy of engaging primarily with senior executives and rejecting more mundane, routinized, and low-margin tasks at the lower rungs of the corporate ladder. He also molded McKinsey's culture into one more akin to a white-shoe law or accounting firm. Bower stressed professionalism and elite recruitment from top business schools.[33] ACME members explicitly rejected "unprofessional practices" such as mass media advertising, cold-calling clients, or contingent billing.[34] The stereotype of management consultants as well-heeled, well-educated, well-dressed gadflies comes from the McKinsey template.

As with think tanks, management consultants played a significant policy role during the Second World War. Booz Allen reorganized the US Navy to prosecute a two-ocean campaign. A. D. Little helped develop operations research to better organize military logistics. After the war, the Eisenhower administration hired McKinsey to reorganize White House operations.[35] Many of the big corporate trends of the past fifty years—the rationalizations of the 1950s, the widespread adoption of information technology in the 1980s, the global business strategies of the 1990s, and the rise of offshore outsourcing in the 2000s—can be traced to management consultants.[36]

Management consultants quickly became an essential component of American multinational corporations in the second half of the twentieth century. This permitted them to act as "knowledge brokers" for all of corporate America. The rise of the Boston Consulting Group (BCG) in the early 1960s only reinforced the "intellectualization" of business.[37] First BCG, then its offshoot Bain, and then McKinsey in response developed concepts to theorize business strategy, proselytizing these ideas to most of corporate America. They leveraged premiere access to high-level corporate boardrooms into even more access, generating long-term consulting contracts and advising firms on how they should function. In some years, 85 percent of McKinsey's annual revenue comes from repeat customers, or its "transformational relationships," to use their argot.[38] The sector increased in size to more than $150 billion in operations in recent years. The market is lucrative enough to attract renewed competition from accounting and financial firms.[39]

Management consultancies mostly engage in proprietary work for private-sector firms. How, then, do they influence the marketplace of foreign policy ideas? The first pathway is through their direct consultancy services. Although the bread and butter of management consulting is catering to the private sector, by 2008 more than one-fifth of their business came from advising government and nonprofit clients.[40] As the federal government increased its efforts to outsource services to private contractors, myriad consultants were there to assist and proffer their services.[41] In the United States, Booz Allen and PricewaterhouseCoopers offered to improve government functioning in new security areas such as bioterrorism. McKinsey played a controversial role in health-care privatization in the United Kingdom.[42] The firm also became the "climate consultants *du jour*" in the developing world. The consulting firm's influence over Saudi Arabia's economic reforms has been so pervasive that the joke in Riyadh is that the Saudi Ministry of Planning should be called "the McKinsey Ministry."[43] Governments in emerging markets hired McKinsey as a signal to donors of their seriousness in reducing emissions from deforestation and forest degradation.[44] This eventually led to the McKinsey Center for Government, which offers advice on improving the performance of public sector agencies.[45] With access to governments across the globe, management consultants have direct effects on policy implementation. They can also acquire insider knowledge from their partnerships with governments.

The more significant way that these firms affect the marketplace of ideas is through a conscious strategy of thought leadership. Many smaller firms are centered around management gurus who push big ideas in strategy and management through books, lectures, and media hits. The big firms emulate this strategy and expand upon it through speaking engagements and articles in scholarly and popular outlets.[46] McKinsey invests $400 million a year in such activities; in 2013 Dominic Barton, the firm's global managing partner, bragged to the *Economist* about the firm's "university-like capabilities" in knowledge development.[47] Surveys of corporate officials strongly suggest that this kind of thought leadership has led to additional demand for consulting services.[48] The influence of management consulting ideas in the public sphere can be seen in the spread of their argot: terms like "outside the box," "bandwidth," and "buy-in" all originate with consultants.[49] Consider how one firm historian attempted to define how a McKinsey consultant was viewed by the outside world:

> He has gained money, power, and prestige, as well as the pretense of an intellectually minded pursuit within the corporate sphere. He is not a banker, accountant, or lawyer. He is a thinker. He has had the chance to whisper into the ears of power, to exercise influence while being insulated from responsibility....
>
> McKinsey's ability to take an idea and "leverage" it up using its brand and organizational effectiveness ... made its consultants far

and away the most effective disseminators of ideas via the consulting process.[50]

The most significant exercise in thought leadership is the creation of for-profit think tanks. McKinsey has been a trailblazer in this area. The firm established the management journal *McKinsey Quarterly* in 1964 and then the McKinsey Global Institute (MGI) in 1990. All of McKinsey's literature describes MGI as its in-house "think tank." According to its website, "MGI's mission is to provide leaders in the commercial, public, and social sectors with the facts and insights on which to base management and policy decisions."[51] MGI report topics have ranged from the future of the Chinese economy to the rise of Big Data to the pros and cons of the dollar remaining the world's reserve currency. Since 2009, McKinsey has vastly increased its marketing of MGI products, circulating them widely and making them more freely available to outside observers.

A host of other management consultancies and financial firms have copied McKinsey's template, as Table 6.1 shows.[52] The University of Pennsylvania's 2015 ranking of for-profit think tanks shows that MGI was the top-ranked for-profit think tank in 2015. Ernst & Young, A. T. Kearney, Accenture, Boston Consulting Group, Deloitte, and PricewaterhouseCoopers were behind MGI in the top twenty.

The for-profit think tank world extends beyond management consultants. In recent years, the investment firm Legatum set up the Legatum Institute to focus on promoting economic prosperity. JPMorgan Chase created the JPMorgan Chase Institute to advise policymakers.[53] The firm hired Diana Farrell, a former National Security Council director and the former head of the McKinsey Global Institute, to run it. Similarly, Kohlberg Kravis Roberts created the KKR Global Institute, which "integrates expertise and analysis about emerging developments and long-term trends in geopolitics, macroeconomics, demographics, energy and natural resource markets, technology, and trade policy" and thereby "serves as a platform for thought leadership."[54] KKR hired former four-star general and CIA director David Petraeus to be its chairman.

For-profit actors have pursued other tactics to influence the marketplace of ideas. Many of them have developed the accoutrement of

TABLE 6.1 Best For-Profit Think Tanks, 2015

Rank	Think Tank	Headquarters
1	McKinsey Global Institute	United States
2	Deutsche Bank Research	Germany
3	Economist Intelligence Unit	United Kingdom
4	Oxford Analytica	United States
5	Nomura Research Institute	Japan
6	A.T. Kearney Global Business Policy Council	United States
7	Jigsaw (Google Ideas)	United States
8	Eurasia Group	United States
9	Ernst & Young	United States
10	Samsung Economic Research Institute	Republic of Korea
11	Accenture Institute for High Performance	United States
12	Stratfor	United States
13	Strategy&, FKA Booz and Company	United States
14	Kissinger Associates	United States
15	Calouste Gulbenkian Foundation	Portugal
16	IBM Institute for Business Value	United States
17	GovLab (Deloitte)	United States
18	European House—Ambrosetti	Italy
19	Boston Consulting Group	United States
20	PricewaterhouseCoopers	United States

Source: The Lauder Institute, *2015 Global Go To Think Tank Index Report*, Table 28.

more scholarly organizations. Some of these trappings are superficial, such as Deloitte labeling its publications as coming from "Deloitte University Press."[55] Many investment banks and management consultancies, to further market their wares, offer their reports for free to the business press. They do this in the hopes that their brand gets more media coverage. Several of them publish freely available forecasts of the future of the global economy or world politics. In the past few years alone Credit Suisse has issued a report about the return of multipolarity in world politics; KPMG sketched out what the global economy would look like in 2030. HSBC and PricewaterhouseCoopers went even further into the future than that, offering analyses of what the global economy would look like in 2050.[56] Many of these reports are explicitly labeled as examples of thought leadership. They go far beyond conventional financial analysis to include speculations on geopolitics.

Another tactic is the development of public accessible indices that rank different countries, cities, or other actors on desirable qualities. An increasing array of actors are ranking countries on a welter of desirable criteria, from the World Economic Forum's Global Competitiveness Index to Transparency International's Corruption Perceptions Index. Michael Chui, the head of MGI, told me that the development of such rankings "is a great way to engage people" in McKinsey's work.[57] An observer of the consulting sector blogged, "firms get extra publicity when they become known for a specific topic—they become an obvious source of comment for relevant stories in the media and can get a lot of media coverage on the back of rankings which tend to appeal to the 'Who's beating who?' mentality in all of us."[58] There is growing evidence that countries respond to performing poorly in these ranking exercises by making real-world changes to policy.[59] Not surprisingly, as these indices have gained traction, private-sector actors have jumped in. The Legatum Institute developed a global prosperity index to measure national levels of well-being. Both DHL and McKinsey have marketed their own indices of cross-border connectedness. Deloitte produced a global manufacturing competitiveness index.

Most of these firms are playing catch-up with the management consulting sector. The chastening of the Great Recession has constrained the thought leadership of the traditional financial powerhouses like Goldman Sachs compared to consulting firms like McKinsey. The crisis itself forced many of the financial firms to retrench at the exact moment that consulting firms expanded their thought leadership. The public ignominy suffered by the entire financial sector because of its role in the 2008 financial crisis also tarnished the luster of their thought leadership. The symbolic inflection point might have been 2014, when McKinsey took over from Goldman Sachs to sponsor the *Financial Times* Business Book of the Year award.

For management consulting firms, the intellectual whole of direct client work and thought leadership practices is greater than the sum of those efforts. Their myriad global activities give these firms a particular advantage in combining tacit knowledge with big ideas. They engage in "epistemic arbitrage," applying lessons learned in one sector to another—and generalizing from all of their experiences to propose new ways of thinking in the aggregate. This was a key source of McKinsey's "war for talent" or BCG's prediction of the "homeshoring" of American manufacturing.[60] The combination of the location of these networked firms and their ideas make them uniquely situated in the marketplace of ideas.[61]

Of course, the thought leadership from management consultants has not been an unblemished success. One reason the term "thought leader" is so derided is because of its overuse by the consulting sector. The private-sector ranking exercises and projections of the global economy suffer from numerous methodological flaws.[62] Many of the trends that McKinsey, BCG, and others have identified and branded turned out to be wildly overhyped. BCG overestimated the number of jobs that would be created from insourcing. It could be argued that McKinsey's "war for talent" was responsible for Enron's spectacular bankruptcy in 2001. According to Malcolm Gladwell, "[McKinsey] essentially created the blueprint for the Enron culture."[63] McKinsey's participation in Great Britain's privatization of the National Health Service led to a rash of negative media coverage.[64] To celebrate the fiftieth anniversary of the *McKinsey Quarterly*, the firm's best and brightest wrote an essay sketching out the next fifty years of management.[65] The *Financial Times'* Lucy Kellaway was underwhelmed, characterizing the essay as a "sorry exercise in windy platitudes."[66] A scholarly analysis of the field concluded, "It seems amazing that there is so much criticism of consulting, and so much skepticism surrounding it, and yet it is a booming industry."[67]

The other category of firms that rank high on Table 6.1 come from political risk analysis. This sector has a more recent origin story. The modern demand for geopolitical risk assessments began in the early 1970s. Expropriations of foreign direct investment swept across newly independent countries in the developing world. OPEC, through the 1973 oil embargo, demonstrated the ability of a state cartel to radically affect energy prices. While this generated interest in political risk, there was not much in the way of systemic analysis.[68]

A generation later, the demand for political risk surged again.[69] Economic globalization opened up new markets for cross-border investment and enabled the creation of complex global supply chains. These, in turn, created the need for estimating the geopolitical risk to physical plants and key links in countries across the world.[70] The proliferation of economic sanctions in this century introduced an added layer of political uncertainty for global firms, leading some sectors to seek advice for how to "de-risk" their overseas investments. The aftermath of the 2008 financial crisis made it clear that political risk was a consideration in developed as well as developing markets. Indeed, over the past decade the biggest risks to global financial markets have come from political instability in the European Union and United States. Bank of England surveys show that between 2013 and 2014, business executives citing geopolitical risk as a concern for their operations increased from 13 percent to 57 percent; McKinsey surveys reflect the same concerns.[71] In September 2014, the *Financial Times* reported that "political risk is now a growth industry in its own right."[72] As the Eurasia Group's David Gordon phrased it to me, political risk is now a "c-suite conversation."

The supply side expanded for another reason: political consulting became a preferred landing spot for former policymakers. As noted in the previous chapter, the traditional route for ex-policy principals was to take a sinecure at a think tank. A successful for-profit consultancy, however, is far more lucrative than a think tank fellowship. Henry Kissinger pioneered this approach in 1982 when he and Brent Scowcroft founded Kissinger Associates to offer advisory services for corporate clients. In this century the number of these Washington firms specializing in political consulting and strategic communications has mushroomed. They include Albright Stonebridge Group (founded by three former policy principals in Bill Clinton's administration), RiceHadleyGates (founded by three former policy principals in George W. Bush's administration), The Scowcroft Group (founded by the two-time former national security advisor), and Teneo (founded by former Clinton administration officials).[73] Almost all of their work is "bespoke" research—work directly contracted by a client—and therefore not directly accessible in the public sphere. Nevertheless, it is an important part of the Ideas Industry. This research often informs the public discourse of the actors who procure the research. Furthermore, the employees at these firms can wear multiple hats, serving on various foreign affairs advisory groups and helping to draft think tank reports.[74]

Increasingly, firms contract for political risk assessments as part of their due diligence before making significant decisions involving cross-border investments. Public-sector agencies like the US National Intelligence Council also look to private-sector consultants to buttress their own research. As Table 6.1 shows, the Economist Intelligence Unit (EIU), Oxford Analytica, Eurasia Group, Kissinger Associates, and Stratfor all are in the top twenty for-profit think tanks. With the exception of EIU, none of these firms existed prior to 1975.

In essence, the current state of political risk consulting echoes the nascent stages of the management consulting industry. The product generated by this sector remains amorphous. There is, at this point, no such thing as "political risk insurance." Geopolitical risk consultants advise their clients, and then those firms respond with a variety of hedging and insurance subcomponents.[75] There are no professional political risk associations, nor are there accepted best practices. The firms in this sector recruit an eclectic mix of international relations analysts, former intelligence officials, and retired special forces operators. This mix sometimes produces culture clashes within these consultancies. The firms in this sector engage in many of the aggressive marketing gambits that the founders of management consultancies disdained.

Both outsider and insider assessments of geopolitical risk analysts are ambivalent about their performance. There have been some positive press portrayals. One of the leading firms, Stratfor, received glowing press coverage at the beginning of this century. Barron's referred to it as a "shadow CIA."[76] EIU was the top-ranked for-profit think tank in 2014, and the presence of these firms at the top of the rankings suggests that they produce quality analysis some of the time. Having reviewed one of these firms' exercises in geopolitical scenario planning for a US government agency, I would conclude that their bespoke research can be quite rigorous.

Nevertheless, this part of the Ideas Industry has its issues. Many ex-policymakers who are involved in consulting firms avoid disclosing possible conflicts of interest between their for-profit activities and their other roles in think tanks and policy boards.[77] The *Financial Times* cheekily noted this sector's "love of colored maps of varying sophistication."[78] The opacity of the sector was pierced in 2012, when WikiLeaks published more than five million Stratfor emails. WikiLeaks declared that the so-called "Global Intelligence Files" revealed "the inner workings of a company that fronts as an intelligence publisher, but provides confidential intelligence services to large corporations . . . and government agencies."[79] In truth, the emails revealed the shoddy nature of the firm's work—or, as the *Guardian* observed, "the extremely low quality of the information available to the highest bidder."[80] One commentator joked at the time of the email release, "Stratfor is just *The Economist* a week later and several hundred times more expensive."[81] Even industry insiders have acknowledged the variegated quality of geopolitical risk analysis.[82] One former political risk analyst concluded, "While there are some notable exceptions, most political risk assessment remains both superficial and subjective."[83]

Despite precarious intellectual standing, political risk consultancies are a key component of the for-profit sector of the Ideas Industry for two reasons. The first is that the very nature of geopolitical risk analysis means that these firms employ implicit theories of how the world works. As one scholarly assessment of the industry notes, "although theories are seldom explicated by the various [risk] ratings systems, they exist nevertheless."[84] Private-sector theories about what causes wars, crises, or revolutions clearly affect the public discourse on these issues—particularly if public-sector agencies and large multinational corporations consume their research as part of their geopolitical due diligence.[85]

The second reason is that many geopolitical risk firms are also engaging in thought leadership activities akin to management consultants and financial services firms. Like these other sectors, geopolitical risk analysts have also developed long-term projections of the global economy. EIU has published its own macroeconomic forecasts out to

2050.[86] These firms have also introduced headline-grabbing indices as well. EIU has a Democracy Index. Verisk Maplecroft, Political Risk Services, Eurasia, and others offer a suite of rankings and indices of political risk. Every January, Eurasia publishes its "Top Risks" list for the upcoming year, an exercise that generates considerable media coverage and commentary.

Like other for-profit sectors, the political risk industry also relies on gurus. Indeed, because of the recent emergence of this sector, most of these gurus are also the firm founders. George Friedman, the founder of Stratfor, published multiple books predicting what world politics will look like in the next decade and the next century when he was CEO of the firm.[87] Ian Bremmer, the CEO of the Eurasia Group, is also a widely published author, and has written columns for *Foreign Policy* and *Time*. Bremmer has a close relationship with the World Economic Forum, furthering his network with possible clients and influencers. According to its website, "Bremmer and other top analysts at the firm frequently address high-level executive briefings, large conferences, and international summits."[88]

Clearly, some elements of the political risk industry try to use thought leadership to mimic the evolution of management consulting firms. Compared to that sector, however, the reputation of political risk firms presents a challenge. Political psychologist Philip Tetlock has devoted his life to studying the ability of experts to make accurate predictions, and he concludes, "There is a paucity of evidence—peer-reviewed scientific evidence—that forecasters know how to deliver the goods: reliably accurate political, economic and technological predictions."[89] The quality of their thought leadership products is even lower than their bespoke research. The marketing aspect of their thought leadership guarantees certain biases in their analysis. One well-placed member of the geopolitical risk industry told me that all publicly accessible work done by this sector should be viewed as marketing rather than analysis. By producing eye-opening, easily digestible content, these firms get on the radar of potential clients, luring them in for more granular, firm-specific analysis. This lends to obvious biases in their public work. Or, as he put it more crudely to me: "You scare the shit out of them first. That's what gets the clients through the front door."

A final glance at Table 6.1 reveals one oddity in the top twenty list: Jigsaw, née Google Ideas. As previously noted, twenty-first-century plutocrats direct and organize philanthropic giving in ways different from their twentieth-century predecessors. Consistent with that vein, it is thus unsurprising that Jigsaw was described by its head as "a think/do tank that aims to explore how technology can make a difference to people working on the front lines of global issues."[90] In a *Financial Times* interview at the time of its founding, Google chairman Eric Schmidt explained that Jigsaw "is built on this assumption that technology is part of every challenge in the world and also part of every solution in the world. It empowers people both for good and for ill . . . where does that leave us as a technology company? Where it leaves us is recognizing that technology is now relevant to every single challenge in the world in some way, shape, or form."[91]

That kind of mission statement would not sound out of place from other Silicon Valley philanthropies. There were subtle differences, however, suggesting that it represented a new organizational form for the Ideas Industry. For one thing, unlike the Gates Foundation or Google's charity organization Google.org, Google Ideas Jigsaw was neither a corporate foundation nor a nonprofit entity. It originally existed as a unit within Google's business operations and strategy division.[92] Another distinction is that Google named Jared Cohen to be the first director of Google Ideas. Cohen served on the State Department's policy planning staff during the Bush and Obama administrations. His prior claim to fame was convincing Twitter to delay its scheduled maintenance in the summer of 2009 to allow Iranian protestors to communicate with each other and the outside world.[93] This suggested that Jigsaw was intended to be an alchemy of business strategy and policy advocacy.

It is noteworthy that in their 2013 coauthored book on the digital transformation of world politics, Schmidt and Cohen mentioned Google Ideas only once.[94] Its initial focus seemed narrowly tailored, focusing primarily on combating extremist rhetoric on the Internet.[95] Its most high-profile initiative was the Against Violent Extremism (AVE) network. Founded at a June 2011 summit in Dublin of former gang members, jihadists, right-wing extremists, and other militants, the network exists to "prevent the recruitment of 'at risk' youths and encourage the disengagement of those already involved."[96] The idea behind the AVE network is to provide "counter-narratives" that push back against extremist narratives that flourish online. It is too soon and too difficult to assess the impact of AVE on countering violent extremism. One review of such efforts, however, pointed out the private-sector nature of Jigsaw endowed it with greater credibility than state-led efforts. The backing of Google "allows [AVE] to stand independent of governments, avoiding the usual political sensitivities that can follow state involvement in such initiatives."[97]

The mere existence of Jigsaw generates considerable paranoia from some quarters. WikiLeaks founder Julian Assange wrote in *Newsweek* that "Cohen's directorate appeared to cross over from public relations and 'corporate responsibility' work into active corporate intervention in foreign affairs at a level that is normally reserved for states. Jared Cohen could be wryly named Google's 'director of regime change.' "[98] Other critics lodged similar accusations when Schmidt announced in February 2016 that Google Ideas would be renamed Jigsaw and turned into a "technology incubator."[99] Jigsaw has released an array of new products, including Google Shield, designed to prevent DDoS attacks on vulnerable websites.[100]

There is a business element to Jigsaw's initiatives—but that has been clear since its inception. The firm has expressed interest in how to export Google products to countries currently under heavy US sanctions, such as Iran and North Korea. I participated in one brainstorming meeting on this question under the auspices of a think tank that shall remain nameless. For all the paranoia about Google's motives in some quarters, it seems obvious that its motives are simultaneously altruistic and self-serving. On the one hand, it argues that unless it can export software updates and patches to these countries, dissidents and human rights activists could be left vulnerable to government cyber-intrusions. On the other hand, this is part and parcel of Google's business strategy of expanding their global footprint, and consistent with Schmidt's travels to Myanmar and North Korea to push for greater online openness.[101] A critical scholarly take on Google's influence concludes: "While it seems clear that Googlers do genuinely support freedom of expression as a fundamental human right, there is little evidence that this is the reason the company pursues greater global connectivity.... the simple fact that its survival (in the political-economy sense of the word) depends on getting more and more people online to use its complimentary services."[102] Jigsaw is clearly trying to do good *and* do well.

The private-sector portion of the Ideas Industry is a motley collection. None of the for-profit think tanks has come close to being in the overall top twenty since the University of Pennsylvania started its ranking exercise. The thought leadership of both management consultants and political risk analysts serves a marketing objective as much as any intellectual purpose. The for-profit sector also suffers from certain heuristic biases. Market analysts are prone to "chartism" in their forecasts. Chartists look for regular patterns in their data to develop short-term predictions—but they do not necessarily possess a causal logic for *why* any particular pattern is significant. As a result, private-sector thought leaders often engage in "overfitting": over-interpreting statistical noise as representing an underlying trend. As Nate Silver has cautioned, "overfitting represents a double whammy: it makes our model look *better* on paper but perform *worse* in the real world."[103] Worse, because for-profit thought leaders are convinced that they have found a true predictor, they will often hype its value far beyond its true worth.

The private sector also demonstrates some serious weaknesses in applying its tools to explain politics. Ironically, since 2008, more and more financial actors have invested in political analysis—but actual political behavior can flummox them. Market participants are adept at identifying the economic pressures that could force politicians to act. It is in predicting how politicians will react to those pressures that the consultants and traders fall down. In my conversations with management consultants and investment bankers during the 2013 debt-ceiling showdowns, for example, they were constantly surprised at the political bargaining failures that kept recurring. Politicians have different incentives than market participants—a fact that sometimes escapes for-profit actors when they think about the world.

Nonprofit think tanks must defend themselves against conflict of interest claims; surely, the private sector should face even harsher scrutiny. Conflicts of interest in the consulting world have led to criminal prosecution.[104] Furthermore, while for-profit actors like McKinsey or Goldman Sachs offer many useful analyses, they are biased toward highlighting market opportunities for potential clients. A decade ago, management consultants overhyped the offshore outsourcing phenomenon in part to encourage US firms to contract their services for their own offshoring efforts. Many of these offshoring moves yielded lower-than-expected cost savings, triggering a reverse wave of "homeshoring" this decade—a trend that was also hyped by management consultants.[105] Similarly, numerous financial advisors have authored papers and op-eds defending sovereign wealth funds from greater federal regulation. An undeniable incentive for this defense was that these firms wanted to earn commissions advising sovereign wealth fund investments in the United States.[106]

Despite these obvious concerns, the private-sector portion of the Ideas Industry appears to be doing quite well. In my survey of opinion leaders, top-ranked think tanks like the Brookings Institution and Center for Strategic and International Studies were trusted more than either MGI or the Eurasia Group. As Figure 6.1 shows, however, those two for-profit think tanks earned greater confidence scores than the

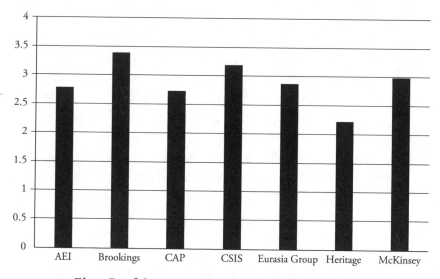

FIGURE 6.1 Elite Confidence in Think Thanks

Notes: Ideas Industry elite survey response to: "In writing about a new topic, your research will yield relevant papers from different sources. All else equal, how much confidence would you place in a report's findings based on the institutional origins listed below?" (Number of respondents = 193, possible 1–4 ranking).

Source: Author survey.

more partisan think tanks, such as AEI, Heritage, or the Center for American Progress. Indeed, thought leaders from the private sector are increasingly prevalent in prestigious conferences, prestigious journals, and airport bookstores. Why hasn't the for-profit sector faced the same challenges to its thought leadership as nonprofit think tanks?

The provisional answers go to style as well as substance. Stylistically, the private sector is far better at conveying ideas than university professors or think tank fellows. Management consultants figured out the power of graphs and charts long before *Vox* or *Business Insider* appeared on the scene. There are many ways in which the foreign policy community is allergic to numbers—but that allergy makes them more likely to accept data presentations at face value. The for-profit sector excels at finding the one number, metric, or chart that will capture the attention of the audience, the "takeaway" stat that even the innumerate can comprehend. Their ideas about the state of the world are therefore easier to understand and carry more heuristic punch. This does not mean that these ideas are necessarily correct, but it does mean that the private sector is far better placed to exploit the tectonic shifts in the modern Ideas Industry.

Substantively, the explicitly for-profit nature of organizations such as McKinsey and Stratfor also endows them with some powerful advantages in the marketplace of ideas.[107] The most obvious one is the implicit inference that audiences draw from their for-profit nature: *if someone is willing to pay for their services then they must have value.* Outside observers naturally infer from their continued existence as viable businesses that the advice Credit Suisse or the Eurasia Group proffers is high quality.[108] This is why so many management consultants and geopolitical risk analysts advertise their connections with blue-chip firms and official intelligence agencies. The inference that they want their audience to draw is that if large organizations trust their advice, then it must be valuable. This extends to the particular ideas that they market. "We try to monetize ideas," Credit Suisse's Krithika Subramanian explained to me: "but it's not just an idea, it is an idea that has been tested in the marketplace."[109]

The for-profit nature of these ventures gives these firms another advantage. The proprietary information they gather and provide for their clients allows access to information that more traditional public intellectuals might lack. This gives them a decided edge in presenting arguments about how the world works. When the McKinsey Global Institute issues reports, or when its directors coauthor books, they draw on both publicly available and proprietary information.[110] Similarly, when JPMorgan Chase launched the JPMorgan Chase Institute, it stressed that it would rely on "the broad spectrum of data within the firm to use for the public good."[111]

The reliance on both anecdotes and data from proprietary sources plays to the cognitive biases of potential clients. Individuals are far more likely to value information derived from firsthand narratives than detached analyses.[112] Not surprisingly, management consultants excel at marrying such narratives to their predictions.[113] Even beyond anecdotes, proprietary data is a strength and not a weakness for corporate thought leaders. It is information that more traditional intellectual outlets lack. Proprietary information also gives the private sector a justifiable excuse for opacity. Neither consultants nor tech firms will divulge all their data or methodologies, for fear of exposing their customers to unwarranted scrutiny. This obviously makes it easier for public audiences to cast a skeptical eye at their analysis and allege conflicts of interest. At the same time, however, it makes it impossible for outside observers to falsify their arguments.

The constant interaction with clients also gives private-sector intellectuals an added advantage over more traditional foreign policy analysts: speed. In recent years, I have researched the geopolitical effect of sovereign wealth funds, the relative financial power of China, and the political economy of the 2008 financial crisis. For each of these research endeavors, market analysts produced sophisticated analyses quicker than either academics or think-tankers. Whenever a new issue crops up on the radar, it is Goldman Sachs or McKinsey or State Street that often emerges with the first substantive report. When the private sector assesses and interprets the state of the world, they are usually relying on the freshest data. For example, I attended multiple foreign policy conferences in early 2008 in which academics and wonks talked about what the next US president would get to do once in office. All of the market participants at these conferences insisted that the subprime mortgage crisis was a bigger deal than people realized, and that its effects would constrain any ambitious policy agenda.

After the 2008 financial crisis, market analysts were also far quicker than inside-the-Beltway intellectuals to downgrade China's long-term growth trajectory.

Finally, the tectonic shifts driving the modern marketplace of ideas tilt the playing field in favor of the private sector. The erosion of trust in traditional sources of authority means that the prestige gap between private-sector thought leaders and traditional public intellectuals has narrowed considerably. The rise in partisanship affects private-sector thought leaders less than either the academy or think tanks. As agents of business, they arouse less suspicion among conservatives than academics or members of left-of-center think tanks. Most importantly, private-sector thought leaders are the intellectuals most comfortable interacting with plutocrats. In many cases, the private-sector thought leader *is* an entrenched part of the benefactor class. By their nature, management consultants and political risk analysts are geared to cater to this constituency in their bespoke research. That allows them to gain the social intelligence and network ties to successfully navigate the waters of the plutocracy. To put matters more simply, when dealing with potential benefactors, management consultants are better able to network than professors or think tank denizens.

It used to be that foreign policy professionals had a choice: take the credit or take the money. Those intellectuals who wanted to own the ideas they ginned up, such as academics, were happy to promote them to others. Those intellectuals who were comfortable with outsourced and subcontracted work could earn generous consulting contracts, while policymakers could take credit for their ideas. That tradeoff still exists to some extent, but it is not as strong. The emergence of the modern Ideas Industry has enabled for-profit thought leaders to have it all. Through their thought leadership, they can claim credit as a marketing device. Through their bespoke work, they can earn the money as well.

The rise of the private sector for intellectuals parallels the rise of the BRICS. Its emergence is undeniable, the effects are observable, and yet the real significance is heavily contested. Some scholars decry the rise of for-profit thought leaders. One recent academic op-ed groused that these private-sector actors are "aggressively marketing their research to media outlets," going on to warn that "for-profit public intellectuals frequently have questionable motives and funding sources."[114] At the same time, it is intrinsic to the business model of these private-sector actors that they hype their importance and access. It is undeniable that management consultants, investment bankers, and political risk analysts have increased their influence over the marketplace of ideas. But it is possible that these actors have exaggerated that influence.

Influence is a relative commodity; if one actor gains it, another actor inevitably loses some. There is constant churn in the marketplace of foreign policy ideas, but the last few chapters suggest that traditional public intellectuals in the nonprofit sector have merely survived, while for-profit thought leaders have thrived. The growth in numbers and legitimacy of private-sector think tanks, geopolitical risk analysts, and tech firms suggests that these thought leaders cannot be ignored by more traditional intellectuals.

The more interesting question to ask is what it all means for the marketplace of ideas. And that is the topic we turn to in the next few chapters.

PART III

7

The Promise and Perils of Intellectual Brands

Articles and ideas are only as good as the fees you can get for talking about them. They are merely billboards for the messengers.

— Stephen Marche

THE NOSTALGIC ARGUMENT IS a powerful one when talking about the modern marketplace of ideas. In both my survey of opinion leaders and my conversations with foreign policy experts, I heard variations of "Who is our generation's Walter Lippmann?" numerous times. To appreciate the ways that the modern Ideas Industry is different from last century's marketplace of ideas, it is worth considering whether there is a twenty-first-century equivalent to Lippmann. Of course, that raises a more immediate question: Just who was Walter Lippmann?

A strong case can be made that Lippmann was nothing less than the most influential public intellectual of his generation.[1] A Harvard student under the noted philosopher George Santayana, Lippmann dropped out of graduate school to write for a socialist newspaper. He was one of the founding editors of the *New Republic* in 1914, propounding pro-interventionist sentiments at the start of the Great War. He served in the Wilson administration and managed The Inquiry, a brain trust set up to think about the postwar order and advise US officials at the Versailles peace conference. Soon after Versailles, Lippmann returned to newspapers. He wrote editorials for the *New York World* and, later, the *New York Herald-Tribune*. In 1931, he turned down offers to be a Harvard professor and the president of the University of North

Carolina to start his syndicated column, "Today and Tomorrow." It lasted more than thirty-five years and earned Lippmann two Pulitzer prizes for commentary. In his later years, he wrote for the *Washington Post* as well as *Newsweek*. The ideas he articulated were influential enough for *Reader's Digest* to publish condensed versions of his bestsellers and for the *Ladies Home Journal* to present them to its readers in comic-book form.[2]

Lippmann's politics ran the gamut during his professional life, which is a polite way of saying that he often changed his mind. His biographer Ronald Steel wrote that Lippmann's views had the habit of "not straying too far from the main thrust of public opinion."[3] One of Lippmann's rivals, the columnist Joseph Alsop, noted more caustically that "Walter's column was saved from constant repetition only by the simple fact that he changed his views roughly once every eight months."[4] One could also argue, however, that Lippmann's political arc revealed a long, variegated path away from socialism toward a conservative skepticism about America and American power. In his college years, Lippmann was considered more radical than his classmate John Reed, but he eschewed socialism soon afterwards. Lippmann then grew enamored with Teddy Roosevelt's brand of progressivism, but parted ways with him during the First World War. An enthusiastic supporter of US entry into the First World War when writing at the *New Republic*, Lippmann grew more and more disenchanted with American statecraft. He opposed containment in the late 1940s because he believed it would be too aggressive and militaristic. In his last years as a columnist, Lippmann railed against the Johnson administration's expansion of the war in Vietnam.

Lippmann's abilities as an essayist would have been enough to earn him a hefty intellectual obituary. Yet he added at least two other dimensions to his role as a public intellectual. Lippmann counseled a number of American presidents and politicians. He advised President Wilson on his Fourteen Points, prepped Wendell Wilkie and Dwight Eisenhower as presidential candidates, and befriended both John Kennedy and Lyndon Johnson. He urged Republican senator Arthur Vanderberg to move the GOP in a more internationalist direction at the dawn of the Cold War. During the 1940s, Lippmann was deemed so important a player in the crafting of American foreign policy that the

British Embassy appointed an official to stay informed about the columnist's thinking.[5] The KGB, which monitored influential members of the Washington press corps, gave Lippmann the codename "Hub."[6] President Kennedy ordered his press secretary to put Lippmann directly through to him if he called the White House.[7]

Lippmann also developed arguments that had lasting effects on several areas of scholarship. His more ambitious tomes affected research in public opinion, foreign policy analysis, and media studies for the next half century.[8] His books, particularly *U.S. Foreign Policy: Shield of the Republic* and *The Cold War*, helped define the foreign policy debate for the postwar era. Indeed, Lippmann is credited with popularizing the very term "Cold War" itself.[9] In *The Cold War*—and the columns that comprised it—Lippmann penned the most high-profile contemporaneous rebuttal to George Kennan's doctrine of containment.[10] Soon afterwards, Kennan came around to Lippmann's worldview on the flaws of America's Cold War policies.

Lippmann's lasting legacy in political science came from one of the few constants of his political worldview: his skepticism about the merits of public opinion and democratic control of foreign affairs. In one of his early books, *Public Opinion*, Lippmann's elitism shines through: "Representative government . . . cannot be worked successfully, no matter what the basis of election, unless there is an independent, expert organization for making the unseen facts intelligible to those who have to make the decisions."[11] More than thirty years later, in *The Public Philosophy*, he warned, "The unhappy truth is that the prevailing public opinion has been destructively wrong at the critical junctures. The people have imposed a veto upon the judgments of informed and responsible officials. . . . Mass opinion has acquired mounting power in this country. It has shown itself to be a dangerous master of decisions when the stakes are life and death."[12] Lippmann's pessimism about public attitudes affected a generation of public opinion scholarship. That generation of research culminated in the "Almond-Lippmann consensus," which suggests that mass attitudes toward foreign policy are inconstant, irrational, and ill-considered.[13]

Is there a modern equivalent to Lippmann? Let me suggest one possible candidate: Fareed Zakaria.

In my survey of opinion leaders, Zakaria was considered to be one of the three most influential foreign policy writers, behind only Henry Kissinger and Thomas Friedman. Zakaria's life and worldview parallel Lippmann's much more strongly than either Kissinger's or Friedman's. Both were born into well-off families. Like Lippmann, Zakaria spent some of his formative years at Harvard. While Lippmann dropped out of his graduate program, Zakaria completed his Ph.D. in political science. His mentor was Samuel Huntington, who chaired his all-star dissertation committee. Like Lippmann, Zakaria could have become a professor but chose to eschew the academy, taking a positon as the managing editor of *Foreign Affairs* at the tender age of twenty-eight (where he would publish his mentor's "Clash of Civilizations" essay). He moved on to become editor of *Newsweek International* in 1999, writing a syndicated column for both *Newsweek* and the *Washington Post*. In the wake of the September 11 terrorist attacks, Zakaria authored a seven-thousand-word *Newsweek* cover essay on the roots of anti-Americanism in the Arab Middle East.[14] Widely cited and circulated inside the Beltway, it lifted Zakaria into a whole new level of acclaim.

Like Lippmann, Zakaria's politics and place of employment have been peripatetic. The myriad profiles of Zakaria have variably described him as a liberal, a conservative, and a neoconservative.[15] He supported the 2003 invasion of Iraq, and in January 2004 he was still arguing that the benefits outweighed the costs.[16] Nonetheless, just as the invasion was to begin, he published a scathing critique of the Bush administration's diplomacy surrounding Operation Iraqi Freedom. He later excoriated the Bush administration for its reckless bungling of the invasion and occupation.[17]

Professionally, Zakaria moved on from *Newsweek* to become a columnist for *Time* and a contributing editor of *The Atlantic* while still continuing to write for the *Washington Post*. Zakaria made the jump into television in 2002 as a panelist for ABC's *This Week with George Stephanopoulos*. Three years later, he began hosting a weekly program, *Foreign Exchange*, for PBS. Three years after that, he moved to CNN. *Fareed Zakaria GPS* is currently the only major cable news show in the United States to focus on international affairs. The program won a Peabody Award in 2011.

Zakaria's career also parallels Lippmann's in his activities outside his column. Zakaria's influence as a foreign policy intellectual and his mainstream media platforms have given him greater access in the corridors of power. He met with myriad senior officials from the Clinton and Bush administrations. He interacted with President Obama enough for Zakaria to have to clarify on air that he was not an Obama adviser. And, like Lippmann, Zakaria's longform writing has had impact as well. His 1997 *Foreign Affairs* essay on "illiberal democracy" presaged twenty-first-century problems with the US policy of democracy promotion. In that essay—eventually expanded into 2003's *The Future of Freedom*—Zakaria articulated concerns about democratization without democratic culture in ways that echoed Lippmann's frequent warnings about public opinion. Though Zakaria remains less prolific than Lippmann, both political scientists and foreign policy cognoscenti have widely cited Zakaria's books on world politics.

The magazine profiles of Zakaria through the years have been just as effusive in their praise as the biographies of Lippmann. As early as 1999, Walter Russell Mead described Zakaria as "the most influential foreign-policy adviser of his generation." Henry Kissinger praised Zakaria to *New York* magazine, raving that "he has a first-class mind and likes to say things that run against conventional wisdom."[18] One review of Zakaria's *The Post-American World* suggested that "he may have more intellectual range and insights than any other public thinker in the West."[19] All of those quotes would have described Walter Lippmann at comparable stages of his career.

It would seem that apart from a few minor details, Lippmann and Zakaria share similar intellectual DNA. It is worth noting two important distinctions, however. One difference is that when Lippmann was opining about foreign affairs, he possessed a near-monopoly on that part of the public sphere. Zakaria might be a superstar in the modern marketplace of ideas, but it is a much more crowded market now than during Lippmann's life.

The other difference is more significant: unlike Lippmann, Zakaria has in recent years battled serious charges of plagiarism. This chapter—about the life of superstar intellectuals in the Ideas Industry—suggests that the two differences might be related.

Walter Lippmann was a man of considerable intellectual gifts, but he had one structural advantage over Fareed Zakaria: less competition. Lippmann towered over the foreign policy public sphere in part because he was so big but also because that sphere was so small. This was particularly true during the early years of the Cold War. Lippmann's heyday as a foreign policy intellectual was also the heyday of the "Georgetown Set" that debated American foreign policy over DC dinners.[20] This coterie of academics, columnists, publishers, and policymakers was small enough to exercise real leverage over the marketplace of ideas. George Kennan's direct influence over politicians and policy principals was small. The one arena where he did exercise soft power, however, was over the Georgetown crowd of columnists.[21] Those opinion writers cemented Kennan's reputation for foreign policy gravitas in the public's mind.[22]

The early Cold War commentators who opined about American foreign policy had their rivalries and jealousies, but there was also significant amounts of shared social capital that helped to sustain the entire group through adversity. Most of them had gone to the same schools and served together in the Second World War. The common background helped them trust each other even when they disagreed. As a managed oligopoly, the Cold War intellectuals were also able to keep assorted personal scandals under wraps and away from the public eye. While married to his first wife, Walter Lippmann had an affair with the wife of longtime *Foreign Affairs* editor Hamilton Fish Armstrong, triggering multiple divorces. The KGB tried to blackmail Joseph Alsop from a homosexual dalliance during a 1957 trip to Moscow. Neither indiscretion derailed the careers of those involved.[23] As Fareed Zakaria told me, somewhat wistfully, about this past era, "it used to be a cartel."[24]

If the Cold War foreign policy pond was small, it was also a bit shallow. Historians and political scientists continue to debate the precise carbon dating of the Cold War consensus, but they do agree that it existed. By the 1950s, the degree of intellectual consensus about American foreign policy during the Cold War spanned the ideological spectrum.[25] Graham Allison described the consensus as a compilation of several key axioms: "The pre-eminent feature of international politics is the conflict between Communism and the Free World"; and

"The surest simple guide to U.S. interests in foreign policy is opposition to Communism"; and "The United States has the *power, responsibility,* and *right* to defend the Free World and maintain international order."[26] That consensus limited the range of acceptable disagreement within the foreign policy establishment. Andrew Bacevich notes, "The signature of American public intellectuals at the beginning of the Cold War was not breadth but narrowness, not playfulness but rigidity. When it came to politics, they were doctrinaire and inflexible. As a consequence, they accepted an oversimplified framework of analysis that foreclosed alternatives and impoverished debate."[27] Lippmann stood out in part because he was on the dovish edge of the spectrum of respectable opinion. Even acolytes of Lippmann's acknowledge that he was operating in a constrained marketplace of ideas.[28]

The old public sphere was a genteel oligopoly; the current Ideas Industry is something else entirely. In one sense, it is far more competitive. The explosion of outlets eager for copy has enlarged the number of intellectuals who can write about foreign policy for a living. This does not mean that any foreign policy intellectual can or will crack the top tier, but the ability of anyone to establish a personal intellectual empire has increased dramatically. Such a description might sound over the top, but it fairly characterizes *Vox*'s Ezra Klein, *Talking Points Memo*'s Josh Marshall, *FiveThirtyEight*'s Nate Silver, and *Pajamas Media*'s Glenn Reynolds.

In another sense, greater competition has not leveled the playing field all that much. In my survey of opinion leaders in the foreign policy community, I asked them to name who they thought were the most influential intellectuals at the current moment. Table 7.1 shows the results. That list suggests that credentials and elite pedigrees still matter a great deal. Thomas Friedman became a bestselling author because of his perch on the *New York Times* op-ed page; Krauthammer, Ignatius, and Kagan all have *Washington Post* columns, while Krugman is at the *New York Times.* Joseph Nye is a professor at Harvard University. Neither Henry Kissinger's nor Francis Fukuyama's foreign policy bona fides need further elaboration. Niall Ferguson was an award-winning historian at Oxford and Harvard. This is not a group of upstarts; it is a group

TABLE 7.1 Most Influential Foreign Policy Intellectuals

Rank	Name	Affiliation	Alma Mater	Gender
1	Henry Kissinger	Kissinger Associates	Harvard University	M
2	Thomas Friedman	*New York Times*	Brandeis College	M
3	Fareed Zakaria	CNN/*Washington Post*	Yale University	M
4	Robert Kagan	Brookings Institution	Yale University	M
5	Joseph Nye	Harvard University	Princeton University	M
6	Charles Krauthammer	*Washington Post*	McGill University	M
7	Walter Russell Mead	Bard College	Yale University	M
8	David Ignatius	*Washington Post*	Harvard University	M
9	Francis Fukuyama	Hoover Institution	Cornell University	M
10	Robert D. Kaplan	Center for New American Security	University of Connecticut	M
11	Richard Haass	Council on Foreign Relations	Oberlin College	M
11	Jeffrey Goldberg	*The Atlantic*	University of Pennsylvania	M
12	Paul Krugman	*New York Times*	Yale University	M
13	William Kristol	*Weekly Standard*	Harvard University	M
14	Samantha Power	Harvard University*	Yale University	F
14	Nicholas Kristof	*New York Times*	Harvard University	M
14	Stephen Walt	Harvard University	Stanford University	M
14	Zbigniew Brzezinski	CSIS/SAIS	McGill University	M
15	Niall Ferguson	Hoover Institution	Oxford University	M

TABLE 7.1 *Continued*

Rank	Name	Affiliation	Alma Mater	Gender
15	Bret Stephens	*Wall Street Journal*	University of Chicago	M
15	David Sanger	*New York Times*	Harvard University	M
15	John Mearsheimer	University of Chicago	West Point	M

* Last non-government position at the time of the survey.
Source: Author survey.

of people lousy with Ivy League degrees, Council on Foreign Relations memberships, and other prestigious affiliations. There are almost no women. The list is about as close to an old boys' club as one can get in the twenty-first century.

How can the elite nature of the top tier of foreign policy intellectuals be reconciled with the lowered barriers to entry? As the modern Ideas Industry has grown, the economics of superstars has kicked in.[29] In these markets a few people at the top earn a disproportionate share of the income and attention. This holds in fields as diverse as journalism and athletics. For athletes, skill and ability determine the pecking order of the superstar phenomenon. For other groups, such as foreign policy intellectuals, a greater element of caprice is involved. The nature of the modern Ideas Industry is such that one Big Idea can thrust anyone into the stratosphere. One well-timed essay can vault an intellectual into the top tier.

Most of the individuals listed in Table 7.1 achieved wider public prominence with one big idea in one big essay. Fukuyama's moment came when he published "The End of History" in *The National Interest* just as the Cold War was coming to an end. Krauthammer's "The Unipolar Moment" has been widely cited since it was first published in *Foreign Affairs* at the end of the Cold War. Nye's notion of soft power has been a mainstay of international relations discourse since he introduced it in a 1990 *Foreign Policy* essay. And Robert Kagan rose to prominence with his 2002 *Policy Review* essay on how Americans are from Mars and Europeans are from Venus, just as transatlantic tensions flared over Iraq.

The effect exists beyond the names listed in Table 7.1. Parag Khanna, for example, was a nondescript graduate student when he pitched the New America Foundation for a grant to travel the world and write about shifts in world politics. He received a fellowship that led him to write his first book.[30] In a display of fortuitous timing and uncanny marketing, Khanna's book was excerpted as the cover story of the *New York Times Magazine* at a moment of American anxiety about its superpower status.[31] Khanna's argument became "one of the most globally debated and influential essays since the end of the Cold War," according to his website.[32] Hyperbole aside, that essay catapulted Khanna into a higher tier. He has written four more books, secured a commenting gig for CNN, and consulted for the National Intelligence Council. Khanna's online bio states that he is now "a widely cited global intellectual" who "lectures frequently at international conferences and gives executive briefings to government leaders and major corporations on global trends and scenarios, systemic risks and technological disruptions, and market entry strategies and economic master planning." The point here is not whether Khanna deserves his elite status; it is that through a combination of skill, will, and *fortuna*, he accomplished it in relatively short order.

The top tier is far more enticing now than it was during Lippmann's time, for a very simple reason. In the twenty-first century, intellectual superstardom comes with both influence *and* affluence.

Much like other markets with network externalities, the modern Ideas Industry can be competitive and simultaneously skew the rewards to those at the top. As in other superstar economies, those who can attain the highest rank in the Ideas Industry will command a disproportionate share of the rewards. Book advances are fatter, television appearances are paid, and the conference swag improves dramatically. They become more than just intellectuals; they become brands.

Indeed, it is striking how much the public profiles of foreign policy intellectuals like Friedman, Zakaria, or Ferguson rely on the terminology of branding. One of Friedman's longtime friends told the *New Yorker*, "What I appreciate in Tom, and what I think is maybe his greatest skill, is he's tremendous at what advertising people call positioning, or brand-ing. He's created a brand for himself."[33] Friedman would concur. A core argument of his biggest book, *The World is Flat*, is that to thrive in the global economy one needs to be "special," a unique brand like Michael Jordan, because such people "have a global market for their goods and services and can command global wages."[34] Friedman is hyperconscious about his own brand; he will tell other writers if they fail to ascribe the provenance of Friedman's neologisms to Friedman.[35]

Ferguson has displayed similar marketing savvy. In a skillful display of synergy, five of the books he wrote in this century were designed from their inception as television documentaries also featuring Ferguson.[36] The *Guardian* described his 2011 book *Civilization* as "a book of a TV series of a university course on the rise and fall of the west."[37] Eric Alterman has criticized Ferguson severely but nonetheless conceded that "Ferguson, perhaps more than any other academic of his generation, has built an extremely successful intellectual brand for himself."[38] As for Zakaria, one former colleague at *Time* noted, "This guy is his own brand." Zakaria's successor at *Newsweek*, Tunku Varadarajan, wrote that "he is as much a brand as he is a journalist: he has 'inc.' in his veins."[39]

Intellectuals expend enormous effort to develop and sustain their brand. As a 2012 *New York Times* story about Zakaria noted,

> Not that long ago, getting a column in *Time* would have been the pinnacle of a journalist's career. But expectations and opportunities have grown in the last few years. Many writers now market them-selves as separate brands, and their journalism works largely as a pro-motion for more lucrative endeavors like writing books and public speaking.[40]

The financial benefits of this strategy are significant. Brand-name in-tellectuals can crack the top tier of the lecture circuit and sign with a speakers bureau. Such bureaus can enable someone to deliver variations of the same speech multiple times for a princely sum. *Foreign Policy's* Katie Peek concludes that, "a few keynote addresses are all it could take for one to jump into a new tax bracket." [41] According to *Fortune* maga-zine, the speaking fees Thomas Friedman collects have helped boost his annual income "into CEO range." Fareed Zakaria earns in the high five figures for his speeches.[42] Ferguson went so far as to relinquish his academic sinecure at Harvard Business School—though not his other academic affiliations at Harvard—because the rewards from public speaking exceed business school salaries. When I asked Ferguson what motivated him to write for a public audience, he responded immediately, "I did it all for the money."[43]

The superstar economics rewarding those at the top creates a powerful incentive to stay active in the Ideas Industry. Those rewards are lucrative enough to foster the professional and financial dreams of an entire underclass of underpaid intellectuals. The modern marketplace of ideas now resembles the market for acting: a few celebrities making millions, and many others doing other menial jobs and dreaming of making millions.

Of course, those rewards have other effects as well. *Esquire*'s Stephen Marche reported that Ferguson receives between $50,000 and $75,000 per speech. Ferguson told me he gives, on average, one of these speeches a month. As Marche wrote, this kind of revenue stream affects one's intellectual arc.

> The entire economics of Ferguson's writing career, and many other writing careers, has been permanently altered. Nonfiction writers can and do make vastly more [money], and more easily, than they could ever make any other way, including by writing bestselling books or being a Harvard professor. Articles and ideas are only as good as the fees you can get for talking about them. They are merely billboards for the messengers.
>
> That [speaker's fee] means that Ferguson doesn't have to please his publishers; he doesn't have to please his editors; he sure as hell doesn't have to please scholars. He has to please corporations and high-net-worth individuals, the people who can pay 50 to 75K to hear him talk.[44]

To stay in the superstar rank, intellectuals need to be able to speak fluently to the plutocratic class. In the case of Friedman or Ferguson, this is unproblematic. Businessmen adore Friedman's writings on how technology and globalization transform the global economy. Salesforce

CEO Marc Benioff has said that he is in awe of Friedman's intellect, and he is hardly the only corporate mogul in that category. Venture capitalist John Doerr described Friedman as "the most cited thinker in business conversations."[45] Similarly, Ferguson told me in an interview that he is a "classical liberal" whose corpus of work is extremely supportive of free markets and a robust American foreign policy.[46] Both Friedman and Ferguson are thought leaders who truly believe in the ideas that also resonate with the movers and shakers of the modern Ideas Industry. For less confident public intellectuals, however, it is not so simple. If they want to make potential benefactors happy, they cannot necessarily afford to speak truth to money.

Another effect of intellectual brands is that superstars have to expend considerable effort to maintain their status. Those at the top garner an outsized fraction of opportunities in which superstars are asked to speak and write a lot more than anyone else. If they decline such offers repeatedly, however, their status can decline as well. More than one participant of the Ideas Industry has told me about the pressure that they feel to constantly produce more think pieces and accept speaking offers in order to maintain their place in the intellectual food chain.

Friedman, Ferguson, and Zakaria might be superstars, but they are extremely busy superstars. Like their plutocratic peers, they work hard to earn their income. In addition to his *New York Times* column, Friedman has written five books and hosted at least three documentary television series. In 2013 he launched, with the *Times*, his own Davos-style conference, called the Friedman Forum.[47] Every profile of Friedman stresses his indefatigable work ethic.[48]

Like Friedman, Ferguson has taken to converting his books into other media outlets. He has also been prolific in his public commentary, with a weekly column for the *Daily Telegraph* as well as other columns for the *Financial Times, Newsweek*, and other venues. A 2007 *Harvard* magazine profile of Ferguson noted his prodigious workload during his career, including: "eight meaty, weighty books, and has another two in progress; hundreds of scholarly articles, tumbles of introductions and book chapters, and an assembly line of regular columns and op-eds for American, British, and German newspapers, all while editing the *Journal of Contemporary History*."[49] He subsequently founded Greenmantle, a macroeconomic and geopolitical advisory firm that employs seven full-time employees. In 2012, when Ferguson permanently relocated to the United States, he told the *Daily Telegraph*, "I'm over-industrious, so I don't feel quite such a deviant in America as I did in England."[50]

As for Zakaria, Varadarajan's praise of him also covers his workload:

> Zakaria ... is insanely successful by the standards of his profession: he has a TV show to which few people of any prominence would refuse an invitation, plus columns at *Time*, CNN.com, and the *Washington Post*. He also writes academic-lite books that presidents clutch as they clamber aboard planes, and gives speeches at—it is said—$75,000 a pop.[51]

When I interviewed Zakaria, he explained how he divides his days between crafting his *Washington Post* column, preparing for his CNN show, and his other responsibilities. He acknowledged that he hasn't yet found the time to write the longer essays he wants to for *The Atlantic*. He has simply been stretched too thin.

Most people who wind up as intellectual superstars do not just snap their fingers and take on all of these jobs at once. There is a slow accretion of opportunities that are hard to refuse, until one is overextended. The process can lead to one of two outcomes. If the intellectual continues past practices, then he or she will inevitably become overworked from mounting obligations. In this situation, the superstar continues to write and research everything as if nothing has changed. The increased demand, however, can cause the intellectual to self-plagiarize or slack off as a survival tactic. Ferguson has admitted to this in interviews, telling the *Washington Monthly* that his books on empire could be described as "edutainment at best."[52] He told me, "I think overstretch is good."

The other outcome is that a solitary intellectual becomes a brand manager with subordinates. To be sure, professors, think tank fellows, and management consultants frequently rely on research assistants. Nevertheless, a brand-name intellectual can require a staff—and most people who are good at being intellectuals are lousy at managing subordinates. It becomes all too easy for a superstar to outsource research to assistants. To run his show and to write his column, for example,

Zakaria has a staff of eight people—and he takes great pride in doing most of the research for his column himself.[53] Ferguson hired a full-time researcher, as well as a "cottage industry" of bright undergraduates, to assist him with his research. Comparable superstars can choose to delegate research and writing tasks to coauthors or research assistants.

Outsourcing research and writing tasks is a natural shortcut for intellectual superstars to meet the Ideas Industry's demands. But such delegation increases the probability of errors seeping into published work. If small shortcuts or errors are not caught the first time a writer uses them, they become crutches that pave the way for bigger short-cuts, which then become cheats. It is rare for a public intellectual or a thought leader to willfully commit plagiarism or fraud. But there have been enough intellectual scandals in this century for a familiar narrative to emerge: a confusion of notes, or a miscommunication between assistants and writers.[54] Corners are not cut, but perhaps they are rounded.

The combination of overstretched superstars and an underclass of intellectuals eager to move to the top tier creates an interesting ecosystem for ideas. Critics often treat intellectual superstars like music groups, extolling their earlier work while disparaging their more recent, commercial output.[55] And because superstars are more likely to err as they try to sustain their brand, they inexorably create intellectual firestorms that invite critical calumny. If a superstar stumbles, there are plenty of lower-tier intellectuals ready to pounce on the mistake.

Both Zakaria and Ferguson have encountered critical backlash in recent years in response to their work. The source of their controversies—and their responses to them—highlight the perils of intellectual superstardom. They also highlight the advantage that thought leaders like Ferguson possess relative to public intellectuals like Zakaria.

In August 2012, accusations of plagiarism threatened Zakaria's career. He had cut and pasted unattributed text from a Jill Lepore *New Yorker* essay into one of his *Time* columns about gun control. Zakaria quickly admitted and apologized for the "terrible mistake," attributing the error to a mixing up of his source notes.[56] After a temporary suspension and investigation by his employers at CNN and *Time*, Zakaria returned to work with the mini-scandal ostensibly behind him. He endured some blowback, but the reputational damage was largely contained.[57]

A few years later, however, two anonymous bloggers at the website Our Bad Media began publishing numerous other alleged instances of plagiarism by Zakaria that stretched back decades; their examples included more than forty of his columns for the *Washington Post, Time, Newsweek*, and *Slate*. The bloggers offered up comparisons of Zakaria's essays with material from *Foreign Affairs, Time*, and other sources that he appeared to copy without proper attribution.[58]

The effect of these anonymous charges on Zakaria's intellectual standing was mixed. On the one hand, the publications listed above dismissed the overwhelming majority of the accusations. The anonymous nature of the accusers also rankled many within the mainstream media, as did some of the exaggerated accusations. Nevertheless, some of the charges stuck. Three different outlets amended a total of thirteen Zakaria columns to note an insufficient degree of attribution.[59] Media critics concluded that he had indeed crossed a line. Dylan Byers wrote in *Politico*, "For years now, Zakaria has made a habit of borrowing facts, language and style from other sources without attributing the work to its original authors, and he has presented such material as if it were his own." In *Vanity Fair*, Michael Kinsley concluded that "somewhere between plagiarism and homage, there is a line. Fareed stepped over it."[60]

Niall Ferguson has also run into controversies in his recent public musings, but they are of a different sort. He is a classic thought leader. A 2004 *Washington Monthly* profile of him observed, "In a moment of profound, and deeply felt, confusion at what our national direction ought to be, Ferguson offered extreme certainty. And his claims caught on when no one was able to make a counter-argument with such confidence and clarity."[61] Rather than plagiarism, Ferguson has been accused of being a hack. He has taken to coining Friedmanesque neologisms like "Chimerica" and "IOU-solationism" and "the six killer apps of Western civilization" to explain some of his ideas.[62] As Justin Fox observed in *Harvard Business Review*: "In recent years he's become more of a generalist, and has focused more on current events. . . . Ferguson has been so good at it, and can express himself so charmingly, and handsomely, and swashbucklingly, that some people are willing to pay him to yammer on about pretty much anything."[63]

However, some of his more contentious claims have drawn wider criticism. In the aftermath of the 2008 financial crisis, Ferguson began issuing clarion calls about the dangers of excessive US federal government debt. He joined an open letter to the Federal Reserve chairman, signed by more than twenty conservative economists and opinion leaders, warning that additional rounds of quantitative easing would "risk currency debasement and inflation, and we do not think they will achieve the Fed's objective of promoting employment."[64] This did not make Ferguson unusual among conservative thought leaders. Ferguson, however, went further in his doomsaying. In a spring 2010 *Foreign Affairs* essay, he compared the United States to other empires that had collapsed suddenly. Ferguson suggested that a sudden shift in expectations could destroy America's ability to recover from the crisis.[65] He persistently predicted the return of double-digit inflation and a revolt of the bond market against quantitative easing.

By the end of 2016, the American economy had develeraged significantly, the federal budget deficit had shrunk at the fastest rate in postwar history, the economy had approached full employment, the dollar had surged in value, and the Fed had started to raise interest rates. At a minimum, Ferguson's concerns seemed wildly misplaced. Joe Weisenthal concluded in *Business Insider*, "As you read Niall Ferguson, it's worth noting that he has been wrong on economics ever since Obama took office."[66]

Ferguson has run afoul of critics beyond his advocacy for macroeconomic austerity. In August 2012, he penned a cover story in *Newsweek* entitled "Hit the Road, Barack."[67] He blasted Obama's first term as president with a barrage of damning economic statistics. As Paul Krugman and other fact-checkers observed, however, Ferguson jerry-rigged some of the negative numbers, wildly exaggerating the fiscal effects of Obama's healthcare reform.[68] Ferguson's defense of his data triggered another round of criticism from fact-checkers.[69] The *New Yorker*'s John Cassidy noted, "What is pretty remarkable about the latest dustup is the weakness of the arguments presented by Ferguson." A former *Wall Street Journal* reporter concluded in the *Columbia Journalism Review*: "It's been a long time since I've seen a cover story so comprehensively demolished."[70]

Ferguson was also called to task in recent years for other misstatements. In 2013 he gave a speech at an investor conference claiming that John Maynard Keynes's homosexuality and failure to have children caused him to prefer short-term solutions to long-term ones.[71] The *Financial Times* was also forced to issue a correction to a May 2015 column by Ferguson in which he misstated figures concerning UK economic confidence and wage growth to make David Cameron's Conservative government look better.[72]

Zakaria's and Ferguson's responses to their controversies, and the Ideas Industry's reactions to these responses, suggest the ways in which the modern marketplace of ideas favors thought leaders over public intellectuals. Ferguson responded to his critics by giving little quarter and politicizing their attacks. He blasted those who fact-checked his *Newsweek* cover story: "The spectacle of the American liberal blogosphere in one of its almost daily fits of righteous indignation is not so much ridiculous as faintly sinister." He concluded that "*not one* of my critics has addressed [my argument]. Instead, they have unleashed a storm of nit-picking and vilification."[73] Ferguson also resisted backing down from his warnings about the risks of inflation and dollar debasement. In 2013 he insisted that "there is in fact still a risk of currency debasement and inflation." He reiterated that concern in 2014 as well.[74] By 2016, however, he acknowledged that he had erred.

Ferguson was more contrite in response to the Keynes kerfuffle, offering an unqualified apology.[75] As liberals continued to hound him, however, Ferguson wrote an open letter to the *Harvard Crimson* concluding, "what that the self-appointed speech police of the blogosphere forget is that to err occasionally is an integral part of the learning process."[76] In making this complaint, Ferguson omitted the fact that the "speech police" consisted primarily of professors of economics and history.[77] Similarly, in response to the *Financial Times* correction, Ferguson wrote a jeremiad against what he called "correct politicalness" in the *Spectator*: "The essence of correct politicalness is to seek to undermine an irrefutable argument by claiming loudly and repetitively to have found an error in it." He heaped disdain on the former policymaker who challenged his FT column, noting, "[he] has no PhD and has published painfully few articles in peer-reviewed journals."[78]

The response pattern is clear. Ferguson has acknowledged some small factual mistakes in recent years. He told me that the Keynes kerfuffle taught him to "speak more like a central banker" in public talks to avoid needless controversies.[79] At the same time, however, he has also argued that his critics' liberal bias invalidates their attacks. According to Ferguson, the exercise of picayune fact checking does not undercut his grander arguments. Rather, the failure by his liberal critics to directly engage those arguments therefore invalidates their minor criticisms. He takes great pride in pushing back on his liberal critics with as much brio as possible.[80]

The effect on Ferguson's status as a thought leader has been minimal. As a longstanding conservative, he has been a perennial target of liberal ire.[81] They repeatedly accuse Ferguson of converting his academic bona fides into a license to write mendacious op-eds. *Dissent's* Mark Engler wrote in 2008 that Ferguson "is trading on his status as an acclaimed historian to give weight to arguments that regularly fail to rise above the predictable biases of conservative punditry." More recently, *New York* magazine's Jonathan Chait argued, "Only a figure of [Ferguson's] standing would have the ability to publish wildly erroneous claims in major mainstream publications."[82] On the other hand, conservatives have offered him intellectual succor. Ferguson's critique of fact checking resonates with ongoing conservative criticism of the phenomenon.[83] Numerous right-wing luminaries and corporate executives have defended Ferguson during his myriad contretemps.[84]

In October 2015 Ferguson announced that he would be leaving Harvard full time and moving to the Hoover Institution, a conservative think tank based in Stanford.[85] By moving to Hoover, Ferguson was able to relinquish all of his teaching responsibilities, which had become a distraction for him.[86] Moving to Hoover freed up more time for his public commentary and book writing. He told me that he would not miss teaching, as it was "not the most efficient way to change the world." [87]

In one way, Zakaria reacted to his scandal in a manner akin to Ferguson. He also reduced his responsibilities. After apologizing for the initial case of plagiarism, Zakaria resigned from the Yale board of governors, scaled back his activities at the Council on Foreign Relations, and abstained from attending all but one conference a year.[88] He cut down significantly on his social schedule and social media to prioritize his family and his work. "Otherwise, the noise is overwhelming," he told me.[89]

Zakaria's response has otherwise differed from Ferguson in its lack of pugnacity. As previously noted, he quickly apologized for the plagiarism in his 2012 column for *Time*. His response to the next wave of plagiarism accusations was far more muted. He did not issue a public response beyond, "I will leave it to viewers and readers to make their own decisions. I'm fully focused on putting out the best work I can." CNN ordered him not to say anything further on the record.[90] The reason for this has less to do with Zakaria's guilt or innocence and more to do with his superstar status. As he told me, one problem with having such a high profile is that, "if you respond, then it's another story." He told me that he now embraces the ethos of his mentor, Samuel Huntington: research something, write something, and then move on to the next topic.

On the whole, Zakaria has retained the support of those in the media and politics who could have turned on him. The media outlets and book publishers have not fired him. Compared to the fabulists and pure partisans in the Ideas Industry, Zakaria's missteps could be judged as a venial and not a mortal sin.[91] Even reporters who feel that Zakaria appropriated quotes from them have been only mildly critical of those actions.[92] Nonetheless, Zakaria's brand has been tarnished. In my interactions with him on this subject, the experience has clearly left a mark. Part of this is likely due to his own sense of intellectual identity. As he put it to me, "I think of myself as a lapsed academic and writer who does television."[93] For true academics, allegations of plagiarism cut deep.

Both Ferguson and Zakaria continue to thrive in the modern Ideas Industry, but in somewhat different ways. Ferguson has fully embraced his status as a thought leader. He embraces a conservative worldview and attacks his critics as petty, envious liberals. He continues to write, speak, and provoke at will. He has willingly shed his status as a professor to fully engage in his role as a thought leader. The controversies surrounding his public commentary only endear him more to conservative sympathizers, not to mention plutocrats. Zakaria remains a public intellectual, someone who prefers to critique all sides. He embraces a nonpartisan worldview and allies himself with like-minded institutions. He has sacrificed some opportunities in order to maintain independence. The controversies surrounding his public commentary have not seriously wounded his reputation—but they have not helped either. Based on my survey results, Zakaria's star continues to shine brighter. Still, even for superstars, it is easier to be a thought leader.

What lessons can be drawn in searching for the modern Walter Lippmann? The first is that Lippmann had it easy. Compared to him, Fareed Zakaria has to compete in a much more intense and crowded marketplace for ideas.

The next lesson is that the benefits of being seen as the modern Lippmann are also greater. Even though the current Ideas Industry is more competitive, it has boosted the rewards of intellectual life for those at the top of the pecking order. David Brooks identified this trend fifteen years ago in *Bobos in Paradise*, but the effect has become even more amplified in the twenty-first century.[94] The rise in economic inequality identified in Chapter 2 has altered the marketplace of ideas in several ways. The most awkward effect has been to increase the variance of rewards that intellectuals themselves earn from hawking their wares. Superstars can become their own brands, commanding bigger book advances, larger media platforms, and lucrative lecture fees. As with the global economy, in the current marketplace of ideas the elite can command the overwhelming majority of the income.

Another lesson is that even at the superstar level, it is easier to be a thought leader than a public intellectual. The recent travails of Zakaria and Ferguson illuminate how superstar intellectuals can face fierce criticism for any missteps. As Ferguson has embraced his role as a happy warrior for economic and foreign policy conservatism, however, he has withstood waves of substantive criticism of his public writings. Zakaria has positioned himself as more of a public intellectual. This has made it more difficult for him to easily dismiss criticism—and therefore more wary of engaging with such criticism.

No matter what Thomas Friedman says, the intellectual world is not flat. The modern marketplace of ideas is competitive but not perfectly competitive; there are behemoths and there are minnows. If intellectual life is treacherous for intellectual superstars, their rise creates an even more problematic incentive structure. Becoming a thought leader now is almost like making it as an entertainer or entrepreneur. The rewards at the top are lucrative enough to foster the professional and financial dreams of an entire underclass of underpaid intellectuals. The superstar economics rewarding those at the top guarantees that the incentives for joining the Ideas Industry will not dissipate over time.

The pathway to superstardom seems enticing enough to warp the incentives of new entrants into the Ideas Industry. David Carr observed in 2012 that for journalists, "the now ancient routes to credibility at small magazines and newspapers—toiling in menial jobs while learning the business—have been wiped out, replaced by an algorithm of social media heat and blog traction."[95] Similarly, Justin Fox notes:

> The path to lucrative thought-leaderdom blazed over the past couple of decades was to establish yourself with dense, serious work (or a big, important job) and *then* move on to catch-phrase manufacturing. Nowadays ambitious young people looking to break into the circuit often just aim straight for the catch-phrases. Speakers bureaus need pithy sales pitches, not complex erudition ... for journalists and academics they often represent their only real shot at a top-tax-bracket income.
>
> The result is an intellectual environment that seems to increasingly reward the superficial, and keeps rewarding those who make it into the magic circle of top-flight speakers even if they don't have anything new or interesting to say.[96]

As the previous chapters demonstrate, there is still a middle class of intellectuals housed in the academy, think tanks, and private firms. Still, in a superstar economy, younger members of the Ideas Industry might take aim at being a superstar before becoming a true intellectual. Whether one agrees with Niall Ferguson's writings or not, it is impossible to deny that he earned his scholarly bona fides before reaching for the lucre of lectures and television series. Even Ferguson's liberal critics praise his scholarly work. Thomas Friedman served in a variety of journalistic postings before talking about how the world was flat. Fareed Zakaria earned a doctorate and managed America's leading foreign policy journal before becoming a columnist. All of the top-tier foreign policy intellectuals wrote a lot before achieving superstar status. The economics of the modern Ideas Industry, however, incentivizes younger intellectuals to hit the lecture circuit before doing the research necessary to justify the lecture circuit.

The modern Ideas Industry rewards superstar intellectuals and superstar notions. Does the marketplace regulate these superstars as well, however? To put it another way: As the marketplace of ideas has become more competitive, has it also become more efficient?

8

Is the Ideas Industry Working?

The first lesson the student of international politics must learn and never forget is that the complexities of international affairs make simple solutions and trustworthy prophecies impossible. Here the scholar and the charlatan part company.

— Hans Morgenthau

THE EMERGENCE OF THE Ideas Industry has created new winners and new losers. It has empowered thought leaders more than public intellectuals, economists more than political scientists, management consultants more than think tank fellows, superstars more than anyone else. So are these changes good for the ideas? There is no denying that the public sphere is home to a far more heterogeneous array of intellectuals than in the past. The barriers to entry in American foreign policy debates are lower, and the variation of thought is wider than during the height of the Cold War. But a key test of a well-functioning marketplace of ideas is also the ease of exit. Bad or bankrupt ideas should exit the stage. Has the transformation of the marketplace of ideas improved debates about American foreign policy?

To answer that question, this chapter will take a deep dive into the uses and abuses of "disruption" in debates about the US economy and American foreign policy. As we shall see, it is the ideal case for looking at how a new notion can spread across the marketplace of ideas. The evolution of disruptive innovation as a way of thinking about how to change the world explains an awful lot about how the modern Ideas Industry functions. For good and ill, the modern marketplace of ideas strongly resembles modern financial markets. Usually, the system works. On occasion, however, there can be asset bubbles.

Economists have been aware of the importance of innovation since Adam Smith's *Wealth of Nations*. When Joseph Schumpeter coined the term "creative destruction," he captured the degree to which radical innovations could disrupt as well as create economic growth. Indeed, Schumpeter fretted that the huge fixed costs of technological innovation, combined with the risk-averse nature of bureaucratized corporations, would lead to a tapering off of radical innovations.[1] The consensus among modern growth theorists is that at least 75 percent of American economic growth can be attributed to innovation. Distinguished economists from Robert Solow to Paul Romer to Robert Gordon have devoted their lives to understanding the relationship between innovation and growth.[2] The most visible working theory of innovation comes not from an economist, however, but from a professor of business strategy.

A half century after Schumpeter, Harvard Business School professor Clayton Christensen coauthored a *Harvard Business Review* article on disruptive technologies that extended the concept of creative destruction even further.[3] Christensen argued that firms generate two kinds of innovations. *Sustaining innovations* lead to a steady rate of product improvement over time. These incremental upgrades are necessary for leading firms in any sector to retain their customers. *Disruptive innovations*, in contrast, introduce an alternative set of attributes to a product. These new attributes, while promising, can also worsen performance on key dimensions, alienating mainstream customers. Leading firms in a sector will be wary of adopting disruptive technologies; understandably, they prioritize customer satisfaction over innovations that might not attract many new clients.

New attributes, however, can attract an underserved niche market. Over time, an upstart firm with a disruptive innovation will corner that niche market. Then, through sustaining innovations, the upstart can improve the quality and efficiency of the product across all dimensions. Eventually, the firm that controls the disruptive innovation outclasses the industry leader, acquires a dominant market share, and becomes the new standard for that sector. In the past decade alone, one could argue that Apple, Netflix, and Airbnb all used this strategy to upend the markets for mobile phones, movie rentals, and hotels.

In a 2013 *Harvard Business Review* article, Christensen and his co-authors distilled the essence of disruptive innovation down to a single paragraph:

> The pattern of industry disruption is familiar: new competitors with new business models arrive; incumbents choose to ignore the new players or to flee to higher-margin activities; a disrupter whose product was once barely good enough achieves a level of quality acceptable to the broad middle of the market, undermining the position of longtime leaders and causing the "flip" to a new level of competition.[4]

Christensen's theory had profound implications for the study and practice of business strategy. He was arguing that all of the longstanding principles that made companies great also made them vulnerable to extinction. This was especially true given that, at first glance, most disruptive innovations appear to be flawed. By staying too attuned to their customer base, Christensen argued, these firms developed blinders about possible game-changing innovations. As he wrote in his first book, *The Innovator's Dilemma*, "there are times when it is right not to listen to customers, right to invest in developing lower-performance products that promise lower margins, and right to aggressively pursue small, rather than substantial, markets."[5] This was a legitimately counterintuitive idea. His theory implied that disruption could upend the market dominance of industry leaders at any time. Furthermore, the necessary survival strategies to cope with potential disruptions appeared to be counterintuitive at best and counterproductive at worst. As Joshua Gans, author of *The Disruption Dilemma*, notes, "Christensen's observations have led to widespread fear and paranoia" in the business world.[6]

As a field, business strategy is shot through with thought leaders. Christensen took this approach to the next level. As the *Economist* observed, "Mr. Christensen is a hedgehog (someone who knows one big thing) rather than a fox (who knows lots of little things)."[7] Christensen's model and Christensen himself exemplify how a theory could catch on the modern marketplace of ideas. Disruptive innovation was a simple, clearly communicable, counterintuitive thesis. Christensen built it up from a single, big case—the computer disk drive industry—and made it easily digestible to others. Its implications were wide ranging. From his very first essay on the subject, Christensen argued that disruptive innovation could explain the widespread decline and fall of industry leaders. Even if it was not observable, the prospect of disruption put the fear of God into business executives at leading firms.

Beyond the theory's intrinsic appeal, Christensen's approach synced up perfectly with the forces of change in the Ideas Industry. His thesis was that the conventional wisdom regarding sound business strategy was fatally flawed. This resonated with skeptics of traditional business school scholarship. Furthermore, Christensen was not shy about his devout Mormon beliefs and Republican political leanings.[8] This made him a more appealing figure to conservative executives than if he had been a stereotypical left-leaning academic.

Most importantly, Christensen's message of disruption hit the plutocratic sweetspot. He depicted a world in which the new New Thing could happen at any time and radically transform an entire economic sector. This conformed to a plutocratic worldview in which success favors the bold, risk-taking entrepreneur. Christensen only enhanced his plutocratic appeal in his follow-up book *The Innovator's Solution*, in which he asserted that founders of firms were better prepared to cope with disruption than managers.[9] This fit perfectly with a sector dominated by founder-owners. As one of Christensen's coauthors observed, the idea of disruptive innovation really took off in 1999 when Andy Grove, then the CEO of Intel, posed next to Christensen on the cover of *Forbes*. The headline read: "Andy Grove's Big Thinker."[10] Other Silicon Valley luminaries such as Steve Jobs, Eric Schmidt, Peter Thiel, and Marc Andreessen embraced the thesis, arguing that disruptive innovations rocked the IT sector on an almost monthly basis. Other moguls, including Michael Bloomberg, heartily endorsed Christensen's message.

Some management experts had formulated similar arguments prior to Christensen, but his timing was also perfect.[11] He articulated the theory just as the dot-com boom was beginning in the mid-1990s. Older firms were starting to realize the massive productivity gains that came from incorporating information technologies into their internal processes.[12] The theory of disruptive innovation appeared to explain far more than computer disk drives. It offered a lens to view how the entire world worked. As Evan Goldstein wrote in a *Chronicle of Higher Education* profile of Christensen, the idea of disruption "is nothing less than the mechanism at work behind the boom-bust churn of capitalism.... To true believers, it's something more: a gospel of progress for the Internet age, a democratic force that makes more things—education, air travel, health care—more accessible to more people."[13]

After the successful publication of *The Innovator's Dilemma* in 1997, Christensen built an intellectual empire around disruptive innovation. He authored or coauthored eight books on the concept, each one covering an area further afield from the manufacturing sector.[14] He coauthored a paper on religion and capitalism entitled "Disrupting Hell." At Harvard Business School, he created the Forum for Growth and Innovation, a center designed to advance further research in the relationship between management and disruptive innovation. In 2000, Christensen co-created the Disruptive Growth Fund, designed to buy stock in companies on the cusp of developing disruptive technologies. That same year he founded a consulting firm, Innosight, designed to work "with Fortune 100 companies that are seeking to defend their core businesses and adapt to disruptive environments," according to a glowing *Harvard Magazine* profile of Christensen.[15] In 2007 he opened Rose Park Advisors, a boutique investment firm in which, according to his website, "decisions are driven by Christensen's theories in disruptive innovation and related fields and therefore invests exclusively in companies where Christensen's research gives unique and differential insights to the investment thesis."[16] As a Harvard professor who created both nonprofit and for-profit structures to hawk his ideas, Christensen seemed to embody the best attributes of both the academy and the consulting world.

These myriad efforts paid off in numerous ways. Christensen was hailed as one of the most important management theorists of the last half century. In the two decades since the original *Harvard Business Review* article appeared, media and journal uses of the terms "disruptive innovation" and "disruptive technology" went from just two mentions in 1995 to more than 4,500 mentions in 2015.[17] The *Economist* declared

The Innovator's Dilemma to be one of the top business books published in the past half century. He topped the Thinkers50 ranking, "the Oscars of the 'management guru' world," twice in the last ten years. His speaker fee is well in excess of $40,000.[18] In the world of business, Christensen became the *ne plus ultra* of thought leaders. In 2014, *Business Insider*'s Henry Blodget dubbed him "today's most influential modern management thinker."[19]

If this was the end of the story, Christensen's rise to intellectual superstar status would echo a familiar narrative about the rise of a business management guru to prominence. But Christensen's idea did not stay confined to the world of business. Nor did Christensen want it confined there. As with other asset bubbles, the market overvalued the idea and believed that it applied far beyond business applications. That, in turn, generated its own critical reaction.

Christensen and his acolytes spread the theory of disruptive innovation in two ways. His supporters tried to bolster the empirical foundations of the theory.[20] Christensen himself expanded it by applying it to areas far beyond traditional business sectors. Three of his later books applied the model of disruptive innovation to nonprofit areas: primary education, higher education, and healthcare.[21] He argued that his theory could be extended from the microeconomic realm to the macroeconomic realm and explain sluggish post-2008 economic growth.[22] He founded the Christensen Institute, a nonpartisan think tank that is, according to its website, "redefining the way policymakers, community leaders, and innovators address the problems of our day by distilling and promoting the transformational power of disruptive innovation."[23] He is a cofounder of the Disruptor Foundation, an organization dedicated to "rais[ing] awareness of and encourag[ing] the advancement of disruptive innovation theory and its application in societally-critical domains," according to its website. It also sponsors Disruption Foundation Fellows and a "Disruptor Cup" competition.[24] In 2015, Christensen insisted that there remained additional areas ripe for applying his theory, including traditional foreign policy bailiwicks like conflict resolution, environmental policy, and counterterrorism.[25] In one interview, he used his theory to explain the challenges with postwar statebuilding in Iraq.[26]

Christensen was not shy about trying to apply his theory to a vast array of policy arenas. But he was far from the only person to do this with disruptive innovation. Indeed, it would seem that every thought leader has embraced the concept of disruption to explain his or her own professional bailiwick. The language of disruption completely took over the field of management consulting. It is virtually impossible to read a management consulting report without warning about a coming "disruption," "discontinuity," "trend-break," or "revolution."[27] In 2015, Accenture released a report with the rather grandiose title "Be the Disruptor, not the Disrupted," about compliance with financial regulation.[28] Three McKinsey consultants crystallized this style of discourse with *No Ordinary Disruption*, which contains sentences like "Ours is a world of near-constant discontinuity" and "[Disruptions] are causing trends to break down, to break up, or simply to break."[29] The media sector has been obsessed with disruption; the *New York Times'* 2014 *Innovation Report* is clearly predicated on Christensen's theory, using it to explain the rise of competitors like *BuzzFeed, Politico*, and *Vox*.[30] As Harvard historian Jill Lepore noted in the *New Yorker*, "ever since *The Innovator's Dilemma*, everyone is either disrupting or being disrupted."[31]

Lepore is correct; thought leaders have spread the gospel of disruption far beyond the business world. In recent years it has permeated the policy discourse on foreign affairs and international relations. To those who believe in the theory of disruptive innovation, such an intellectual leap makes perfect sense. As the McKinsey consultants who wrote *No Ordinary Disruption* explain, "the trend break era is imposing uncertainties and pressures on governments and policy makers that are as significant and meaningful as those it is placing on companies and executives."[32] Indeed, a quick glance at covers of *Foreign Affairs* and *Foreign Policy* suggest that their editors believe that disruptive innovations are affecting world politics as much as global markets. In the two years prior to a 2013 *Foreign Affairs* redesign, for example, only one of its twelve lead articles touched on anything remotely related to disruptive innovation. In the two years after its redesign, half of its cover packages touched on some kind of disruptive innovation, including such titles as "The Rise of Big Data," "Next Tech," and "Here Come the Disruptors."[33] *Foreign Policy* made a similar pivot toward disruption-friendly cover art. Its 2014 issue promoting its leading one hundred global thinkers was entitled "A World Disrupted."

Disruption discourse has penetrated deeper than the covers of these magazines. Google CEO Eric Schmidt coauthored a 2010 *Foreign Affairs* article with Google Ideas Director Jared Cohen entitled "The Digital Disruption." Their essay took the concept of disruption and applies it to international relations.

> The advent and power of connection technologies—tools that connect people to vast amounts of information and to one another—will make the twenty-first century all about surprises. . . .
>
> In the interconnected estate, a virtual space that is constrained by different national laws but not national boundaries, there can be no equivalent to the Treaty of Westphalia—the 1648 agreement that ended the Thirty Years' War and established the modern system of nation-states. Instead, governments, individuals, nongovernmental organizations, and private companies will balance one another's interests. . . .
>
> In an era when the power of the individual and the group grows daily, those governments that ride the technological wave will clearly be best positioned to assert their influence and bring others into their orbits. And those that do not will find themselves at odds with their citizens.[34]

The idea that innovations are disrupting twenty-first-century international relations is not unique to tech entrepreneurs. Foreign affairs pundits have been making similar arguments.[35] Parag Khanna's intellectual trajectory has been a slow migration away from traditional geopolitics and toward technological determinism. Khanna's first two books discussed how the rise of advanced developing economies such as China or India affects conventional international relations. His third book, *Hybrid Reality*, published by TED and coauthored with his wife Ayesha, was consciously designed to be far more in the spirit of Alvin Toffler than Henry Kissinger. Echoing Christensen's rhetoric, the Khannas posited that "the great disruptive trends of the 21st century—the shift to multipolarity, shrinking of space, economic convergence, and new forms of collaboration—all have technology at their root."[36] He went even further in *Connectography*, arguing that global supply chains have completely disrupted great power politics: "We are moving into an era when cities will matter more than states and supply chains will be a more important source of power than militaries—whose main purpose will be to protect supply chains rather than borders."[37]

The notion that disruptive innovations transform world politics has also been a key theme of Thomas Friedman's oeuvre since the start of the century. *The World Is Flat* is a tome about the ways that the global political economy faces constant disruption. In a 2009 column, he warned of "the Great Inflection," which he characterized as "the mass diffusion of low-cost, high-powered innovation technologies—from hand-held computers to Web sites that offer any imaginable service— plus cheap connectivity." In 2013, he reiterated his warning about the Great Inflection, noting that when "the world gets this hypercon- nected . . . the speed with which every job and industry changes also goes into hypermode." He explicitly cited Christensen in talking about how higher education was about to be disrupted. By 2015, Friedman had widened the scope of the Great Inflection's effects, concluding in one column, "We're in the middle of some huge disruptive inflections in technology, the labor market and geopolitics that will raise funda- mental questions about the future of work and the social contracts between governments and their people and employers and employ- ees."[38] Friedman's rhetoric for the past decade has been a homage to Christensen's big idea.

It is not merely foreign policy pundits who have latched on to the idea of disruption as a lens to explain world politics. International rela- tions scholars seized upon disruptive innovation to explain phenom- ena in security studies such as military doctrine and weapons procure- ment strategies.[39] Traditional foreign policy hands have also trafficked in disruption metaphors. As noted in Chapter 2, David Rothkopf was born again through the gospel of disruptive innovation at TED. He warned DC policymakers that "because so many of those new trends are tied to scientific and technological developments, and because our leaders are undereducated in these areas, and because the historical technology-government partnership that helped build America has broken down, we are ill-prepared to cope with this new era."[40] In a 2009 *Foreign Affairs* essay, Anne-Marie Slaughter argued that networks were a disruptive innovation in world politics that "exists above the state, below the state, and through the state."[41]

This kind of discourse affects how foreign policy professionals talk about international relations. Echoing the language of McKinsey's consultants, USAID administrators have extolled the virtues of disruptive innovation as a force for poverty reduction.[42] Slaughter's *Foreign Affairs* article captured the attention of Hillary Clinton, who consequently made Slaughter her first director of policy planning at the State Department.[43] Slaughter's staff included Jared Cohen, who went on to Jigsaw, and Alec Ross, who went on to be the secretary of state's senior advisor on innovation. Slaughter advised Clinton to take a number of steps designed to empower civil society activists through public-private partnerships and economic diplomacy. These were signature elements of Clinton's "21st Century Statecraft" initiative. According to the State Department's website explaining the initiative, "the 21st century statecraft agenda addresses new forces propelling change in international relations that are pervasive, disruptive and difficult to predict."[44] One *Huffington Post* story declared that Clinton was the Obama administration's "improbable MVP in the technology realm."[45]

Clinton continued to embrace disruption discourse long after leaving the State Department. While campaigning for president in the summer of 2015, the former secretary of state called for "innovative, disruptive ideas that will save capitalism for the 21st century." Six months later, when she outlined her counterterrorism strategy, Clinton argued that Silicon Valley needed to be at the forefront: "We need to put the great disrupters at work at disrupting ISIS."[46] At the same time, policy analysts were complimenting Donald Trump's rhetoric in *Foreign Policy*: "Trump is a disruptor, and international relations are certainly a sector in need of disruption."[47] Pundits like Friedman and policymakers like Clinton argue that the digitally connected individual is *the* disruptive innovation of twenty-first-century world politics. The overarching theme is that the world has encountered a genuine trend break and that the future of world politics will look radically different from the Westphalian order of the past.

An additional appeal of disruption theory to the foreign policy community is its bias for preemptive action. Christensen's theory argues that even if all seems well, disruptive innovation can happen at any time, threatening the survival of leading firms. Proactive steps are encouraged to cope with this possibility. This argument mirrors the bias in foreign policy for action over inaction. In an environment of asymmetric threats and Dick Cheney's "One Percent Doctrine," the logic of disruption seemed to perfectly capture early twenty-first-century world politics.

The irony is that, just as the argot of disruptive innovation permeated the foreign policy community, the original idea became enmeshed in one hell of an intellectual debate.

Over the years there had been some sharp scholarly critiques of Christensen's work. They questioned the causal logic or the general applicability of disruptive innovation.[48] A few popular articles had also lamented the spread of the disruption gospel.[49] This pushback, however, was neither influential nor widespread. Christensen's idea continued to gain traction within and beyond his field of business strategy.

In 2014, however, Harvard University historian Jill Lepore took to the pages of the *New Yorker* to write a six-thousand-word takedown of Christensen and his idea of disruptive innovation.[50] Lepore did not pull her punches. She posited that the theory had caught on because the rhetoric of disruption—"a language of panic, fear, asymmetry, and disorder"—fit well with the twenty-first-century concern with terrorism. Absent that context, Lepore suggested that the theory had been massively oversold. Christensen's first investment fund predicated on picking firms ripe to generate disruptive innovations went bankrupt within a year, suggesting that perhaps his theory was not predictive. She criticized Christensen's reliance on "handpicked case studies" to develop his theory and questioned whether even those cases played out as Christensen described. She wrote, in language that no academic would ever want to read about their scholarship, that "Christensen's sources are often dubious and his logic questionable." Despite all of these charges, however, Lepore's deepest outrage was devoted to how the idea of disruptive innovation was being applied beyond the business world.

> Innovation and disruption are ideas that originated in the arena of business but which have since been applied to arenas whose values and goals are remote from the values and goals of business. . . .

Disruptive innovation is a theory about why businesses fail. It's not more than that. It doesn't explain change. It's not a law of nature. It's an artifact of history, an idea, forged in time; it's the manufacture of a moment of upsetting and edgy uncertainty. Transfixed by change, it's blind to continuity. It makes a very poor prophet.[51]

Previous scholarship had raised several of Lepore's points. Still, her essay was the most high-profile attack on Christensen's theory, and it got considerable traction. The immediate response to it was a flurry of press stories, including multiple interviews with Christensen.[52] Lepore's supporters saw it as evidence that the theory had been overblown and the word "disruption" had been devalued to the point of meaninglessness.[53] One management journal editor noted, in support of Lepore, that "Christensen's concept of disruptive innovation is clearly a theory focused on failure and driven by anxiety."[54]

The social media pushback from Silicon Valley was ferocious; in response to Lepore, venture capitalist Marc Andreessen tweeted, "I've probably been on the receiving end of disruption 30 times in the last 20 years—almost as many times as I've been on the giving end."[55] Several columnists defended Christensen, arguing that Lepore had gone too far in trying to debunk the entire idea.[56] Christensen's coauthors also came to his defense, contending that Lepore was attacking a "caricature of the theory" and that the paradigm had evolved since *The Innovator's Dilemma*.[57] Christensen stressed this point in his own interviews on the subject—although he also accused Lepore of "lies" and performing "a criminal act of dishonesty" in the article.

The debate did produce some areas of consensus. The first point of agreement was that Lepore had illuminated real problems with Christensen's theory. The fact that even Christensen's original case—the disk drive industry—did not evolve according to his theory suggested that a closer empirical look was warranted. The second point of consensus was that the theory of disruptive innovation was a legitimately interesting idea that should not be completely discarded. Lepore doubted the theory's applicability beyond business but was noncommittal on its applicability within the business world. *Slate*'s Will Oremus, *Vox*'s Timothy B. Lee, and the *Financial Times*' Andrew Hill were all sympathetic to much of Lepore's critique. Nevertheless, they all argued that Lepore had gone too far; as Lee put it, "Lepore's nitpicking aside, Christensen's theory has a lot of explanatory power."[58]

The last and most interesting area of consensus was that Christensen's idea had been applied far too indiscriminately. All of Lepore's supporters agreed that the word "disruption" had been debased to the point of meaninglessness. But defenders of disruptive innovation claimed that Lepore was critiquing a caricature more than Christensen's actual theory. The *Financial Times'* Hill observed, " 'Disruption' has become a distracting buzzword. It has fueled conferences, consultancies and corporate strategies. In the process, the idea got distorted.... *The New Yorker* article is a useful corrective for overzealous executives and consultants who took a 17-year-old idea and turned it into a religion."[59] In his interviews on the subject, Christensen himself acknowledged that "[disruption] is used to justify whatever anybody—an entrepreneur or a college student—wants to do" and that "this is something that happens over and over again, where an important idea is bastardized."[60]

Of course, such statements minimize Christensen's own culpability in proselytizing the idea. As noted repeatedly in this chapter, Christensen has not been shy in setting up a plethora of for-profit and nonprofit initiatives related to disruptive innovation. It was Christensen who claimed that disruptive innovation could explain nonprofit sectors such as healthcare and education. Given that these sectors exist largely because of market failure, the assumptions of disruptive innovation theory do not hold. And as one scholarly review of the contretemps concluded, "Christensen's own research has been too loose with the term, its applications, and its implications."[61]

If Lepore's article was the first major critique of Christensen to gain intellectual traction, it was not the last. A more devastating article appeared in the September 2015 *MIT Sloan Management Review.*[62] Andrew King and Baljir Baatartogtokh dissected the core of Christensen's theory. They re-examined all of the cases that formed the empirical backbone of *The Innovator's Dilemma* and *The Innovator's Solution.* They interviewed and surveyed industry experts in each sector to see if the cases fit Christensen's model of disruptive innovation. Their results were sobering: of the seventy-seven cases under examination, only seven—9 percent of the total—met all the characteristics of disruptive innovation theory. King and Baatartogtokh were particularly skeptical of any possible application of Christensen's theory to nonprofit or government organizations.[63]

The effect of this study on support for Christensen's theory was more substantial.[64] Those who had either praised Christensen or stayed silent found their critical voice. The *Economist* concluded that "[Christensen's] hedgehog mind leads him to ignore or belittle companies or market forces that do not fit his template."[65] One management professor told the *Chronicle of Higher Education*, "All the evidence suggests that Christensen genuinely believes his theory. All the evidence also suggests that he doesn't know how to reform his theory in the face of new evidence."[66] Economic observers noted the disconnect between the widespread perception of disruptive innovation and the lack of actual growth in US total factor productivity.[67] In contrast to his reaction to Lepore's article, Christensen did not publicly respond to this study beyond telling reporters that he now worried his colleagues viewed him as an intellectual lightweight.[68]

Christensen did try to parry the intellectual onslaught in a December 2015 *Harvard Business Review* article that directly addressed critics. Regardless of its intent, the essay reads more like a strategic retreat than a robust defense.[69] After stating that conceptual sloppiness has debased the concept of disruptive innovation, Christensen and his coauthors acknowledge that "identifying true disruptive innovation is tricky" and that "not every disruptive path leads to a triumph, and not every triumphant newcomer follows a disruptive path." In essence, the paper radically restricted the theory's explanatory domain, going so far as to dismiss a company like Uber as not being disruptive. As one postmortem of the theory observed, "Christensen has gotten disruption theory into such a tangle that even he is tripping over it."[70] It turns out that Christensen and his critics agree that the theory has been overexposed in the marketplace of ideas. Furthermore, it remains an open question as to whether his theory of disruption even explains that much about technological innovation and market churn. As King and Baatartogtokh conclude, "stories about disruptive innovation can provide warnings of what may happen, but they are no substitute for critical thinking."[71]

In the wake of the controversy, Christensen finds himself on uncertain ground. In interviews to promote his next book in October 2016, he vacillated in his response. In an interview with the *Washington*

Post, he sounded determined to proceed as if was a minor kerfuffle. He claimed that "there actually hasn't been a lot of criticism" of disruptive innovation.[72] At the same time, in talking to the *Financial Times*, his grievances towards Lepore and others were more pronounced.[73] His new book did not find the same kind of intellectual traction as *The Innovator's Dilemma*.

After almost twenty years, Christensen's theory has encountered fresh intellectual criticism in the world of business strategy. What about his foreign policy counterparts? Have those who have adopted the language of disruption to describe twenty-first-century world politics also received some pushback? To be fair, while the disruption meme has become more popular in foreign policy discourse, it was never as prevalent as in other areas of public debate such as education and healthcare. The scholarly uses of disruptive innovation in international relations, for example, have largely been confined to the study of defense acquisition.[74] Such a framework can be perfectly applicable to this area.

There has also been critical feedback at efforts to apply the disruption discourse more widely to explain world politics. Because the language of disruptive innovation is so intertwined with the gospel of Silicon Valley, critic Evgeny Morozov has conducted a one-man crusade against this kind of rhetoric—what he labels "rupture talk."[75] In his indictment of technological "solutionism," *To Save Everything, Click Here*, Morozov rails against the idea that Silicon Valley innovations have created a trend-break era in which nothing is as it was before. He notes, correctly, that much of the talk about how the Internet has transformed twenty-first-century politics echoes discourse from the twentieth century about how nuclear weapons had revolutionized international relations. More generally, the rhetoric of disruption "overlaps with and feeds on several earlier fetishes and discourses about technology, information, innovation, and digitality."[76]

Morozov's most acidic take on the rhetoric of disruption in international relations came in a review of the Khannas' book for the *New Republic*. He blasted not only the Khannas but the intellectual trajectory that they represented in the foreign policy community.

The "technological" turn in Khanna's "thought" is hardly surprising. As he and others have discovered by now, one can continue fooling the public with slick ahistorical jeremiads on geopolitics by serving them with the coarse but tasty sauce that is the Cyber-Whig theory of history. The recipe is simple. Find some peculiar global trend—the more arcane, the better. Draw a straight line connecting it to the world of apps, electric cars, and Bay Area venture capital. Mention robots, Japan, and cyberwar. Use shiny slides that contain incomprehensible but impressive maps and visualizations. Stir well. Serve on multiple platforms. With their never-ending talk of Twitter revolutions and the like, techno-globalists such as Khanna have a bright future ahead of them.[77]

If Morozov's last assertion about the bright future of "techno-globalists" was accurate, it would certainly be a sign that the marketplace of foreign policy ideas is not functioning terribly well. Surveying the landscape, however, it is not clear at all that Morozov's prediction has come to pass. To be sure, the paradigm of disruptive innovation has not disappeared. But there is evidence that in places where disruption discourse should be thriving, the rhetorical wheel has turned.

Consider, for example, the foreign policy debate over the Islamic State's online presence. In many ways, ISIS's social media strategy represents fertile ground for foreign policy intellectuals to opine about disruptive innovation. The Islamic State does appear to be adept at using the Internet for both recruitment and trolling other actors in world politics. One US senator noted at a 2015 public hearing on this issue, "I know something about memes. . . . Look at their fancy memes compared to what we're not doing."[78]

As noted in Chapter 6, this has been a particular area of emphasis for Jigsaw. Its director Jared Cohen contributed to this debate with a November 2015 essay in *Foreign Affairs* on how to cope with ISIS online, entitled "Digital Counterinsurgency."[79] It would have been predictable had Cohen talked about how the Pentagon needs to adapt to the disruptive architecture of the Internet in order to cope with this asymmetrical threat. Intriguingly, Cohen's essay went in the opposite direction. Rather than use the language of disruption to explain to national security officials what they need to do, Cohen applied conventional foreign policy discourse to describe and propose solutions to this twenty-first-century problem. Instead of talking about decentralized networks, Cohen noted the clear hierarchy of the Islamic State's online disciples. He argued in favor of both multilateral coalition building and law enforcement tactics. He suggested that any suspension policy of ISIS social media accounts "needs to be targeted—more like kill-or-capture raids than strategic bombing campaigns."[80] If the director of Jigsaw and the co-author of "Digital Disruption" and *The New Digital Age* talks about this issue without stressing disruptive innovation, then maybe that discourse has jumped the shark in the world of foreign policy.

As the intellectual luster of Christensen's theory continues to wane, it is likely that the disruption discourse will also fade in debates about American foreign policy. World politics is experiencing considerable disruption, but if anything this has revived populist nationalism, not a waning of the Westphalian nation-state. This does not mean that thought leaders from the business world will not continue to affect foreign policy debates. Even as disruption theory has fallen from grace, other Silicon Valley fads, like "design thinking," have come into vogue within the foreign policy community. One author has argued that American foreign policy suffers from an "innovation deficit" and is in need of a "National Security Innovation Lab" to counter threats like the Islamic State: "If U.S. policymakers want to succeed in managing future threats, then they need to start thinking more like business innovators who integrate human needs with technology and economic feasibility."[81] Even as business fads wax and wane, private-sector ideas will continue to receive a sympathetic ear in national security debates.

What does the rise and fall of disruption discourse tell us about the functioning of the Ideas Industry? Reality provides something of a messy picture. On the one hand, it would seem that public intellectuals like Jill Lepore and Evgeny Morozov offered a valuable check on thought leaders like Clayton Christensen and Parag Khanna. To be sure, acolytes of disruptive innovation still exist. It is probably fair to conclude that the idea still retains some intellectual value in thinking about business management. As the economist Joshua Gans notes, "just because the hypothesized link between disruptive technologies and the failure of a company is weak does not necessarily mean disruption cannot happen."[82] Still, by inserting critiques into the public sphere, public intellectuals have demonstrated the vital role they play in maintaining a healthy marketplace of ideas.

This is particularly true given the fact that business scholars, left to their own devices, failed at the same task. Christensen was able to proselytize the explanatory power of disruptive innovation for two decades with minimal levels of critical disciplinary feedback. That allowed his idea and his acolytes to permeate the entire Ideas Industry, including the realm of international affairs. As Andrew King told the *Chronicle of Higher Education* about this episode, "a theory is like a weed. Unless it is pruned back by empirical testing, it will grow to fill any void."[83] In this sense, Lepore and Morozov and King himself functioned as expert gardeners. Other management scholars were less vigilant. Why did disruptive innovation go mainstream if scholars found the theory even somewhat flawed on its home ground? Or, as King put it, "why didn't they rein in the theory? Why didn't they engage in the conversation?"[84]

There are several possible answers. Part of it is that key components of the Ideas Industry found the theory of disruptive innovation to be so appealing. Christensen's theory was more precise than much of the strategic management literature, while being conceptually fuzzy enough to ward off efforts at outright falsification. Another part is that for many management scholars, the risks of alienating the funders of the Ideas Industry was a significant barrier to engaging in criticism.[85] Silicon Valley remains the last redoubt of disruptive innovation, as debates about the effect of its innovations on productivity growth continue to persist.[86] Crossing that stream of revenue is a risky undertaking for even the most rebellious of thinkers. Furthermore, within a scholarly discipline, concerns about taking on one of the field's titans no doubt offered an additional disincentive. Why risk challenging such a widely cited scholar?

As it turns out, when scholarly norms failed to do the job adequately, the very public nature of critiques like Lepore's and Morozov's provided the necessary intellectual checks and balances. The modern marketplace of ideas generates interesting reactions to notions that go viral. The Ideas Industry functions as a tremendous amplifier for attractive ideas. Much like the superstar intellectuals discussed in the previous chapter, there are superstar ideas that will soak up a disproportionate share of attention. This practically guarantees that as ideas gain cachet, they will become overexposed. This, in turn, offers a chance for outsiders to provide the intellectual feedback that insiders might be reluctant to proffer. Thought leaders can clearly thrive in the Ideas Industry, but they also create new opportunities for public intellectuals to engage in useful corrections. Even though these public clashes of ideas can be unpleasant to the individual participants themselves, the public sphere benefits enormously from it.

This process takes time, of course, which leads to an undeniable downside of the modern Ideas Industry. In order for public intellectuals to recognize the need to prune a thought leader's intellectual excesses, the thought leader's reach must have already exceeded what is merited. The phenomenon seems akin to an asset bubble in finance. Most asset bubbles begin for valid reasons; in Christensen's case, there was an interesting idea to be had. As the idea becomes more and more popular, its intellectual appeal rises even more. Eventually, intellectual arbitrage by the thought leader or by acolytes leads to even wider application of the concept. An idea will garner public criticism from the Ideas Industry only after it has been inflated past the point of rational valuation. Really popular ideas will experience booms and then busts. That can incur an intellectual cost on how to think about foreign policy. If the modern marketplace of ideas was populated by more public intellectuals, such overshoots would be less likely to occur.

As previously noted, the Ideas Industry has lowered the barriers to entry for outside thought leaders. Any admirer of John Stuart Mill's *On Liberty* would likely welcome such a trend. What this chapter suggests, however, is that the barriers to exit have also been raised. Once ideas gain popular currency, they can be pruned back, but not extinguished. In some cases, this is for valid reasons. The value of disruptive innovation to management theorists has been diminished but not eliminated. In other cases, the ideas still seem politically appealing to some segment of intellectuals. In the Ideas Industry as it is currently constituted, there are many booms, fewer busts, and even fewer intellectual bankruptcies.

9

Tweeting Ideas: Or, the Requisite Chapter on Social Media

As the frequency of expression grows, the force of expression diminishes: Digital expectations of alacrity and terseness confer the highest prestige on the twittering cacophony of one-liners and promotional announcements.

— Leon Wieseltier

THE DIFFERENT COMPONENTS OF the Ideas Industry clearly possess different subcultures. Even if Harvard professors, Brookings fellows, and McKinsey consultants were educated in a similar manner, their professional surroundings inevitably shape the way they think about ideas. They all care about "impact," but to varying degrees and for various reasons. But there is one thing that all thought leaders and public intellectuals from each of these different groups have in common: they will hawk their wares on Twitter.

Every component of the Ideas Industry uses the Internet to advertise and debate foreign policy concepts. An increasing fraction of peer-reviewed journals, think tank reports, and multimedia consulting presentations exist only online. The intellectuals behind these longform works will promote them by blogging short excerpts, sending mass emails, and exploiting social media as best they can. Indeed, online social networks are a place where thought leaders and public intellectuals and everyone else can interact. Even straight-laced academics recognize the need to use online outlets to promote scholarship.[1]

In theory, the ease of online interaction should facilitate the market-place of ideas. While many focus on social media's utility for advertising finished work, that focus marginalizes the degree to which online interactions improve arguments that are still in flux. Blogs and social media act as de facto notebooks for nascent ideas. Queries for citations and sources are likely to be answered more quickly on Facebook or Twitter than through other methods. Online exchanges can open up debate about politics and policy with individuals that stretch well beyond one's own perspective and profession—an "invisible college," as economist Brad DeLong put it.[2] In my own scholarly research, as well as my public writings, I have found social media to be extremely useful as a sounding board. My online interactions have introduced me to smart people who are interested in foreign policy but have very different experiences and training from my own. These are precisely the kind of critics who can offer variegated feedback when I am playing with new ideas. The book you are reading has been improved countless times over because people I met through Twitter were kind enough to read drafts of it.

The dark side to online discourse is by now well known. It has only gotten darker as social media has become a massive amplifier of the Ideas Industry's outputs. The very forces that have shaped the modern marketplace of ideas have also degraded the state of online debate. The erosion of authority has increased the costs of online interaction. The rise of political polarization has intensified the degree of internecine ideological conflict. The growth of inequality within the Ideas Industry itself has incentivized more extreme reactions to the work of intellectual superstars. The necessity for writers to use social media has also caused many intellectuals—myself included—to reveal less flattering aspects of their personality. These combined effects have made it much easier for superstars to ignore all online criticism—to their detriment.

How can online discourse cause all of these problems? To properly understand the downsides of the online world of intellectuals, you have to understand a small, sad website called Political Science Rumors.

Google's descriptor for Political Science Rumors (PSR) is "the forum for Political Scienctists (sic) to discuss Political Science and rumors in the profession."[3] Other descriptions of the site are less charitable. One political scientist blogged: "PSR represents political scientists as angry, hungry, hunted people whose ranks you wouldn't want to join." He hypothesized that "there is really no hyperbolic expression that one could use to describe PSR that would outdo something already written by someone on PSR."[4]

When PSR and its precursors emerged more than a decade ago, their purpose was salutary. "Rumor-mill" sites like PSR were created to provide information about the academic job market: what political science departments were really looking for in their job searches, whom they were interviewing, who got job offers, who accepted jobs, and so forth. There remains an undeniable utility for clearinghouses of this sort. Other social science disciplines have spawned websites akin to PSR.[5]

PSR nonetheless fails at its core mission of providing accurate information about the job market. There is no fact checking on threads offering alleged details about job searches. PSR posts about who has interviewed where and who has received or rejected a job offer are strewn with errors.[6] One colleague learned from her department that she had been tenured, only to read that same day on PSR that she had been denied. Fortunately—and typically—PSR was wrong.

False rumors existed long before PSR came into existence. What makes it stand out is its ability to amplify bad information. One obvious reason for this is anonymous posting; many contributors masquerade as informed insiders when they know nothing about the job search being discussed. Unsurprisingly, a website based on rumor traffics mostly in malicious gossip, ill-informed speculation, and petty back stabbing.[7] This leads to another possible reason for the absence of credible information: people who get jobs are scared of being the object of PSR discussion threads. Explanations offered at PSR for *why* someone got a job make paranoid conspiracy websites seem civilized by comparison.

PSR's failure at its original mission is its most obvious flaw. Its biggest flaw lies in the 90 percent of the site not devoted to job searches. A decade ago, as rumor-mill sites were just emerging, the president of the American Political Science Association warned about "anonymous postings on these lists making racist, sexist, and homophobic attacks on political scientists."[8] As PSR crowded out the other rumor mills, this problem got worse. The garden-variety PSR discussion thread is a toxic alchemy of rage and resentment that most closely resembles the burn book from *Mean Girls. New York* science reporter Jesse Singal characterized it as a "cesspool" that makes his "eyes start bleeding," concluding that "posts on it have a tendency to devolve into attacks, rumor-mongering, and bitterness fueled by an apocalyptic academic job market."[9] PSR's creator has tried to address the problem by empowering moderators who are fellow political scientists. But even PSR users acknowledge that the anonymity of the comments is a perfect breeding ground for personal attacks ranging from sexist insults to actual doxxing.[10] Moderators admit that they constantly second-guess their contributions to the site.[11]

When political scientists talk publicly about PSR, they do not say very nice things. Daniel Nexon, a professor of political science at Georgetown University and a co-editor of *International Studies Quarterly*, described PSR as "the website that makes us all ashamed to be Political Scientists."[12] Duke University professor Michael Munger wrote in the *Chronicle of Higher Education* that PSR is "juvenile, full of gossip and scabrous trolling."[13] Political scientists who have been the object of PSR vitriol are even more disgusted by its existence. Joshua Cohen read a PSR discussion thread devoted to his recent changes of employment. Cohen noted that the PSR thread consisted of "four claims: each confidently asserted, each completely wrong." He concluded, "these claims are not simply mistakes. They are bullshit, and of an especially execrable variety. . . . [PSR] does not simply exhibit indifference to reality. It actively recruits the value of truth without submitting at all to its discipline."[14]

I have never posted a comment at PSR, but I have been the object of the occasional discussion thread. The comments are not pretty. One discussion thread was titled "Why hasn't anyone smacked Drezner in the face?" before a moderator deleted it. Below is a small sampling of PSR comments between 2014 and 2016 that were not deleted:

- "Drezner is a phony motherf**ker. I've been seriously considering writing an open letter to him detailing the ways in which I think he is a charlatan."
- "F**k you, Dan Drezner. You are old. Act like it."
- "Drezner, you are such a loser. Nobody likes you and we all think you're a hack."

- "If you are assigning the Drezner book for IR theory it means you have a very shallow understanding of theory. Have you actually read it?"
- "Drezner has been proven an idiot. My hypothesis is that people around him don't want to break it to him, so he continues to express his opinion as if he isn't an idiot."

I got off easy. I am a straight white man who holds mainstream opinions on American foreign policy. As the science fiction writer John Scalzi has noted, if the real world was a video game, "Straight White Male" would be the beginner setting.[15] If I was a woman, a minority, or someone working in a less mainstream part of the discipline, the comments would have been nastier.[16]

It is easy for me to dismiss PSR as a source of analysis of my work. The overarching theme of the site is resentment against anyone who achieves a modicum of success. The anonymity of PSR commenters makes it a fertile breeding ground for commentary ranging from indignant rants to full-blown slander. The website seems about as far as one can get from anything resembling reasoned criticism.

One obvious lesson to draw from PSR is that learning how to filter out unhinged criticism is crucial for anyone who wants to contribute to the public sphere. Online sites devoted to foreign policy or domestic politics can generate even more traffic and vitriol. An ease at dismissing hyperbolic critiques is a useful skill for anyone trying to contribute to the marketplace of ideas. That ease, however, also contains the kernel of a growing problem.

Success in the Ideas Industry generates two opposing effects on the critical reception of new interventions from successful intellectuals. The first reaction is bandwagoning; junior members of the Ideas Industry will praise the work of senior members. This may be for reasons of genuine agreement, but it is also based on self-interest. Brand-name thought leaders have the ability to corral attention and sell books. Publishers and editors will not necessarily push back on their dubious ideas. For example, Thomas Friedman has admitted in interviews that he can pretty much publish whatever book he wants: "I'm in this scary and enviable position. I can go to my publisher and say, 'I want to write a book.' 'Here's the check.' 'Don't you want to know what it's about?' 'No, we don't care.' It isn't quite like that, but it's pretty much like that."[17] Being constantly in demand means that superstar intellectuals have their choice of venues, and therefore face fewer critical gatekeepers before publication. The more successful an intellectual's past efforts, the easier it will be for them to place their future efforts.

High-profile intellectuals also exert tremendous power in the marketplace of ideas. Through their own outlets, they have the power to call attention to the work of others in the Ideas Industry. This is the "mention" economy—for lower-tier foreign policy writers, a favorable public mention by Paul Krugman or Peggy Noonan or Francis Fukuyama can drive web traffic and book sales. I have a much smaller profile than any of these people, but in recent years I have found myself on the receiving end of numerous requests from senior scholars to blurb or write or tweet about their books. The capacity to direct attention creates an incentive for lower-profile intellectuals to curry favor with brand-name thinkers. This leads, inevitably, to a soft-pedaling of criticism directed at superstar intellectuals. Why savage someone who might blurb your book in a year?

For successful intellectuals, this can be a problem. If all they hear is positive feedback, then how can they improve their arguments? For the marketplace of ideas to produce good work, intellectuals need constructive criticism of their embryonic ideas. Indeed, quality criticism should constitute a healthy fraction of the Ideas Industry. But the mention economy can blunt many a foreign policy observer's critical faculties, as can simple human frailty.

Of course, not all lower-tier intellectuals will take the accommodationist path. Success in the Ideas Industry can also produce an equal and opposite reaction to bandwagoning: the brutal takedown.

Takedowns are hardly an online-only phenomenon, as anyone who has read about vicious twentieth-century intellectual feuds knows. The Internet tends to exacerbate the nastiness of criticism, however. The very nature of interactive, online discourse is different from previous forms of intellectual interaction. The progenitors of the modern Internet were aware of the problem long before the existence of social media. A 1985 RAND analysis warned about the different nature of online communications:

Perhaps the attribute ... that most distinguishes them from other forms of communication is their propensity to evoke emotion in the recipient—very likely because of misinterpretation of some portion of the form or content of the message—and the likelihood that the recipient will then fire off a response that exacerbates the situation. . . .

These media are quite different from any other means of communication. Many of the old rules do not apply.[18]

Similarly, Godwin's law—the adage that "as an online discussion grows longer, the probability of a comparison involving Nazis or Hitler approaches one"—was first introduced in 1990, more than a decade before Reddit, Facebook, or Twitter emerged.[19] The dark side of Internet discourse has been present since the invention of the Internet.

In discussing negative feedback, we need to start from the ground and work our way up, because that is often how intellectuals experience it over the course of their careers. And the absolute bottom starts with the vituperative criticism at online comment boards like PSR, which display all of the pathologies mentioned in the previous paragraphs. These online forums feature attacks so unhinged that one begins to question the sanity of the critic. Take the rage and resentment of Political Science Rumors, amplify it by several orders of magnitude, and one can approximate the negative feedback that superstars receive. Fareed Zakaria told me that about one-third of all the feedback he gets on his column is racist in nature. He stressed the need for a thick skin when dealing with negative feedback but acknowledged that, "temperamentally, it's harder than people realize."[20]

Zakaria told me this about a month before he became the target of an absurd online slander. A malware site tried to attract traffic by claiming that Zakaria had called for the "jihad rape of white women" on his private blog and in deleted tweets. He has no such blog and never tweeted anything remotely like that. Zakaria described what happened next:

Hundreds of people began linking to it, tweeting and retweeting it, and adding their comments, which are too vulgar or racist to repeat. A few ultra-right-wing websites reprinted the story as fact. With each new cycle, the levels of hysteria rose, and people started demanding

that I be fired, deported or killed. For a few days, the digital intimi-
dation veered out into the real world. Some people called my house
late one night and woke up and threatened my daughters, who are
7 and 12. . . .

It would have taken simple common sense to realize the absurdity
of the charge. But none of this mattered. The people spreading this
story were not interested in the facts; they were interested in feeding
prejudice.[21]

Niall Ferguson has encountered similar difficulties, both because of his
own public profile and that of his wife, anti-Islamist activist Ayaan Hirsi
Ali. She has received death threats for her severe criticisms of Islam,
leading her and Ferguson to be more circumspect in their daily lives. As
noted in Chapter 7, Ferguson has also had to cope with his own online
contretemps, in which he has given as good as he has gotten. He holds
a special contempt for Twitter, describing it as "a giant urinal wall for
the world" that he predicts will be bankrupt by 2020. Nonetheless,
Ferguson acknowledges that "the experience of being dragged through
the mud on Twitter is an unpleasant one."[22]

This is, by and large, how most intellectuals feel about the fetid
swamp of online criticism. A mantra for anyone who writes for a public
outlet is, "Never read the comments." Godwin's law applies with particular force to comments sections. *Slate*'s Justin Peters encapsulates the
consensus when he notes, "Every person who writes for the Web has,
at one point or another, been driven to the brink of insanity by a commenter—usually a skeptical or resentful reader who has made it his or
her personal mission to convince a [writer] to go die in a fire."[23]

Online publications continually debate how to moderate their
comments sections, or whether to have comments at all.[24] There is
no easy answer. The conundrum is that the more successful the publication, the more likely the comments deteriorate in quality. When
I started my blog, I found the comments to be substantive and engaging. That was less true, however, for posts that generated more
traffic. Once I moved to *Foreign Policy*, and especially after I moved
to the *Washington Post*, the comments changed for the worse. Some
sites, like Ta-Nehisi Coates's blog at *The Atlantic*, used heavy mod-
eration to preserve some degree of quality for a period of time. As

Coates's intellectual star rose, his comments section deteriorated.[25] The self-regulation of comments sections by other commenters also does not work. One recent study of such self-regulation concluded that under such systems "authors of negatively evaluated content are encouraged to post more, and their future posts are also of lower quality."[26] Comments sections are the intellectual equivalent of Gresham's law: the bad ones drive out the good.

The problem metastasizes when a writer has made an actual mistake. "Twitter mobs" responding to real intellectual transgressions can overreact so wildly that they engender sympathy for the original transgressor. The waves of online calumny targeted at science writer Jonah Lehrer for his admitted plagiarism, for example, appalled even *Daily Beast* columnist Michael Moynihan, the person who discovered Lehrer's fraud: "You turn around and you suddenly realize that you're the head of a pitchfork mob."[27] Wael Ghonim, one of the online architects behind the 2011 Tahrir Square protests in Egypt, concedes that "online discussions quickly descend into angry mobs.... It's as if we forget that the people behind screens are actually real people and not just avatars."[28]

For many intellectuals, the easy anonymity of the online world is particularly odious. As Peters notes, "the pseudo-anonymity of a Comments section can inspire rudeness, truculence, callow dismissals, angry accusations, endless arguments characterized by bile, and mutual disingenuousness."[29] Most writers respond by not engaging these discussions at all—or when they do, to excoriate them. In the fall of 2015, the *Financial Times'* Edward Luce intervened in a discussion thread to address a frequent commenter to his articles. It was, according to the *Financial Times'* global media editor, an "epic takedown" by Luce:

> My colleagues are professional, diligent and hard-working. They do not deserve these kinds of snide noises-off. You know who we are. We have no idea who you are.... I urge you to submit reasonable and constructive criticism that encourage rather than deter a response from the authors and other readers, rather than heaping them with derision. If you are as brave as you clearly think you are, you should do it under your own name. My name is Edward Luce. What is yours? [30]

Clearly, when public intellectuals and thought leaders dismiss the world of online criticism, they are doing so for justifiable reasons. This is doubly true for women, who bear a disproportionate burden of vile attacks.[31] On Political Science Rumors, commenters routinely question whether successful women in political science have slept their way to the top. Annie Lowrey, an economics writer, quit Twitter after receiving too many waves of sexist abuse. She asked, "Why put things out there if you're not going to be able to have even a semblance of a good conversation about them? Why put things out there if people are going to attack you rather than the work?"[32]

The ways of coping with these kinds of criticism all lead to the same outcome: tuning it out. One can try engagement. The instinctive response of any intellectual is to engage online critics. Most intellectuals enjoy the thrust and parry of debate. And, of course, the desire to be right on the Internet is natural to us all.[33] Online engagement carries its own costs and risks, however. Over time, online debates tend to splinter into smaller and smaller squabbles over who said what about the response to the response to the initial spark of the controversy. No fight on social media is ever worth having.[34] Responding to criticism amplifies the initial critique. Even a perfect retort—and those do exist[35]—turns one's original forceful point into a debate. This is why CNN prevented Zakaria from publishing his response to anonymous claims of plagiarism.

The Internet has slowly evolved to make it easier for public intellectuals and thought leaders to cope with online abuse and inanity. No sane person expects a writer to actually read their comments. Twitter allows a user to block others from reading their feed; even better is to mute their responses, so the critics do not even know that they are going unread. Verified users on Twitter have even more powerful filtering options at hand. It is easy to unfriend or unfollow irascible acquaintances on Facebook. Most social media enterprises now have reporting mechanisms to handle particularly abusive critics. Dedicated email cranks can be quickly dispatched to the spam folder. Over time, one can learn how to filter out toxic feedback. But this method of coping brings its own set of intellectual blinders.

The most obstreperous critics are trolls, but on occasion trolls serve a useful purpose. To successfully troll in intellectual affairs is to disrupt someone else's official narrative. Trolls do this through put-downs; over-the-top accusations; or sheer, unflagging annoyance. As Bloomberg columnist Eli Lake put it, "the best trolls are provocateurs. Their language is meant to expose a fallacy or weakness in the opponent's position as opposed to offering a constructive alternative."[36] Trolls agree with this characterization; one explained his strategy to the *New Yorker*: "I read postmodernist theory in college. If everything is a narrative, then we need alternatives to the dominant narrative."[37] Anyone can engage in trolling, and it certainly pre-dates the Internet era. In their 1968 televised exchanges during the Republican and Democrat national conventions, Gore Vidal repeatedly goaded, needled, and trolled William F. Buckley. Vidal finally got Buckley to lose his cool after calling him a "crypto-Nazi." This prompted Buckley to call Vidal a "queer" and threaten to punch him. By flustering the previously unflappable Buckley, Vidal achieved his intended purpose of cutting Buckley down to size.

As a general rule, trolling is a weapon of the weak designed to harass the powerful into engaging their arguments. In the modern world, many online trolls advance arguments that tend toward the insipid. When they are not invoking conspiracy theories, they veer toward racism, sexism, and xenophobia. Crafting arguments that add value to the public debate can be challenging work on a good day. Coping with trolls simply adds to the transaction costs of participating in the Ideas Industry.

This is the biggest problem with updating John Stuart Mill's argument in favor of unfettered inquiry to the twenty-first century. Mill was adamant that unquestioned doctrines be interrogated on a regular basis. He argued that the ideational power of cults, sects, and extremists came from their status as aggrieved minorities. Because they had to constantly defend their views to a hostile public, their skill at intellectual engagement only increased.[38] Mill presumed that cumulative nature of debate would lead to a cessation of serious controversy on some issues. He bemoaned such consensus, arguing that it sapped the vitality of the ideas.

There are debates in American foreign policy that should be ongoing: the importance of credibility in international relations, or the economic effects of immigration, for example. Mill, however, never addressed the opportunity costs of engaging in constant debate over first principles. In an age of outsized trolls, what used to be accepted as stylized facts are litigated anew: Was 9/11 an inside job? Is Barack Obama an American citizen? And so on. Constant engagement with critics makes it difficult for intellectuals to think of anything new. The costs in time and mental energy are significant. Whether Mill would have endorsed unvarnished debate in the Internet age is an interesting proposition to consider.

I have encountered this problem firsthand, as the expressive quotes from Political Science Rumors suggest. My online criticisms of Donald Trump led to a wave of anti-Semitic feedback. So I understand the impulse to ignore critics and trolls—and yet sometimes they can highlight the problems with a heretofore unchallenged set of ideas. There is a fine line between tuning out trolls and tuning out those with different ideological viewpoints. As social media sites have cracked down on online abuse, legitimate questions are being asked about whether arrangements like Twitter's "Trust and Safety Council" are unintentionally Orwellian.[39]

Which brings us back to PSR and the curious case of Michael LaCour.

In December 2014, Michael LaCour, a UCLA graduate student, coauthored a paper in *Science* with Don Green, a full professor at Columbia, exploring the effects of face-to-face conversations on individual preferences regarding same-sex marriage.[40] They conducted an experiment to see if the personal narratives of gay canvassers would have an effect on voters they interacted with. The existing scholarly consensus was that exposure to alternative narratives did not have an appreciable effect on voter preferences. The published results of Green and LaCour's experiment were surprising and counterintuitive: personal interactions with gay canvassers had a pronounced effect on voter preferences, causing them to be significantly more receptive to gay marriage. Not only was the effect significant, later surveys suggested it was durable over time. LaCour told the *Los Angeles Times*, "I was totally surprised that it worked at all."[41] The findings were significant enough to merit coverage in the *New York Times, Washington Post*, Bloomberg, and other news outlets.[42] The results also had global implications; gay activists in Ireland based their campaign strategy for a 2015 gay marriage referendum on the findings.[43] Unsurprisingly, LaCour made a big splash in the academic job market during the 2014–2015 academic year. Princeton University looked set to hire him; he was a budding superstar.

Eight days after the *Science* paper was published, however, a comment by "Reannon" appeared on a PSR discussion thread devoted to the LaCour and Green paper.[44] Beginning with, "Just took a look at the data. Kind of weird," Reannon questioned some of the oddities with the statistical distribution of the data set. The comment generated some debate but was deleted soon afterwards by one of PSR's moderators.

"Reannon" was David Broockman, then a political science graduate student at Berkeley. He had suspicions about the validity of LaCour's data. His dissertation advisors warned him off of airing such concerns publicly. They told him that, given the seriousness of the allegations, making accusations of this kind could threaten his career as a political scientist.[45] Broockman turned to PSR out of desperation.

Six months later, after running a similar experiment and failing to get similar results, Broockman and two coauthors dug into LaCour's data more closely, and concluded that he had fabricated the survey results. Their findings quickly rocketed around political science. Convinced that LaCour had fabricated the data, Green sought and secured a retraction of the *Science* paper.[46] Soon reporters discovered that LaCour had fabricated other parts of his academic resume, including fake teaching awards and bogus research grants.[47] LaCour published an online defense, but his response raised more questions than it answered. Eventually, Princeton rescinded LaCour's preliminary job offer.

From the time Broockman and his coauthors published their paper to the revocation of LaCour's job offer at Princeton, the central clearing house for information and discussion on what had happened was Political Science Rumors. I checked the site regularly during this period, as did many of my colleagues. Duke University political science professor Michael Munger was one of those colleagues:

At the height of the LaCour revelations I was on that site, refreshing my screen two or three times an hour. There was more, and better, information, minute-by-minute, from PSR than anywhere else. And a diverse crowd of smart people was having a real-time public debate (though admittedly a debate full of expletives and genital references) about an important topic.[48]

This gets to the conundrum that confronts participants in the Ideas Industry. The reaction of online criticism by some academic fields has been to label it as "methodological terrorism."[49] Even if the signal-to-noise ratio is extremely low, however, the lowest levels of online criticism can generate trenchant criticism. When Zakaria's anonymous critics accused him of serial plagiarism across a wide body of his written work, they overreached in their attacks. But they were not completely wrong either.

If even the lowest level of criticism can generate useful feedback, what about higher levels? This is where matters get even trickier. Less anonymous forms of criticism should produce a higher ratio of wheat to chaff—but the chaff is also far more problematic. And some of the forces driving the modern Ideas Industry are also leading to a degradation of online discourse.

Social media aids and abets both the erosion of trust in authority and the rise in political polarization. The erosion of trust makes online discourse more challenging even for groups of experts. Middle East scholar Marc Lynch, for example, notes that the divisive politics of the region makes online activity fraught with risk: "The Middle East is a field that generates enormous passion on all sides, tempers often run hot, and scholars with an online presence run a constant risk of finding one of their tweets or essays at the center of a media firestorm."[50] I know many experts on American foreign policy who shy away from writing about the Middle East because of the online cesspool such interventions inevitably attract.

Social media is the great leveler; anyone can tweet at anyone else. Indeed, as a tactic, trolling can also be a leveler. The explicit aim of most of these online critics is to drag down a more prestigious writer. One explained to *Time*: "Let's say I wrote a letter to the *New York Times*. . . . they throw it in the shredder. On Twitter I communicate directly with the writers. It's a breakdown of all the institutions."[51] Goading a superstar intellectual into paroxysms of rage will be seen by many trolls as an intellectual accomplishment in and of itself. Even if an intellectual excels at parrying trolls, online snark can harm one's reputation among colleagues unaccustomed to social media argot. As Lynch notes, "the attacks, subtweeting, mockery, and play that is completely normal in online spaces suddenly become treacherous inside the discipline."[52] Furthermore, the spontaneity of social media allows emotion to trump reason, causing esteemed individuals to say things that they regret soon afterwards. Such mistakes only erode intellectual authority even further. Particularly for those at the apex of the Ideas Industry, direct engagement with online critics can impose a serious tax on one's time, focus, and sanity. The only winning move is not to play.[53]

This holds true even if the online troll is a serious intellectual. Nassim Taleb, for example, is a professor and distinguished author of the best-selling books *Fooled By Randomness, The Black Swan,* and *Antifragile.* Online, however, Taleb can best be described as an unreconstructed ass. He is quick to disparage people who disagree with him on Twitter as "BS vendors"—myself included.[54] His blanket dismissal of all the social sciences makes him sound more like a troll than an academic.[55] Like many trolls, he questions the motivations of those he disagrees with rather than engages in substantive debate.

Following repeated and nasty online disagreements with Taleb, I finally met him for coffee in 2015. He politely explained his side of an argument we had been having online. I wasn't fully persuaded by his reasoning, but I understood his intellectual position better. After this productive exchange, I asked him point blank why he was so obnoxious online. He smiled, shrugged his shoulders, and compared Twitter to being in a seedy bar at two in the morning with a lot of drunks.[56] To him, bellicosity is the best way to survive online. Perhaps this works for him most of the time. However, such puerile exchanges make it harder to take Taleb's more substantive interventions seriously. It also leads Taleb down unproductive alleys, such as when he got into a Twitter fight with a parody account.[57]

Political polarization has also been exacerbated by social media—and, in turn, polarization has worsened online behavior. On Twitter, both conservatives and liberals are far more likely to follow and reiterate politically congruous sources.[58] Liberals are also more likely to defriend someone on Facebook because of political disagreements.[59]

Polarization has encouraged a secular increase of trolling in recent years—but not in the way one would think. Trolling is a weapon of the weak, but it is also a tactic of the intellectual militant. As philosopher Rachel Barney notes, "some troll for amusement, and a few for profit, but most as enemies and members of a faction."[60] To be sure, liberals troll conservatives and vice versa. At the same time, however, writers on both the hard left and alt-right have embraced such tactics in their sectarian intellectual feuds with ideological neighbors.

On the left, *Jacobin* magazine has revitalized socialist thought in American politics.[61] Its class-based, Marxist intellectual ethos, however, has conflicted with other leftists who prioritize race and gender barriers as issues to be addressed. These disputes have led to charges and countercharges of abusive threats. There are documented examples of leftist writers orchestrating online harassment campaigns against other progressives because of internecine disagreements. One target of harassment warned that:

> We need to start acknowledging that men with real power and authority are fostering online harassment. Such public intellectuals are perhaps even more dangerous—both because they give online harassment a larger and more mainstream audience, and because they give those campaigns the stamp of moral or intellectual seriousness.[62]

Indeed, the think tank Demos fired one of its bloggers, Matt Bruenig, over this kind of bellicose behavior. After Bruenig directed a number of offensive tweets at Center for American Progress president Neera Tanden and refused to apologize for them, Demos announced that they and Bruenig had "agreed to disagree on the value of the attack mode on Twitter."[63] Bruenig, along with ideological allies like The Intercept's Glenn Greenwald, believe that their political message is being censored under the guise of "tone policing."

The conscious rejection of civility is a trait shared by the "alt-right," an agglomeration of loosely connected white nationalists, paleoconservatives, and other reactionaries who embraced the political rise of Donald Trump. The alt-right believes that culture is inherently tied to race, and therefore societies function best when there is some degree of separation between different racial groups. One description of the movement notes the "penchant for aggressive rhetoric and outright racial and anti-Semitic slurs, often delivered in the arch, ironic tones common to modern internet discourse." A quasi-intellectual manifesto written by some alt-right leaders acknowledges the movement's "addiction to provocation," explaining that "it's just fun to watch the mayhem and outrage that erupts when those secular shibboleths are openly mocked."[64] Unsurprisingly, actual targets of the provocations feel differently. The alt-right has focused much of its ire at the online harassment of "cucks"—a racially loaded term for Republicans who reject the alt-righters as antithetical to modern conservatism.[65]

Both ends of the ideological spectrum have increased the toxicity of social media outlets like Twitter and Facebook. One could argue that these are less disputes about ideas rather than raw politics. On the foreign policy front, however, the fractiousness can be equally toxic. Realists have traditionally been on the right of the political spectrum and have focused their ire far more on neoconservatives than liberals. Similarly, leftist Democrats have been far angrier with the hawkishness of liberal internationalism than with conservatives.[66]

The effect of inequality on online interactions has also been to exacerbate resentment against the intellectual superstars discussed in the previous chapters. Thomas Friedman, for example, has spawned his own cottage industry of critics. Matt Taibbi wrote a superbly wicked review of Friedman's *The World Is Flat* more than a decade ago, describing it as "the worst, most boring kind of middlebrow horseshit."[67] Taibbi has regularly lampooned Friedman's musings ever since. *Salon*'s Alex Pareene compiles an annual "Hack 30" list of awful American pundits, and Friedman always does well on the list. These two examples barely scratch the surface of Friedman critiques.[68] There is even a website, www.thomasfriedmanopedgenerator.com, devoted to producing automated, Friedmanesque prose. These computer-generated op-eds are uncannily lifelike.

Most top-tier intellectuals have their own gaggle of outside critics and negative profiles. Many of these critiques might be overly snarky or mean-spirited, but that does not mean they are devoid of merit. Any intellectual targeted for criticism, however, is far more likely to focus on the spirit rather than the substance of any critique. And as Alice Gregory noted in the *New York Times Book Review*, with respect to younger critics, such takedowns are often devoid of a key understanding:

> There's a sense in which such unburdened conditions nurture the fairest criticism. It can be performed coldly, impersonally; the work under review can be taken almost as an authorless artifact. But the same circumstances that allow very young people to write some of the most astonishingly worded praise and boldly argued brutality are the same ones that prevent them from actually taking seriously the fact that they are engaging with the product of someone else's time and effort and intellect.[69]

Takedowns might contain valid intellectual criticisms, but they are also designed to wound. Psychologically, it is easy for intellectuals to lump takedowns in with anonymous attacks and therefore dismiss them out of hand with the trolls of the intellectual world.

Any successful intellectual can tune out the cacophony of opinions that exist in the modern Ideas Industry. As this chapter suggests, the incentives to ignore more obnoxious voices are obvious. The sanity gained from tuning out anonymous cranks and trolls on social media is considerable. But there is a slippery slope to tuning out negative criticism. Once all of the trolls, takedown artists, partisans, and other obstreperous folk are eliminated, who is left to criticize?[70] As they continue to opine, top-tier intellectuals either encounter fawning praise or easily dismissible criticism. If they only internalize the praise, they tend to become even more overconfident in their ideas.

The modern marketplace of ideas works, but it is far from perfect. Is there any way for aspiring intellectuals to survive and thrive in the modern Ideas Industry? Is there any way to make the marketplace better? That is what the concluding chapter will address.

Conclusion: *The Dark Knight* Theory of the Ideas Industry

> Reforming a tyranny may not be within our power, but the exercise of intellectual self-control always is. That is why the first responsibility of a philosopher who finds himself surrounded by political and intellectual corruption may be to withdraw.
>
> —Mark Lilla

THE IDEAS INDUSTRY IS bigger than it has ever been before. It would be great if it was just a little bit better.

As this book has hopefully demonstrated, the twenty-first-century Ideas Industry has altered the marketplace of ideas. The barriers to entry are lower for heterogeneous thinkers. Thought leaders benefit more than public intellectuals. Superstars benefit far more than everyone else. Combined, these effects mean that, despite the larger overall pool of intellectuals, certain thought leaders command a greater influence than they otherwise would in a perfectly functioning market.

Public intellectuals can still act as an important check on thought leaders, but the erosion of trust in authority, the rise of political polarization, and the increase in economic inequality all cut against the ability of public intellectuals to speak truth to other ideas. The easy shortcut of arguing from authority does not work in the same way it used to, because trust in all forms of authority has declined. Liberal thought leaders can dismiss conservative public intellectuals as motivated solely by partisanship, and vice versa. And through their patronage, pluto-crats can ensure that the thought leaders they like will not disappear into the ether. Each of these factors works against the ability of public intellectuals to force recognition of their criticism in the public sphere.

The Ideas Industry has stacked the deck in favor of thought lead-ers, but obviously, valuable intellectual debates still occur. This book has detailed the Sachs/Easterly debate over economic development, the pushback against Nicholas Kristof's claims about the marginaliza-tion of the academy, the battle royale between Jill Lepore and Clayton Christensen over disruptive innovation, and the contretemps between Niall Ferguson and his critics on a welter of subjects. In contrast to previous eras, the barriers to entry in the marketplace of ideas are much lower, which has enabled more people to propose more ideas than ever before about public policy and foreign policy. Still, there has been less churn at the top of the intellectual food chain than one would expect. All of the most influential foreign policy thinkers mentioned previously have been influential for quite some time now. Disruptive innovation has had little effect on the Ideas Industry itself.

The result is a marketplace of ideas that functions imperfectly. Superstar thought leaders cope better than superstar public intellectu-als. Popular ideas, like disruptive innovation, present like asset bubbles in financial markets. They garner too much uncritical attention too quickly, and then are taken down after they have wreaked significant intellectual carnage. The modern Ideas Industry incentivizes thought leaders to ignore public intellectuals until it is too late. The online world incentivizes critics to embrace their inner troll to make their crit-icisms sting even more. Troll tactics might work in the short run. Over the long term, however, such behavior simply encourages intellectual superstars to tune out negative feedback even more.

To sum up: Things are not worse than they used to be. They are just bad in a different way.

Can things get better? Can concerted efforts to elevate the level of discourse make a difference? What are individual intellectuals to do in a flawed system? To be sure, there are structural shifts and institutional reforms that can make the marketplace of ideas work better. Another engine for change in the Ideas Industry may well come from the abil-ity of successful intellectuals to regulate from within. But the recent upheaval at the *New Republic* suggests the limits to individual efforts to change things—even if that individual is a very wealthy patron.

However one demarcates the proper boundaries of the marketplace of ideas, the *New Republic* belongs safely inside its borders. From its founding in 1914, the magazine's purpose was, according to cofounder Herbert Croly, to "give certain ideals and opinions a higher value in American public opinion. If these ideas and opinions were accepted as facts it would be unnecessary to start the paper. The whole point is that we are trying to impose views on blind or reluctant people."[1] The *New Republic* proceeded to publish some of the greatest intellectuals of the past century: John Dewey, Walter Lippmann, Louis Menand, Hans Morgenthau, Reinhold Niebuhr, Martha Nussbaum, George Orwell, Bertrand Russell, Andrew Sullivan, Michael Walzer, and Rebecca West all graced its pages. The magazine was also a vital way station for its editorial staff; after a stint, the publication's best and brightest could go on to bolster the intellectual heft of *The New Yorker, Harper's, Commentary, The Atlantic, New York Review of Books, New York Times*, and *Washington Post*. Its "back of the book" featured some of the strongest and longest cultural criticism in print.

Any honest accounting of the *New Republic* must also detail its numerous flaws. It was too enamored of Stalinist economics during the 1930s, and ensnared in a Soviet spy ring in the 1950s. As the magazine revived its intellectual vibrancy in the 1980s, it also published some blinkered perspectives toward race in the United States.[2] Its advocacy of a muscular, interventionist foreign policy in recent decades exhilarated some and exasperated others. Nevertheless, even fierce critics of the magazine, like Ta-Nehisi Coates, acknowledge the centrality of its intellectual legacy.[3] No one ever accused it of not taking ideas seriously.

The *New Republic*'s problem is that it has always been as unprofitable as it has been intellectually stimulating. Former editor Hendrik Hertzberg explained, "There's only one business model for a place like the *New Republic*—and that is an eccentric millionaire who pays the difference between income and outgo."[4] Starting with Willard Straight and proceeding through Marty Peretz, a cavalcade of eccentric millionaires were, for a time, willing to bankroll the magazine's significant achievements in unprofitability in return for the cachet it afforded in political, literary, and academic circles. Eventually, however, the losses would accumulate, forcing its owner to cast about for the next munificent patron.[5]

When Facebook cofounder Chris Hughes bought the *New Republic* in 2012, it seemed that the latest benefactor had been found. Despite how he made his hundreds of millions, Hughes made it clear from the outset that he did not want to transform the publication's intellectual culture into anything resembling a tech startup. Soon after buying the *New Republic*, Hughes told the *New York Times* that he was uninterested in recruiting social media stars and very interested in retaining the magazine's best writers, to "make sure the *New Republic* isn't a place where they work for 10 years and then move on."[6] A *New York* profile noted that "Hughes wants to produce what thoughtful people ought to read, as opposed to churning out what most people like to 'like.'"[7] In a 2013 interview, he said, "We are not the next big trend in Silicon Valley," and swore that "the *New Republic* will not be having an IPO any time soon."[8] Literary editor Leon Wieseltier similarly bragged to the press after Hughes' purchase: "I feel very confident in saying we're not going to become quicker, fuzzier, faster. We're reviving our old standards."[9]

In the first few years of Hughes's reign, the *New Republic* refurbished its website, rehired renowned editor Franklin Foer to run the magazine,[10] and bolstered its staff with many excellent writers. It published some outstanding reportage and criticism, essays that sparked wide-ranging conversations about the Middle East peace process, Russian politics, technological utopianism, and political corruption.[11] It was a finalist for numerous National Magazine Awards under Foer's editorship. One alumnus praised Hughes as a "21st-century Walter Lippmann."[12] A gala, star-studded party, held in the fall of 2014, celebrated the magazine's centennial anniversary.

Nevertheless, the *New Republic*'s unprofitability persisted. Indeed, according to Hughes, the magazine's losses accelerated at an alarming rate.[13] He had plowed significant sums into the magazine, albeit less for reporting than for office redesigns and image consultants.[14] All of the spending dramatically worsened the bottom line.

At this point in past cycles, previous owners had started the search for a new patron. Hughes charted a different course. He brought in

Guy Vidra, a former general manager at Yahoo News, to shake things up. In the press release announcing Vidra's hire, Hughes extolled Vidra's entrepreneurialism and explained, "One thing I've learned over the past two years is that to preserve and strengthen great institutions, you have to change them." In the same press release, Hughes also announced the creation of a new investment vehicle, the New Republic Fund, to finance early stage technology companies.[15] He later explained in an interview that, "in bringing Guy in, we were making a pivot . . . to new kinds of digital storytelling."[16]

According to numerous accounts, Vidra brought with him a lot of talk about disruption and thought leadership. *The New Yorker*'s Ryan Lizza provided the most authoritative account of the first fateful meeting between Vidra and *New Republic* staff:

> [Vidra] offered a series of statements intended to describe a transformation that could make the magazine profitable, but it came across to the editors as a jumble of clichés and tech jargon. "We're going to be a hundred-year-old startup," he said. The magazine needed "to align ourselves from the metabolism perspective" and create "magical experiences for both the content and the product design" and be "fearless in innovation and experimentation" and "change some of the DNA of the organization." He said that he wanted to institute "a process for annual reviews" and effect a "cultural change where we need to just embrace innovation, experimentation, and cross-functional collaboration," and said that the editors, writers, and business side would need to "speak to each other much more effectively and efficiently in our gatherings" in order "to take us to the next stage.". . .
>
> Vidra ended his talk with a speech that TNR writers and editors would quote mockingly for weeks. "They say that there's two types of C.E.O.s," he said. "There's the peacetime C.E.O. and the wartime C.E.O. Not to be overly dramatic about it, but this is sort of a war. This is a wartime period. That just means that we need to change a lot of things. We need to just break shit. Sorry to say, we've got to break shit and embrace being uncomfortable sometimes. And it's scary. It's definitely a scary thing to do. But it's also fun: you know, lean up against the wall and break it."[17]

Although confusing to staffers at the time, readers of this book should by now be familiar with Vidra's argot. Using the language of disruptive innovation, he was arguing in favor of a magazine oriented around thought leadership rather than the traditional public intellectuals of the magazine's heyday.

Repeated discord between Vidra and Foer finally led Hughes to covertly seek out a replacement for the latter. Once wind of this got back to Foer, he quit, along with Wieseltier, setting off considerable turmoil. Vidra announced that the magazine's annual publication rate would be cut in half and that it would be rebranded "as a vertically integrated digital media company."[18] In the media firestorm that ensued, more than thirty editors listed on the masthead quit.

In the wake of that exodus, the new editor wrote that "the best way for any new editor of this magazine to respect the spirit of the institution is to first recognize its defining characteristic is a habit of reinvention."[19] Hughes defended his actions, explaining, "I didn't buy *The New Republic* to be the conservator of a small print magazine."[20] A few months later, the magazine hired a new "chief revenue officer" responsible for "starting a branded-content unit that will produce stories for advertisers."[21] One of the newly hired senior editors described the attraction of joining the staff as "joining a 100-year-old startup," echoing Vidra's mantra. The *New Republic* got another redesign, another refurbishing of its website, and a new credo. It was to be "a mission-driven media organization," one that "promote[d] novel solutions for today's most critical issues."[22] How that ethos differed from a management consulting firm was unclear.

The *New Republic* morphed into an outlet that offered more predictable and partisan liberal analysis. The new TNR focused intensely on identity issues of race and gender, with less of a focus on world politics. Within that bailiwick, it published some agenda-setting intellectual essays.[23] Foer suggested to me that this allowed TNR to brand itself more clearly in a world in which there is an "arms race for audience," echoing statements by other magazine editors that the competition has become ever more intense.[24] The problem was that the audience also grew less interested. Web traffic declined by more than fifty percent immediately after the mass exodus and only weakly recovered over the subsequent year.[25] In January 2016, Hughes decided to sell the magazine, admitting that, "I underestimated the difficulty of transitioning an old and traditional institution into a digital media company in today's quickly evolving climate."[26] The sale to new benefactor Win McCormack was announced six weeks later. Under Hughes, TNR had been thoroughly disrupted, without anything useful in the way of innovation.

What was the effect of the *New Republic's* transformation on the marketplace of ideas? Here matters get murky. Numerous ex-TNR staffers signed petitions and wrote elegies to the magazine-that-was, bemoaning Hughes's desecration of the *New Republic's* century-long intellectual brand.[27] Conservatives bemoaned the demise of its willingness to criticize liberal dogma. Former owner Marty Peretz emerged from semi-seclusion to blast Hughes for not taking ideas seriously.[28] Wieseltier took to the pages of the *New York Times Book Review* to accuse Hughes and his ilk of being "posthumanists" who "deny the importance, and even the legitimacy, of human agency."[29]

Many of the protestations from the magazine's alumni, however, insisted that the publication be treated like a public trust rather than a business. They offered no viable solution to fix the hemorrhaging finances. Writers without a personal tie to the magazine offered a more jaundiced perspective. *Vox* cofounder Ezra Klein, for example, noted that policy magazines like the *New Republic, The American Prospect,* and *Washington Monthly* were "no longer the center of the policy conversation in Washington. That conversation has spilled online, beyond their pages, outside their borders."[30] This included new online sites like *BuzzFeed* and *FiveThirtyEight*, blogs like Marginal Revolution and the Upshot, or individual columnists like Jamelle Bouie, Megan McArdle, or Ramesh Ponnuru. Indeed, *New Republic* staffers who departed with Foer and Wieseltier found excellent sinecures elsewhere. Many other commentators grew exasperated at the sheer number of words devoted to the entire brouhaha.

If the tale of the *New Republic* is not quite the intellectual *götterdämmerung* that some claimed, it is emblematic of trends underlying the twenty-first-century Ideas Industry. For over a century, the magazine had managed to function as a bastion for traditional intellectuals. In its first issue, Rebecca West wrote about "the duty of harsh criticism," a duty that the *New Republic* and others fulfilled with gusto for the next hundred years.[31] The publication's longstanding comparative advantage had been its ability to dissect, interrogate, and skewer ideas so widely accepted that they had congealed into conventional wisdom—John Stuart Mill's "dead dogma." Yet even it was forced to shed its identity as a place for public intellectuals in a desperate bid for thought leadership. The parable suggests the degree to which the marketplace of ideas is facing some serious turmoil. And the *New Republic* is hardly the only outlet to face these pressures in the current moment.[32]

The saga offers some sobering lessons for the Ideas Industry. First, plutocrats might hold greater sway in the marketplace of ideas, but that sway only exists if there is a willingness to absorb financial losses. Second, trying to change entities with strong intellectual cultures will lead to significant discord and likely fail. Third, even the disruption of one of the oldest publication outlets in the marketplace of ideas will not fundamentally affect the modern Ideas Industry.

So how can the modern marketplace of ideas be improved? And what can intellectuals do to survive and thrive in the Ideas Industry?

The danger in writing a book like this one is to fall into the trap of the nostalgic argument, to argue that it was all better back in the day. Hopefully, I have demonstrated that there are decided advantages to the modern Ideas Industry. But neither do I want to make the claim that all is well. The old marketplace of ideas was more cosseted, but within those constraints there were substantive debates. Occasionally, someone actually changed their mind because of those debates. In the modern Ideas Industry, a thousand TED talks have bloomed. But none of them have discussants, none of the speakers appear to be listening to each other, and the audience is attending only a few select presentations.

There are three important guidelines in thinking about how to make the modern marketplace of ideas function better. The first is that we cannot and should not try to go back to the old days. Some aspects of the modern Ideas Industry are irreversible. The proliferation of media platforms, for example, cannot be undone. More importantly, for all of the Ideas Industry's imperfections, there are virtues as well. A world of venerated authorities, minimal polarization, and less inequality might sound good, but it also sounds intellectually bland. A marketplace of ideas that returns power to gatekeepers also stacks the deck against thought leaders. What is needed is equipoise between the different intellectual styles, not a world dominated by public intellectuals.

The second guideline is that some of the drivers shaping the modern Ideas Industry may well reverse themselves over the next decade. Trust in authority has rebounded slightly after hitting all-time lows a few years ago. There is also nascent evidence that political polarization may be abating.[33] The election of Donald Trump suggests that conservative orthodoxy will face serious challenges from more populist forces within the Republican Party. It seems hard to envision right now, but it is possible that partisanship will not run this hot for much longer. Much like previous waves of "creedal passions," this one should subside with time.[34] And it is possible that some wealthy patrons decide to invest their resources into improving the lot of true public intellectuals. There is evidence that some benefactors are moving down the learning curve in their engagement with the Ideas Industry. Some philanthrocapitalists have backed away from efforts to immediately affect political change, and are instead investing in more traditional efforts to fund intellectuals in universities and think tanks. Others are bankrolling traditional public intellectuals as a counterweight to thought leaders.[35] If each of these forces abates somewhat, the demand for ideas will stay high, but the deck will not be as stacked in favor of thought leaders.

The most powerful actors that could correct the ills of the modern Ideas Industry are located in the traditional nonprofit sector. Both universities and think tanks need to redouble their efforts to bolster their endowments. More endowment income is the best way that both types of organizations can ensure intellectual autonomy.

Universities and think tanks also need to revive their institutional prestige. Skeptics might argue that their decline in authority is permanent, but I have witnessed firsthand that this is not necessarily so. Over the past two years I was part of a Fletcher School team that received a Carnegie Corporation grant dedicated to bridging the gap between the academy and policy. In response to the grant, Fletcher put together a multidisciplinary group of scholars that focused on the relevance of political legitimacy to policymakers. My most important takeaway from that experience was that the whole of the team was greater than the sum of the parts. All of the participating scholars had solid reputations in their own bailiwicks. Combined, however, the audiences seemed most impressed by the notion that it was a combined Fletcher School effort. Just as my institution was able to leverage its reputation into more influence, the same would hold for SAIS, Georgetown, Brookings, Heritage, and the rest.[36] A marketplace of ideas with stronger universities and think tanks would be one that empowered traditional public intellectuals. Philanthropic foundations could contribute to this trend if they cared a little less about immediate impact and more about long-term investments. Conservative philanthropies have had far more success in recent decades precisely because they were able to be patient with their giving.[37]

There are also small-bore steps that can be taken to ensure a wider array of critical voices in the foreign policy community. There has been a concerted push in recent years for more inclusive foreign policy conversations—that is, those that do not consist solely of white men. Numerous studies show that men dominate the most high-profile outlets. A 2011 study found that women were responsible for less than 20 percent of *Wall Street Journal* op-eds and only 23 percent of *New York Times* op-eds. In 2014, less than one-quarter of all think tank presenters were women. That same year, fewer than a quarter of all Sunday morning talk show guests were women.[38] Organizations like the Op-Ed Project and Foreign Policy Interrupted have been created to publicize and address these imbalances.

It might seem that altering the ethnic and gender diversity of the Ideas Industry would be unconnected to the problems discussed in this book. There is no guarantee that diversity in race or gender guarantees a healthier intellectual debate—particularly if arguments grounded solely in identity trump arguments grounded in additional theory and evidence. Nonetheless, widening the backgrounds of foreign policy conferences is one possible way to offer a wider perspective of views. If nothing else, increased diversity would act as a useful constraint on the power of superstars. Simply introducing more heterogeneous voices at various intellectual confabs levels the playing field at the margins.

It would be fortuitous if structural factors reversed themselves, or if large organizations reformed themselves. I am too much of a social scientist to expect such phenomena to spontaneously occur, however. These changes will take time. In the meanwhile I am fearful of a future where the flaws of the modern marketplace of ideas overwhelm the benefits. The two most scarring US policy disasters in this short century have been the 2003 invasion of Iraq and the slow-motion response to the subprime mortgage bubble. In both instances, there were critics who highlighted the problems with the hegemonic ideas guiding policymakers. In each case, however, those critics were marginalized as oddballs or extremists. In an optimal marketplace of ideas, establishment figures promoting flawed ideas should be forced to reconsider their premises when confronted with superior arguments and evidence.

Let me close with what sounds like a naïve suggestion. For change to come to the Ideas Industry successful intellectuals must themselves become more self-aware of the sphere in which they operate. The foreign policy community needs to internally resist the ways in which the Ideas Industry makes it easy to tune out constructive criticism. With weak external checks, the importance of internal checks becomes more salient. Conscientious intellectuals can be encouraged to actively seek out intelligent critiques of their work, particularly if it will be read by the rich and the powerful.

Asking intellectuals to police themselves sounds like a very weak reed. It is like asking the scorpion to not sting the frog. By definition, it is not in the nature of a thought leader to contemplate the possibility of being wrong. Expecting such individuals to seek out critical feedback might be asking too much of them. And prominent public intellectuals, particularly those housed in prestigious universities, think tanks, or consultancies, are not exactly the most modest of folk. As Niall Ferguson told me, "In intellectual life, no one declares bankruptcy."[39]

Nonetheless, if there is one thing that intellectuals excel at, it is thinking that they are self-aware. Asking politicians to exercise political will and ignore short-term incentives is like asking politicians to not act like politicians. It is not much easier to ask intellectuals to act against their immediate material interests; like other middle-class denizens, they have mortgages and student loans to pay off. That said, simply highlighting the dynamics of the Ideas Industry can help successful intellectuals—including the most confident of thought leaders—to appreciate the long-term risks of ignoring critical feedback.

Richard Hofstadter noted, "the fate of intellectuals [is] either to berate their exclusion from wealth, success, and reputation, or to be seized by guilt when they overcome this exclusion."[40] Material rewards can corrupt the garden-variety intellectual, but guilt and fear can counteract financial temptations. The guilt that comes with success can be harnessed and redirected toward self-restraint. The fear of failure is also a powerful incentive in the marketplace of ideas. Intellectuals rarely go bankrupt, but they are acutely aware of their place in the pecking order. As this book has demonstrated, foreign and public policy thinkers fall from grace on a regular basis, in the same way that asset bubbles pop. Hopefully, foreign policy intellectuals want to avoid being the subject of a sad parable that older think-tank fellows tell their research assistants late in the day.

For this kind of self-recognition to occur, however, successful intellectuals will need to shed a few bad habits. This is easier said than done. The expansion of the marketplace for ideas has also expanded the rewards for those who thrive in this environment. As one moves up the intellectual food chain, the temptations and rewards also increase. Life as a successful thought leader is clearly hectic but also personally and financially rewarding.

Early in Christopher Nolan's *The Dark Knight*, the charismatic district attorney Harvey Dent tells his dinner companions, "You either die a hero, or live long enough to see yourself become the villain." Beyond offering some foreshadowing for Dent's character arc, a variation of that sentence holds a ring of truth for intellectuals in the Ideas Industry: you either die in noble obscurity or live long enough to see yourself become what you loathed about the marketplace of ideas.

As someone who has avoided (so far) an obscure death, I can bear some witness to this progression.

From the start of my career, I intended my research to speak to both a scholarly and a public audience. In one of my first published articles, I wrote:

> [A] singularly useful purpose of social scientists [is to play] the role
> of the critic. Politicians have the incentive to use dubious theories
> when they are politically expedient. Academics test theories for their

theoretical and empirical rigor to filter out arguments that may be emotionally appealing but wrong. This is useful to policymakers, because it tells them which theories should be ignored and which merit further attention. Scholarly criticism can make a difference.[41]

As my career progressed I continued to publish in peer-reviewed journals, but I also wrote for a larger public. I started a blog in September 2002. I wrote for the *New York Times* and *Foreign Affairs* as well as *International Security* and *International Organization*. In aiming at a wider audience, I relied on a few common themes. One of my tropes was to critique more prominent public intellectuals for mistaken metaphors about world politics. This theme rebounded back into my scholarly work as well.[42]

Experts in political economy and foreign policy work in a countercyclical field. The worse things seem in the world, the more demand there is for experts to weigh in. So, unfortunately for everyone else, the past decade has been excellent for me. On the academic side, life is good: I have been promoted to full professor, awarded some prestigious grants and fellowships, published in numerous scholarly journals, and asked to sit on a number of journal editorial boards. On the public intellectual side, life is even better: my scribblings have migrated toward ever-larger outlets. Foreign governments have asked me to lecture to their officials; on occasion I have consulted for the US government as well. I wrote a short and satirical textbook on international relations theory that has been widely assigned. Academic administrators want their professors to have "impact" in this era of austerity. I score pretty well on those metrics. I proofread this paragraph in a Rockefeller Foundation villa in Bellagio, Italy. I can't complain.

To be absolutely clear, I am nowhere close to the intellectual stratosphere of Fareed Zakaria or Clayton Christensen or Niall Ferguson. Nevertheless, as my own career has progressed, I have had a small taste of what superstar intellectuals enjoy on a regular basis. I can talk about frequent-flyer mile programs with the best of them. When given the opportunity, I have partaken in snack-filled green rooms, business class airport lounges, and swanky conferences in exotic locales. My most life-affirming example was a conference in Portugal, to which I was able to bring my spouse. This was significant, as she has usually been unable to accompany me on these kind of boondoggles. We were met at the Lisbon airport by an entire entourage of staffers. They quickly escorted us to a black SUV and sped us to a luxury hotel in Cascais, close to the casino that was the inspiration for Ian Fleming's *Casino Royale*. In the town there were massive billboards with pictures of all the participants, which included Francis Fukuyama, Nouriel Roubini, and myself, among many others.[43] When my wife saw a ten-foot high picture of me close to the town square, she turned to me and said, "OK, now I'm impressed."

In *Bobos in Paradise*, David Brooks perfectly captured this milieu of "semiprofessional, semisocial institutions" such as TED conferences, Ditchley Park weekends, Salzburg Seminars, and World Economic Forum gatherings, in which the successful mingle with the influential to discuss the intellectual.[44] I am not my own brand and have not been to Davos, but I probably possess upper-middle-class status in the marketplace of ideas. The material rewards of succeeding in the Ideas Industry are nothing compared to the fortunes made in Silicon Valley or Wall Street. Still, for individuals who began their careers by choosing a life of the mind, the benefits are greater than one would expect. Mortgages can be paid; children can be sent to college. A good life can be lived.

The intellectual effects of success and visibility, however, are more problematic, both for the individual and for the marketplace of ideas writ large.

In the modern Ideas Industry, you have not truly succeeded unless you attract an army of critics. In the last chapter, I mentioned some of the less-than-flattering fans I have at Political Science Rumors. Others troll me on social media, populate the comments section of my *Washington Post* comment board, or send me irate emails.[45] Some of these critics are passive-aggressive. Many are just aggressive. After one interview on CNN, conspiracy theorists seized on a mangled sentence of mine to suggest I had revealed evidence that President Obama was in league with the Islamic State.[46] The conservative *Washington Free Beacon* claimed I had legitimized a Holocaust denier.[47] Leftist writers have accused me of articulating positions on American foreign policy for the sole purpose of "careerist posturing."[48]

None of these contretemps has been particularly disturbing. They are inconsequential compared to the harassment that other intellectuals endure because of who they are or what they say. Nevertheless, their combined effect has been the development of a mental callus. It makes it easier to opine and write, but it also means that I do not consider criticism as much as I probably should. David Brooks once warned that "the tragedy of middle-aged fame is that the fullest glare of attention comes just when a person is most acutely aware of his own mediocrity."[49] There is a worse fate, however: to gain attention and be completely unaware of one's flaws. The callus required to engage in the public sphere makes that outcome more likely.

Furthermore, there have been times when my own critical faculties have been blunted a bit. I still critique other foreign affairs pundits, but perhaps not quite as much as before. This might be due to my growing appreciation for how hard it is to craft interesting, original arguments on a regular basis. But it might be due to a simple human failing; it is harder to publicly criticize writers whom one knows.[50] And the more successful one is as an intellectual, the more people one meets.

As my career has progressed, I have experienced the benefits of greater intellectual success, and the effects frankly scare the hell out of me. My intellectual style has evolved, and not always in a good way. With success has come confidence, and a large dollop of arrogance. I have said "yes" to writing assignments that, in retrospect, I should have declined because I lacked the time or expertise to do them justice. As I write and speak more, I read less. It has become more difficult to replenish my intellectual capital beyond listening to others speak at conferences. The more international business class flights I take, the more impatient I become with quotidian responsibilities on the ground. As a graduate student, I would get irked when I contacted a senior scholar and failed to get a response. Now I am that senior scholar.

My favorite Political Science Rumors comment about me is, "99% of cites to his work is to call him the asshole he is." It's funny and over the top, but there are days when I fear that PSR commenter might have hit upon a grain of truth. I have no doubt that, on my short-tempered days, I meet Aaron James's philosophical definition of a smug asshole: someone "comfortable in his sense that others are inferior . . . that others should well expect him to behave as their better."[51]

Unsurprisingly, James's best examples of smug assholes are intellectuals such as Larry Summers and Bernard Henri-Lévy.

If the Ideas Industry is going to improve, this career narrative needs to change. Successful intellectuals need to acknowledge fallibility. The possibility of doing so certainly exists. A student's first exposure to the philosophy of science is learning that the entire social science enterprise revolves around falsification.[52] By proving an existing idea wrong, we refine our understanding of what our ideas can and cannot explain.

The trouble with intellectuals is that the impulse is always to prove the *other* guy is wrong, because that aligns perfectly with our own psychology. As Kathryn Schulz observed in *Being Wrong*, "the thrill of being right is undeniable, universal, and (perhaps most oddly) almost entirely undiscriminating. . . . It's more important to bet on the right foreign policy than the right racehorse, but we are perfectly capable of gloating over either one."[53]

At the same time, there is a positive aspect to the proliferation of contingent writing—the world of social media, blog posts, and op-eds. As someone who has blogged for more than a decade, I have been wrong an awful lot. I have sometimes been wrong in a big way, such as supporting the 2003 invasion of Iraq. I've grown somewhat more comfortable with the feeling of wrongness. I don't want to make mistakes, of course. But if I tweet or blog a half-formed supposition and it then turns out to be wrong, I get more intrigued about *why* I was wrong. That kind of empirical and theoretical investigation seems more interesting than doubling down on my initial opinion. Younger intellectuals, weaned on the Internet, more comfortable with the push and pull of debate on social media, may well feel similarly.

There are two ways my story can end. The first is that I become the villain. Successful intellectuals, whether they are thought leaders or public intellectuals, have the capacity to be major league assholes. If I become a brand, then it will become easier to publish, easier to give speeches, easier to network, easier to send my children to good colleges, easier to neglect students and colleagues and friends—right up to the moment I say or write something that is so egregiously bad that someone jumpstarts their own intellectual career by exposing my flaws. This has happened to smarter, better-spoken, and more gifted intellectuals than myself. It has happened to many of the people discussed in this book. In the modern marketplace of ideas, an awful lot of intellectuals will consciously or unconsciously take this path.

The second way my story can end is the choice Harvey Dent never contemplated: sustainability. If I believe the arguments I have made in this book are correct, then I need to write a bit less and read and think a bit more. Sustainable intellectuals embrace the need for greater self-reflection; they seek out and understand criticism without letting it lead to paralysis. They learn to balance the twin intellectual impulses of play and piety. In the short run, this is the less sexy path. But as more scholars, think tank fellows, and private-sector analysts understand the current state of the Ideas Industry, they might prefer long-term sustainability over short-term superstardom. Such a choice would benefit both their own professional careers and the marketplace of ideas more generally.

The temptation to sacrifice the important for the urgent is not unique to policymakers; it lurks in the heart of ambitious intellectuals as well.

I do not know for sure which way my own story will end. But I have a pretty good idea.

NOTES

―――⋙◆⋘―――

Introduction

1. James Kloppenberg, *Reading Obama: Dreams, Hope, and the American Political Tradition* (Princeton, NJ: Princeton University Press, 2011).

2. Barack Obama, "Renewing American Leadership," *Foreign Affairs* 86 (July/August 2007): 3.

3. Sam Stein, "Obama and Conservatives Break Bread at George Will's House," *Huffington Post*, February 13, 2009; Michael Calderone, "How Obama Plays the Pundits," *Politico*, March 8, 2009; Paul Starobin, "All the President's Pundits," *Columbia Journalism Review*, September/October 2011; Dylan Byers, "President Obama, Off the Record," *Politico*, November 1, 2013.

4. Ryan Lizza, "The Consequentialist," *The New Yorker*, May 2, 2011.

5. Mike Allen, " 'Don't Do Stupid Sh—' (Stuff)," *Politico*, June 2, 2014.

6. Michael Grunwald, "The Selling of Obama: The Inside Story of How a Great Communicator Lost the Narrative," *Politico*, May/June 2016.

7. Clinton quoted in Jeffrey Goldberg, "Hillary Clinton: 'Failure' to Help Syrian Rebels Led to the Rise of ISIS," *The Atlantic*, August 10, 2014.

8. Colin Campbell, "Ted Cruz: 'The World Is on Fire,' " *Business Insider*, December 2, 2014; Jake Sherman, "Boehner in Israel: 'The World Is on Fire,' " *Politico*, April 2, 2015; Charles Krauthammer, "Obama's Ideological Holiday in Havana," *Washington Post*, March 24, 2016.

9. Grunwald, "The Selling of Obama." See also Byers, "President Obama, Off the Record."

10. Derek Chollet, *The Long Game* (New York: Public Affairs, 2016), xvi.

11. Rhodes quoted in Robert Draper, "Between Iraq and a Hawk Base," *New York Times Magazine*, September 1, 2015.

12. Rhodes quoted in David Samuels, "The Aspiring Novelist Who Became Obama's Foreign-Policy Guru," *New York Times Magazine*, May 5, 2016.

13. Jeffrey Goldberg, "The Obama Doctrine," *The Atlantic*, April 2016.

14. Ibid.

15. Daniel W. Drezner, "Swing and a Miss," *Foreign Policy*, September 16, 2013; Max Fisher, "The Credibility Trap," *Vox*, April 29, 2016.

16. See, for example, Mark Landler, "For President, Two Full Terms of Fighting Wars," *New York Times*, May 15, 2016.

17. Tom Wright, "Donald Trump's 19th Century Foreign Policy," *Politico*, January 20, 2016; Jeet Heer, "Donald Trump's Foreign Policy Revolution," *New Republic*, March 26, 2016.

18. Ashley Parker, "Donald Trump Says NATO is 'Obsolete,' UN is 'Political Game,'" *New York Times*, April 2, 2016.

19. Binyamin Appelbaum, "On Trade, Donald Trump Breaks with 200 Years of Economic Orthodoxy," *New York Times*, March 10, 2016.

20. "A Transcript of Donald Trump's Meeting with the *Washington Post* Editorial Board," *Washington Post*, March 21, 2016; Maggie Haberman and David Sanger, "Transcript: Donald Trump Expounds on His Foreign Policy Views," *New York Times*, March 26, 2016; Bob Woodward and Robert Costa, "Transcript: Donald Trump Interview with Bob Woodward and Robert Costa," *Washington Post*, April 2, 2016; Maggie Haberman and David Sanger, "Transcript: Donald Trump on NATO, Turkey's Coup Attempt and the World," *New York Times*, July 21, 2016.

21. Maggie Haberman and David Sanger, "Donald Trump's Trial Balloons Are Catching Up With Him," *New York Times*, April 9, 2016; Zack Beauchamp, "Republican Foreign Policy Experts Are Condemning Trump. It Matters More Than You Think," *Vox*, August 8, 2016.

22. For economists, see Ben Leubsdorf, Eric Morath, and Josh Zumbrun, "Economists Who've Advised Presidents Are No Fans of Donald Trump," *Wall Street Journal*, August 26, 2016. For historians, see http://www.historiansagainsttrump.org/.

23. See, for example, the reactions to his first major foreign-policy speech: Fareed Zakaria, "Trump's Head-Spinning and Secret Plans for Foreign Policy," *Washington Post*, April 28, 2016; Fred Kaplan, "A Mess of Contradictions," *Slate*, April 27, 2016; Julia Ioffe, "On Trump, Gefilte Fish, and World Order," *Foreign Policy*, April 27, 2016; Charles Krauthammer, "The World According to Trump," *Washington Post*, April 28, 2016; Joseph Nye, "How Trump Would Weaken America," *Project Syndicate*, May 10, 2016; "Look Out, World," *Economist*, April 27, 2016.

24. Stephen Walt, "No, @realDonaldTrump Is Not a Realist," *Foreign Policy*, April 1, 2016; Walt, "Donald Trump: Keep Your Hands Off the Foreign-Policy Ideas I Believe In," *Foreign Policy*, August 8, 2016; Emma Ashford, "The Unpredictable Trump Doctrine," *Philadelphia Inquirer*, April 1,

2016; Ryan Cooper, "Donald Trump's Deranged Foreign Policy," *The Week*, August 17, 2016.

25. See the Economist Intelligence Unit explanation at https://gfs.eiu.com/ Article.aspx?articleType=gr&articleId=2866.

26. Tevi Troy, "How GOP Intellectuals' Feud with the Base Is Remaking U.S. Politics," *Politico*, April 19, 2016; Victoria McGrane, "Trump's Policy Stances Baffle Think Tanks," *Boston Globe*, May 27, 2016.

27. Molly Ball, "The Republican Party in Exile," *The Atlantic*, August 18, 2016.

28. The letter can be accessed at http://warontherocks.com/2016/03/open-letter-on-donald-trump-from-gop-national-security-leaders/. I was one of the signatories.

29. Tim Mak, Andrew Desidero, and Alexa Corse, "GOP National Security Experts Are #ReadyForHer," *Daily Beast*, June 30, 2016; Michael Crowley and Alex Isenstadt, "GOP Foreign Policy Elites Flock to Clinton," *Politico*, July 6, 2016; Michael Hirsh, "Role Reversal: The Dems Become the Security Party," *Politico*, July 28, 2016; David Sanger, "50 G.O.P. Officials Warn Donald Trump Would Put Nation's Security 'at Risk,'" *New York Times*, August 8, 2016.

30. Ross Douthat, "Trump and the Intellectuals," *New York Times*, October 1, 2016. Jeremy Herb, "Will Trump Flunk the Commander-in-Chief Test?," *Politico*, January 22, 2016; Victoria McGrane, "Trump's Policy Stances Baffle Think Tanks," *Boston Globe*, May 27, 2016.

31. The full text can be accessed at https://www.donaldjtrump.com/press-releases/donald-j.-trump-foreign-policy-speech.

32. Libby Nelson, "Read Donald Trump's bizarre, frightening speech responding to sexual assault allegations," *Vox*, October 13, 2016; McKay Coppins, "Trump Gets Desperate," *BuzzFeed*, October 13, 2016. Jacob Heilbrunn, "The GOP's New Foreign-Policy Populism," *The National Interest*, February 17, 2016; John Allen Gay, "Trump vs. Conservative Intellectuals," *The National Interest*, June 7, 2016. To be fair to Trump, there were pale echoes of some of his arguments in more mainstream political discourse. Obama, for example, also complained about US allies being "free riders" in providing global security. See Goldberg, "The Obama Doctrine"; Eli Lake, "The Trump-Obama Doctrine," BloombergView, March 11, 2016.

33. See, for example, Peggy Noonan, "A Party Divided, and None Too Soon," *Wall Street Journal*, June 2, 2016.

34. Corker quoted in Gregory Krieg, "Corker Praises Trump for 'Challenging the Foreign Policy Establishment,'" CNN, April 29, 2016; Felipe Cuello, "A Defense of Donald Trump's Foreign Policy Chops," *Foreign Policy*, February 26, 2016; Haberman and Sanger, "Donald Trump's Trial Balloons Are Catching Up With Him."

35. Jeffrey Goldberg, "The Lessons of Henry Kissinger," *The Atlantic*, November 10, 2016. Accessed at http://www.theatlantic.com/magazine/archive/2016/12/the-lessons-of-henry-kissinger/505868/.

36. Michael Grunwald, "Do Ideas Still Matter in the Year of Trump (and Clinton)?" *Politico*, September/October 2016.

37. Zeynep Tufekci, "Adventures in the Trump Twittersphere," *New York Times*, March 31, 2016; Mike Konczal, "Trump is Actually Full of Policy," Medium, September 21, 2016, accessed at https://medium.com/@rortybomb/trump-is-actually-full-of-policy-f8bfdb6389e8#.kaiilnavq; Max Fisher, "Twilight of the Neoconservatives," *Vox*, March 10, 2016.

38. Matthew Continetti, "The Coming Conservative Dark Age," *Commentary*, April 12, 2016; Yuval Levin, "The Next Conservative Movement," *Wall Street Journal*, April 15, 2016; Zack Beauchamp, "A Republican Intellectual Explains Why the Republican Party Is Going to Die," *Vox*, July 25, 2016.

39. Some self-identified intellectuals very much dislike the term "marketplace of ideas" because it uses an economic metaphor to characterize a phenomenon that they feel should be free from the shackles of neoliberalism. Those intellectuals should either accept their Foucauldian defeat on this question or not bother to read any further.

40. Friedrich A. von Hayek, "The Intellectuals and Socialism," *University of Chicago Law Review* 16 (Spring 1949): 417–433. The extant definitions are a bit more expansive than mine. In *Public Intellectuals*, Richard Posner defines the term to mean someone who "opines to an educated public on questions of or inflected by a political or ideological concern." In *The Last Intellectuals*, Russell Jacoby, who popularized the term, defined it as "writers and thinkers who address a general and educated audience." My narrower definition reflects the contrast between public intellectuals and thought leaders—or critics and creators—that will animate the rest of this book.

41. See http://www.google.com/trends/explore#q=public%20intellectual%2C%20thought%20leader, accessed September 1, 2016.

42. David Brooks, "The Thought Leader," *New York Times*, December 17, 2013.

43. The Jeffrey Sachs profiled in Nina Munk's *The Idealist* is clearly acting as a thought leader. The Sachs who writes columns on austerity and foreign policy for *Project Syndicate* is acting as a public intellectual. See the next chapter for more on Sachs.

44. Isaiah Berlin, *The Hedgehog and the Fox: An Essay on Tolstoy's View of History* (Princeton, NJ: Princeton University Press, 2013), 437.

45. David Brooks, *Bobos in Paradise* (New York: Simon and Schuster, 2000), chapter 4. As will be discussed in the next chapter, Brooks's depiction of the 1950s intellectuals was somewhat exaggerated.

46. On Ferguson, see "The History Man and Fatwa Girl," *Daily Mail*, February 12, 2010. Krugman's IMDB page can be found at http://www.imdb.com/name/nm1862259/. On Harris-Perry's MSNBC departure, see Josh Koblin, "After Tense Weeks, Melissa Harris-Perry's MSNBC Show Is Cancelled," *New York Times*, February 28, 2016.

47. Philip Tetlock and Dan Gardner, *Superforecasters: The Art and Science of Prediction* (New York: Crown Books, 2015), 231. See also Daniel Kahneman, *Thinking, Fast and Slow* (New York: Farrar Strauss Giroux, 2011), chapter 10; and Kathryn Schulz, *Being Wrong* (New York: Ecco, 2010).

48. Of course, some intellectuals loathe both terms, because they rely on economic metaphors. Those readers should either proceed to Chapter 4 immediately or simply stop reading.

49. Evgeny Morozov, "The Naked and the TED," *New Republic*, August 2, 2012; Morozov, *To Save Everything, Click Here* (New York: PublicAffairs, 2013); Felix Salmon, "Jonah Lehrer, TED, and the Narrative Dark Arts," Reuters, August 3, 2012. See also Justin Fox, "Niall Ferguson and the Rage Against the Thought-Leader Machine," *Harvard Business Review*, August 23, 2012.

50. See, for example, David Landes, *The Unbound Prometheus* (Cambridge: Cambridge University Press, 1969); Nathan Rosenberg and L. E. Birdzell Jr., *How the West Grew Rich* (New York: Basic Books, 1986); Andrew Clark, *A Farewell to Alms* (Princeton, NJ: Princeton University Press, 2007); Angus Deaton, *The Great Escape: Health, Wealth, and the Origins of Inequality* (Princeton, NJ: Princeton University Press, 2013).

51. Nathan Heller, "Listen and Learn," *New Yorker*, July 9, 2012.

52. George Will, "An Anti-Authority Creed," *Washington Post*, January 23, 2011.

53. David Milne, "America's 'Intellectual' Diplomacy," *International Affairs* 86 (January 2010): 50.

54. Berger quoted in David Rothkopf, "The Urgent vs. the Important," *Foreign Policy*, December 2, 2015.

55. Ronald Krebs, *Narrative and the Making of US National Security* (New York: Cambridge University Press, 2015).

56. Bruce Russett, "Bushwhacking the Democratic Peace," *International Studies Perspectives* 6 (September 2005): 396.

57. See Jack Snyder, "Imperial Temptations," *The National Interest* 71 (Spring 2003): 33–34; Daniel W. Drezner, "The Realist Tradition in American Public Opinion," *Perspectives on Politics* 6 (March 2008): 99–100.

58. Benjamin Barber, *The Truth of Power* (New York: W. W. Norton, 2001), 35.

59. Richard Hofstadter, *Anti-Intellectualism in American Life* (New York: Knopf, 1962), 45.

60.   Paul Johnson, *Intellectuals* (New York: Harper and Row, 1989); Thomas Sowell, *Intellectuals and Society* (New York: Basic Books, 2009); Walter Russell Mead, "The Crisis of the American Intellectual," *The American Interest*, December 8, 2010.

61.   On the atrocious record of twentieth-century intellectuals, see Mark Lilla, *The Reckless Mind: Intellectuals in Politics* (New York: New York Review Books, 2001).

62.   Quoted in Daniel Byman and Matthew Kroenig, "Reaching Beyond the Ivory Tower: A How To Manual," *Security Studies* 25 (May 2016): 317.

63.   The last includes conversations I have held with a bevy of scholars, journalists, practitioners, and thought leaders at a series of "Ideas Industry" conferences I have organized at the Fletcher School over the past two years.

64.   The course, Foundations of Economic Prosperity, was done for the Teaching Company, and can be accessed at http://www.thegreatcourses.com/courses/foundations-of-economic-prosperity.html.

65.   Michael Polanyi, *The Tacit Dimension* (Chicago: University of Chicago Press, 1966).

66.   Let's face it, if you did not think ideas were important, you would not be reading this endnote.

Chapter 1

1.   Jeffrey Sachs, *The End of Poverty: Economic Possibilities for Our Time* (New York: Penguin, 2005), 90–91.

2.   Paul Starobin, "Does It Take a Village?," *Foreign Policy*, June 24, 2013.

3.   Louis Uchitelle, "Columbia Gets Star Professor from Harvard," *New York Times*, April 5, 2002.

4.   Starobin, "Does It Take a Village?"

5.   Nina Munk, *The Idealist: Jeffrey Sachs and the Quest to End Poverty* (New York: Signal, 2013), 32.

6.   Ibid., 2.

7.   Starobin, "Does It Take a Village?"

8.   Munk, *The Idealist*.

9.   William Easterly, *The Tyranny of Experts* (New York: Basic Books, 2013), 6.

10.   Munk, *The Idealist*; Abhijit Banerjee and Esther Duflo, *Poor Economics* (New York: PublicAffairs, 2011).

11.   Starobin, "Does It Take a Village?"

12.   Email correspondence from Jeffrey Sachs, February 13, 2016.

13.   Paul M. Pronyk, Jeffrey Sachs, et al., "The Effect of an Integrated Multisector Model for Achieving the Millennium Development Goals and Improving Child Survival in Rural Sub-Saharan Africa: A Non-Randomised Controlled Assessment," *The Lancet* 379 (May 8, 2012): 2179–2188.

14. Jeffrey Sachs, "Global Health within Our Grasp, if We Don't Give Up," CNN.com, September 12, 2012.

15. Munk, *The Idealist*.

16. Gabriel Demombynes and Sofia Karina Trommlerova, "What Has Driven the Decline of Infant Mortality in Kenya?" World Bank Policy Research Working Paper 6057, May 2012.

17. Gabriel Demombynes, "The Millennium Villages Project Impacts on Child Mortality," *Development Impact*, May 10, 2012.

18. Paul M. Pronyk, "Errors in a paper on the Millennium Villages project," *The Lancet*, May 21, 2012.

19. Jeff Tollefson, "Millennium Villages Project Launches Retrospective Analysis," *Nature*, August 12, 2015.

20. Starobin, "Does It Take a Village?"

21. Bill Gates, "Why Jeffrey Sachs Matters," *Project Syndicate*, May 21, 2014.

22. Email correspondence with Jeffrey Sachs, February 16, 2016.

23. Munk, *The Idealist*, 230 and 232.

24. See, for example, Jeffrey Sachs, "Hillary Clinton and the Syrian Bloodbath," *Huffington Post*, February 15, 2016.

25. Robert Kagan, "Power and Weakness," *Policy Review* 113 (June/July 2002): 3–28; G. John Ikenberry, "Is American multilateralism in Decline?," *Perspectives on Politics* 1 (September 2003): 533–550; David Skidmore, "Understanding the Unilateralist Turn in US Foreign Policy," *Foreign Policy Analysis* 1 (July 2005): 207–228.

26. John Mearsheimer and Stephen Walt, "The Israel Lobby," *London Review of Books* 28 (March 2006): 3–12.

27. See Brian C. Schmidt and Michael C. Williams, "The Bush Doctrine and the Iraq War: Neoconservatives Versus Realists," *Security Studies* 17 (June 2008): 191–220; Francis Fukuyama, *America at the Crossroads: Democracy, Power, and the Neoconservative Legacy* (New Haven, CT: Yale University Press, 2006); Eric Van Rythoven, "The Perils of Realist Advocacy and the Promise of Securitization Theory: Revisiting the Tragedy of the Iraq War Debate," *European Journal of International Relations* 22 (September 2016): 487–511.

28. David Frum, "Foggy Bloggom," *The National Interest* 93 (January/ February 2008): 46–52; Jacob Heilbrunn, "Rank Breakers: Anatomy of an Industry," *World Affairs* 170 (Spring 2008): 36–46.

29. Michael Desch, *The Relevance Question: Social Science's Inconstant Embrace of Security Studies*, forthcoming.

30. See Dina Smeltz and Ivo Daalder, *Foreign Policy in the Age of Retrenchment* (Chicago: Chicago Council on Global Affairs, 2014). See also, more generally, Daniel W. Drezner, "The Realist Tradition in American Public Opinion," *Perspectives on Politics* 6 (March 2008): 51–70; Benjamin Page with Marshall Bouton, *The Foreign Policy Disconnect* (Chicago: University of Chicago Press, 2006).

31. Interview with Gideon Rose, New York, December 9, 2015.

32. Catherine Ho, "Mega-Donors Opposing Iran Deal Have Upper Hand in Fierce Lobbying Battle," *Washington Post*, August 13, 2015; Julie Hirschfield-Davis, "Lobbying Fight over Iran Nuclear Deal Centers on Democrats," *New York Times*, August 17, 2015.

33. Pew Research Center, "Support for Iran Nuclear Agreement Falls," September 8, 2015.

34. Smeltz and Daalder, *Foreign Policy in the Age of Retrenchment*, chapter 3; Stephen Kull and I. M. Destler, *Misreading the Public* (Washington, DC: Brookings Institution, 1999).

35. See Daniel W. Drezner, "Foreign Policy Goes Glam," *The National Interest* 92 (November/December 2007): 22–29.

36. See, for example, Martin Wolf, "The Economic Losers Are in Revolt against the Elites," *Financial Times*, January 26, 2016; Roger Cohen, "The Know-Nothing Tide," *New York Times*, May 16, 2016.

37. David Freedman, "The War on Stupid People," *The Atlantic*, July/August 2016; Edward Luce, "The End of American Meritocracy," *Financial Times*, May 8, 2016. On populism more generally, see Jan-Werner Muller, *What Is Populism?* (Philadelphia: University of Pennsylvania Press, 2016).

38. P. J. O'Rourke, "Let's Cool It with the Big Ideas," *The Atlantic*, July/August 2012.

39. David Halberstam, *War in a Time of Peace* (New York: Scribner, 2001), 408–409.

40. John Lewis Gaddis, "A Grand Strategy of Transformation," *Foreign Policy* 133 (November/December 2002), 51 and 57.

41. Craig Kafura and Dina Smeltz, "Who Matters for US Foreign Policymaking?," Chicago Council on Global Affairs, June 19, 2015.

42. See Jacob Heilbrunn, "The GOP's New Foreign Policy Populism," *The National Interest* (March/April 2016).

43. Charles Murray, "The Tea Party Warns of a New Elite. They're Right," *Washington Post*, October 24, 2010. See, more recently, Thomas Edsall, "How the Other Fifth Lives," *New York Times*, April 27, 2016.

44. Kull and Destler, *Misreading the Public*. For a recent example, see Peter Moore, "Foreign Aid: Most People Think America Gives Too Much Away," YouGov, March 11, 2016.

45. Daniel Brouwer and Catherine Squires, "Public Intellectuals, Public Life, and the University," *Argument and Advocacy* 39 (Winter 2003), 203. See also Amitai Etzioni and Alyssa Bowditch, eds., *Public Intellectuals: An Endangered Species?* (New York: Rowman and Littlefield, 2006); Heilbrunn, "Rank Breakers."

46. Eric Lott, *The Disappearing Liberal Intellectual* (New York: Basic Books, 2006); Howard Jacob Karger and Marie Theresa Hernández, "The Decline of the Public Intellectual in Social Work," *Journal of Sociology and Social Welfare* 31 (September 2004): 51–68; Charlotte Allen, "Feminist Fatale," *Los Angeles Times*, February 13, 2005; Alan Jacobs,

"The Watchmen," *Harper's*, September 2016. For an exception, however, see Michael Eric Dyson, "Think Out Loud," *New Republic*, September 8, 2015.

47. Ezra Klein, "RIP, William F. Buckley," *The American Prospect*, February 27, 2008, accessed at http://prospect.org/article/rip-william-f-buckley. Jacob Heilbrunn echoed this sentiment when he wrote that "today's intellectuals often succumb to celebrity culture, shouting on FOX News and MSNBC rather than arguing about ideas in books or in the pages of magazine." Heilbrunn, "Rank Breakers," 42.

48. Sam Tanenhaus, "Requiem for Two Heavyweights," *New York Times*, April 13, 2008; Klein, "RIP, William F. Buckley"; David Brooks, "The Smile of Reason," *New York Times*, November 19, 2006.

49. See, for example, Ian Bremmer, "George Kennan's Lessons for the War on Terror," *International Herald Tribune*, March 24, 2005; Ian Lustick, *Trapped in the War on Terror* (Philadelphia: University of Pennsylvania Press, 2006); James Goldeiger and Derek Chollet, "The Truman Standard," *The American Interest* 1 (Summer 2006): 107–111; Ian Shapiro, *Containment: Rebuilding a Strategy against Global Terror* (Princeton, NJ: Princeton University Press, 2007); Aziz Huq, "The Ghost of George Kennan," *The American Prospect*, May 15, 2007.

50. Richard Haass, *The Opportunity* (New York: PublicAffairs, 2005); Derek Chollet and James Goldgeier, *America between the Wars: From 11/9 to 9/11* (New York: PublicAffairs, 2008); John Mearsheimer, "Imperial by Design," *The National Interest* 111 (January/February 2011): 16–34.

51. Ronald Krebs, *Narrative and the Making of US National Security* (New York: Cambridge University Press, 2015), chapters 5–7.

52. Zbigniew Brzezinski, *Second Chance: Three Presidents and the Crisis of American Superpower* (New York: Basic Books, 2008).

53. Glenn Greenwald, "The Foreign Policy Community," *Salon*, August 8, 2007.

54. G. John Ikenberry and Anne-Marie Slaughter, *Forging a World of Liberty under Law: U.S. National Security in the 21st Century* (Princeton, NJ: Princeton Project for National Security, 2006), 58. I was one of the many people that participated in the Princeton Project.

55. W.W. Rostow, *The Stages of Economic Growth: A Non-Communist Manifesto* (Cambridge: Cambridge University Press, 1960), 4.

56. See, for example, Peter Hall, "Policy Paradigms, Social Learning, and the State: The Case of Economic Policymaking in Britain," *Comparative Politics* 25 (April 1993): 275–296; Stephen Teles, *The Rise of the Conservative Legal Movement* (Princeton, NJ: Princeton University Press, 2008); Jennifer Burns, *Goddess of the Market: Ayn Rand and the American Right* (New York: Oxford University Press, 2009); Angus Burgin, *The Great Persuasion: Reinventing Free Markets since the Depression* (Cambridge, MA: Harvard University Press, 2012); Dani Rodrik, "When

Ideas Trump Interests: Preferences, Worldviews, and Policy Innovations," *Journal of Economic Perspectives* 28 (January 2014); Deirdre McCloskey, *Bourgeois Equality: How Ideas, Not Capital or Institutions, Enriched the World* (Chicago: University of Chicago Press, 2016).

57. Judith Goldstein and Robert Keohane, eds., *Ideas and Foreign Policy* (Ithaca, NY: Cornell University Press, 1993).

58. Mark Blyth, *Great Transformations: Economic Ideas and Institutional Change in the Twentieth Century* (New York: Cambridge University Press, 2002).

59. Peter Haas, "Banning Chlorofluorocarbons: Epistemic Community Efforts to Protect Stratospheric Ozone," *International Organization* (Winter 1992): 187–224; Daniel Hirschman, "Stylized Facts in the Social Sciences," *Sociological Science* 3 (July 2016): 604–626.

60. Krebs, *Narrative and the Making of US National Security*; Michael Barnett and Raymond Duvall, "Power in International Politics," *International Organization* 59 (January 2005): 39–75.

61. On free trade, see Douglas Irwin, *Against the Tide: An Intellectual History of Free Trade* (Princeton, NJ: Princeton University Press, 1996); and Daniel Yergin and Joseph Stanislaw, *The Commanding Heights* (New York: Simon and Schuster, 1998). See also, more generally, Daniel W. Drezner, *The System Worked: How the World Stopped Another Great Depression* (New York: Oxford University Press, 2014), chapter 6.

62. Andrew Sullivan, "Here Comes the Groom," *New Republic*, August 28, 1989.

63. Tom Ricks, *The Gamble* (New York: Penguin Press, 2009).

64. Quote from http://www.bartleby.com/268/9/23.html.

65. John Maynard Keynes, *The General Theory of Employment, Interest, and Money* (London: MacMillan, 1936), 383.

66. Paul Krugman, "The Outside Man," *New York Times*, January 7, 2013.

67. Rachel Weiner, "Jim DeMint Leaving the Senate," *Washington Post*, December 6, 2012.

68. David Welna, "Outside the Senate, DeMint Appears More Powerful Than Ever," NPR, September 26, 2013.

69. Felix Salmon, "Is There a Wonk Bubble?," *Politico*, April 8, 2014.

70. Jessica Tuchman Matthews, "Why Think Tanks Should Embrace 'New Media,'" *Washington Post*, October 8, 2015.

71. Eliot Cohen, "How Government Looks at Pundits," *Wall Street Journal*, January 23, 2009.

72. See, for example, Simon Owens, "How a Hobby Foreign Affairs Blog Became a Paywalled News Destination—and a Business," *NiemanLab* (blog), March 25, 2015.

73. Justin McCarthy, "Americans Remain Upbeat about Foreign Trade," Gallup, February 26, 2016; Bruce Stokes, "Republicans, Especially Trump Supporters, See Free Trade Deals as Bad for U.S," Pew Research Center,

March 31, 2016; Matthew Yglesias, "Donald Trump Is Counting on an Anti-Trade Backlash That Doesn't Appear to Exist," *Vox*, March 18, 2016.

74. Smeltz and Daalder, *Foreign Policy in the Age of Retrenchment*, 30.

75. Richard Hofstadter, *Anti-Intellectualism in American Life* (New York: Vintage, 1963). See also Louis Menand, *The Metaphysical Club: A Story of Ideas in America* (New York: Farrar Strauss Giroux, 2001).

76. Hofstadter, *Anti-Intellectualism in American Life*, 21.

77. Chaim Kaufmann, "Threat Inflation and the Failure of the Marketplace of Ideas: The Selling of the Iraq War," *International Security* 29 (Summer 2004): 5.

78. See, for example, Jack Snyder, *Myths of Empire: Domestic Politics and International Ambition* (Ithaca, NY: Cornell University Press, 1991).

79. Evan Thomas, "Why We Need a Foreign Policy Elite," *New York Times*, May 4, 2016.

80. Ezra Klein, "The Budget Myth That Just Won't Die: Americans Still Think 28 Percent of the Budget Goes to Foreign Aid," *Washington Post*, November 7, 2013.

81. Ibid.; Kull and Destler, *Misreading the Public*.

82. Richard Posner, *Public Intellectuals* (Cambridge, MA: Harvard University Press, 2001), 33. See also Rick Perlstein, "Thinkers in Need of Publishers," *New York Times*, January 22, 2002.

83. Thomas Wright, "Learning the Right Lessons from the 1940s," in *Avoiding Trivia: The Role of Strategic Planning in American Foreign Policy*, ed. Daniel W. Drezner (Washington, DC: Brookings Institution Press, 2008).

84. George Kennan, *Around the Cragged Hill* (New York: W. W. Norton, 1993), 144.

85. William Easterly, *The Elusive Quest for Growth* (Cambridge, MA: MIT Press, 2001).

Chapter 2

1. David Rothkopf, "Dis Town," *Foreign Policy*, November 28, 2014.

2. Ibid.

3. For critiques, see for starters, Alex Pareene, "Don't Mention Income Inequality Please, We're Entrepreneurs," *Salon*, May 21, 2012; Felix Salmon, "Jonah Lehrer, TED, and the Narrative Dark Arts," Reuters, August 3, 2012; Ted Frank, "TED Talks Are Lying to You," *Salon*, October 13, 2013; Benjamin Bratton, "We Need to Talk about TED," *Guardian*, December 30, 2013; Umaire Haque, "Let's Save Great Ideas from the Ideas Industry," *Harvard Business Review*, March 6, 2013. For satire, see Betsy Morais, "The Onion Tees up TED Talks," *New Yorker*, October 17, 2012.

4. Rothkopf's TED talk can be accessed at http://www.ted.com/talks/david_rothkopf_how_fear_drives_american_politics?language=en.

5. David Rothkopf, "Objects on Your TV Screen Are Much Smaller Than They Appear," *Foreign Policy*, March 20, 2015.

6. Ibid.

7. Carmine Gallo, *Talk Like TED: The Public-Speaking Secrets of the World's Top Minds* (New York: St. Martin's Press, 2014), 5.

8. David Rothkopf, "Davos Haters Gonna Hate, but It's Not Going Anywhere," *Foreign Policy*, January 29, 2016.

9. Michael Barber and Nolan McCarty, "Causes and Consequences of Polarization," in *Negotiating Agreement in Politics*, ed. Jane Mansbridge and Cathie Jo Martin (Washington, DC: American Political Science Association, 2013).

10. The evidence linking public distrust to the other two trends is weak. See Malcolm Fairbrother and Isaac W. Martin, "Does Inequality Erode Social Trust? Results from Multilevel Models of US States and Counties," *Social Science Research* 42 (March 2013): 347–360. For a contrary view, see Dido Kuo and Nolan McCarty, "Democracy in America, 2015," *Global Policy* 6 (June 2015): 49–55.

11. Pew Research Center, "Public Trust in Government: 1958–2014," November 13, 2014, accessed at http://www.people-press.org/2014/11/13/public-trust-in-government/.

12. Gallup, "75% in U.S. See Widespread Government Corruption," September 19, 2015, accessed at http://www.gallup.com/poll/185759/widespread-government-corruption.aspx.

13. Pew Research Center, *Beyond Red & Blue: The Political Typology*, June 26, 2014, accessed at http://www.people-press.org/files/2014/06/6-26-14-Political-Typology-release1.pdf, 37.

14. Gallup, "Public Faith in Congress Falls Again, Hitting Historic Low," June 19, 2014, accessed at http://www.gallup.com/poll/171710/public-faith-congress-falls-again-hits-historic-low.aspx.

15. Gallup, "Americans Losing Confidence in All Branches of Gov't," June 30, 2014, accessed at http://www.gallup.com/poll/171992/americans-losing-confidence-branches-gov.aspx.

16. Gallup, "Trust in Federal Gov't on International Issues at New Low," September 10, 2014, accessed at http://www.gallup.com/poll/175697/trust-federal-gov-international-issues-new-low.aspx

17. Gallup, "Trust in U.S. Judicial Branch Sinks to New Low of 53%," September 18, 2015, accessed at http://www.gallup.com/poll/185528/trust-judicial-branch-sinks-new-low.aspx.

18. Tom W. Smith and Jaesok Son, *Trends in Public Attitudes about Confidence in Institutions*, National Opinion Research Center, University of Chicago, May 2013, accessed at http://www.norc.org/PDFs/GSS%20Reports/Trends%20in%20Confidence%20Institutions_Final.pdf.

19. Institute of Politics, *Survey of Young Americans' Attitudes Toward Politics and Public Service: 25th Edition*, Harvard University, April 29, 2014,

accessed at http://www.iop.harvard.edu/sites/default/files_new/Harvard_
ExecSummarySpring2014.pdf, 17–20. See also Yascha Mounk and
Roberto Foa, "The Democratic Disconnect," *Journal of Democracy* 27
(July 2016): 5–17.

20. Gallup, "75% in U.S. See Widespread Government Corruption."
21. Gallup, "Honesty/Ethics in Professions," accessed at http://www.gallup.
com/poll/1654/honesty-ethics-professions.aspx.
22. Smith and Son, *Trends in Public Attitudes about Confidence in Institutions.*
23. Ibid.
24. National Science Board, *Science and Engineering Indicators 2014*,
accessed at http://www.nsf.gov/statistics/seind14/content/chapter-7/
chapter-7.pdf, 32.
25. Cary Funk and Lee Rainie, "Public and Scientists' Views on Science and
Society," Pew Research Center, January 29, 2015, accessed at http://www.
pewinternet.org/2015/01/29/public-and-scientists-views-on-science-and-
society/.
26. National Science Board, *Science and Engineering Indicators 2014.*
27. Funk and Rainie, "Public and Scientists' Views on Science and Society";
Gabriel R. Ricci, "The Politicization of Science and the Use and Abuse of
Technology." *International Journal of Technoethics* 6 (Fall 2015): 60–73.
28. Bryan Caplan, Eric Crampton, Wayne Grove, and Ilya Somin,
"Systemically Biased Beliefs about Political Influence," *PS: Political
Science and Politics* 46 (October 2013): 760–767.
29. The SurveyMonkey questionnaire was conducted via electronic mail
between January 20, 2016, and February 7, 2016. A total of 440
academics, columnists, journalists, editors, think tank officials, and
former policymakers were surveyed. The response rate was over 47
percent, which for an elite survey is an extremely high yield.
30. Organization for Economic Cooperation and Development, *Government at
a Glance* (Paris: OECD, 2013), accessed at http://www.oecd.org/governance/
governments-can-do-more-to-regain-trust-says-oecd-report.htm.
31. Foa and Mounk, "The Democratic Disconnect"; Roberto Foa and
Yascha Mounk, "The Signs of Deconsolidation," *Journal of Democracy* 26
(January 2017): 5–15.
32. The 2015 Edelman Trust Barometer can be accessed at http://www.
edelman.com/insights/intellectual-property/2015-edelman-trust-
barometer/trust-around-world.
33. For a survey of expert opposition to Brexit, see Keith Breene, "What
Would Brexit Mean for the UK Economy?," World Economic Forum,
March 23, 2016. For Gove's remarks, see Robert Colville, "Britain's
Truthiness Moment," *Foreign Policy*, June 9, 2016.
34. Tobias Buck, "Middle England Drives Brexit Revolution," *Financial
Times*, June 15, 2016.
35. Steven Teles, Heather Hurlburt, and Mark Schmitt, "Philanthropy in a
Time of Polarization," *Stanford Social Innovation Review* (Summer 2014): 47.

36. Christopher Hayes, *Twilight of the Elites: America after Meritocracy* (New York: Crown Books, 2012), 13 and 25.

37. Yuval Levin, "The Next Conservative Movement," *Wall Street Journal*, April 15, 2016.

38. Tom Nichols, "The Death of Expertise," *The Federalist*, January 17, 2014.

39. See Benjamin Page with Marshall Bouton, *The Foreign Policy Disconnect* (Chicago: University of Chicago Press, 2006).

40. Lawrence Jacobs and Benjamin Page, "Who Influences U.S. Foreign Policy?," *American Political Science Review* 99 (February 2005): 113.

41. On journalists, see Zixue Tai and Tsan-Kuo Chanfe, "The Global News and the Pictures in their Heads," *Gazette: The International Journal For Communications Studies* 64 (June 2002): 251–265. On academics, see Susan Peterson, Michael Tierney, and Daniel Maliniak, "Inside the Ivory Tower," *Foreign Policy* 151 (November/December 2005): 58–63. On businessmen, see PricewaterhouseCoopers, "9th Annual Global CEO Survey," January 2006.

42. Francis Fukuyama, *America at the Crossroads* (New Haven, CT: Yale University Press. 2006); Jacob Heilbrunn, *They Knew They Were Right: The Rise of the Neocons* (New York: Doubleday, 2008).

43. Richard Burt and Dmitri Simes, "Foreign Policy by Bumper Sticker," *The National Interest*, August 17, 2015.

44. See Mill, *On Liberty* for more on dead dogma.

45. Christopher Hitchens, "The Plight of the Public Intellectual," *Foreign Policy* 166 (May/June 2008): 64.

46. Gordon Gauchat, "Politicization of Science in the Public Sphere: A Study of Public Trust in the United States, 1974 to 2010," *American Sociological Review* 77 (April 2012): 167–187; Gauchat, "The Political Context of Science in the United States: Public Acceptance of Evidence-Based Policy and Science Funding," *Social Forces* (February 2015): 1–24.

47. For the former, see Jacob Hacker and Paul Pierson, *Off Center: The Republican Revolution and the Erosion of American Democracy* (New Haven, CT: Yale University Press, 2005); and Thomas Mann and Norman Ornstein, *It's Even Worse Than It Looks: How the American Constitutional System Collided with the New Politics of Extremism* (New York: Basic Books, 2012). For a taste of the latter, see Stefan Halper and Jonathan Clarke, *The Silence of the Rational Center* (New York: Basic Books, 2007).

48. Marina Azzimonti, "Partisan Conflict," Federal Reserve Bank of Philadelphia Working Paper No. 14–19, June 2014.

49. Pew Research Center, "Political Polarization in the American Public," June 12, 2014, available at http://www.people-press.org/2014/06/12/political-polarization-in-the-american-public/.

50. Joseph Bafumi and Michael C. Herron, "Leapfrog Representation and Extremism: A Study of American Voters and Their Members in Congress," *American Political Science Review* 104 (September

2010): 519–542; see also Marc J. Hetherington, "Resurgent Mass Partisanship: The Role of Elite Polarization," *American Political Science Review* 95 (September 2001): 619–631.

51. Pew Research Center, "Political Polarization in the American Public."

52. Andrew Garner and Harvey Palmer, "Polarization and Issue Consistency over Time," *Political Behavior* 33 (June 2011): 225–246; Edward Carmines, Michael Ensley, and Michael Wagner, "Who Fits the Left-Right Divide? Partisan Polarization in the American Electorate," *American Behavioral Scientist* 56 (October 2012): 1631–1653; Seth J. Hill and Chris Tausanovitch, "A Disconnect in Representation? Comparison of Trends in Congressional and Public Polarization," *Journal of Politics* 77 (December 2015): 1058–1075.

53. Lilliana Mason, "'I Disrespectfully Agree': The Differential Effects of Partisan Sorting on Social and Issue Polarization," *American Journal of Political Science* 59 (January 2015): 128–145.

54. Shanto Iyengar, Gaurav Sood, and Yphtach Lelkes. "Affect, not Ideology: A Social Identity Perspective on Polarization," *Public Opinion Quarterly* 76 (Fall 2012): 405–431.

55. Daron Shaw, "If Everyone Votes Their Party, Why Do Presidential Election Outcomes Vary So Much?," *The Forum* 10 (October 2012).

56. Pew, "Political Polarization in the American Public."

57. Shanto Iyengar and Sean Westwood, "Fear and Loathing across Party Lines: New Evidence on Group Polarization," *American Journal of Political Science* 59 (July 2015): 690–707.

58. Quoted in Marc Fisher, "The Evolution of David Brooks," *Moment*, January/February 2016.

59. Cass Sunstein, *Republic.com 2.0* (Princeton, NJ: Princeton University Press, 2009).

60. Julian Sanchez, "Frum, Cocktail Parties, and the Threat of Doubt," March 26, 2010, accessed at http://www.juliansanchez.com/2010/03/26/frum-cocktail-parties-and-the-threat-of-doubt/.

61. Paul Krugman, "Other Stuff I Read," *New York Times*, March 8, 2011.

62. Andrea Nuesser, Richard Johnston, and Marc A. Bodet, "The Dynamics of Polarization and Depolarization: Methodological Considerations and European Evidence," presented at the American Political Science Association annual meeting, Washington, DC, August 2014; Larry M. Bartels, "Party Systems and Political Change in Europe," presented at the American Political Science Association annual meeting, Chicago, August 2013.

63. Tom Pepinsky, "The Global Economic Crisis and the Politics of Non-Transitions," *Government and Opposition* 47 (April 2012): 135–161.

64. Clifford Bob, *The Global Right Wing and the Clash of World Politics* (New York: Cambridge University Press, 2012).

65. Gabrielle Tétrault-Farber, "Russian, European Far-Right Parties Converge in St. Petersburg," *Moscow Times*, March 22, 2015; Rosie Gray, "U.S.

Journalist Regrets Attending Conspiracy Conference in Tehran," *BuzzFeed*, October 6, 2014.

66. An obvious exception is if an intellectual from the other side of the spectrum breaks ranks to agree to a particular issue.

67. Brendan Nyhan and Jason Reifler, "When Corrections Fail: The Persistence of Political Misperceptions," *Political Behavior* 32 (June 2010): 303–330.

68. Dinesh D'Souza, *Illiberal Education: The Politics of Race and Sex on Campus* (New York: Free Press, 1991).

69. Mark Stricherz, "What Happened to Dinesh D'Souza?," *The Atlantic*, July 25, 2014.

70. Dinesh D'Souza, *The End of Racism* (New York: Free Press, 1995); D'Souza, *The Enemy at Home: The Cultural Left and its Responsibility for 9/11* (New York: Doubleday, 2007); D'Souza, *The Roots of Obama's Rage* (New York: Regnery, 2010); D'Souza, *Obama's America: Unmaking the American Dream* (New York: Regnery, 2012).

71. Evgenia Peretz, "Dinesh D'Souza's Life after Conviction," *Vanity Fair*, May 2015. Indeed, according to Andrew Sullivan, D'Souza's nickname in *New Republic* offices after that book came out was "Distort Denewsa."

72. Andrew Ferguson, "The Roots of Lunacy," *The Weekly Standard*, October 25, 2010.

73. Peretz, "Dinesh D'Souza's Life after Conviction."

74. Stricherz, "What Happened to Dinesh D'Souza?"

75. Sam Tannenhaus, "Dinesh D'Souza Is Planning His Prison Memoir," *New Republic*, September 16, 2014.

76. See the discussion of the economy of speaking engagements in Chapter 7.

77. Jonathan Mahler, "Heady Summer, Fateful Fall for Dinesh D'Souza, a Conservative Firebrand," *New York Times*, July 24, 2014.

78. David Weigel, "Dinesh D'Souza and the Soft Bigotry of Low Expectations," *Slate*, July 25, 2014.

79. See, for example, Ramesh Ponnuru, "Explaining Obama," *Claremont Review*, May 2, 2011.

80. Pamela Geller, "The Political Persecution of Dinesh D'Souza," *Breitbart*, July 15, 2015; Andrew McArthy, "How Dinesh D'Souza Became a Victim of Obama's Lawless Administration," *National Review*, December 19, 2015.

81. Charles A. Kupchan and Peter L. Trubowitz, "Dead Center: The Demise of Liberal Internationalism in the United States," *International Security* 32 (Fall 2007): 7–44; Joshua W. Busby and Jonathan Monten, "Without Heirs? Assessing the Decline of Establishment Internationalism in US Foreign Policy," *Perspectives on Politics* 6 (September 2008): 451–472; Helen V. Milner and Dustin H. Tingley, "Who Supports Global

Economic Engagement? The Sources of Preferences in American Foreign Economic Policy," *International Organization* 65 (January 2011): 37–68;

82. Kupchan and Trubowitz, "Dead Center," 9.

83. Dina Smeltz, Ivo Daalder, Karl Friedhoff, and Craig Kafura, *America Divided: Political Partisanship and US Foreign Policy* (Chicago: Chicago Council on Global Affairs, 2015).

84. Alexandra Guisinger and Elizabeth Saunders, "Mapping the Boundaries of Elite Cues: How Elites Shape Mass Opinion Across International Issues," working paper, George Washington University, April 2016.

85. Thomas Piketty, *Capital in the Twenty-First Century* (Cambridge, MA: Belknap Press, 2014), Figure 8.5.

86. Ibid., Figure 8.6.

87. Brenda Cronin, "Some 95% of 2009–2012 Income Gains Went to Wealthiest 1%," *Wall Street Journal*, September 10, 2013.

88. Atif Mian and Amir Sufi, "Measuring Wealth Inequality," *House of Debt* (blog), March 29, 2014, accessed at http://houseofdebt.org/2014/03/29/measuring-wealth-inequality.html; see also Derek Thompson, "How You, I, and Everyone Got the Top 1 Percent All Wrong," *The Atlantic*, March 30, 2014.

89. Credit Suisse Research Institute, *Global Wealth Report 2014*, 28–30.

90. Ibid., 27.

91. Elhannan Helpman, *The Mystery of Economic Growth* (Cambridge, MA: Belknap Press, 2004); Piketty, *Capital in the Twenty-First Century.*

92. For an interesting debate on this very question, see Daron Acemoglu and James Robinson, "The Rise and Decline of General Laws of Capitalism," *Journal of Economic Perspectives* 29 (January 2015): 3–28; and Thomas Piketty, "Putting Distribution Back at the Center of Economics: Reflections on *Capital in the Twenty-First Century*," *Journal of Economic Perspectives* 29 (January 2015): 67–88.

93. Fay Lomax Cook, Benjamin I. Page, and Rachel Moskowitz, "Political Engagement by Wealthy Americans," *Political Science Quarterly* 129 (Fall 2014): 396.

94. Benjamin I. Page, Larry M. Bartels, and Jason Seawright, "Democracy and the Policy Preferences of Wealthy Americans," *Perspectives on Politics* 11 (March 2013): 54–55.

95. Nicholas Confessore, "The Families Funding the 2016 Election," *New York Times*, October 10, 2015. See also, more generally, Benjamin I. Page, Jason Seawright, and Matthew LaCombe, "Stealth Politics by U.S. Billionaires," paper presented at the 2015 annual meeting at the American Political Science Association, San Francisco, CA.

96. Matea Gold and Anu Narayanswany, "The New Gilded Age: Close to Half of All Super-PAC money Comes from 50 Donors," *Washington Post*, April 15, 2016.

97.   Gallup, "Satisfaction with the United States," available at http://www.
       gallup.com/poll/1669/general-mood-country.aspx.

98.   David Rothkopf, *Superclass* (New York: Farrar Strauss Giroux,
       2008); Rubin Rogers, "Why Philanthro-Policymaking Matters,"
       Society 48 (September 2011): 376–381; Chrystia Freeland, *Plutocrats*
       (New York: Penguin, 2012); Gara Lamarche, "Democracy and the
       Donor Class," *Democracy* 34 (Fall 2014): 48–59; Alessandra Stanley,
       "Silicon Valley's New Philanthropy," *New York Times*, October 31,
       2015; Kristin Goss, "Policy Plutocrats: How America's Wealthy Seek
       to Influence Governance," *PS: Political Science and Politics* 49 (July
       2016): 442–448.

99.   On the Big History Project and his love of Common Core, see Andrew
       Ross Sorkin, "So Bill Gates Has This Idea for a History Class . . .,"
       New York Times Magazine, September 5, 2014. On Common Core, see
       Lyndsey Layton, "How Bill Gates Pulled Off the Swift Common Core
       Revolution," *Washington Post*, June 7, 2014.

100.   Richard Pérez-Pena, "Facebook Founder to Donate $100 Million to Help
       Remake Newark's Schools," *New York Times*, September 22, 2010; Amit
       Chowdhry, "Mark Zuckerberg Starts a Book Club as His New Year's
       Resolution," *Forbes*, January 5, 2015.

101.   Stephen Foley, "Lunch with the FT: Charles Koch," *Financial Times*,
       January 8, 2016.

102.   See, for example, Andrew Carnegie, "Wealth," *North American Review* 148
       (June 1889): 653–664.

103.   Quoted in Paul Weingarten, "Chicago's Billion-Dollar Baby," *Chicago
       Tribune*, May 9, 1982. It should be noted that the first generation of
       plutocrats, like the current crop, strongly believed in "giving while
       living" and in directing their foundations to pursue specific policy aims.
       See Carnegie, "Wealth." For a more radical take, see Inderjeet Parmar,
       Foundations of the American Century (New York: Columbia University
       Press, 2012).

104.   Adam Meyerson, "When Philanthropy Goes Wrong," *Wall Street Journal*,
       March 9, 2012. See also Naomi Schaefer Riley and James Piereson, "What
       Today's Philanthropoids Could Learn from Andrew Carnegie," *National
       Review*, December 22, 2015.

105.   Sean Parker, "Philanthropy for Hackers," *Wall Street Journal*, June
       26, 2015.

106.   For a fuller explanation of the sociology of venture philanthropy, see
       Matthew Bishop and Michael Green, *Philanthrocapitalism: How the
       Rich Can Save the World* (New York: Bloomsbury Press, 2008); and
       Darrell West, *Billionaires: Reflections on the Upper Crust* (Washington,
       DC: Brookings Institution Press, 2014).

107.   Rogers, "Why Philanthro-Policymaking Matters," 378.

108.   Quoted in Stanley, "Silicon Valley's New Philanthropy."

109. Gautam Mukunda, "The Price of Wall Street's Power," *Harvard Business Review* 92 (June 2014): 77.

110. Steven Teles, "Foundations, Organizational Maintenance, and Partisan Asymmetry," *PS: Political Science and Politics* 49 (July 2016): 457. See also Jeffrey Berry, "Negative Returns: The Impact of Impact Investing on Empowerment and Advocacy," *PS: Political Science and Politics* 49 (July 2016): 437–441.

111. Kavita Ramdas, "Philanthrocapitalism: Reflections on Politics and Policy Making," *Society* 48 (September 2011): 395.

112. West, *Billionaires*, 9.

113. Page, Bartels, and Seawright, "Democracy and the Policy Preferences of Wealthy Americans."

114. See, for example, Robert Frank, "For the New Superrich, Life is Much More Than a Beach," *New York Times*, June 20, 2015.

115. Freeland, *Plutocrats*, 67.

116. Ibid. See also West, *Billionaires*.

117. Rael J. Dawtry, Robbie M. Sutton, and Chris G. Sibley, "Why Wealthier People Think People Are Wealthier, and Why It Matters: From Social Sampling to Redistributive Attitudes," *Psychological Science* 26 (September 2015): 1389–1400.

118. Stéphane Côté, Julian Hose, and Robb Willer, "High Economic Inequality Leads Higher-Income Individuals to Be Less Generous," *Proceedings of the National Academy of Sciences* 112 (November 2015): 15838–15843.

119. Musk quoted in Leila Janah, "Shouldn't We Fix Poverty before Migrating to Mars?," *Medium*, May 27, 2015, accessed at https://medium.com/@leilajanah/migration-is-the-story-of-my-life-my-parents-and-grandparents-journeyed-across-four-continents-to-2ef2ced74bf#.yx7wtrxyq.

120. Thomas Perkins, "Progressive Kristallnacht Coming?," letter to the *Wall Street Journal*, January 24, 2014. For a related example, see Monica Langley, "Texas Billionaire Doles Out Election's Biggest Checks," *Wall Street Journal*, January 22, 2013.

121. All results from Greg Ferenstein, "What Silicon Valley Really Thinks about Politics," *Medium*, November 6, 2015, accessed at https://medium.com/the-ferenstein-wire/what-silicon-valley-really-thinks-about-politics-an-attempted-measurement-d37ed96a9251#.yvzcss002.

122. See Daniel W. Drezner, *All Politics Is Global* (Princeton, NJ: Princeton University Press, 2007).

123. George Packer, "Change the World," *New Yorker*, May 27, 2013. See also Evgeny Morozov, *To Save Everything, Click Here* (New York: PublicAffairs, 2013); and David Roberts, "Tech Nerds Are Smart. But They Can't Seem to Get Their Heads around Politics," *Vox*, August 27, 2015.

124. David Frum, "The Great Republican Revolt," *The Atlantic*, January–February 2016.

125. Richard Hoftstadter, *Anti-Intellectualism in American Life* (New York: Random House, 1962); Samuel Huntington, *American Politics: The Promise of Disharmony* (Cambridge, MA: Belknap, 1981).

126. Edward G. Andrew, *Patrons of Enlightenment* (Toronto: University of Toronto Press, 2006).

127. Daniel Hirschman, "Stylized Facts in the Social Sciences," *Sociological Science* 3 (July 2016): 604–626.

128. Drezner, *The System Worked*, 191.

129. Nathan Heller, "Listen and Learn," *New Yorker*, July 9, 2012.

Chapter 3

1. Nicholas Kristof, "Professors, We Need You!," *New York Times*, February 15, 2014.

2. Alan Wolfe, "Reality in Political Science," *Chronicle of Higher Education*, November 4, 2005; Joseph Nye, "Scholars on the Sidelines," *Washington Post*, April 13, 2009; Robert Gallucci, "How Scholars Can Improve International Relations," *Chronicle of Higher Education*, November 26, 2012.

3. Vernon Louis Parrrington, *Main Currents in American Thought, Volume III* (New York: Harcourt, Brace, 1930), xxvii. Quoted in Robert S. Lynd, *Knowledge for What: The Place of Social Science in American Culture* (Princeton, NJ: Princeton University Press, 1939), 4.

4. Josh Marshall, "Goodbye to All That—Why I Left the Academic Life," *Talking Points Memo*, February 24, 2014.

5. Tweets accessed at https://twitter.com/RichardHaass/status/435605662199201793; https://twitter.com/djrothkopf/status/435028506984980480. Given that I was a contributing editor at *Foreign Policy* at the time, and writing a weekly column for them, this pronouncement came as something of a surprise. To save Rothkopf some time with his dialing back, I quit *Foreign Policy* soon afterwards.

6. Erik Voeten, "Dear Nicholas Kristof: We Are Right Here!," *Washington Post*, February 15, 2014.

7. Ibid. See also Samuel Goldman, "Where Have All the Public Intellectuals Gone?," *The American Conservative*, February 17, 2014; Corey Robin, "Look Who Nick Kristof's Saving Now," February 16, 2014, accessed at http://coreyrobin.com/2014/02/16/look-who-nick-kristofs-saving-now/; Wei Zhu, "Are Academics Cloistered?," *The Immanent Frame* (blog), March 5, 2014, accessed at http://blogs.ssrc.org/tif/2014/03/05/are-academics-cloistered/.

8. See, on this point, Michael Horowitz, "What Is Policy Relevance?," *War on the Rocks*, June 17, 2015.

9. Erica Chenoweth, "A Note on Academic (Ir)relevance," *Political Violence at a Glance* (blog), February 17, 2014, accessed at http://

politicalviolenceataglance.org/2014/02/17/a-note-on-academic-irrelevance/.

10. Kristof's first quote is from his Facebook response to the column, accessed at https://www.facebook.com/kristof/posts/10153827908840389; Joshua Rothman, "Why Is Academic Writing so Academic?," *The New Yorker*, February 20, 2014; personal email correspondence with Kristof, July 10, 2015.

11. Russell Jacoby, *The Last Intellectuals: American Culture in the Age of Academe* (New York: Basic Books, 1987), 5. For a more recent iteration of this argument, see Craig Timberg, *Culture Crash: The Killing of the Creative Class* (New Haven, CT: Yale University Press, 2015).

12. Jacoby, *The Last Intellectuals*, 220.

13. Bruce Kuklick, *Blind Oracles: Intellectuals and War from Kennan to Kissinger* (Princeton, NJ: Princeton University Press, 2006), chapter 1; Michael Desch, *The Relevance Question: Social Science's Inconstant Embrace of Security Studies*, forthcoming.

14. Rebecca Lowen, *Creating the Cold War University* (Los Angeles: University of California Press, 1997).

15. C. Wright Mills, *The Power Elite* (New York: Oxford University Press, 1958), 217.

16. Lowen, *Creating the Cold War University*; Edward Shils, "Intellectuals, Tradition, and the Traditions of Intellectuals: Some Preliminary Considerations," *Daedalus* 101 (Spring 1972): 21–34; Thomas Mahnken, "Bridging the Gap between the Worlds of Ideas and Action," *Orbis* 54 (Winter 2010): 4–13.

17. Robert Jervis, "Security Studies: Ideas, Policy, and Politics," in *The Evolution of Political Knowledge: Democracy, Autonomy and Conflict in Comparative and International Politics*, ed. Edward Mansfield and Richard Sisson (Columbus: Ohio State University Press, 2004), 101.

18. Charles King, "The Decline of International Studies," *Foreign Affairs* 94 (July/August 2015): 90.

19. Fred Kaplan, *The Wizards of Armageddon* (New York: Simon and Schuster, 1983); William Poundstone, *Prisoner's Dilemma* (New York: Doubleday, 1992); Lowen, *Creating the Cold War University*; S. M. Amadae, *Rationalizing Capitalist Democracy: The Cold War Origins of Rational Choice Liberalism* (Chicago: University of Chicago Press, 2003).

20. Theodore White, "The Action Intellectuals," *Life*, June 9, 1967, 48.

21. Irving Howe, "This Age of Conformity," *Partisan Review* 21(1): 13 and 26.

22. Seymour Martin Lipset and Richard Dobson, "The Intellectual as Critic and Rebel: With Special Reference to the United States and the Soviet Union," *Daedalus* 101 (Summer 1972): 137–198. The removal of the New York intellectuals from the market was also somewhat exaggerated. On this point, see Irving Howe, "The

New York Intellectuals: A Chronicle and a Critique," *Commentary*, October 1, 1968.

23. Noam Chomsky, "The Responsibility of Intellectuals," *New York Review of Books*, February 23, 1967.

24. See Brooks, *Bobos in Paradise*, 142–145.

25. Andrew Bennett and G. John Ikenberry, "The *Review*'s Evolving Relevance for US Foreign Policy 1906–2006," *American Political Science Review* 100 (November 2006): 651–658.

26. Schelling quoted in Gregg Herken, *Counsels of War* (New York: Knopf, 1985), 313.

27. Jacoby, *The Last Intellectuals*, 190.

28. Shils, "Intellectuals, Tradition, and the Traditions of Intellectuals"; Mark Lilla, *The Reckless Mind: Intellectuals in Politics* (New York: NYRB, 2001).

29. Lipset and Dobson, "The Intellectual as Critic and Rebel," 146–47.

30. See also Stephen Walt, "The Relationship between Theory and Policy in International Relations," *Annual Review of Political Science* 8 (2005): 41; Ernest J. Wilson III, "Is There Really a Scholar-Practitioner Gap? An Institutional Analysis," *PS: Political Science and Politics* 40 (January 2007): 147–151.

31. Daniel Byman and Matthew Kroenig, "Reaching beyond the Ivory Tower: A How To Manual," *Security Studies* 25 (May 2016): 309.

32. Francis Fukuyama, "The End of History?," *The National Interest* 16 (Summer 1989): 3–18; Fukuyama, *The End of History and the Last Man* (New York: Free Press, 1992); John J. Mearsheimer, "Why We Will Soon Miss the Cold War," *The Atlantic Monthly* 266 (August 1990): 35–50; Mearsheimer, "Back to the Future: Instability in Europe after the Cold War," *International Security* 15 (Summer 1990): 5–56; Joseph Nye, "Soft Power," *Foreign Policy* 80 (Autumn 1990): 153–171; Nye, *Bound to Lead: The Changing Nature of American Power* (New York: Basic Books, 1990); Samuel Huntington, "The Clash of Civilizations?," *Foreign Affairs* 72 (Summer 1993): 22–49; Huntington, *The Clash of Civilizations and the Remaking of World Order* (New York: Simon and Schuster, 1996); Michael Brown, Sean Lynn-Jones, and Steven Miller, eds., *Debating the Democratic Peace* (Cambridge, MA: MIT Press, 1996); Charles Krauthammer, "The Unipolar Moment," *Foreign Affairs* 70 (1990/1991): 23–33.

33. Stephen Walt, "Theory and Policy in International Relations: Some Personal Reflections," *Yale Journal of International Affairs* 7 (September 2012): 39.

34. Nye has published numerous iterations of his "soft power" thesis. Huntington participated in multiple symposia on the clash of civilizations, and wrote an even more controversial sequel to that work. Fukuyama has been commissioned to write essays commemorating "End of History" anniversaries. And the debate over the sustainability of the

democratic peace has been a staple of international relations scholarship for decades.

35. Christopher J. Fettweis, "Evaluating IR's Crystal Balls: How Predictions of the Future Have Withstood Fourteen Years of Unipolarity," *International Studies Review* 6 (Winter 2004): 79–104.

36. Steven Pinker, *The Better Angels of Our Nature: The Decline of Violence in History and Its Causes* (London: Penguin, 2011); Joshua S. Goldstein, *Winning the War on War: The Decline of Armed Conflict Worldwide* (New York: Penguin, 2011).

37. Quoted in Steven Del Rosso, "Our New Three Rs: Rigor, Relevance, and Readability," *Governance* 28 (April 2015): 127.

38. Francis Fukuyama, *Political Order and Political Decay* (New York: Farrar Strauss Giroux, 2014).

39. Joseph Nye, "The Decline of America's Soft Power," *Foreign Affairs* 83 (May/June 2004): 16–21.

40. King, "The Decline of International Studies."

41. Daniel W. Drezner, "The Realist Tradition in American Public Opinion," *Perspectives on Politics* 6 (March 2008): 51–70; John E. Rielly, ed., *American Public Opinion and U.S. Foreign Policy 1999* (Chicago: Chicago Council on Foreign Relations, 1999), 8.

42. David Abel, "War's Fall from Grace," *Boston Globe*, January 30, 2001.

43. Chaim Kaufmann, "Threat Inflation and the Failure of the Marketplace of Ideas: The Selling of the Iraq War," *International Security* 29 (Summer 2004): 45.

44. Fred Kaplan, *The Insurgents: David Petraeus and the Plot to Change the American Way of War* (New York: Simon and Schuster, 2013).

45. "The Minerva Initiative," accessed at http://minerva.dtic.mil/overview. html.

46. Gates's April 14, 2008, speech to the Association of American Universities can be accessed at http://archive.defense.gov/Speeches/Speech. aspx?SpeechID=128. See also Patricia Cohen, "Pentagon to Consult Academics on Security," *New York Times*, June 18, 2008.

47. Cohen, "Pentagon to Consult Academics on Security." See also Scott Jaschik, "Embedded Conflicts," *Inside Higher Ed*, July 7, 2015.

48. David Milne, "America's 'Intellectual' Diplomacy," *International Affairs* 86 (January 2010): 49–68.

49. Lynn Vavreck and Steve Friess, "An Interview with Lynn Vavreck," *PS: Political Science and Politics* 48 (September 2015): 43–46; Stephen M. Walt, "How to Get Tenure," *Foreign Policy*, February 17, 2016.

50. This is true even in public policy schools, which are ostensibly more concerned about the policy impact of scholarship.

51. There is money to be made by some enterprising university-affiliated person to act as a conduit between academic publications and journalists

interested in reading them. Or, in return, business journalists could provide interested academics with research notes from financial firms.

52.   See, for example, Douglas A. Borer, "Rejected by the *New York Times*? Why Academics Struggle to Get Published in National Newspapers," *International Studies Perspectives* 7 (September 2006): vii–x.

53.   Steven Pinker, "Why Academics Stink at Writing," *Chronicle of Higher Education*, September 26, 2014, quoted in Victoria Clayton, "The Needless Complexity of Academic Writing," *The Atlantic*, October 26, 2015.

54.   See, for example, Peter Dreier, "Academic Drivel Report," *The American Prospect*, February 22, 2016.

55.   I've written enough for the popular press to recognize print media terms like "lede" and "tk" and "kicker," but to the lay person they are gobbledygook.

56.   Vavreck and Friess, "An Interview with Lynn Vavreck," 43.

57.   Rose McDermott, "Learning to Communicate Better with the Press and the Public," *PS: Political Science and Politics* 48 (September 2015): 86.

58.   George Orwell, "Politics and the English Language," in *Why I Write* (New York: Penguin Books, 1984), 120.

59.   One could argue that a hidden strength of Donald Trump's presidential campaign was that while he was not always factually correct, his plain language nonetheless resonated with voters. See Salena Zito, "Take Trump Seriously, Not Literally," *The Atlantic*, September 23, 2016.

60.   They also hired me after I quit *Foreign Policy*.

61.   See, for example, Kieran Healy, "Public Sociology in the Age of Social Media," *Perspectives on Politics*, forthcoming.

62.   Walt, "The Relationship between Theory and Policy in International Relations," 38.

63.   Lest one think my case was unusual, Kathleen McNamara received a similar reprimand from Princeton for publishing in *Foreign Affairs* five years before me. See Alexander Kafka, "How the Monkey Cage Went Ape," *Chronicle of Higher Education*, January 10, 2016.

64.   Scott Jaschik, "Too Much Information?," *Inside Higher Ed*, October 11, 2005; Steve Johnson, "Did Blogging Doom Prof's Shot at Tenure?," *Chicago Tribune*, October 14, 2005; Robert Boynton, "Attack of the Career-Killing Blogs," *Slate*, November 16, 2005.

65.   Ivan Tribble, "Bloggers Need Not Apply," *Chronicle of Higher Education*, July 8, 2005; Tribble, "They Shoot Messengers, Don't They?," *Chronicle of Higher Education*, September 2, 2005; Jeffrey Young, "How Not to Lose Face on Facebook, for Professors," *Chronicle of Higher Education*, February 6, 2009. The warnings include the perils of offending senior scholars, revealing one's political partisanship, and being perceived as investing too much time in a non-scholarly activity to the detriment of the traditional scholarly responsibilities. See Christine Hurt and Tung

Yin, "Blogging While Untenured and Other Extreme Sports," *Washington University Law Review* 84 (April 2006): 1235–1255. Some bloggers quit due to the pressures of conventional academic work. See James Lang, "Putting the Blog on Hold," *Chronicle of Higher Education*, January 12, 2007. Others expressed the fear that integrating new forms of information technology into their professional activities had cost them. See Brandon Withrow, "Not Your Father's Ph.D.," *Chronicle of Higher Education*, April 18, 2008.

66. Cheryl Boudreau, "Read but Not Heard? Engaging Junior Scholars in Efforts to Make Political Science Relevant," *PS: Political Science and Politics* 48 (September 2015): 51.

67. Vavreck and Friess, "An Interview with Lynn Vavreck," 44. See also Walt, "How to Get Tenure."

68. Boudreau, "Read but Not Heard?"

69. Charli Carpenter and Daniel W. Drezner, "International Relations 2.0: The Implications of New Media for an Old Profession," *International Studies Perspectives* 11 (August 2010): 255–272.

70. John Kenneth Galbraith, "Writing, Typing, and Economics," *The Atlantic*, March 1978, 104.

71. Boudreau, "Read but Not Heard?," 52.

72. Galbraith, "Writing, Typing, and Economics." See also Kieran Healy, "Fuck Nuance," *Sociological Theory*, forthcoming.

73. And in my experience, if there is one thing professors are loath to say out loud, it is "I'm confused."

74. Theda Skocpol, "How the Scholars Strategy Network Helps Academics Gain Public Influence," *Perspectives on Politics* 12 (September 2014): 695–703.

75. Lawrence Mead, "Scholasticism in Political Science," *Perspectives on Politics* 8 (June 2010), 459.

76. See results at https://trip.wm.edu/reports/2014/rp_2014/index.php.

77. Daniel Maliniak, Sue Peterson, and Michael Tierney, "TRIP Around the World," accessed at http://www.wm.edu/offices/itpir/_documents/trip/trip_around_the_world_2011.pdf.

78. James Fearon, "Data on the Relevance of Political Scientists to the NYT," *Washington Post*, February 23, 2014.

79. Ezra Klein, "Poli Sci 101: Presidential Speeches Don't Matter, and Lobbyists Don't Run D.C.," *Washington Post*, September 12, 2010; Klein, "How Political Science Conquered Washington," *Vox*, September 2, 2014.

80. Greg Lukianoff and Jonathan Haidt, "The Coddling of the American Mind," *The Atlantic*, September 2015.

81. See Morton Schapiro, "The New Face of Campus Unrest," *Wall Street Journal*, March 18, 2015; Judith Shulivetz, "In College and Hiding from Scary Ideas," *New York Times*, March 21, 2015; Edward Schlosser, "I'm a Liberal Professor, and My Liberal Students Terrify Me," *Vox*, June 3, 2015; Nathan Heller, "The Big Uneasy," *New Yorker*, May 30, 2016.

82. Laura Kipnis, "My Title IX Inquisition," *Chronicle of Higher Education*, May 29, 2015; Jake New, "Defunding for Diversity," *Inside Higher Ed*, September 23, 2015; Catherine Rampell, "Free Speech is Flunking Out on College Campuses," *Washington Post*, October 22, 2015.

83. For a sampling, see Louis Menand, *The Marketplace of Ideas* (New York: W. W. Norton, 2010); Benjamin Ginsberg, *The Fall of the Faculty: The Rise of the All-Administrative University and Why It Matters* (New York: Oxford University Press, 2011); Mark C. Taylor, *Crisis on Campus* (New York: Knopf, 2011); William Deresiewicz, *Excellent Sheep: The Miseducation of the American Elite and the Way to a Meaningful Life* (New York: Simon and Schuster, 2014).

84. Deresiewicz, *Excellent Sheep*.

85. William Deresiewicz, "The Neoliberal Arts," *Harper's*, September 2015.

86. Fredrik DeBoer, "Closed Campus," *New York Times Magazine*, September 13, 2015. See also Rebecca Schuman, "College Students Are Not Customers," *Slate*, May 20, 2015; Jeffrey Di Leo, "Public Intellectuals, Inc.," *Inside Higher Ed*, February 4, 2008; Ginsberg, *The Fall of the Faculty*.

87. Lukianoff and Haidt, "The Coddling of the American Mind."

88. Jessica Carrick-Hagenbarth and Gerald A. Epstein, "Dangerous Interconnectedness: Economists' Conflicts of Interest, Ideology and Financial Crisis," *Cambridge Journal of Economics* 36 (January 2012): 43–63. See also Neil Parmar, "Beware of 'Independent' Investing Research," *Wall Street Journal*, August 15, 2010.

89. Benedict Carey and Pam Belluck, "Doubts about Study of Gay Canvassers Rattle the Field," *New York Times*, May 25, 2015.

90. Adam Marcus and Ivan Oransky, "What's Behind Big Science Frauds?," *New York Times*, May 22, 2015.

91. Andrew C. Chang and Phillip Li, "Is Economics Research Replicable? Sixty Published Papers from Thirteen Journals Say 'Usually Not,'" Finance and Economics Discussion Series 2015–083, Board of Governors of the Federal Reserve System, October 2015, http://dx.doi.org/10.17016/FEDS.2015.083, 3.

92. Open Science Collaboration, "Estimating the Reproducibility of Psychological Science," *Science* 349 (August 28, 2015): 4716. For press coverage of that finding, see Benedict Carey, "Many Psychology Findings Not as Strong as Claimed, Study Says," *New York Times*, August 27, 2015. For the critique, see Daniel Gilbert, Gary King, Stephen Pettigrew, and Timothy Wilson, "Comment on 'Estimating the Reproducibility of Psychological Science,'" *Science* 351 (March 4, 2016): 1037a.

93. See, for example, Jeffrey Isaac, "For a More *Public* Political Science," *Perspectives on Politics* 13 (June 2015): 269–283.

94. Nicholas Kristof, "A Confession of Liberal Intolerance," *New York Times*, May 9, 2016; Kristof, "The Dangers of Echo Chambers on Campus," *New York Times*, December 10, 2016.

95. On campaign contributions, see Andy Kierscz and Hunter Walker, "These Three Charts Confirm Conservatives' Worst Fears about American Culture," *Business Insider*, November 3, 2014.

96. Heterodox Academy, "The Problem," accessed at http://heterodoxacademy.org/problems/. See also Scott Jaschik, "Moving Further to the Left," *Inside Higher Ed*, October 24, 2012.

97. Reprinted as Max Weber, "Science as a Vocation," *Daedalus* 87 (Winter 1958): 111–134.

98. Phoebe Maltz-Bovy, "Straight Outta Chappaqua," *Tablet*, January 7, 2015.

99. José L. Duarte et al., "Political Diversity Will Improve Social Psychological Science," *Behavioral and Brain Sciences* 38 (January 2015): 5.

100. Chris Martin, "How Ideology Has Hindered Sociological Insight," *The American Sociologist* 47 (March 2016): 115–130.

101. For international relations, see Brian Rathbun, "Politics and Paradigm Preferences: The Implicit Ideology of International Relations Scholars," *International Studies Quarterly* 56 (September 2012): 607–622. For law, see Adam S. Chilton and Eric A. Posner, "An Empirical Study of Political Bias in Legal Scholarship," Coase-Sandor Institute for Law and Economics Research Paper No. 696, University of Chicago, August 2014.

102. Anemona Hartocollis, "College Students Protest, Alumni's Fondness Fades and Checks Shrink," *New York Times*, August 4, 2016.

103. Paul Brest and Hal Harvey, *Money Well Spent* (New York: Bloomberg Press, 2008).

104. West, *Billionaires*, 85.

105. Glenn Reynolds, "Scott Walker's National Education Effect," *USA Today*, February 15, 2015. On the evidence supporting the economic benefits of a college degree, see Pew Research Center, "The Rising Cost of Not Going to College," February 11, 2014, accessed at http://www.pewsocialtrends.org/2014/02/11/the-rising-cost-of-not-going-to-college/.

106. See the Thiel Fellowship's June 2015 press release archived at http://www.thielfellowship.org/2015/06/2015-thiel-fellows-press-release/.

107. Transcript of Kristol's interview with Thiel can be accessed at http://conversationswithbillkristol.org/wp-content/uploads/2014/09/Thiel_conversations_transcript.pdf.

108. Peter Thiel, "Thinking Too Highly of Higher Ed," *Washington Post*, November 21, 2014; Conor Friedersdorf, "Peter Thiel Compares Elite Education to a Night Club with a Long Line," *The Atlantic*, June 1, 2015.

109. Weber, "Science as a Vocation," 125 and 128.

110. Corey Robin, "How Intellectuals Create a Public," *Chronicle of Higher Education*, January 22, 2016.

111. Tom Wolfe, "In the Land of the Rococo Marxists," *Harper's*, June 2000, 82.

Chapter 4

1. Nicholas Kristof, "Professors, We Need You!," *New York Times*, February 15, 2014.
2. Tom Ricks, "Given All That Is Going On, Why Is *International Security* So Damn Boring?," *Foreign Policy*, September 15, 2014.
3. Robert Putnam "The Public Role of Political Science," *Perspective on Politics* 1 (June 2003), 250.
4. Steven Van Evera, "U.S. Social Science and International Relations," *War on the Rocks*, February 9, 2015; Michael Desch, "Technique Trumps Relevance: The Professionalization of Political Science and the Marginalization of Security Studies," *Perspectives on Politics* 13 (June 2015), 378.
5. Charles Beard, "Time, Technology, and the Creative Spirit in Political Science," *American Political Science Review* 21 (February 1927): 8; Robert S. Lynd, *Knowledge for What: The Place of Social Science in American Culture* (Princeton, NJ: Princeton University Press, 1939), 138–39; David Easton, "The Decline of Modern Political Theory," *Journal of Politics* 13 (February 1951): 48.
6. Paul Krugman, "Economic Culture Wars," *Slate*, October 25, 1996.
7. Beard, "Time, Technology, and the Creative Spirit in Political Science," 10; John Kenneth Galbraith, "Power and the Useful Economist," *American Economic Review* 63 (March 1973): 6; Gordon Tullock, "Economic Imperialism," in *Theory of Public Choice*, ed. James Buchanan (Ann Arbor: University of Michigan Press, 1972), 325.
8. Marion Fourcade, Etienne Ollion, and Yann Algan, "The Superiority of Economists," *Journal of Economic Perspectives* 29 (January 2015), 89.
9. Dani Rodrik, *Economics Rules: The Rights and Wrongs of the Dismal Science* (New York: W. W. Norton, 2015), 80.
10. Ibid., 110.
11. John Balz, "The Absent Professor," *Washington Monthly*, January/February/March 2008.
12. Henry Farrell and John Quiggin, "Consensus, Dissensus and Economic Ideas: The Rise and Fall of Keynesianism During the Economic Crisis," manuscript, George Washington University, fall 2013; Drezner, *The System Worked*, chapter 6.
13. Patrick Thaddeus Jackson and Stuart J. Kaufman, "Security Scholars for a Sensible Foreign Policy: A Study in Weberian Activism," *Perspectives on Politics* 5 (March 2007): 96.
14. Paul C. Avey and Michael C. Desch, "What Do Policymakers Want from Us? Results of a Survey of Current and Former Senior National Security Decision Makers," *International Studies Quarterly* 58 (December 2014): 227–246.
15. Avey and Desch, "What Do Policymakers Want from Us?"

16. Bruce W. Jentleson and Ely Ratner, "Bridging the Beltway–Ivory Tower Gap," *International Studies Review* 13 (March 2011): 8.

17. Melissa Harris-Perry and Steve Friess, "An Interview with Melissa Harris-Perry," *PS: Political Science and Politics* 48 (September 2015): 28.

18. *Economist*, "Pushback," March 5, 2016; Kieran Healy, "Public Sociology in the Age of Social Media," *Perspectives on Politics*, Figures 1 and 2.

19. Richard Posner, *Public Intellectuals: A Study of Decline* (Cambridge, MA: Harvard University Press, 2000), 215.

20. Karin Frick, Detlef Guertler, and Peter A. Gloor, "Coolhunting for the World's Thought Leaders," accessed at http://www.ickn.org/documents/COINs13_Thoughtleaders4.pdf.

21. Piketty, *Capital in the Twenty-First Century*.

22. American Political Science Association, *Improving Public Perceptions of Political Science's Value* (Washington: APSA, 2014), 15.

23. Stephen Walt, "Theory and Policy in International Relations: Some Personal Reflections," *Yale Journal of International Affairs* 7 (September 2012): 35.

24. Stephen D. Krasner, "The Garbage Can Framework for Locating Policy Planning," in *Avoiding Trivia: The Role of Strategic Planning in American Foreign Policy*, ed. Daniel W. Drezner (Washington, DC: Brookings Institution Press, 2009).

25. Andrew Bennett and G. John Ikenberry, "The *Review*'s Evolving Relevance for US Foreign Policy 1906–2006," *American Political Science Review* 100 (November 2006): 651–658; Daniel Maliniak, Amy Oakes, Susan Peterson, and Michael J. Tierney, "International Relations in the US Academy," *International Studies Quarterly* 55 (June 2011): 437–464.

26. APSA, *Improving Public Perceptions of Political Science's Value*, 11.

27. Cowen quoted in Alexander Kafka, "How the Monkey Cage Went Ape," *Chronicle of Higher Education*, January 10, 2016.

28. Robert E. Lucas, "Macroeconomic Priorities," *American Economic Review* 93 (March 2003): 1.

29. Olivier Blanchard, "The State of Macro," NBER Working Paper No. 14259, August 2008, 2.

30. Nate Silver, *The Signal and the Noise* (New York: Penguin, 2012), 20.

31. See, for example, John Quiggin, *Zombie Economics* (Princeton, NJ: Princeton University Press, 2012).

32. Richard H. Thaler, *Misbehaving: The Making of Behavioral Economics* (New York: W. W. Norton, 2015), 4.

33. Davide Furcer et al., "Where Are We Headed? Perspectives on Potential Output," in *World Economic Outlook* (Washington: International Monetary Fund, 2015).

34. Noah Smith, "Economists' Biggest Failure," BloombergView, March 5, 2015.

35. Quoted in David Colander, "Intellectual Incest on the Charles: Why Economists Are a Little Bit Off," *Eastern Economic Journal* 41 (January 2015): 156.

36. Alberto Alesina and Silvia Ardagna, "Large Changes in Fiscal Policy: Taxes Versus Spending," NBER Working Paper no. 15438, October 2009; Carmen Reinhart and Kenneth Rogoff, "Growth in a Time of Debt," NBER Working Paper No. 15639, January 2010.

37. Paul Krugman, "How the Case for Austerity Has Crumbled," *New York Review of Books*, June 6, 2013.

38. Mark Blyth, *Austerity: The History of a Dangerous Idea* (New York: Oxford University Press, 2013); Drezner, *The System Worked*, chapter 6.

39. Jaime Guajardo, Daniel Leigh, and Andrea Pescatori, "Expansionary austerity? International evidence," Journal of the European Economic Association 12 (August 2014): 949–968; Thomas Herndon, Michael Ash and Robert Pollin, "Does High Public Debt Consistently Stifle Economic Growth? A Critique of Reinhart and Rogoff," Political Economy Research Institute Working Paper no. 322, University of Massachusetts at Amherst, April 2013.

40. Paul Romer, "The Trouble with Macroeconomics," *The American Economist*, forthcoming. See also Olivier Blanchard, "Do DSGE Models Have a Future?," Peterson Institute for International Economic Policy Brief 16-11, August 2016.

41. Luigi Zingales, "Does Finance Benefit Society?," AFA Presidential Address, January 2015, 3, accessed at http://faculty.chicagobooth.edu/luigi.zingales/papers/research/Finance.pdf.

42. Paul Pfleiderer, "Chameleons: The Misuse of Theoretical Models in Finance and Economics," *Revista de Economía Institucional* 16 (July/December 2014): 23–60.

43. Barry Ritholz, "Why Don't Bad Ideas Ever Die?" *Washington Post*, December 15, 2012; Ritholz, "Zombie Ideas That Keep on Losing," BloombergView, October 20, 2014.

44. Raghuram Rajan, *Fault Lines* (Princeton, NJ: Princeton University Press, 2010); Simon Johnson and James Kwak, *13 Bankers* (New York: Pantheon, 2010).

45. Alan Blinder, *Hard Heads, Soft Hearts* (Boston: Addison-Wesley, 1988).

46. This is almost the exact way the question was phrased in this survey of elite economists: http://www.igmchicago.org/igm-economic-experts-panel/poll-results?SurveyID=SV_0dfr9yjnDcLh17m.

47. Rodrik, *Economics Rules*.

48. David Autor, David Dorn, and Gordon Hanson, "The China Shock: Learning from Labor Market Adjustment to Large Changes in Trade," NBER Working Paper No. 21906, January 2016.

49. Rodrik, *Economics Rules*; Noah Smith, "Free Trade with China Wasn't Such a Great Idea for the U.S.," BloombergView, January 26, 2016.

50. Binyamin Appelbaum, "On Trade, Donald Trump Breaks with 200 Years of Economic Orthodoxy," *New York Times*, March 10, 2016.

51. Dani Rodrik, "Economists vs. Economics," *Project Syndicate*, September 10, 2015; Rodrik, *Economics Rules*; and Paul Romer, "Mathiness in the Theory of Economic Growth." *American Economic Review* 105 (May 2015): 89–93.

52. Paul Krugman, "How Did Economics Get It So Wrong?," *New York Times Magazine*, September 2, 2009; Barry Eichengreen, "The Last Temptation of Risk," *The National Interest* 101 (May/June 2009): 8.

53. Romer, "Mathiness in the Theory of Economic Growth."

54. Clive Crook, "The Trouble with Economics," BloombergView, October 11, 2015.

55. Federico Fubini, "The Closed Marketplace of Ideas," *Project Syndicate*, January 4, 2016.

56. John Lewis Gaddis, "International Relations Theory and the End of the Cold War," *International Security* 17 (Winter 1992/93): 5–58; Marc Morjé Howard and Meir Walters, "Explaining the Unexpected: Political Science and the Surprises of 1989 and 2011," *Perspectives on Politics* 12 (June 2014): 394–408.

57. Christopher J. Fettweis, "Evaluating IR's Crystal Balls: How Predictions of the Future Have Withstood Fourteen Years of Unipolarity," *International Studies Review* 6 (Winter 2004): 79–104; Philip Tetlock, *Expert Political Judgment* (Princeton, NJ: Princeton University Press, 2005).

58. Benjamin Valentino, "Why We Kill: The Political Science of Political Violence against Civilians," *Annual Review of Political Science* 17 (2014): 89–103.

59. James Long, Daniel Maliniak, Sue Peterson, and Michael Tierney, "International Relations Scholars, U.S. Foreign Policy, and the Iraq War," working paper, The College of William & Mary, December 2013. In the spirit of full disclosure, I was not one of the smart political scientists that opposed the war.

60. Daniel W. Drezner, "Why political science is not an election casualty," Washington Post, November 15, 2016; Seth Masket, "Did political science, or 'political science,' get it wrong?," *Vox*, November 15, 2016.

61. See, with respect to political science, Thomas Pepinsky and David Steinberg, "Is International Relations Relevant for International Money and Finance?," working paper, Cornell University, December 2014.

62. Thaler, *Misbehaving*, 5.

63. Harris-Perry and Friess, "An Interview with Melissa Harris-Perry," 28.

64. Daniel T. Rodgers, *Age of Fracture* (Cambridge, MA: Belknap, 2011), chapter 2; Blinder, *Hard Heads, Soft Hearts*.

65. Eliza Evans, Charles Gomez, and Daniel McFarland, "Measuring Paradigmaticness of Disciplines Using Text," *Sociological Science* 3 (August 2016): 757–778.

66. See also Deirdre McCloskey, *Knowledge and Persuasion in Economics* (New York: Cambridge University Press, 1994).

67. See the citations in fn. 7, as well as Barry Eichengreen, "Dental Hygiene and Nuclear War: How International Relations Looks from Economics," *International Organization* 52 (1998), 993–1061; Noah Smith, "Why Economists Are Paid So Much," BloombergView, December 2, 2014.

68. Rodrik, *Economics Rules*, 31. See also 30, 78–79, as well as Richard Freeman, "It's Better Being an Economist (But Don't Tell Anyone)," *Journal of Economic Perspectives* 13 (Summer 1999): 139–145.

69. Carmen Reinhart and Kenneth Rogoff, *This Time Is Different: Eight Centuries of Economic Folly* (Princeton, NJ: Princeton University Press, 2009), 30.

70. Freeman, "It's Better Being an Economist (But Don't Tell Anyone)."

71. Lawrence Mead, "Scholasticism in Political Science," *Perspectives on Politics* 8 (June 2010): 460.

72. APSA, *Improving Public Perceptions of Political Science's Value*, 11.

73. "A Different Agenda," *Nature* 487 (271), July 18, 2012; Kenneth Prewitt, "Is Any Science Safe?," *Science* 340 (6132), May 3, 2013, 525.

74. John Sides, "Why Congress Should Not Cut Funding to the Social Sciences," *Washington Post*, June 10, 2015.

75. Jeffrey Isaac, "For a More *Public* Political Science," *Perspectives on Politics* 13 (June 2015): 269.

76. See, for example, David A. Lake, "Why "isms" Are Evil: Theory, Epistemology, and Academic Sects as Impediments to Understanding and Progress," *International Studies Quarterly* 55 (June 2011): 465–480.

77. The best example of this approach can be seen in Jeffry Frieden, David A. Lake, and Kenneth Schultz, *World Politics: Interests, Interactions, Institutions*, 2nd ed. (New York: W. W. Norton, 2012).

78. Mead, "Scholasticism in Political Science," 454.

79. Lynn Vavreck and Steve Friess, "An Interview with Lynn Vavreck," *PS: Political Science and Politics* 48 (September 2015), 43.

80. Eliot Cohen, "How Government Looks at Pundits," *Wall Street Journal*, January 23, 2009. It is possible that this could change over time, as younger foreign service officers more comfortable with econometrics accept such methods as legitimate. See, on this point, Tanisha Fazal, "An Occult of Irrelevance? Multimethod Research and Engagement with the Policy World," *Security Studies* 25 (January 2016): 34–41.

81. Robert Jervis, "Bridges, Barriers, and Gaps: Research and Policy," *Political Psychology* 29 (Summer 2008): 576.

82. Susan Jacoby, *The Age of American Unreason* (New York: Vintage Books, 2008), 228.

83. Rodgers, *Age of Fracture*, 63.

84. Rodrik, *Economics Rules*, 170.

85. Piketty, *Capital in the Twenty-First Century*, 296. See also N. Gregory Mankiw, "Yes, the Wealthy Can Be Deserving," *New York Times*, February 15, 2014; Mankiw, "Defending the One Percent," *Journal of Economic Perspectives* 27 (Summer 2013): 21–24.

86. Chrystia Freeland, *Plutocrats* (New York: Penguin, 2012), 268.
87. Quote from Alan Jay Levinovitz, "The New Astrology," *Aeon*, April 4, 2016.
88. Whenever I have written about this subject for an online outlet, some variation of "Political science is not a real science, and you can tell because they put 'science' in the title" will appear in the comments section.
89. *Nature*, "A Different Agenda."
90. Brendan P. Foht, "Who Decides What Scientific Research to Fund?," *National Review*, July 25, 2012. It should be noted that prominent political scientists agree with this formulation. As Arthur Lupia noted, "Congress is not obligated to spend a single cent on scientific research. Its obligation is to the American people under the framework of the Constitution." Arthur Lupia, "What is the Value of Social Science? Challenges for Researchers and Government Funders," *PS: Political Science and Politics* 47 (January 2014): 5.
91. Daniel B. Klein and Charlotta Stern, "Economists' Policy Views and Voting," *Public Choice* 126 (March 2006): 331–342; Neil Gross and Solon Simmons, "The Social and Political Views of American Professors," Harvard University working paper, September 2007; Jon Shields and Joshua Dunn, *Passing on the Right: Conservative Professors in the Progressive University* (New York: Oxford University Press, 2016).
92. Daniel B. Klein and Charlotta Stern, "Professors and Their Politics: The Policy Views of Social Scientists," *Critical Review* 17 (March 2005): 278.
93. Zubin Jelveh, Bruce Kogut, and Suresh Naidu, "Political Language in Economics," Columbia Business School Research Paper No. 14–57, December 2014.
94. Ibid., 372.
95. Ronald Rogowski, "Shooting (or Ignoring) the Messenger," *Political Studies* 11 (May 2013): 216.
96. Jervis, "Bridges, Barriers, and Gaps: Research and Policy."
97. See, for example, Steven F. Hayward, "Is Political Science Dying?," *The Weekly Standard*, December 21, 2015.
98. Michael Stratford, "Symbolic Slap at Social Sciences," *Inside Higher Ed*, June 2, 2014.
99. APSA, *Improving Public Perceptions of Political Science's Value*, 31.
100. Michael C. Horowitz, "Joe Public v. Sue Scholar: Support for the Use of Force," *Political Violence at a Glance* (blog), July 27, 2015, accessed at http://politicalviolenceataglance.org/2015/07/27/joe-public-v-sue-scholar-support-for-the-use-of-force/; Institute for the Theory and Practice of International Relations, "Opinions of IR Scholars, Public Differ on World Crises," July 9, 2015, accessed at http://www.wm.edu/offices/itpir/news/Opinions-of-ir-scholars,-public,-differ-on-world-crises.php.

101. Charles Lane, "Congress Should Cut Funding for Political Science Research," *Washington Post*, June 4, 2012. To be fair, there are also areas of consensus among political scientists that are more sympathetic to the conservative worldview. Most political science research, for example, is skeptical of the notion that the Supreme Court's *Citizens United* decision has had a profound effect on legislative elections.

102. Ezra Klein, "How Political Science Conquered Washington," *Vox*, September 2, 2014.

103. Bryan Caplan, Eric Crampton, Wayne Grove, and Ilya Somin, "Systemically Biased Beliefs about Political Influence," *PS: Political Science and Politics* 46 (October 2013): 760–767.

104. Hochschild quoted in Marc Perry, "Is Political Science Too Pessimistic," *Chronicle of Higher Education*, September 19, 2016.

105. This has changed in recent years, however. Prominent exceptions include Allan C. Stam, Michael C. Horowitz, and Cali M. Ellis, *Why Leaders Fight* (New York: Cambridge University Press, 2015); and Elizabeth Saunders, *Leaders at War: How Presidents Shape Military Interventions* (Ithaca, NY: Cornell University Press, 2011).

106. Kenneth Waltz, *Theory of International Politics* (New York: McGraw Hill, 1979), 66 and 110.

107. For a primer on open economy politics, see David A. Lake, "Open Economy Politics: A Critical Review," *Review of International Organizations* 4 (September 2009): 219–244. For an application of open economy politics to explaining American foreign policy, see Helen Milner and Dustin Tingley, *Sailing the Water's Edge: The Domestic Politics of American Foreign Policy* (Princeton, NJ: Princeton University Press, 2016).

108. Stephen Walt, "The Relationship between Theory and Policy in International Relations," *Annual Review of Political Science* 8 (2005): 37.

109. Keren Yarhi-Milo, *Knowing the Adversary: Leaders, Intelligence, and Assessment of Intentions in International Relations* (Princeton, NJ: Princeton University Press, 2014).

110. Alexander George, *Bridging the Gap* (Washington: US Institute for Peace, 1993), 6–7.

111. Many presidential aspirants share the same attitudes toward risk. See, for example, most of the politicians profiled in McKay Coppins, *The Wilderness* (Boston: Little, Brown, 2015).

112. Rodrik, *Economics Rules*, 151.

113. Ibid., 175.

114. Smith, "Political Science and the Public Sphere Today," 369. Charli Carpenter, " 'You Talk Of Terrible Things So Matter-of-Factly in This Language of Science': Constructing Human Rights in the Academy," *Perspectives on Politics* 10 (June 2012): 363–383.

Chapter 5

1. Crane quoted in Lee Edwards, *Leading the Way: The Story of Ed Feulner and the Heritage Foundation* (New York: Crown Books, 2013), 372; Marshall quoted in Lee Edwards, *The Power of Ideas: The Heritage Foundation at 25 Years* (New York: Jameson Books, 1997), 200.

2. The quotes are from, in order: Molly Ball, "The Fall of the Heritage Foundation and the Death of Republican Ideas," *The Atlantic*, September 25, 2013; Julia Ioffe, "A 31-Year-Old Is Tearing Apart the Heritage Foundation," *New Republic*, November 24, 2013; Jenifer Steinhauser and Jonathan Weisman, "In the DeMint Era at Heritage, a Shift From Policy to Politics," *New York Times*, February 23, 2014. See also Edwards, *Leading the Way*, 372–75. For a contrarian take, see Jacob Weisberg, "Happy Birthday, Heritage Foundation," *Slate*, January 9, 1998.

3. Josh Barro, "The Odd Choice of Jim DeMint at Heritage," BloombergView, December 6, 2012.

4. John Podhoretz, "DeMint Takes Over the Heritage Foundation," *Commentary*, December 6, 2012; Kristol quoted in Dylan Byers, "With a new leader, Heritage rising," *Politico*, December 6, 2012.

5. Ezra Klein, "Jim DeMint and the Death of Think Tanks," *Washington Post*, December 6, 2012.

6. Mike Gonzalez, "Jim DeMint to Become Heritage's Next President," December 6, 2012, accessed at http://dailysignal.com/2012/12/06/jim-demint-to-become-heritages-next-president/.

7. Rachel Weiner, "Jim DeMint Leaving the Senate," *Washington Post*, December 6, 2012; Daniel Henninger, "Sen. Jim DeMint to Head Heritage Foundation," *Wall Street Journal*, December 6, 2012.

8. Suzy Khimm, "The Right's Latest Weapon: Think-Tank Lobbying Muscle," *Washington Post*, January 24, 2013.

9. Steinhauser and Weisman, "In the DeMint Era at Heritage."

10. Ibid.

11. Joshua Green, "The Tea Party Gets into the News Biz," BloombergBusiness, May 8, 2014.

12. Steinhauser and Weisman, "In the DeMint Era at Heritage."

13. Jim DeMint, *Falling in Love with America Again* (New York: Center Street, 2014).

14. Most think tanks, including Heritage, exist under the Internal Revenue Service's 501(c)(3) status, which allows organizations to educate legislators about broad-based policy but not lobby directly for specific legislation. 501(c)(4) organizations are allowed to lobby legislators, however. See Khimm, "The Right's Latest Weapon," and Ioffe, "A 31-Year-Old Is Tearing Apart the Heritage Foundation."

15. Edward Feulner and Michael Needham, "New Fangs for the Conservative 'Beast,'" *Wall Street Journal*, April 12, 2010.

16. Ioffe, "A 31-Year-Old Is Tearing Apart the Heritage Foundation."

17. Robert Rector and Jason Richwine, "The Fiscal Cost of Unlawful Immigrants and Amnesty to the U.S. Taxpayer," Heritage Foundation Special Report No. 133, May 6, 2013.

18. Walter Hickey, "Here's The Massive Flaw with the Conservative Study That Says Immigration Reform Will Cost Taxpayers Nearly $7 Trillion," *Business Insider*, May 6, 2013.

19. Keith Hennessey, "Eight Problems with the Heritage Immigration Cost Estimate," May 9, 2013, accessed at http://keithhennessey.com/2013/05/09/heritage-immigration-study-problems/.

20. Tim Kane, "Immigration Errors," May 6, 2013, accessed at http://balanceofeconomics.com/2013/05/06/immigration-errors/.

21. Daniel W. Drezner, "Regarding Richwine," *Foreign Policy*, May 11, 2013.

22. Jennifer Rubin, "Jim DeMint's Destruction of the Heritage Foundation," *Washington Post*, October 21, 2013; Shane Harris, "How the NSA Scandal is Roiling the Heritage Foundation," *Foreign Policy*, October 16, 2013.

23. Rubin, "Jim DeMint's destruction of the Heritage Foundation"; Lauren French, Anna Palmer, and Jake Sherman, "GOP Lawmakers Confront Demint over Ratings," *Politico*, January 28, 2015, accessed at http://www.politico.com/story/2015/01/gop-lawmakers-jim-demint-heritage-foundation-ratings-114672.html.

24. Jake Sherman, "Heritage Will Honor Ryan's Top Staffer Even as It Tries to Upend GOP Budget," *Politico*, February 9, 2016, accessed at http://www.politico.com/story/2016/02/heritage-foundation-paul-ryan-219028#ixzz3zosoEfHb.

25. See, for example, Weisberg, "Happy Birthday, Heritage Foundation."

26. See the references in footnote 2.

27. Harris, "How the NSA Scandal is Roiling the Heritage Foundation."

28. Jim DeMint, "Free Trade in Name Only," *The National Interest*, June 16, 2015.

29. Matt Fuller, "Donald Trump and the Heritage Foundation: Friends with Benefits," *Huffington Post*, August 10, 2016.

30. Compare the 2012 Go To Think Tank Report, accessed at http://repository.upenn.edu/cgi/viewcontent.cgi?article=1006&context=think_tanks, with the 2015 report, accessed at http://repository.upenn.edu/think_tanks/10/.

31. John B. Judis, "The Little Think Tank That Could," *Slate*, August 18, 2015.

32. Ball, "The Fall of the Heritage Foundation and the Death of Republican Ideas."

33. Ibid.

34. James Jay Carafano, "Think Tanks Aren't Going Extinct. But They Have to Evolve." *The National Interest*, October 21, 2015.

35. In the 2012 Go To Think Tank Index Report, Heritage ranked fifteenth in advocacy; in its 2015 report, Heritage had moved up to third place. In impact, it moved from tenth to eighth.

36. Philip Wegmann, "Heritage Foundation takes risk and wins big with Trump," *Washington Examiner*, November 10, 2016; Kelefa Sanneh, "Secret Admirers," *New Yorker*, January 9, 2017.

37. Amanda Bennett, "Are Think Tanks Obsolete?," *Washington Post*, October 5, 2015.

38. Tom Medvetz, *Think Tanks in America* (Chicago: University of Chicago Press, 2012), 18.

39. See Donald Abelson, *Do Think Tanks Matter? Assessing the Impact of Public Policy Institutes* (Montreal: McGill-Queens Press, 2009); Andrew Selee, *What Should Think Tanks Do? A Strategic Guide to Policy Impact* (Stanford, CA: Stanford University Press, 2013).

40. Christopher DeMuth, "Think-Tank Confidential," *Wall Street Journal*, October 17, 2007.

41. Nathan Russell, "An Introduction to the Overton Window of Political Possibilities," Mackinac Center for Public Policy, 2006, accessed at http://www.storyboardproductions.com/ehc/circle6/30verton-window.pdf. The term is better known to conservatives because Glenn Beck used it as the title to one of his novels.

42. It is noteworthy that during the debate over Iraq in the fall of 2002, academics had much less influence than a Brookings Institution scholar named Kenneth Pollack, whose book, *The Threatening Storm*, was the go-to citation for Democrats to justify their support for invasion.

43. David Rothkopf, *National Insecurity: American Leadership in an Age of Fear* (New York: PublicAffairs, 2014), 15–17.

44. See, for example, Tevi Troy, "Devaluing the Think Tank," *National Affairs* 10 (Winter 2012): 75–90; Klein, "Jim DeMint and the Death of Think Tanks"; Anne-Marie Slaughter and Ben Scott, "Rethinking the Think Tank," *Washington Monthly*, November/December 2015. It is also possible that this nostalgia is misplaced. See Medvetz, *Think Tanks in America*, chapters 2 and 3.

45. David Rothkopf, "Dis Town," *Foreign Policy*, November 28, 2014.

46. High-ranking official referred to Massachusetts Avenue, where many foreign think tanks are headquartered, as "Arab-occupied territory." Jeffrey Goldberg, "The Obama Doctrine," *The Atlantic*, April 2016.

47. "Why think tanks are concerned about a Trump administration," *Economist*, November 17, 2016.

48. James McGann, "For Think Tanks, It's Either Innovate or Die," *Washington Post*, October 6, 2015.

49. Bryan Bender, "Many DC Think Tanks Now Players in Partisan Wars," *Boston Globe*, 11 August 2013; Eric Lipton, Brooke Williams, and Nicholas Confessore, "Foreign Powers Buy Influence at Think Tanks," *New York Times*, September 6, 2014; Tom Hamburger and Alexander Becker, "At Fast-Growing Brookings, Donors May Have an Impact on Research Agenda," *Washington Post*, October 30, 2014; Eric Lipton and Brooke

Williams, "How Think Tanks Amplify Corporate Influence," *New York Times*, August 7, 2016.

50. See, for example, James A. Smith, *The Idea Brokers* (New York: Free Press, 1991); Andrew Rich, *Think Tanks, Public Policy, and the Politics of Expertise* (Cambridge: Cambridge University Press, 2004).

51. Richard Hoftstadter, *Anti-Intellectualism in American Life* (New York: Random House, 1962), 199.

52. Jeffry Frieden, *Banking On the World* (New York: Harper and Row, 1987), 33–34; Slaughter and Scott, "Rethinking the Think Tank."

53. Bruce Smith, *The RAND Corporation: Case Study of a Nonprofit Advisory Corporation* (Cambridge, MA: Harvard University Press, 1966), 6.

54. Rich, *Think Tanks*, 42; Smith, *The Idea Brokers*; David R. Jardini, "Out of the Blue Yonder: The RAND Corporation's Diversification into Social Welfare Research, 1946–1968" (PhD dissertation, Carnegie Mellon University, 1996); David Hounshell, "The Cold War, RAND, and the Generation of Knowledge, 1946–1962," *Historical Studies in the Physical and Biological Sciences* 27 (Spring 1997): 237–267.

55. Peter W. Singer, "Factories to Call Our Own," *Washingtonian*, August 2010.

56. Rich, *Think Tanks*, 37.

57. Ibid., 56. See also Lee Edwards, *Leading the Way: The Story of Ed Feulner and the Heritage Foundation* (New York: CrownForum, 2013).

58. Khimm, "The Right's Latest Weapon"; Ioffe, "A 31-Year-Old Is Tearing Apart the Heritage Foundation."

59. Troy, "Devaluing the Think Tank," 86.

60. Quoted in Medvetz, *Think Tanks in America*, 138.

61. Donald Abelson, "Old World, New World: The Evolution and Influence of Foreign Affairs Think-Tanks," *International Affairs* 90 (January 2014): 129.

62. Tom Ricks, *The Gamble* (New York: Penguin Press, 2009), chapters 3 and 4.

63. For a droll account of this dynamic, see Jeremy Shapiro, "Who Influences Whom? Reflections on U.S. Government Outreach to Think Tanks," Brookings Institution, June 4, 2014, accessed at http://www.brookings.edu/blogs/up-front/posts/2014/06/04-us-government-outreach-think-tanks-shapiro. For a more despairing account, see Shadi Hamid, "What is Policy Research For? Reflections on the United States' Failures in Syria," *Middle East Law and Governance* 7 (Summer 2015): 373–386.

64. Quoted in Rich, *Think Tanks*, 72–73.

65. Troy, "Devaluing the Think Tank," 87.

66. Slaughter and Scott, "Rethinking the Think Tank."

67. Benjamin I. Page with Marshall M. Bouton. *The Foreign Policy Disconnect* (Chicago: University of Chicago Press, 2008); Joshua Busby and Jonathan Monten, "Republican Elites and Foreign Policy Attitudes," *Political Science Quarterly* 127 (Spring 2012): 105–142.

68. Ken Silverstein, "The Great Think Tank Bubble," *New Republic*, February 19, 2013.

69. Hamburger and Becker, "At Fast-Growing Brookings."

70. Ken Silverstein, "Pay to Play Think Tanks: Institutional Corruption and the Industry of Ideas," Edmund J. Safta Institute for Ethics, Harvard University, June 2014.

71. Robert Gates, speech as delivered at the Eisenhower Library, Abilene, KS, May 8, 2010. Accessed at http://www.defense.gov/speeches/speech.aspx?speechid=1467.

72. Marcus Weisgerber, "Shake-Up Underway at Prominent Washington Think Tank," *Defense One*, July 15, 2015.

73. Heritage Foundation's 2014 annual report, accessed at https://s3.amazonaws.com/thf_media/2015/pdf/2014annualreport.pdf, 46. Heritage Action's funding appears to come primarily from small donations. See Robert Maguire, "More than Kochs, Small Donors Fueled Heritage Action in 2012," OpenSecrets, October 14, 2013, accessed at http://www.opensecrets.org/news/2013/10/more-than-kochs-small-donors-fueled/.

74. Carafano, "Think Tanks Aren't Going Extinct."

75. Steven Teles, "Foundations, Organizational Maintenance, and Partisan Asymmetry," *PS: Political Science and Politics* 49 (July 2016): 455–460.

76. Weisgerber, "Shake-Up Underway at Prominent Washington Think Tank."

77. CFR, "Benefits of Corporate Membership," accessed at http://www.cfr.org/about/corporate/corporate_benefits.html.

78. Brookings Institution, "Brookings Corporate Council Donor Privileges," accessed at http://www.brookings.edu/~/media/About/development/Brookings-Donor-PrivilegesCorporate.pdf. Center for New American Security, "Corporate Partnership Program," accessed at http://www.cnas.org/sites/default/files/CNAS%20Corporate%20partnership%20program_042815.pdf.

79. Hamburger and Becker, "At Fast-Growing Brookings."

80. Lipton and Williams, "How Think Tanks Amplify Corporate America's Influence."

81. Ibid.

82. Dylan Matthews, "Elizabeth Warren Exposed a Shocking Instance of How Money Corrupts DC Think Tanks," *Vox*, September 30, 2015.

83. Nicholas Confessore, Eric Lipton, and Brooke Williams, "Think Tank Scholar or Corporate Consultant? It Depends on the Day," *New York Times*, August 8, 2016.

84. Ryan Grim and Paul Blumenthal, "The Vultures' Vultures: How A Hedge-Fund Strategy Is Corrupting Washington," *Huffington Post*, May 16, 2016.

85. Warren quoted from September 28, 2015, letter to Strobe Talbott, accessed at http://www.warren.senate.gov/files/documents/2015-9-28_Warren_Brookings_ltr.pdf; Helaine Olen, "Wonks for Hire," *Slate*, October 2, 2015.

86. John B. Judis, "Foreign Funding of Think Tanks Is Corrupting Our Democracy," *New Republic*, September 9, 2014.

87. Quoted in Lipton, Williams, and Confessore, "Foreign Powers Buy Influence at Think Tanks."

88. Judis, "The Little Think Tank That Could"; Eli Clifton, "Home Depot Founder's Quiet $10 Million Right-Wing Investment," *Salon*, August 5, 2013; Eric Lichtblau, "Financier's Largess Shows G.O.P.'s Wall St. Support," *New York Times*, August 27, 2010.

89. Slaughter and Scott, "Rethinking the Think Tank."

90. Jane Harman, "Are Think Tanks Too Partisan?," *Washington Post*, October 7, 2015.

91. Steven Teles, Heather Hurlburt, and Mark Schmitt, "Philanthropy in a Time of Polarization," *Stanford Social Innovation Review*, Summer 2014, 44–49.

92. J. K. Trotter, "Leaked Files Show How the Heritage Foundation Navigates the Reactionary Views of Wealthy Donors," *Gawker*, September 9, 2015.

93. David Weigel, "Cato Goes to War," *Slate*, March 5, 2012.

94. David Weigel, "Cato at Peace," *Slate*, June 25, 2012.

95. David Weigel, "Cato Shrugged: Panic about An Incoming Leader's Admiration for Ayn Rand," *Slate*, August 30, 2012.

96. McGann quoted in Bennett, "Are Think Tanks Obsolete?"; Ellen Lapison, "Why Our Demand for Instant Results Hurts Think Tanks," *Washington Post*, October 9, 2015. Brookings managing director quoted in Lipton and Williams, "How Think Tanks Amplify Corporate America's Influence."

97. Quoted in Silverstein, "Pay to Play Think Tanks," 10. See also Slaughter and Scott, "Rethinking the Think Tank."

98. Jamie Kirchick, "How a U.S. Think Tank Fell for Putin," *Daily Beast*, July 27, 2015.

99. See, for example, Leonid Bershidsky, "Putin Hurts a Think Tank by Not Banning It," BloombergView, July 29, 2015.

100. Ali Gharib and Eli Clifton, "Dissent Breaks Out at the Center for American Progress Over Netanyahu's Visit," *The Nation*, November 10, 2015. See also John Hudson, "Netanyahu Visit Sparks Internal Backlash at Powerhouse D.C. Think Tank," *Foreign Policy*, November 9, 2015.

101. For the Center for the National Interest, see John Hudson, "Think Tank Fires Employee Who Questioned Ties to Donald Trump," *Foreign Policy*, May 20, 2016. On Demos, see Kevin Drum, "The Great Matt Bruenig-Neera Tanden Kerfuffle Sort of Explained," *Mother Jones*, May 20, 2016.

102. Michael Tanji, "The Think Tank is Dead. Long Live the Think Tank," http://www.haftofthespear.com/wp-content/uploads/2010/08/The-Think-Tank-is-Dead-Final-Online.pdf, August 2010.

103. Carafano, "Think Tanks Aren't Going Extinct."

104.   Slaughter and Scott, "Rethinking the Think Tank."

Chapter 6

1.   Richard Posner, *Public Intellectuals: A Study of Decline* (Cambridge, MA: Harvard University Press, 2000), 58.

2.   For a conventional treatment of how the private sector affects American foreign policy, see Helen Milner and Dustin Tingley, *Sailing the Water's Edge: The Domestic Politics of American Foreign Policy* (Princeton, NJ: Princeton University Press, 2015). The classic explanation of how the private sector provides information to the public sector is Mathew McCubbins and Thomas Schwartz, "Congressional Oversight Overlooked: Police Patrols versus Fire Alarms," *American Journal of Political Science* 28 (February 1984): 165–179.

3.   South Africa did not join until 2010. In this chapter, "BRICS" refers to all five countries; "BRICs" refers to the pre-2010 grouping.

4.   For more information see the University of Toronto's "BRICS Information Centre" website at http://www.brics.utoronto.ca/docs/index. html.

5.   Christian Brütsch and Mihaela Papa, "Deconstructing the BRICS: Bargaining Coalition, Imagined Community, or Geopolitical Fad?," *Chinese Journal of International Politics* 6 (Autumn 2013): 300.

6.   Barry Eichengreen, *Exorbitant Privilege: The Rise and Fall of the Dollar and the Future of the International Monetary System* (New York: Oxford University Press, 2011), 142–45.

7.   BRICS Fortaleza Declaration, July 15, 2014, accessed at http://brics. itamaraty.gov.br/media2/press-releases/214-sixth-brics-summit-fortaleza-declaration; Simon Romero, "Emerging Nations Bloc to Open Development Bank," *New York Times*, July 16, 2014.

8.   The summit communiqué can be accessed at http://www.brics.utoronto. ca/docs/081107-finance.html.

9.   Daniel W. Drezner, *The System Worked* (New York: Oxford University Press), 149–150; and Miles Kahler, "Conservative Globalizers: Reconsidering the Rise of the Rest," *World Politics Review*, February 2, 2016.

10.   On the exaggeration of the BRICS, see Harsh V. Pant, "The BRICS Fallacy," *Washington Quarterly* 36 (Summer 2013): 91–105; Drezner, *The System Worked*, 149–150; Bruce Jones, *Still Ours to Lead: America, the Rising Powers, and the Myths of the Coming Disorder* (Washington, DC: Brookings Institution Press, 2014). On the potential of the BRICS, see Parag Khanna, *The Second World: Empires and Influence in the New Global Order* (New York: Random House, 2008); Moisés Naim, *End of Power* (New York: Basic Books, 2013); Naazneen Barma, Ely Ratner, and Steven Weber, "Welcome to the World Without the West," *The National Interest*, November 12, 2014; Helmut Reisen, "Will the AIIB and the NDB Help Reform Multilateral Development Landing?," *Global Policy* 6 (September 2015): 297–304.

11.   See http://infobrics.org/history-of-brics/, accessed October 15, 2015.

12.   Jim O'Neill, "Building Better Global Economic BRICs," Goldman
       Sachs Global Economics Paper No. 66, November 30, 2001, 3 and
       10. To O'Neill's credit, he noted at the time that the G-20 grouping
       of finance ministers was "arguably an extended club version of this
       proposal."

13.   Dominic Wilson and Roopa Purushothaman, "Dreaming with
       BRICs: The Path to 2050," Goldman Sachs Global Economics Paper No.
       99, October 1, 2003.

14.   See, for example, Philip Stephens, "A Story of Brics without Mortar,"
       Financial Times, November 24, 2011; Pant, "The BRICS Fallacy."

15.   Brütsch and Mihaela Papa, "Deconstructing the BRICS"; Drezner, The
       System Worked, chapters 6 and 7.

16.   Gillian Tett, "The Story of the Brics," Financial Times, January 15, 2010.

17.   Ye Xie, "Goldman's BRIC Era Ends as Fund Folds after Years of Losses,"
       BloombergBusiness, November 8, 2015.

18.   Barma, Ratner, and Weber, "Welcome to the World without the West";
       Parag Khanna, Connectography (New York: Random House, 2016).

19.   Evan Osnos, "Born Red," New Yorker, April 6, 2015; David Shambaugh,
       "The Coming Chinese Crackup," Wall Street Journal, March 6, 2015;
       Kahler, "Conservative Globalizers."

20.   Drezner, The System Worked, chapter 6; "The Headwinds Return,"
       Economist, September 13, 2014.

21.   Ruchir Sharma, "Broken BRICs: Why the Rest Stopped Rising," Foreign
       Affairs 91 (November/December 2012): 4. See also Ruchir Sharma, "How
       Emerging Markets Lost Their Mojo," Wall Street Journal, June 26, 2013.

22.   Pant, "The BRICS Fallacy"; Marcos Degaut, "Do the BRICS Still
       Matter?," CSIS Americas Program, October 2015.

23.   Sinead Cruise and Chris Vellacott, "Emerging Markets Mania Was a
       Costly Mistake: Goldman Executive," Reuters, July 4, 2013; Luciana
       Megalhanes, "China only BRIC Country Worthy of the Title—O'Neill,"
       Wall Street Journal, August 23, 2013.

24.   Xie, "Goldman's BRIC Era Ends as Fund Folds after Years of Losses."

25.   Ibid. See also Michael Patterson and Shiyin Chen, "BRIC Decade Ends
       with Record Fund Outflows as Growth Slows," BloombergBusiness,
       December 28, 2011; Ye Xie, "As Emerging-Market Debt Crisis Talk
       Grows, Some Investors Scoff," BloombergBusiness, April 1, 2015;
       Mohammed El-Erian, "Rethinking Emerging Markets," BloombergView,
       April 3, 2015; Eric Balchunas, "ETF Investors Are Unbundling Emerging
       Markets," BloombergBusiness, November 4, 2015.

26.   For BRICSAM, see Alan Alexandroff and Andrew Cooper, eds., Rising
       States, Rising Institutions: Challenges for Global Governance (Washington,
       DC: Brookings Institution Press, 2010); for MIKTA, see Scott Snyder,
       "Korean Middle Power Diplomacy: The Establishment of MIKTA," Asia

Unbound, Council on Foreign Relations, October 1, 2013, accessed at http://blogs.cfr.org/asia/2013/10/01/korean-middle-power-diplomacy-the-establishment-of-mikta/; for MINTs, see Jim O'Neill, "Who You Calling a BRIC?," BloombergView, November 12, 2013.

27. Tett, "The Story of the Brics," emphasis added.

28. Christopher McKenna, *The World's Newest Profession: Management Consulting in the Twentieth Century* (New York: Cambridge University Press, 2006), 16–17.

29. Ibid.

30. Walter Kiechel, *The Lords of Strategy: The Secret Intellectual History of the New Corporate World* (Cambridge, MA: Harvard Business Press, 2010), x.

31. Robert J. David, Wesley D. Sine, and Heather A. Haveman, "Seizing Opportunity in Emerging Fields: How Institutional Entrepreneurs Legitimated the Professional Form of Management Consulting," *Organization Science* 24 (March/April 2013): 367–368.

32. McKenna, *The World's Newest Profession*; Duff McDonald, *The Firm: The Inside Story of McKinsey* (London: OneWorld, 2013).

33. McDonald, *The Firm*; McKenna, *The World's Newest Profession*, chapter 8; Joe O'Mahoney and Andrew Sturdy, "Power and the Diffusion of Management Ideas: The Case of McKinsey & Co," *Management Learning* 47 (July 2016): 247–265.

34. David, Sine, and Haveman, "Seizing Opportunity in Emerging Fields," 369.

35. Ibid., 370–371.

36. McDonald, *The Firm*, 5.

37. Kiechel, *The Lords of Strategy*.

38. McDonald, *The Firm*, chapter 6.

39. "To the brainy, the spoils," *Economist*, May 11, 2013.

40. Andrew Gross and Jozef Poor, "The Global Management Consulting Sector," *Business and Economics* 43 (October 2008): 62; Bessma Momani, "Management Consultants and the United States' Public Sector," *Business and Politics* 15 (October 2013): 381–399; Bessma Momani, "Professional Management Consultants in Transnational Governance," working paper, University of Waterloo; Irvine Lapsley and Rosie Oldfield, "Transforming the Public Sector: Management Consultants as Agents of Change," *European Accounting Review* 10 (October 2001): 523–543.

41. Alison Stanger, *One Nation under Contract: The Outsourcing of American Power and the Future of Foreign Policy* (New Haven, CT: Yale University Press, 2009).

42. O'Mahoney and Sturdy, "Power and the Diffusion of Management Ideas."

43. Anjli Raval and Neil Hume, "Saudi Aramco Listing Presents Challenges for Investors," *Financial Times*, January 10, 2016; Nick Butler, "Saudi Arabia—the Dangers of a Fanciful Vision," *Financial Times*, May 9, 2016;

Adel Abdel Ghafar, "Saudi Arabia's McKinsey Reshuffle," Brookings Institution, May 11, 2016.

44. Sebastian Bock, "Politicized expertise—an Analysis of the Political Dimensions of Consultants' Policy Recommendations to Developing Countries with a Case Study of McKinsey's Advice on REDD+ Policies," *Innovation: The European Journal of Social Science Research* 27 (December 2014): 387.

45. See, for example, Diana Farrell and Andrew Goodman, "Government by design: Four principles for a better public sector," McKinsey, December 2013, accessed at http://economicgrowthdc.org/work/assets/McKinsey-Building-Better-Government.pdf.

46. Gross and Poor, "The Global Management Consulting Sector," 65. See also O'Mahoney and Sturdy, "Power and the Diffusion of Management Ideas."

47. "To the brainy, the spoils."

48. Fiona Czerniawska and Edward Haigh, "Understanding the Impact of Thought Leadership," *Source Point Global* (blog), September 21, 2014, accessed at http://www.sourceglobalresearch.com/blog/2014/09/21/understanding-the-impact-of-thought-leadership; "Big Impact Thought Leadership," *Source Point Global*, July 2015.

49. David Leonhardt, "Consultant Nation," *New York Times*, December 10, 2011.

50. McDonald, *The Firm*, 7 and 289.

51. See MGI's "About Us" page at http://www.mckinsey.com/insights/mgi/about_us, accessed October 16, 2015.

52. Anne-Marie Slaughter and Ben Scott, "Rethinking the Think Tank," *Washington Monthly*, November/December 2015.

53. http://www.jpmorganchase.com/corporate/institute/about.htm, accessed October 16, 2015.

54. http://www.kkr.com/our-firm/kkr-global-institute, accessed October 16, 2015.

55. See http://dupress.com/, accessed October 21, 2015.

56. Credit Suisse, *The End of Globalization or a More Multipolar World?* (London: Credit Suisse Research Institute, 2015); KPMG International, *Future State 2030: The Global Megatrends Shaping Governments* (Toronto: Mowatt Centre for Policy Innovation, 2014); HSBC, *The World in 2050* (London: HSBC Global Research, 2011); PricewaterhouseCoopers, *The World in 2050: Will the Shift in Global Economic Power Continue?* (London: PricewaterhouseCoopers, 2015);

57. Presentation by Michael Chui, Ideas Industry conference, The Fletcher School, Medford, MA, October 7, 2016.

58. Rachel Ainsworth, "Annual Publications in Financial Services: How to Avoid Yours Going Bad," *Source Point Global* (blog), February 5, 2015, accessed at http://www.sourceglobalresearch.com/blog/2015/02/05/annual-publications-in-financial-services-how-to-avoid-yours-going-bad.

59. Judith Kelley and Beth Simmons, "Politics by Number: Indicators as Social Pressure in International Relations," *American Journal of Political Science* 59 (January 2015): 55–70; Kelley and Simmons, "The Power of Performance Indicators: Rankings, Ratings and Reactivity in International Relations," presented at the annual meeting of the American Political Science Association, August 27–September 1, 2014, Washington, DC.

60. Harold Sirkin, Michael Zinser, and Douglas Hohner, "Made in America, Again," Boston Consulting Group, August 2011, accessed at https://www.bcg.com/documents/file84471.pdf; Malcolm Gladwell, "The Talent Myth," *New Yorker*, July 22, 2002.

61. See Ronald S. Burt, *Neighbor Networks* (New York: Oxford University Press, 2010); Leonard Seabrooke, "Epistemic arbitrage: Transnational Professional Knowledge in Action," *Journal of Professions and Organization* 1 (January 2014): 49–64.

62. On the former, see Kelley and Simmons, "The Power of Performance Indicators"; on the latter, see Daniel W. Drezner, "Five Known Unknowns about the Next Generation Global Economy," Brookings Institution, May 2016.

63. Gladwell, "The Talent Myth."

64. O'Mahoney and Sturdy, "Power and the Diffusion of Management Ideas."

65. Richard Dobbs, Sree Ramaswamy, Elizabeth Stephenson, and Patrick Viguerie, "Management Intuition for the Next 50 Years, *McKinsey Quarterly* (September 2014).

66. Lucy Kellaway, "McKinsey's Airy Platitudes Bode Ill for Its Next Half Century," *Financial Times*, September 14, 2014.

67. Lapsley and Oldfield, "Transforming the public sector: management consultants as agents of change," 541.

68. Rudolph J. Rummel and David A. Heenan, "How Multinationals Analyze Political Risk," *Harvard Business Review* 56 (January/February 1978): 67–76; Mark Fitzpatrick, "The Definition and Assessment of Political Risk in International Business: A Review of the Literature," *Academy of Management Review* 8 (April 1983): 249–254.

69. Brian Bremmer and Simon Kennedy, "Geopolitical Risk Rises for Global Investors," Bloomberg, July 29, 2014.

70. Malini Natarajarathinam, Ismail Capar, and Arunachalam Narayanan, "Managing Supply Chains in Times of Crisis: A Review of Literature and Insights," *International Journal of Physical Distribution and Logistics Management* 39 (July 2009): 535–573.

71. John Chipman, "Why Your Company Needs a Foreign Policy," *Harvard Business Review* 94 (September 2016): 36; Drew Erdmann and Ezra Greenberg, "Geostrategic Risks on the Rise," McKinsey survey, May 2016, accessed at http://www.mckinsey.com/business-functions/strategy-and-corporate-finance/our-insights/geostrategic-risks-on-the-rise.

72. Barney Thompson, "Political Risk Is Now a Growth Industry in Its Own Right," *Financial Times*, September 28, 2014.

73. Jeffrey Birnbaum, "Taking Costly Counsel from A Statesman," *Washington Post*, March 29, 2004.

74. Bartholomew Sparrow, *The Strategist: Brent Scowcroft and the Call for National Security* (New York: PublicAffairs, 2015), 501. See also Jeff Gerth and Sarah Bartlett, "Kissinger and Friends and Revolving Doors," *New York Times*, April 30, 1989; Eric Lipton, Nicholas Confessore, and Brooke Williams, "Think Tank Scholar or Corporate Consultant? It Depends on the Day," *New York Times*, August 8, 2016.

75. Llewellyn D. Howell, "Evaluating Political Risk Forecasting Models: What Works?," *Thunderbird International Business Review* 56 (July/August 2014): 305–316.

76. Jonathan R. Laing, "The Shadow CIA," *Barron's*, October 15, 2001; see also Sam C. Gwynne, "Spies Like Us," *Time*, January 25, 1999.

77. Gerth and Bartlett, "Kissinger and Friends and Revolving Doors"; Alec MacGillis, "Scandal at Clinton, Inc.," *New Republic*, September 22, 2013; Rachel Bade, "How a Clinton Insider Used His Ties to Build a Consulting Giant," *Politico*, April 13, 2016; Lipton, Confessore, and Williams, "Think Tank Scholar or Corporate Consultant?" See, more generally, Mark Leibovich, *This Town* (New York: Blue Rider Press, 2013).

78. Thompson, "Political Risk Is Now a Growth Industry in Its Own Right."

79. See WikiLeaks' announcement at http://wikileaks.org/the-gifiles.html, accessed October 18, 2015.

80. Pratap Chatterjee, "WikiLeaks' Stratfor Dump Lifts Lid on Intelligence-Industrial Complex," *Guardian*, February 28, 2012.

81. Max Fisher, "Stratfor Is a Joke and So Is Wikileaks for Taking It Seriously," *The Atlantic*, February 27, 2012.

82. See, for example, Milena Rodban's analysis of the industry at http://www.milenarodban.com/myths-vs-realities-series, accessed October 18, 2015.

83. Bruce Gale, "Identifying, Assessing and Mitigating Political Risk," INSEADKnowledge, http://knowledge.insead.edu/economics-finance/identifying-assessing-and-mitigating-political-risk-2013, February 26, 2008.

84. Howell, "Evaluating Political Risk Forecasting Models," 309.

85. Chipman, "Why Your Company Needs a Foreign Policy."

86. Economist Intelligence Unit, *Long-term Macroeconomic Forecasts: Key Trends to 2050* (London: The Economist, June 2015).

87. George Friedman, *The Next 100 Years* (New York: Doubleday, 2009); Friedman, *The Next Decade* (New York: Doubleday, 2011).

88. See the Eurasia Group's webpage devoted to "Speaking Engagements" at http://www.eurasiagroup.net/client-services/speaking-engagements, accessed October 18, 2015.

89. Philip Tetlock, "Reading Tarot on K Street," *The National Interest* 103 (September/October 2009): 57.

90. Jared Cohen, "Tech for Change," *Think with Google* (blog), https://www. thinkwithgoogle.com/articles/tech-for-change.html, October 2012.

91. Shawn Donnan, "Think Again," *Financial Times*, July 8, 2011.

92. Ibid.

93. Mark Landler and Brian Stetler, "Washington Taps into a Potent New Force in Diplomacy," *New York Times*, June 17, 2009.

94. Eric Schmidt and Jared Cohen, *The New Digital Age: Reshaping the Future of People, Nations and Business* (New York: Knopf, 2013), 176.

95. See, most recently, Jared Cohen, "Digital Counterinsurgency," *Foreign Affairs* 94 (November/December 2015): 53–58.

96. Rachel Briggs and Sebastien Feve, "Review of Programs to Counter Narratives of Violent Extremism," Institute for Strategic Dialogue, April 2013, accessed at http://www.againstviolentextremism.org/faq.

97. Ibid.

98. Julian Assange, "Google Is Not What It Seems," *Newsweek*, October 13, 2014. See, more generally, Julian Assange, *When Google Met WikiLeaks* (New York: OR Books, 2014).

99. For the announcement, see Eric Schmidt, "Google Ideas Becomes Jigsaw," *Medium*, accessed at https://medium.com/jigsaw/google-ideas-becomes-jigsaw-bcb5bd08c423#.fr3jbfy7q. For a critical take, see Julia Powles, "Google's Jigsaw Project Has New Ideas, but an Old Imperial Mindset," *Guardian*, February 18, 2016.

100. See the description of Project Shield at https://www.google.com/ideas/products/project-shield/, accessed October 18, 2015.

101. Bruce Einhorn, "In India, Google's Eric Schmidt Explains Why He Went to North Korea," BloombergBusiness, March 23, 2013.

102. Shawn Powers and Michael Jablonski, *The Real Cyberwar: The Political Economy of Internet Freedom* (Urbana: University of Illinois Press, 2015), 97.

103. Nate Silver, *The Signal and the Noise* (New York: Penguin, 2012), 167.

104. John Gapper, "McKinsey Model Springs a Leak," *Financial Times*, March 9, 2011; Andrew Hill, "Inside McKinsey," *Financial Times*, November 25, 2011; Leonhardt, "Consultant Nation."

105. Sirkin, Zinser, and Hohner, "Made in America, Again."

106. Daniel W. Drezner, "Sovereign Wealth Funds and the (In)Security of Global Finance," *Journal of International Affairs* 62 (Fall/Winter 2008): 115–130.

107. The revolving door between government service and the private sector also helped. The cycling of individuals between Goldman Sachs and the Treasury Department is well known. The number of ex-management consultants in government is more surprising. As of December 2015,

McKinsey alumni alone occupy two cabinet-level positions, two Federal Reserve board of governor slots, and at least one governorship. Other consultancies have their own alumni in government as well.

108. Gautam Mukunda, "The Price of Wall Street's Power," *Harvard Business Review* 92 (June 2014): 70–78.

109. Presentation by Krithika Subramanian, Ideas Industry conference, The Fletcher School, Medford, MA, October 7, 2016.

110. For example, at the outset of a recent book, three McKinsey consultants explained that, "our thinking stems from McKinsey's work with companies and organizations around the world; meaningful conversations about the challenges and opportunities inherent in our world with corporate, government, and NGO leaders, *deep, proprietary quantitative research by MGI over the last twenty-five years*; and extensive and diverse personal experiences" (emphasis added). Richard Dobbs, James Manyika, and Jonathan Woetzel, *No Ordinary Disruption* (New York: PublicAffairs, 2015), 11. See also Momani, "Professional Management Consultants in Transnational Governance."

111. Owen Davis, "JPMorgan Chase & Co Launches Think Tank: The JPMorgan Chase Institute," *International Business Times*, May 21, 2015.

112. Keren Yarhi-Milo, *Knowing the Adversary: Leaders, Intelligence, and Assessment of Intentions in International Relations* (Princeton, NJ: Princeton University Press, 2014).

113. See, for example, Dobbs, Manyika, and Woetzel, *No Ordinary Disruption*.

114. Ryanne Pilgeram and Russell Meeuf. "For-Profit Public Intellectuals." *Contexts* 13 (Fall 2014), 84.

Chapter 7

1. The definitive Lippmann biography is Ronald Steel's *Walter Lippmann and the American Century* (Boston: Little, Brown, 1980).

2. Ibid., 406. See also Patrick Porter, "Beyond the American Century: Walter Lippmann and American Grand Strategy, 1943–1950," *Diplomacy and Statecraft* 22 (July 2011): 569.

3. Steel, *Walter Lippmann and the American Century*, 496.

4. Gregg Herken, *The Georgetown Set: Friends and Rivals in Cold War Washington* (New York: Knopf, 2014), 58.

5. Eric Alterman, *Sound and Fury: The Washington Punditocracy and the Collapse of American Politics* (New York: HarperCollins, 1992), 43–44.

6. Herken, *The Georgetown Set*, 64.

7. The only other reporters with that access were Joe Alsop, Phil Graham, and Scotty Reston. Herken, *The Georgetown Set*, 256–257. See also, "The Columnists JFK Reads Every Morning," *Newsweek*, December 18, 1961, 65–70.

8. Steel, *Walter Lippmann and the American Century*; Stephen Blum, *Walter Lippmann: Cosmopolitanism in the Century of Total War* (Ithaca, NY: Cornell University Press, 1984).

9. Steel, *Walter Lippmann and the American Century*, 445.
10. Ibid., 444–446.
11. Walter Lippmann, *Public Opinion* (New York: Harcourt, Brace, 1922), 31.
12. Walter Lippmann, *The Public Philosophy* (Boston: Little, Brown, 1955), 20.
13. Ibid. See also Gabriel Almond, *The American People and Foreign Policy* (New York: Praeger, 1950); Almond, "Public Opinion and National Security," *Public Opinion Quarterly* 20 (Summer 1956): 371–378; V. O. Key, *Public Opinion and American Democracy* (New York: Knopf, 1961); James Rosenau, *Public Opinion and Foreign Policy* (New York: Random House, 1961); and Philip Converse, "The Nature of Belief Systems in Mass Publics," in *Ideology and Discontent*, ed. David Apter (New York: Free Press, 1964); Christopjer Achen and Larry Bartels, *Democracy for Realists* (Princeton, NJ: Princeton University Press, 2016).
14. Fareed Zakaria, "The Politics of Rage: Why Do They Hate Us?," *Newsweek*, October 14, 2001.
15. For "liberal," see "The 25 Most Influential Liberals in the U.S. Media," *Forbes*, January 22, 2009. For "conservative," see Marion Maneker, "Man of the World," *New York*, April 14, 2003. For "neoconservative," see Joy Press, "The Interpreter," *The Village Voice*, August 9, 2005.
16. See Fareed Zakaria, "Changing the Middle East," *Slate*, January 20, 2004, as well as Maneker, "Man of the World."
17. Zakaria, "The Arrogant Empire," *Newsweek*, March 23, 2003; Zakaria, ""Rethinking Iraq: The Way Forward," *Newsweek*, November 5, 2006; Zakaria, "Who Lost Iraq? The Iraqis Did, with an Assist from George W. Bush," *Washington Post*, June 12, 2014.
18. Maneker, "Man of the World."
19. Mead's quote can be found at http://www.esquire.com/news-politics/a127/twenty-one-more-1199/. Kissinger quoted in Maneker, "Man of the World." The last quote is from David M. Shribman, "Globalization, Its Discontents, and Its Upside," *Boston Globe*, June 1, 2008.
20. Herken, *The Georgetown Set*. See also Robert Merry, *Taking on the World: Joseph and Stewart Alsop, Guardians of the American Century* (New York: Viking, 1996); Maureen Orth, "When Washington Was Fun," *Vanity Fair*, December 2007.
21. Wilson D. Miscamble, *George F. Kennan and the Making of American Foreign Policy, 1947–1950* (Princeton, NJ: Princeton University Press, 1992), 36; Walter Hixson, *George F. Kennan: Cold War Iconoclast* (New York: Columbia University Press, 1989.), 134; Herken, *The Georgetown Set*, 51.
22. See John Lewis Gaddis, *George F. Kennan: An American Life* (New York: Penguin, 2011), 270–75.
23. Steel, *Walter Lippmann and the American Century*, 346–363; Herken, *The Georgetown Set*, 204–209. To be sure, these scandals were not costless for either party. After the affair, Armstrong banned any mention or citation of Lippmann in *Foreign Affairs* during his tenure.

24. Interview with Fareed Zakaria, New York, NY, December 8, 2015.

25. Rob Krebs, *Narrative and the Making of US National Security* (New York: Cambridge University Press, 2015), chapter 6.

26. Graham Allison, "Cool It: The Foreign Policy of Young America," *Foreign Policy* 1 (Winter 1970/71), 150. See also Krebs, *Narrative and the Making of US National Security*, 192.

27. Andrew Bacevich, "American Public Intellectuals and the Early Cold War, or, Mad about Henry Wallace," in Michael Desch, ed., *Public Intellectuals in the Global Arena* (South Bend: University of Notre Dame Press, 2017), 83.

28. Alterman, *Sound and Fury*, 46–47.

29. Sherwin Rosen, "The Economics of Superstars," *American Economic Review* 71 (December 1981): 845–858.

30. Parag Khanna, *The Second World* (New York: Random House, 2008).

31. Parag Khanna, "Waving Goodbye to Hegemony," *New York Times Magazine*, January 27, 2008.

32. http://paragkhanna.com/about-parag-khanna/, accessed December 14, 2015.

33. Quoted in Ian Parker, "The Bright Side," *The New Yorker*, November 10, 2008.

34. Thomas Friedman, *The World Is Flat: A Brief History of the Twenty-First Century* (New York: Farrar Strauss Giroux, 2005), 279–280.

35. Friedman made sure that Bob Woodward knew that he had coined the "Pottery Barn rule" about invading other countries, not Secretary of State Colin Powell. Parker, "The Bright Side."

36. Information from Ferguson's biographical sketch accessed at http://www.niallferguson.com/about. Ferguson explicitly stated this in *The Ascent of Money* (New York: Penguin, 2008), 360.

37. That description of Ferguson's *Civilization* comes from a June 26, 2012, interview with the *Guardian*, accessed at http://www.theguardian.com/books/2012/jun/26/niall-ferguson-civilization-paperback-q-a.

38. Eric Alterman, "Niall Ferguson's Gay Theory for the World's Economic Problems Is Nothing If Not Novel," *Huffington Post*, July 9, 2013.

39. Tunku Varadarajan, "Fareed Zakaria's Plagiarism and the Lynch Mob," *Newsweek*, August 20, 2012.

40. Christine Haughney, "A Media Personality, Suffering a Blow to His Image, Ponders a Lesson," *New York Times*, August 19, 2012.

41. Katie Peek, "Keynote Cosmos," *Foreign Policy*, September/October 2016.

42. Justin Fox, "Rockin' in the Flat World," *Fortune*, September 19, 2005. On the rise of speaker fees for pundits more generally, see also Ben Smith, "Paid to Speak," *Politico*, October 11, 2010; Jason Horowitz, "At the Washington Speakers Bureau, Talk Isn't Cheap," *Washington Post*, October 10, 2011.

43. Interview with Niall Ferguson, Cambridge, MA, April 22, 2016.

44. Stephen Marche, "The Real Problem with Niall Ferguson's Letter to the 1%," *Esquire*, August 21, 2012.

45. Benioff quoted in Felix Salmon, "What on Earth was Thomas Friedman Talking About?" *Fusion*, January 23, 2015; Doerr quoted in Parker, "The Bright Side."

46. Interview with Niall Ferguson, Cambridge, MA, April 22, 2016. See also Mark Engler, "The Ascent of Niall Ferguson," *Dissent* (Spring 2009): 118–124.

47. After conferences in 2013 and 2014, there have been no subsequent Friedman Forums.

48. Parker, "The Bright Side."

49. Janet Tassel, "The Global Empire of Niall Ferguson," *Harvard Magazine*, May–June 2007, accessed at http://harvardmagazine.com/2007/05/the-global-empire-of-nia.html.

50. Richard Eden, "Historian Niall Ferguson: Why I Am Quitting Britain for 'Intellectual' America," *Daily Telegraph*, February 5, 2012.

51. Varadarajan, "Fareed Zakaria's Plagiarism and the Lynch Mob."

52. Benjamin Wallace-Wells, "Right Man's Burden," *Washington Monthly*, June 2004.

53. Zakaria interview, December 8, 2015.

54. See Alexander Abad-Santos, "We've Heard Fareed Zakaria's Excuse Before," *Atlantic Wire*, August 20, 2012, accessed at http://www.thewire.com/business/2012/08/weve-heard-fareed-zakarias-excuse/55952/; David Plotz, "The Plagiarist," *Slate*, January 11, 2002.

55. Every profile of Friedman or review of his work extols his first book, *From Beirut to Jerusalem*. Similarly, articles about Niall Ferguson praise his first major book, a history of the Rothschilds in the nineteenth century.

56. Haughney, "A Media Personality, Suffering a Blow to His Image, Ponders a Lesson"; Zakaria Interview, December 8, 2015.

57. For the harshest takes, see Steven Brill, "Stories I'd Like to See: Fareed Zakaria's 'mistake,'" Reuters, August 21, 2012; and Ta-Nehisi Coates, "How Plagiarism Happens," *The Atlantic*, August 27, 2012.

58. See, for example, https://ourbadmedia.wordpress.com/2014/11/10/newsweek-corrected-7-of-fareed-zakarias-plagiarized-articles-the-washington-post-needs-to-do-the-same-for-these-6/.

59. Dylan Byers, "Fareed Zakaria's Anonymous Pursuers: We're Not Done Yet," *Politico*, November 13, 2014.

60. Dylan Byers, "The Wrongs of Fareed Zakaria," *Politico*, September 16, 2014; Michael Kinsley, "Parsing the Plagiarism of Fareed Zakaria," *Vanity Fair*, February 28, 2015.

61. Wallace-Wells, "Right Man's Burden."

62. Niall Ferguson, "Not two countries, but one: Chimerica," *Daily Telegraph*, March 4, 2007; Ferguson, "The Real Costs of Isolationism," *Newsweek*, June 26, 2011.

63. Justin Fox, "Niall Ferguson and the Rage against the Thought-Leader Machine," *Harvard Business Review*, August 23, 2012.

64. The full text of the letter can be accessed at http://www.hoover.org/research/open-letter-ben-bernanke.

65. Niall Ferguson, "Complexity and Collapse," *Foreign Affairs* 89 (March/April 2010): 18–32.

66. Joe Weisenthal, "Niall Ferguson Has Been Wrong on Economics," *Business Insider*, August 19, 2012.

67. Niall Ferguson, "Hit the Road, Barack," *Newsweek*, August 19, 2012.

68. See Paul Krugman, "Unethical Commentary, Newsweek Edition," *New York Times*, August 19, 2012; Matthew O'Brien, "A Full Fact-Check of Niall Ferguson's Very Bad Argument against Obama," *The Atlantic*, August 20, 2012; Dylan Byers, "Niall Ferguson's Ridiculous Defense," *Politico*, August 20, 2012; Joe Weisenthal, "Niall Ferguson Publishes Embarrassing Defense of Newsweek Article," *Business Insider*, August 20, 2012.

69. For Ferguson's defense, see "Correct This, Bloggers," *Daily Beast*, August 21, 2012. For the responses to Ferguson's response, see Dylan Byers, "Niall Ferguson ducks, nitpicks, vilifies," *Politico*, August 21, 2012; and David Weigel, "Leave Niall Ferguson Alone!," *Slate*, August 21, 2012.

70. John Cassidy, "Ferguson vs. Krugman: Where are the Real Conservative Intellectuals?," *New Yorker*, August 20, 2012; Ryan Chittum, "*Newsweek*'s Niall Ferguson Debacle," *Columbia Journalism Review*, August 21, 2012.

71. Henry Blodget, "Harvard's Niall Ferguson Blamed Keynes' Economic Philosophy on His Being Childless and Gay," *Business Insider*, May 4, 2013.

72. "Correction: UK Confidence," *Financial Times*, June 2, 2015; see also Greg Callus's adjudication of Ferguson's column for the *Financial Times* at http://aboutus.ft.com/files/2010/09/Ferguson-Adjudication-with-PS.pdf.

73. Ferguson, "Correct this, Bloggers."

74. Niall Ferguson, "Quantitative Teasing," http://www.niallferguson.com/blog/quantitative-teasing, December 5, 2013; Caleb Melby, Laura Marcinek, and Danielle Burger, "Fed Critics Say '10 Letter Warning Inflation Still Right," *BloombergBusiness*, October 2, 2014.

75. Niall Ferguson, "An Unqualified Apology," http://www.niallferguson.com/blog/an-unqualified-apology, May 4, 2013.

76. Niall Ferguson, "An Open Letter to the Harvard Community," *Harvard Crimson*, May 7, 2013.

77. Daniel W. Drezner, "Oh, Niall," *Foreign Policy*, May 9, 2013.

78. Ferguson, "Jonathan Portes, Master of the Political Correction."

79. Interview with Ferguson, April 22, 2016.

80. See, for example, Niall Ferguson, "Civilizing the Marketplace of Ideas," *Project Syndicate*, October 14, 2013.

81. Tassel, "The Global Empire of Niall Ferguson." See also Michael Lind, "Niall Ferguson and the Brain-Dead American Right," *Salon*, May 24, 2011, accessed at http://www.salon.com/2011/05/24/lind_niall_fergsuon/.

82. Jonathan Chait, "Niall Ferguson Fights Back against Smear Campaign
     by Fact-checkers, Facts," *New York*, June 11, 2015. See also Fox, "Niall
     Ferguson and the Rage against the Thought Leader Machine."

83. Mark Hemingway, "Lies, Damned Lies, and 'Fact Checking,'" *Weekly
     Standard*, December 19, 2011; Matt Welch, "The 'Truth' Hurts," *Reason*,
     January 7, 2013; Sean Davis, "PunditFact: A Case Study in Face-Free
     Hackery," *The Federalist*, April 29, 2015.

84. See, for example, the contemporaneous defenses of Ferguson's *Newsweek*
     essay at http://www.newsweek.com/responses-niall-fergusons-newsweek-
     cover-story-obama-64559, including from the donor of Ferguson's
     endowed chair at Harvard; Glenn Beck's defense of Ferguson can be
     heard at http://www.glennbeck.com/2012/08/20/newsweek-hit-the-road-
     barack/; Jonah Goldberg, "Niall Ferguson's Real Mistake," *National
     Review* online, http://www.nationalreview.com/article/347651/niall-
     fergusons-real-mistake-jonah-goldberg, May 8, 2013.

85. Meg P. Bernhard and Mariel A. Klein, "Historian Niall Ferguson Will
     Leave Harvard for Stanford," *Harvard Crimson*, October 8, 2015.

86. When the *Financial Times* was forced to issue a factual correction of one
     of his 2015 columns, he responded by noting, "We all make mistakes,
     especially if we are busy, as I am, teaching students and writing books."
     Niall Ferguson, "Jonathan Portes, Master of the Political Correction," *The
     Spectator*, June 13, 2015.

87. Ferguson interview, April 22, 2016.

88. It should be noted that the one conference he still attends is the World
     Economic Forum in Davos. There are worse handicaps.

89. Zakaria interview, December 8, 2015.

90. Michael Kinsley corresponded by email with Zakaria, but noted, "On
     instructions from his bosses at CNN, anything about plagiarism is strictly
     off the record." Kinsley, "Parsing the Plagiarism of Fareed Zakaria." The
     same was true for my own interview with Zakaria.

91. David Carr, "Journalists Dancing on the Edge of Truth," *New York Times*,
     August 19, 2012.

92. See Jeffrey Goldberg, "Fareedenfreude (or, Alternatively, Schadenfareed),"
     The Atlantic, August 14, 2012.

93. Interview with Zakaria, December 8, 2015.

94. Brooks, *Bobos in Paradise*, chapter 4.

95. Carr, "Journalists Dancing on the Edge of Truth."

96. Fox, "Niall Ferguson and the Rage against the Thought Leader Machine."

Chapter 8

1. Joseph Schumpeter, *Capitalism, Socialism, and Democracy*
    (New York: Harper and Row, 1950).

2. Robert Solow, "Technical Change and the Aggregate Production
    Function," *Review of Economics and Statistics* 39 (August 1957): 312–320;

Paul Romer, "Endogenous Technological Change," *Journal of Political Economy* 98 (October 1990): S71–S102; Robert Gordon, *The Rise and Fall of American Growth: The U.S. Standard of Living since the Civil War* (Princeton, NJ: Princeton University Press, 2016).

3. Joseph L. Mower and Clayton Christensen, "Disruptive Technologies: Catching the Wave," *Harvard Business Review* 73 (January/February 1995): 43–53.

4. Clayton Christensen, Dina Wang, and Derek van Bever, "Consulting on the Cusp of Disruption," *Harvard Business Review* 91 (October 2013): 109.

5. Clayton Christensen, *The Innovator's Dilemma* (Cambridge, MA: Harvard Business School Press, 1997), xii.

6. Joshua Gans, "Keep Calm and Manage Disruption," *MIT Sloan Management Review* 57 (Spring 2016): 83.

7. "Disrupting Mr. Disrupter," *Economist*, November 28, 2015.

8. For more on Christensen's faith, see http://www.claytonchristensen.com/beliefs/; for a glimpse into his political worldview, see Nicholas Fandos, "Conversations: Clayton Christensen," *Harvard Crimson*, November 1, 2012.

9. Clayton Christensen and Michael Raynor, *The Innovator's Solution* (Cambridge, MA: Harvard Business School Press, 2003).

10. Michael E. Raynor, "Of Waves and Ripples: Disruption Theory's Newest Critics Tries to Make a Splash," Deloitte University Press, July 8, 2014, accessed at http://dupress.com/articles/disruptive-innovation-theory-lepore-response/.

11. See, for example, Richard N. Foster, *Innovation: The Attacker's Advantage* (New York: Summit Books, 1986).

12. William W. Lewis, *The Power of Productivity* (Chicago: University of Chicago Press, 2004).

13. Evan Goldstein, "The Undoing of Disruption," *Chronicle of Higher Education*, September 15, 2015.

14. See, for example, Clayton Christensen, James Allworth, and Karen Dillon, *How Will You Measure Your Life?* (New York: Harper Business, 2012).

15. Craig Lambert, "Disruptive Genius," *Harvard Magazine*, July–August 2014.

16. See http://www.claytonchristensen.com/ideas-in-action/rose-park-advisors/.

17. Lexis/Nexis news search; see also *Economist*, "Disrupting Mr. Disrupter."

18. Goldstein, "The Undoing of Disruption"; Jena McGregor, "The World's Most Influential Management Thinker?," *Washington Post*, November 12, 2013.

19. Henry Blodget, "Harvard Management Legend Clay Christensen Defends His 'Disruption' Theory, explains the Only Way Apple Can Win," *Business Insider*, November 2, 2014.

20. See, for example, Michael Raynor, "Disruption Theory as a Predictor of Innovation Success/Failure," *Strategy and Leadership* 39 (July 2011): 27–30.

21. Clayton Christensen, Jerome Grosman, and Jason Hwang, *The Innovator's Prescription* (New York: McGraw-Hill, 2008); Clayton Christensen, Curtis Johnson, and Michael Horn, *Disrupting Class* (New York: McGraw-Hill, 2008); Clayton Christensen and Henry Eyring, *The Innovative University* (San Francisco: Jossey-Bass, 2011).

22. Clayton Christensen, "A Capitalist's Dilemma, Whoever Wins on Tuesday," *New York Times*, November 3, 2012; Christensen and Derek Van Bever, "The Capitalist's Dilemma," *Harvard Business Review* 92 (June 2014): 60–68.

23. See http://www.claytonchristensen.com/ideas-in-action/christensen-institute/.

24. See http://disruptorfoundation.org/.

25. Goldstein, "The Undoing of Disruption."

26. Blodget, "Harvard Management Legend Clay Christensen Defends His 'Disruption' Theory."

27. See, for example, McKinsey Global Institute, "Big Data: The Next Frontier for Innovation, Competition, and Productivity," or "Disruptive Technologies: Advances That Will Transform Life, Business, and the Global Economy."

28. Accenture, "Be the Disruptor, Not the Disrupted," accessed at https://www.accenture.com/ae-en/insight-compliance-risk-study-2015-financial-services.aspx.

29. Richard Dobbs, James Manyika, and Jonathan Woetzel, *No Ordinary Disruption: The Four Global Forces Breaking All The Trends* (New York: PublicAffairs, 2015), 3 and 8.

30. The *Times'* Innovation Report can be accessed at https://www.scribd.com/doc/224332847/NYT-Innovation-Report-2014. See also Rhys Grossman, "The Industries That Are Being Disrupted the Most by Digital," *Harvard Business Review*, March 21, 2016.

31. Jill Lepore, "The Disruption Machine: What the Gospel of Innovation Gets Wrong," *New Yorker*, June 23, 2014.

32. Dobbs, Manyika, and Woetzel, *No Ordinary Disruption*, 199.

33. See the covers at https://www.foreignaffairs.com/issues/2016/95/1#browse-past-issues.

34. Eric Schmidt and Jared Cohen, "The Digital Disruption," *Foreign Affairs* 89 (November/December 2010): 75 and 85.

35. See also, for example, Mohamed El-Erian, "Governments' Self-Disruption Challenge," *Project Syndicate*, October 13, 2015.

36. Parag Khanna and Ayesha Khanna, *Hybrid Reality* (TED Conferences, 2012).

37. Parag Khanna, *Connectography* (New York: Random House, 2016), 6.

38. Thomas Friedman, "The Do-It-Yourself Economy," *New York Times*, December 12, 2009; Friedman, "It's P.Q. and C.Q. as Much as I.Q.,"

New York Times, January 29, 2013; Friedman, "The Professors' Big Stage," *New York Times*, March 5, 2013; Friedman, "Hillary, Jeb, Facebook and Disorder," *New York Times*, May 20, 2015.

39. Peter J. Dombrowski and Eugene Gholz, *Buying Military Transformation: Technological Innovation and the Defense Industry* (New York: Columbia University Press, 2006); Gautam Makunda, "We Cannot Go On: Disruptive Innovation and the First World War Royal Navy," *Security Studies* 19 (February 2010): 124–159; Jonathan Caverley and Ethan Kapstein, "Who's Arming Asia?" *Survival* 52 (Spring 2016): 167–184.

40. David Rothkopf, "Objects on Your TV Screen Are Much Smaller Than They Appear," *Foreign Policy*, March 20, 2015.

41. Anne-Marie Slaughter, "America's Edge," *Foreign Affairs* 88 (January/February 2009): 94–95.

42. Alex Thier, "Disruptive Innovations Bringing Nepal Closer to Ending Extreme Poverty," *USAID Impact* (blog), January 5, 2015, accessed at https://blog.usaid.gov/2015/01/disruptive-innovations-bringing-nepal-closer-to-ending-extreme-poverty/.

43. Hillary Clinton, *Hard Choices* (New York: Simon and Schuster, 2014).

44. US Department of State, "21st Century Statecraft," accessed at http://www.state.gov/statecraft/overview/index.htm. See also Clinton, *Hard Choices*, chapter 24; Alec Ross, "Digital Diplomacy and US Foreign Policy," *The Hague Journal of Diplomacy* 6.3–4 (2011): 451–455.

45. Marvin Ammori, "Obama's Unsung Tech Hero: Hillary Clinton," *Huffington Post*, May 25, 2011.

46. First Clinton quote from Natalie Kitroeff, "Is the Theory of Disruption Dead Wrong?," *BloombergBusiness*, October 5, 2015; second Clinton quote from David Sanger, "Hillary Clinton Urges Silicon Valley to 'Disrupt' ISIS," *New York Times*, December 6, 2015.

47. Felipe Cuello, "A Defense of Donald Trump's Foreign Policy Chops," *Foreign Policy*, February 26, 2016.

48. See, for example, Andrew King, and Christopher Tucci, "Incumbent Entry into New Market Niches: The Role of Experience and Managerial Choice in the Creation of Dynamic Capabilities," *Management Science* 48 (February 2002): 171–186; Erwin Danneels, "Disruptive Technology Reconsidered: A Critique and Research Agenda," *Journal of Product Innovation Management* 21 (July 2004): 246–258; Vijay Govindarajan and Praveen Kopalle, "The Usefulness of Measuring Disruptiveness of Innovations Ex Post in Making Ex Ante Predictions," *Journal of Product Innovation Management* 23 (January 2006): 12–18; Constantinos Markides, "Disruptive Innovation: In Need of Better Theory" *Journal of Product Innovation Management* 23 (January 2006): 19–25.

49. Maxwell Wessel, "Stop Reinventing Disruption," *Harvard Business Review*, March 7, 2013; Judith Shulevitz, "Don't You Dare Say 'Disruptive," *New Republic*, August 16, 2013.

50. Lepore, "The Disruption Machine."
51. Ibid.
52. Richard Feloni, "The *New Yorker*'s Takedown of Disruptive Innovation Is Causing a Huge Stir," *Business Insider*, June 19, 2014; Steven Syre, "Harvard Professors Clash over Rebuke of Business Theory," *Boston Globe*, July 8, 2014; Drake Bennett, "Clayton Christensen Responds to *New Yorker* Takedown of 'Disruptive Innovation,'" *BloombergBusiness*, June 20, 2014; MaryAnne M. Gobble, "The Case against Disruptive Innovation," *Research Technology Management* 58 (January/February 2015): 59–61.
53. Paul Krugman, "Creative Destruction Yada Yada," *New York Times*, June 16, 2014; Kevin Roose, "Let's All Stop Saying 'Disrupt' Right This Instant," *New York*, June 16, 2014; Timothy B. Lee, "Disruption Is a Dumb Buzzword. It's Also an Important Concept," *Vox*, June 17, 2014.
54. Gobble, "The Case against Disruptive Innovation," 61.
55. https://twitter.com/pmarca/status/479297963831738368.
56. Blodget, "Harvard Management Legend Clay Christensen Defends His 'Disruption' Theory"; Drake Bennett, "Clayton Christensen Responds to *New Yorker* Takedown of 'Disruptive Innovation,'" *BloombergBusiness*, June 20, 2014; Andrew Hill, "Attack on Clayton Christensen's Theory Falls Wide of the Mark," *Financial Times*, June 23, 2014; Clive Crook, "An Incompetent Attack on the Innovator's Dilemma," Bloomberg, June 30, 2015; Irving Wladawsky-Berger, "A Growing Backlash against the Relentless Advances in Technology?," *Wall Street Journal*, July 3, 2014. In fairness, Lepore's criticism of Christensen's inductive generalization seemed particularly off. It is true that social science usually frowns on inductive methods over deductive theory building. That said, there are obvious examples of excellent theoretical work emerging from inductive case studies. See, on this methodological question, Alexander George and Andrew Bennett, *Case Studies and Theory Development in the Social Sciences* (Cambridge: MIT Press, 2005).
57. Raynor, "Of Waves and Ripples."
58. Lee, "Disruption Is a Dumb Buzzword."
59. Hill, "Attack on Clayton Christensen's theory falls wide of the mark."
60. Blodget, "Harvard Management Legend Clay Christensen Defends his 'Disruption' Theory."
61. Michael R. Weeks, "Is Disruption Theory Wearing New Clothes or Just Naked? Analyzing Recent Critiques of Disruptive Innovation Theory," *Innovation: Management, Policy and Practice* 17 (Winter 2015) 417–428.
62. Andrew King and Baljir Baatartogtokh, "How Useful Is the Theory of Disruptive Innovation?," *MIT Sloan Management Review* 57 (Fall 2015): 77–90.
63. Ibid, 82.
64. Goldstein, "The Undoing of Disruption"; Bhaskar Chakravorti, "The Problem with the Endless Discussion of Disruptive Innovation," *Washington Post*, November 24, 2015.

65. *Economist*, "Disrupting Mr. Disrupter."
66. Quoted in Goldstein, "The Undoing of Disruption."
67. Greg Ip, "Beyond the Internet, Innovation Struggles," *Wall Street Journal*, August 12, 2015; James Heskett, "What Happened to the 'Innovation, Disruption, Technology' Dividend?," August 5, 2015, accessed at http://hbswk.hbs.edu/item/what-happened-to-the-innovation-disruption-technology-dividend.
68. Goldstein, "The Undoing of Disruption."
69. Clayton Christensen, Michael Raynor, and Rory McDonald, "What Is Disruptive Innovation?," *Harvard Business Review* (December 2015), 44–53.
70. Frank Rose, "Disruption . . . Disrupted," *Milken Institute Review* 18 (Third Quarter 2016): 34.
71. King and Baatartogtokh, "How Useful Is the Theory of Disruptive Innovation?," 88.
72. Jena McGregor, "What this Harvard innovation guru thinks can protect companies from disruption," *Washington Post*, October 5, 2016.
73. Andrew Hill, "Clayton Christensen moves on from the dissing of disruption," *Financial Times*, October 3, 2016.
74. See the citations in footnote 39.
75. Evgeny Morozov, *To Save Everything, Click Here: The Folly of Technological Solutionism* (New York: PublicAffairs, 2013), 44. See also Morozov, "Beware: Silicon Valley's Cultists Want to Turn You into a Disruptive Deviant," *Guardian*, January 3, 2016.
76. Morozov, *To Save Everything, Click Here*, 35.
77. Evgeny Morozov, "The Naked and the TED," *New Republic*, August 2, 2012.
78. Quoted in Daniel W. Drezner, "How Trolling Could Become the New International Language of Diplomacy," *Washington Post*, May 15, 2015.
79. Jared Cohen, "Digital Counterinsurgency," *Foreign Affairs* 94 (November/December 2015): 53–58.
80. Ibid, 55.
81. Elizabeth Radziszewski, "Foreign Policy Has Lost Its Creativity. Design Thinking Is the Answer," *Wilson Quarterly* (Winter 2015), accessed at http://wilsonquarterly.com/stories/foreign-policy-has-lost-its-creativity-design-thinking-is-the-answer/.
82. Gans, "Keep Calm and Manage Disruption," 84.
83. Goldstein, "The Undoing of Disruption."
84. Ibid.
85. One management expert suggested to me that Christensen's myriad health issues over the past decade also acted as a deterrent, in that no scholar wanted to take on someone suffering from serious ailments.
86. Timothy Aeppel, "Silicon Valley Doesn't Believe U.S. Productivity Is Slowing Down," *Wall Street Journal*, July 16, 2015.

Chapter 9

1. John Sides, "The Political Scientist as a Blogger," *PS: Political Science and Politics* 44 (April 2011): 267–271.

2. J. Bradford DeLong, "The Invisible College," *Chronicle of Higher Education*, July 28, 2006. See also Henry Farrell, "The Blogosphere as a Carnival of Ideas," *Chronicle of Higher Education*, October 7, 2005.

3. Google descriptor accessed at https://www.google.com/search?q=political +science+rumours&rlz=1C1CHFX_enUS529US529&oq=political+science +rumours&aqs=chrome.69i57j69i59j0l3j69i64.6965j0j4&sourceid=chrom e&es_sm=0&ie=UTF-8.

4. Chris Barker, "Surfing the Cesspool: Political Science Rumors and the LaCour Scandal," *Duck of Minerva* (blog), June 16, 2015, accessed at http://duckofminerva.com/2015/06/surfing-the-cesspool-political-science-rumors-and-the-lacour-scandal.html.

5. See, for example, http://www.econjobrumors.com/ and http://www. socjobrumors.com/. On the utility of these sites, see Rebecca Schuman, "'Demoralizing but Informative,'" *Slate*, December 22, 2016.

6. Scott Jaschik, "Job Market Realities," *Inside Higher Ed*, September 8, 2009.

7. Megan MacKenzie, "Why I Don't Participate at Political Science Rumors," *Duck of Minerva* (blog), April 12, 2014, accessed at http:// duckofminerva.com/2014/04/why-i-dont-participate-in-political-science-rumors.html.

8. Letter from APSA president Robert Axelrod to department chairs, posted at IR Rumor Mill, "Robert Axelrod on Academic Rumor Mills and Gossip Blogs," April 3, 2007, accessed at http://irrumormill.blogspot. com/2007/04/robert-axelrod-on-academic-rumor-mills.html.

9. Quotes from https://twitter.com/jessesingal/status/604739770200276992 and Jesse Singal, "The Case of the Amazing Gay-Marriage Data: How a Graduate Student Reluctantly Uncovered a Huge Scientific Fraud," *New York*, May 29, 2015.

10. For a Political Science Rumors thread on this very topic, see http://www. polscirumors.com/topic/this-site-has-to-go.

11. Steve Saideman, "Why I Participate at Political Science Rumors," *Duck of Minerva* (blog), April 20, 2014, accessed at http://duckofminerva. dreamhosters.com/2014/04/why-i-participate-at-political-science-rumors. html.

12. Daniel Nexon, "'Overheard' on Political Science Job Rumors," *Duck of Minerva* (blog), March 13, 2013, accessed at http://duckofminerva.com/ 2009/03/overheard-on-political-science-job.html.

13. Michael Munger, "L'Affaire LaCour," *Chronicle of Higher Education*, June 15, 2015.

14. Joshua Cohen, "On Bullshit, and Especially Execrable Bullshit," September 1, 2015, accessed at http://leiterreports.typepad.com/files/ cohenonbullshit.pdf.

15. John Scalzi, "Straight White Male: The Lowest Difficulty Setting There Is," *Whatever*, May 15, 3012, accessed at http://whatever.scalzi.com/2012/05/15/straight-white-male-the-lowest-difficulty-setting-there-is/.

16. See Megan MacKenzie, "You Make My Work (Im)Possible: Reflections on Professional Conduct in the Discipline of International Relations," *Duck of Minerva* (blog), April 9, 2014, accessed at http://duckofminerva.dreamhosters.com/2014/04/you-make-my-work-impossible-reflections-on-professional-conduct-in-the-discipline-of-international-relations.html; MacKenzie, "Why I Don't Participate at Political Science Rumors."

17. Friedman quoted in Ian Parker, "The Bright Side," *New Yorker*, November 10, 2008.

18. Norman Shapiro and Robert Anderson, "Toward an Ethics and Etiquette for Electronic Mail," RAND report R-3283-NSF/RC, July 1985, accessed at http://www.rand.org/pubs/reports/R3283/index1.html.

19. Mike Godwin, "I Created Godwin's Law in 1990, but It Wasn't a Prediction—It Was a Warning," *International Business Times*, May 27, 2016.

20. Interview with Fareed Zakaria, New York, December 9, 2015.

21. Fareed Zakaria, "Bile, Venom and Lies: How I Was Trolled on the Internet," *Washington Post*, January 14, 2016.

22. Interview with Niall Ferguson, Cambridge, MA, April 22, 2016.

23. Justin Peters, "I Was Afraid of Slate Commenters. So I Became One," *Slate*, November 5, 2015.

24. Elizabeth Jensen, "NPR Website to Get Rid of Comments," NPR, August 17, 2016.

25. Eva Holland, " 'It's Yours': A Short History of the Horde," Longreads, Febeuary 4, 2015, accessed at http://blog.longreads.com/2015/02/04/its-yours-a-short-history-of-the-horde/.

26. Justin Cheng, Christian Danescu-Niculescu-Mizil, and Jure Leskovec, "How Community Feedback Shapes User Behavior," May 6, 2014, 9.

27. Moynihan quoted in Jon Ronson, *So You've Been Publicly Shamed* (New York: Riverfront Books, 2015), 50.

28. Quoted in Thomas Friedman, "Social Media: Destroyer or Creator?," *New York Times*, February 3, 2016.

29. Peters, "I Was Afraid of Slate Commenters. So I Became One."

30. https://twitter.com/mattgarrahan/status/664104973735694336.

31. See, for example, Amanda Hess, "Why Women Aren't Welcome on the Internet," *Pacific Standard*, January 6, 2014; Maeve Duggan, "Online Harrassment," Pew Research Center, October 22, 2014.

32. Annie Lowrey and Abraham Riesman, "Goodbye to All That, Twitter," *New York*, January 19, 2016.

33. Rachel Barney, "[Aristotle], On Trolling," *Journal of the American Philosophical Association*, available on CJO 2016 doi:10.1017/apa.2016.9, 3.

34. Sonny Bunch, "How to Use Twitter without Going Insane," *Washington Post*, January 20, 2016.

35. Most perfect online retorts involve the author J. K. Rowling. See, for example, Amanda Taub, "JK Rowling Had the Best Possible Reaction to Rupert Murdoch's Anti-Muslim Tweet," *Vox*, January 11, 2015.

36. Eli Lake, "How Ted Cruz Trolls Obama's Foreign Policy," *Daily Beast*, July 29, 2014.

37. Andrew Marantz, "Trolls for Trump," *New Yorker*, October 31, 2016.

38. John Stuart Mill, *On Liberty*, 40–41.

39. See, for example, Robert Tracinski, "#FreeStacy: The Old Regime and the Twitter Revolution," *The Federalist*, February 22, 2016.

40. Michael LaCour and Don Green, "When Contact Changes Minds: An Experiment on Transmission of Support for Gay Equality," *Science* 346 (December 12, 2014): 1366–1369.

41. Monte Morin, "Doorstep Visits Change Attitudes on Gay Marriage," *Los Angeles Times*, December 12, 2014.

42. Sasha Issenberg, "How Do You Change Someone's Mind about Abortion? Tell Them You Had One," BloombergPolitics, October 6, 2014; Benedict Carey, "Gay Advocates Can Shift Same-Sex Marriage Views," *New York Times*, December 11, 2014.

43. Carl Bialik, "As a Major Retraction Shows, We're All Vulnerable to Faked Data," *FiveThirtyEight*, May 20, 2015.

44. Accessed at http://www.poliscirumors.com/topic/gelmans-monkey-cage-post/page/2#post-240222.

45. Singal, "The Case of the Amazing Gay-Marriage Data."

46. David Broockman, Joshia Kalla, and Peter Aronow, "Irregularities in LaCour (2014)," working paper, May 19, 2015, accessed at http://stanford.edu/~dbroock/broockman_kalla_aronow_lg_irregularities.pdf. On Green's reaction, see Bialik, "As a Major Retraction Shows, We're All Vulnerable to Faked Data"; Singal, "The Case of the Amazing Gay-Marriage Data."

47. Jesse Singal, "Michael LaCour Made Up a Teaching Award, Too," *New York*, May 27, 2015.

48. Munger, "L'Affaire LaCour."

49. Jesse Singal, "Inside Psychology's 'Methodological Terrorism' Debate," New York, October 12, 2016.

50. Marc Lynch, "Political Science in Real Time: Engaging the Middle East Policy Public," *Perspectives on Politics* 14 (March 2016): 128.

51. Quoted in Joel Stein, "How Trolls Are Ruining the Internet," *Time*, August 18, 2016.

52. Ibid., 128.

53. Lowrey and Riesman, "Goodbye to All That, Twitter."

54. See, for example, Matthew Boesler, "Nassim Taleb Gets into Historic Twitter Brawl, Shows Everyone How ANTIFRAGILE He Is," *Business Insider*, April 23, 2013; Joe Weisenthal, "Nassim Taleb Tells Us Why He

Goes Nuclear on His Critics on Twitter," *Business Insider*, January 4, 2014. For an example of him insulting me, see https://twitter.com/nntaleb/status/755051465719283712.

55. See, for example, Nasim Taleb, "Intellectual Yet Idiot," Medium, September 16, 2016, accessed at https://medium.com/@nntaleb/the-intellectual-yet-idiot-13211e2d0577#.ienj9raar.

56. Conversation with Nicholas Nassim Taleb, Cambridge, MA, June 2, 2015.

57. David Weigel, "Watch Nassim Taleb Debate Twitter's Greatest Tech Jargon Parody Account," *Slate*, August 12, 2014.

58. M. D. Conover, J. Ratkiewicz, M. Francisco, B. Goncalves, A. Flammini, and F. Menczer, "Political Polarization on Twitter," Proceedings of the Fifth International AAAI Conference on Weblogs and Social Media, 2011, accessed at https://www.aaai.org/ocs/index.php/ICWSM/ICWSM11/paper/viewFile/2847/3275;

59. Pew Research Center, "Political Polarization and Media Habits," October 21, 2014.

60. Barney, "[Aristotle,] On Trolling," 2.

61. Dylan Matthews, "Inside *Jacobin*: How a Socialist Magazine Is Winning the Left's War of Ideas," *Vox*, March 21, 2016.

62. See Sady Doyle, "Beware of the Angry White Male Public Intellectual," *Quartz*, February 16, 2016.

63. Kevin Drum, "The Great Matt Bruenig-Neera Tanden Kerfuffle Sort of Explained," *Mother Jones*, May 20, 2012.

64. The description of the alt-right comes from Rosie Gray, "How 2015 Fueled the Rise of the Freewheeling, White Nationalist Alt Right Movement," *Buzzfeed*, December 27, 2015. For the manifesto, see Allum Bokhari and Milo Yiannopoulos, "An Establishment Conservative's Guide to the Alt-Right," *Breitbart*, March 29, 2016.

65. See Jesse Singal, "Explaining Ben Shapiro's Messy, Ethnic-Slur-Laden Breakup With Breitbart," *New York*, May 26, 2016; Jonathan Weisman, "The Nazi Tweets of 'Trump God Emperor,'" *New York Times*, May 26, 2016; Jamie Kirchick, "Donald Trump's Little Boy Is a Gay Half-Jew with Jungle Fever," *Tablet*, June 1, 2016.

66. To use Walter Russell Mead's typology of American foreign policy schools of thought, the Jeffersonians are most angry with the Wilsonians, and the Jacksonians are most angry with the Hamiltonians. See Walter Russell Mead, *Special Providence: American Foreign Policy and How It Changed the World* (New York: Knopf, 2001).

67. Matt Taibbi, "Flathead," *New York Press*, April 26, 2005.

68. The definitive archive of Tom Friedman takedowns, curated by Jillian York, can be accessed at http://jilliancyork.com/2011/12/14/the-definitive-collection-of-thomas-friedman-takedowns/. It is continually updated. In the interest of full disclosure, I have contributed to this oeuvre: Daniel W. Drezner, "Suffering from Friedman's Disease in Beijing," *Foreign Policy*, June 9, 2011.

69. Alice Gregory, "When Is Criticism Unfair?" *New York Times Book Review*, February 2, 2016.

70. Perhaps other superstars traveling in the same conference circuits can serve as useful critics. But the clubbiness that comes with this circuit can also mute criticism more than would otherwise be desirable.

Conclusion

1. Croly quoted in Franklin Foer, "The Story of How the *New Republic* Invented Modern Liberalism," *New Republic*, November 8, 2014.

2. Jeet Heer, "The *New Republic*'s Legacy on Race," *New Republic*, January 29, 2015.

3. Ta-Nehisi Coates, "The *New Republic*: An Appreciation," *The Atlantic*, December 9, 2014.

4. Hertzberg quoted in Lloyd Grove, "Is This the End of 'The New Republic'?" *Daily Beast*, January 11, 2016.

5. This pattern was not unique to the *New Republic*, though perhaps it had the most regular cycle. See Jack Shafer, "The New Vanity Press Moguls," *Slate*, February 27, 2004.

6. Julie Bosman and Christina Haughney, "Foer Returns to *New Republic* as Editor," *New York Times*, May 20, 2012.

7. Carl Swanson, "Chris Hughes Is about to Turn 100," *New York*, December 2, 2012.

8. David Holmes, "The *New Republic*'s Chris Hughes in 2013: 'We Are Not the Next Big Trend in Silicon Valley,' " Pando, http://pando.com/2014/12/05/the-new-republics-chris-hughes-in-2013-we-are-not-the-next-big-trend-in-silicon-valley/, December 5, 2014.

9. Wieseltier quoted in Paul Farhi, "Chris Hughes, Once a New Media Pioneer, Makes Bet on Old Media with the *New Republic*," *Washington Post*, July 8, 2012. See also Bosman and Haughney, "Foer Returns to *New Republic* as Editor"; David Weigel, "How #Disruption Broke the *New Republic*," *Bloomberg Politics*, December 5, 2014.

10. In hiring Foer, Hughes pushed aside Richard Just, the editor who had, ironically, recruited Hughes to buy the magazine two months earlier.

11. Evgeny Morozov, "The Naked and the TED," *New Republic*, August 2, 2012; Alec MacGillis, "Scandal at Clinton Inc.," *New Republic*, September 23, 2013; Ben Birmbaum and Amir Tohon, "The Explosive, Inside Story of How John Kerry Built an Israel-Palestine Peace Plan—and Watched It Crumble," *New Republic*, July 20, 2014; Julia Ioffe, "Vladimir Putin Might Fall. We Should Consider What Happens Next," *New Republic*, August 6, 2014.

12. Dana Milbank, "The *New Republic* Is Dead, Thanks to Its Owner, Chris Hughes," *Washington Post*, December 8, 2014.

13. Sarah Ellison, "The Complex Power Coupledom of Chris Hughes and Sean Eldridge," *Vanity Fair*, July 2015.

14. Erik Wemple, "Chris Hughes at the *New Republic*: A Wasteful Experiment in Modern Design," *Washington Post*, January 22, 2016.

15. The news release can be accessed at http://www.newrepublic.com/article/ 119470/press-release-guy-vidra-general-manager-yahoo-news-tnr-ceo. The New Republic Fund is explained at http://fund.newrepublic.com/.

16. Ellison, "The Complex Power Coupledom of Chris Hughes and Sean Eldridge."

17. Ryan Lizza, "Inside the Collapse of the *New Republic*," *New Yorker*, December 12, 2014. See also Dylan Byers, "Implosion of a DC Institution, *Politico*, December 4, 2014.

18. Ravi Somaiya, "Shake-Up at the *New Republic*: Franklin Foer and Leon Wieseltier Are Out," *New York Times*, December 4, 2014.

19. Gabriel Snyder, "A Letter from the Editor," *New Republic*, December 22, 2014.

20. Chris Hughes, "Crafting a Sustainable *New Republic*," *Washington Post*, December 7, 2014.

21. Lukas I. Alpert, "*New Republic* to Start Producing Content for Advertisers," *Wall Street Journal*, March 19, 2015.

22. Last two quotes from Benjamin Mullin, "The (new) *New Republic*: How the Magazine's Bosses Are Building a Company around 'Novel Solutions,'" Poynter, August 11, 2015, accessed at http://www.poynter. org/news/mediawire/364679/the-new-new-republic-how-the-magazines-bosses-are-building-a-company-around-novel-solutions/.

23. Michael Eric Dyson, "The Ghost of Cornel West," *New Republic*, April 19, 2015.

24. Foer interview via Skype, December 24, 2015; interview with Gideon Rose, New York, December 8, 2015.

25. Lukas Alpert, "*New Republic* Owner Chris Hughes Puts Magazine Up for Sale," *Wall Street Journal*, January 11, 2016. See also Megan McArdle, "Next Owner of the *New Republic* Needs a Better Vision," BloombergView, January 11, 2016.

26. Chris Hughes, "The *New Republic*'s Next Chapter," *Medium*, January 11, 2016, accessed at https://medium.com/@chrishughes/the-new-republic-s-next-chapter-69f6772606#.usb0t78c9.

27. Michael Calderone, "New Republic Exodus: Dozens of Editors Resign over Management Changes," *Huffington Post*, December 5, 2014; Jonathan Chait, "A Eulogy for the *New Republic*," *New York*, December 4, 2014; Lizza, "Inside the Collapse of the *New Republic*."

28. Martin Peretz, "Why Doesn't the *New Republic*'s New Owner Take Ideas Seriously?" *Washington Post*, December 10, 2014.

29. Leon Wieseltier, "Among the Disrupted," *New York Times Book Review*, January 7, 2015.

30. Ezra Klein, "Even the Liberal *New Republic* Needs to Change," *Vox*, December 5, 2014.

31. Rebecca West, "The Duty of Harsh Criticism," *New Republic*, November 7, 1914.

32. Kelsey Sutton and Peter Sterne, "The Fall of Salon.com," *Politico*, May 27, 2016.

33. Lee Drutman, "What Paul Ryan's House Budget Woes Tell Us about the Continued Crack-Up of the Republican Party," *Vox*, April 11, 2016.

34. On creedal passions, see Samuel Huntington, *American Politics: The Promise of Disharmony* (Cambridge, MA: Belknap Press, 1981). For an updating of Huntington's thesis to the near-present, see George Will, "An Anti-Authority Creed," *Washington Post*, January 23, 2011.

35. For an example of the former, see Tim Alberta and Eliana Johnson, "In Koch World 'Realignment,' Less National Politics," *National Review*, May 16, 2016. For an example of the latter, see Carl Swanson, "Leon Wieseltier Is Not Buying the *New Republic*—But He Is Teaming up with Steve Jobs's Widow to Start a New Publication," *New York*, January 21, 2016.

36. Indeed, one of the relative advantages of the private sector in the Ideas Industry is a tendency to promote the corporate brand over those of individual employees.

37. Steven Teles, "Foundations, Organizational Maintenance, and Partisan Asymmetry," *PS: Political Science and Politics* 49 (July 2016): 455–460.

38. Tamara Cofman Wittes and Marc Lynch, "The Mysterious Absence of Women from Middle East Policy Debates," *Washington Post*, January 20, 2015; Elmira Bayrasli and Lauren Bohn, "Binders Full of Women Foreign Policy Experts," *New York Times*, February 10, 2015; Jane Greenway Carr, "The Underrepresentation of Women in Foreign Policy Is a Huge Problem," *Vox*, February 16, 2015.

39. Interview with Niall Ferguson, Cambridge, MA, April 22, 2016.

40. Richard Hofstadter, *Anti-Intellectualism in American Life* (New York: Knopf, 1962), 417.

41. Daniel W. Drezner, "Globalizers of the World, Unite!," *The Washington Quarterly* 21 (Winter 1998): 222–223.

42. Daniel W. Drezner, "Bad Debts: Assessing China's Financial Influence in Great Power Politics," *International Security* 34 (Fall 2009): 7–45; Drezner, "The System Worked: Global Economic Governance during the Great Recession," *World Politics* 66 (January 2014): 123–164.

43. The keynote speaker was, for reasons I will never completely comprehend, Larry King. He was fantastic, by the way.

44. Brooks, *Bobos in Paradise*, 175.

45. It has gotten to the point where an actual crank letter, sent through the Post Office, seems quaint and even charming.

46. Daniel W. Drezner, "An Open Letter to the Conspiracy Theorists of 2016," *Washington Post*, October 5, 2015.

47. Alana Goodman, "Antiwar Conference Featured Panelist Who Spoke at Holocaust Denial Conference," *Washington Free Beacon*, July 3, 2014;

Michael Goldfarb, "Not All Liberty Conservatives Are Jew-Baiting Paleocons," *Washington Free Beacon*, July 11, 2014.

48. See https://twitter.com/adamjohnsonNYC/status/736626454935392256.

49. David Brooks, "The Thought Leader," *New York Times*, December 16, 2013.

50. In contrast, I have no problem critiquing academic papers in various conferences and in peer refereeing. That might be because the former is an accepted norm and the latter is double blind.

51. Aaron James, *Assholes: A Theory* (New York: Anchor Books, 2012), 39–41.

52. Imre Lakatos, "Falsification and the Methodology of Scientific Research Programmes," in *Criticisms and the Growth of Knowledge*, ed. Lakatos and Alan Musgrave (Cambridge: Cambridge University Press, 1970).

53. Kathryn Schulz, *Being Wrong: Adventures in the Margin of Error* (New York: HarperCollins, 2010), 3.

BIBLIOGRAPHY

Abelson, Donald. 2009. *Do Think Tanks Matter? Assessing the Impact of Public Policy Institutes.* Montreal: McGill-Queens Press.

Abelson, Donald. 2014. "Old World, New World: The Evolution and Influence of Foreign Affairs Think-Tanks." *International Affairs* 90 (January 2014): 125–142.

Achen, Christopher, and Larry Bartels. 2016. *Democracy for Realists.* Princeton, NJ: Princeton University Press.

Alterman, Eric. 1992. *Sound and Fury: The Washington Punditocracy and the Collapse of American Politics.* New York: HarperCollins.

American Political Science Association. 2014. *Improving Public Perceptions of Political Science's Value.* Washington, DC: APSA.

Andrew, Edward G. 2006. *Patrons of Enlightenment.* Toronto: University of Toronto Press.

Avey, Paul C., and Michael C. Desch. 2014. "What Do Policymakers Want from Us? Results of a Survey of Current and Former Senior National Security Decision Makers." *International Studies Quarterly* 58 (December): 227–246.

Bacevich, Andrew. 2016. "American Public Intellectuals and the Early Cold War, or, Mad about Henry Wallace." In *Public Intellectuals in the Global Arena*, edited by Michael Desch. South Bend, IN: University of Notre Dame Press.

Bafumi, Joseph, and Michael C. Herron. 2010. "Leapfrog Representation and Extremism: A Study of American Voters and Their Members in Congress." *American Political Science Review* 104 (September): 519–542.

Barnett, Michael, and Raymond Duvall. 2005. "Power in International Politics." *International Organization* 59 (January): 39–75.

Barber, Benjamin. 2001. *The Truth of Power.* New York: W. W. Norton.

Barber, Michael, and Nolan McCarty. 2013. "Causes and Consequences of Polarization." In *Negotiating Agreement in Politics*, edited by Jane Mansbridge and Cathie Jo Martin. Washington, DC: APSA.

Beard, Charles. 1927. "Time, Technology, and the Creative Spirit in Political Science." *American Political Science Review* 21 (February): 1–11.

Bennett, Andrew, and G. John Ikenberry. 2006. "The *Review*'s Evolving Relevance for US Foreign Policy 1906–2006." *American Political Science Review* 100 (November): 651–658.

Berlin, Isaiah. 2013. *The Hedgehog and the Fox: An Essay on Tolstoy's View of History*. Princeton, NJ: Princeton University Press.

Berry, Jeffrey. 2016. "Negative Returns: The Impact of Impact Investing on Empowerment and Advocacy." *PS: Political Science and Politics* 49 (July): 437–441.

Bishop, Matthew, and Michael Green. 2008. *Philanthrocapitalism: How the Rich Can Save the World*. New York: Bloomsbury Press.

Blanchard, Olivier. 2008. "The State of Macro." NBER Working Paper 14259.

Blinder, Alan. 1988. *Hard Heads, Soft Hearts*. Boston: Addison-Wesley.

Blyth, Mark. 2002. *Great Transformations: Economic Ideas and Institutional Change in the Twentieth Century*. New York: Cambridge University Press.

Blyth, Mark. 2013. *Austerity: The History of a Dangerous Idea*. New York: Oxford University Press.

Bock, Sebastian. 2014. "Politicized Expertise—An Analysis of the Political Dimensions of Consultants' Policy Recommendations to Developing Countries with a Case Study of McKinsey's Advice on REDD+ Policies." *Innovation: The European Journal of Social Science Research* 27 (December): 379–397.

Boudreau, Cheryl. 2015. "Read but Not Heard? Engaging Junior Scholars in Efforts to Make Political Science Relevant." *PS: Political Science and Politics* 48 (September): 51–54.

Brest, Paul, and Hal Harvey. 2008. *Money Well Spent*. New York: Bloomberg Press.

Brooks, David. 2000. *Bobos in Paradise*. New York: Simon and Schuster.

Brouwer, Daniel, and Catherine Squires. 2003. "Public Intellectuals, Public Life, and the University." *Argument and Advocacy* 39 (Winter): 201–213.

Brown, Michael, Sean Lynn-Jones, and Steven Miller, eds. 1996. *Debating the Democratic Peace*. Cambridge, MA: MIT Press.

Busby, Joshua W., and Jonathan Monten. 2008. "Without Heirs? Assessing the Decline of Establishment Internationalism in US Foreign Policy." *Perspectives on Politics* 6 (September): 451–472.

Busby, Joshua W., and Jonathan Monten. 2012. "Republican Elites and Foreign Policy Attitudes." *Political Science Quarterly* 127 (Spring): 105–142.

Burgin, Angus. 2012. *The Great Persuasion: Reinventing Free Markets since the Depression*. Cambridge, MA: Harvard University Press.

Burns, Jennifer. 2008. *Goddess of the Market: Ayn Rand and the American Right*. New York: Oxford University Press.

Byman, Daniel, and Matthew Kroenig. 2016. "Reaching beyond the Ivory Tower: A How To Manual," *Security Studies* 25 (May): 289–319.

Caplan, Bryan, Eric Crampton, Wayne Grove, and Ilya Somin. 2013. "Systemically Biased Beliefs about Political Influence." *PS: Political Science and Politics* 46 (October): 760–767.

Carmines, Edward, Michael Ensley, and Michael Wagner. 2012. "Who Fits the Left-Right Divide? Partisan Polarization in the American Electorate." *American Behavioral Scientist* 56 (October): 1631–1653.

Carnegie, Andrew. 1889. "Wealth." *North American Review* 148 (June): 653–664.

Carpenter, Charli. 2012. "'You Talk of Terrible Things So Matter-of-Factly in This Language of Science': Constructing Human Rights in the Academy." *Perspectives on Politics* 10 (June): 363–383.

Carpenter, Charli, and Daniel W. Drezner. 2010. "International Relations 2.0: The Implications of New Media for an Old Profession." *International Studies Perspectives* 11 (August): 255–272.

Carrick-Hagenbarth, Jessica, and Gerald A. Epstein. 2012. "Dangerous Interconnectedness: Economists' Conflicts of Interest, Ideology and Financial Crisis." *Cambridge Journal of Economics* 36 (January): 43–63.

Chilton, Adam S., and Eric A. Posner. 2014. "An Empirical Study of Political Bias in Legal Scholarship." Coase-Sandor Institute for Law and Economics Research Paper no. 696, University of Chicago.

Chipman, John. 2016. "Why Your Company Needs a Foreign Policy." *Harvard Business Review* 94 (September): 36–45.

Chollet, Derek. 2016. *The Long Game.* New York: PublicAffairs.

Christensen, Clayton. 1997. *The Innovator's Dilemma.* Cambridge, MA: Harvard Business School Press.

Christensen, Clayton, and Michael Raynor. 2003. *The Innovator's Solution.* Cambridge, MA: Harvard Business School Press.

Christensen, Clayton, and Derek Van Bever. 2014. "The Capitalist's Dilemma." *Harvard Business Review* 92 (June): 60–68.

Christensen, Clayton, Dina Wang, and Derek van Bever. 2013. "Consulting on the Cusp of Disruption." *Harvard Business Review* 91 (October): 106–114.

Christensen, Clayton, Michael Raynor, and Rory McDonald. 2015. "What Is Disruptive Innovation?" *Harvard Business Review* (December): 45–53.

Cohen, Jared. 2015. "Digital Counterinsurgency." *Foreign Affairs* 94 (November/December): 53–58.

Colander, David. 2015. "Intellectual Incest on the Charles: Why Economists Are a Little Bit Off." *Eastern Economic Journal* 41 (January): 155–159.

Cook, Fay Lomax, Benjamin I. Page, and Rachel Moskowitz. 2014. "Political Engagement by Wealthy Americans." *Political Science Quarterly* 129 (Fall): 381–398.

Côté, Stéphane, Julian Hose, and Robb Willer. 2015. "High Economic Inequality Leads Higher-Income Individuals to Be Less Generous." *Proceedings of the National Academy of Sciences* 112 (November): 15838–15843.

David, Robert J., Wesley D. Sine, and Heather A. Haveman. 2013. "Seizing Opportunity in Emerging Fields: How Institutional Entrepreneurs

Legitimated the Professional Form of Management Consulting." *Organization Science* 24 (March/April): 356–377.

Deaton, Angus. 2013. *The Great Escape: Health, Wealth, and the Origins of Inequality.* Princeton, NJ: Princeton University Press.

Del Rosso, Steven. 2015. "Our New Three Rs: Rigor, Relevance, and Readability." *Governance* 28 (April): 127–130.

Deresiewicz, William. 2014. *Excellent Sheep: The Miseducation of the American Elite and the Way to a Meaningful Life.* New York: Simon and Schuster.

Desch, Michael. 2015. "Technique Trumps Relevance: The Professionalization of Political Science and the Marginalization of Security Studies." *Perspectives on Politics* 13 (June): 377–393.

Desch, Michael. 2017. *The Relevance Question: Social Science's Inconstant Embrace of Security Studies.* Ithaca, NY: Cornell University Press.

Dobbs, Richard, James Manyika, and Jonathan Woetzel. 2015. *No Ordinary Disruption.* New York: PublicAffairs.

Dobbs, Richard, Sree Ramaswamy, Elizabeth Stephenson, and Patrick Viguerie. 2014. "Management Intuition for the Next 50 Years." *McKinsey Quarterly* (September).

Drezner, Daniel W. 1998. "Globalizers of the World, Unite!" *The Washington Quarterly* 21 (Winter): 207–225.

Drezner, Daniel W. 2007. "Foreign Policy Goes Glam." *The National Interest* 92 (November/December): 22–29.

Drezner, Daniel W. 2007. *All Politics Is Global: Explaining International Regulatory Regimes.* Princeton, NJ: Princeton University Press.

Drezner, Daniel W. 2008. "The Realist Tradition in American Public Opinion." *Perspectives on Politics* 6 (March): 51–70.

Drezner, Daniel W., ed. 2009. *Avoiding Trivia: The Role of Strategic Planning in American Foreign Policy.* Washington, DC: Brookings Institution Press.

Drezner, Daniel W. 2014. *The System Worked: How the World Stopped Another Great Depression.* New York: Oxford University Press.

Duarte, José L, et al. 2015. "Political Diversity Will Improve Social Psychological Science." *Behavioral and Brain Sciences* 38 (January): 130.

Easterly, William. 2013. *The Tyranny of Experts.* New York: Basic Books.

Easton, David. 1951. "The Decline of Modern Political Theory." *Journal of Politics* 13 (February): 36–58.

Eichengreen, Barry. 1998. "Dental Hygiene and Nuclear War: How International Relations Looks from Economics." *International Organization* 52 (October): 993–1061.

Etzioni, Amitai, and Alyssa Bowditch, eds., 2006. *Public Intellectuals: An Endangered Species?* New York: Rowman and Littlefield.

Evans, Eliza, Charles Gomez, and Daniel McFarland. 2016. "Measuring Paradigmaticness of Disciplines Using Text." *Sociological Science* 3 (August): 757–778.

Fairbrother, Malcolm, and Isaac W. Martin. 2013. "Does Inequality Erode Social Trust? Results from Multilevel Models of US States and Counties." *Social Science Research* 42 (March): 347–360.

Fazal, Tanisha. 2016. "An Occult of Irrelevance? Multimethod Research and Engagement with the Policy World." *Security Studies* 25 (January): 34–41.

Fettweis, Christopher. 2004. "Evaluating IR's Crystal Balls: How Predictions of the Future Have Withstood Fourteen Years of Unipolarity." *International Studies Review* 6 (Winter): 79–104.

Ferguson, Niall. 2010. "Complexity and Collapse." *Foreign Affairs* 89 (March/April): 18–32.

Foa, Roberto Stefan, and Yascha Mounk. 2016. "The democratic disconnect." *Journal of Democracy* 27 (July 2016): 5–17.

Foa, Roberto Stefan, and Yascha Mounk. 2017. "The Signs of Deconsolidation." *Journal of Democracy* 28 (July 2016): 5–15.

Fourcade, Marion, Etienne Ollion, and Yann Algan. 2015. "The Superiority of Economists." *Journal of Economic Perspectives* 29 (January): 13–43.

Freeland, Chrystia. 2012. *Plutocrats: The Rise of the New Global Super-Rich and the Fall of Everyone Else*. New York: Penguin.

Friedman, Thomas. 2005. *The World Is Flat: A Brief History of the Twenty-First Century*. New York: Farrar Strauss Giroux.

Frum, David. 2008. "Foggy Bloggom." *The National Interest* 93 (January/February): 46–52.

Fukuyama, Francis. 1989. "The End of History?" *The National Interest* 16 (Summer): 3–18.

Fukuyama, Francis. 1992. *The End of History and the Last Man*. New York: Free Press.

Fukuyama, Francis. 2006. *America at the Crossroads: Democracy, Power, and the Neoconservative Legacy*. New Haven, CT: Yale University Press.

Fukuyama, Francis. 2014. *Political Order and Political Decay*. New York: Farrar Strauss Giroux.

Gaddis, John Lewis. 1992/93. "International Relations Theory and the End of the Cold War." *International Security* 17 (Winter): 5–58.

Galbraith, John Kenneth. 1973. "Power and the Useful Economist." *American Economic Review* 63 (March): 1–11.

Gallo, Carmine. 2014. *Talk Like TED: The Public-Speaking Secrets of the World's Top Minds*. New York: St. Martin's Press.

Gans, Joshua. 2016. "Keep Calm and Manage Disruption." *MIT Sloan Management Review* 57 (Spring): 83–90.

Garner, Andrew, and Harvey Palmer. 2011. "Polarization and Issue Consistency over Time." *Political Behavior* 33 (June): 225–246.

Gauchat, Gordon. 2012. "Politicization of Science in the Public Sphere a Study of Public Trust in the United States, 1974 to 2010." *American Sociological Review* 77 (April): 167–187.

Gauchat, Gordon. 2015. "The Political Context of Science in the United States: Public Acceptance of Evidence-Based Policy and Science Funding." *Social Forces* (February): 1–24.

George, Alexander. 2013. *Bridging the Gap.* Washington, DC: US Institute for Peace.

Ginsberg, Benjamin. 2011. *The Fall of the Faculty: The Rise of the All-Administrative University and Why it Matters.* New York: Oxford University Press.

Goldeiger, James, and Derek Chollet. 2006. "The Truman Standard." *The American Interest* 1 (Summer): 107–111.

Goldstein, Judith, and Robert Keohane, eds. 1993. *Ideas and Foreign Policy.* Ithaca, NY: Cornell University Press.

Goss, Kristin. 2016. "Policy Plutocrats: How America's Wealthy Seek to Influence Governance." *PS: Political Science and Politics* 49 (July): 442–448.

Gross, Andrew, and Jozef Poor. 2008. "The Global Management Consulting Sector." *Business and Economics* 43 (October): 59–68.

Guisinger, Alexandra, and Elizabeth Saunders. 2016. "Mapping the Boundaries of Elite Cues: How Elites Shape Mass Opinion Across International Issues." Working paper, George Washington University, April.

Haas, Peter. 1992. "Banning Chlorofluorocarbons: Epistemic Community Efforts to Protect Stratospheric Ozone." *International Organization* (Winter): 187–224.

Haass, Richard. 2005. *The Opportunity.* New York: PublicAffairs.

Hacker, Jacob, and Paul Pierson. 2005. *Off Center: The Republican Revolution and the Erosion of American Democracy.* New Haven, CT: Yale University Press.

Halberstam, David. 2001. *War in a Time of Peace.* New York: Scribner.

Hall, Peter. 1993. "Policy Paradigms, Social Learning, and the State: the Case of Economic Policymaking in Britain." *Comparative Politics* 25 (April): 275–296.

Halper, Stefan, and Jonathan Clarke. 2007. *The Silence of the Rational Center.* New York: Basic Books.

Hamid, Shadi. 2015. "What is Policy Research For? Reflections on the United States' Failures in Syria." *Middle East Law and Governance* 7 (Summer): 373–386.

Harris-Perry, Melissa, and Steve Friess. 2015. "An Interview with Melissa Harris-Perry." *PS: Political Science and Politics* 48 (September): 26–30.

von Hayek, Friedrich A. 1949. "The Intellectuals and Socialism." *University of Chicago Law Review* 16 (Spring): 417–433.

Hayes, Christopher. 2012. *Twilight of the Elites: America after Meritocracy.* New York: Crown Books.

Helpman, Elhannan. 2004. *The Mystery of Economic Growth.* Cambridge, MA: Belknap Press.

Hetherington, Marc J. 2001. "Resurgent Mass Partisanship: The Role of Elite Polarization." *American Political Science Review* 95 (September): 619–631.

Heilbrunn, Jacob. 2008. "Rank Breakers: Anatomy of an Industry." *World Affairs* 170 (Spring): 36–46.

Heilbrunn, Jacob. 2008. *They Knew They Were Right: The Rise of the Neocons.*
New York: Doubleday.

Heilbrunn, Jacob. 2016. "The GOP's New Foreign Policy Populism." *The National Interest* (March/April).

Herken, Gregg. 1985. *Counsels of War.* New York: Knopf.

Herken, Gregg. 2014. *The Georgetown Set: Friends and Rivals in Cold War Washington.* New York: Knopf.

Hill, Seth J., and Chris Tausanovitch. 2015. "A Disconnect in Representation? Comparison of Trends in Congressional and Public Polarization." *Journal of Politics* 77 (December 2015): 1058–1075.

Hirschman, Daniel. 2016. "Stylized Facts in the Social Sciences." *Sociological Science* 3 (July): 604–626.

Hofstadter, Richard. 1962. *Anti-Intellectualism in American Life.* New York: Knopf.

Howe, Irving. 1954. "This Age of Conformity." *Partisan Review* 21 (January): 1–33.

Howell, Llewellyn D. 2014. "Evaluating Political Risk Forecasting Models: What Works?" *Thunderbird International Business Review* 56 (July/August): 305–316.

Huntington, Samuel. 1981. *American Politics: The Promise of Disharmony.* Cambridge: Belknap.

Huntington, Samuel. 1993. "The Clash of Civilizations?" *Foreign Affairs* 72 (Summer): 22–49.

Huntington, Samuel. 1996. *The Clash of Civilizations and the Remaking of World Order.* New York: Simon and Schuster.

Ikenberry, G. John. 2003. "Is American Multilateralism in Decline?" *Perspectives on Politics* 1 (September): 533–550.

Ikenberry, G. John, and Anne-Marie Slaughter. 2006. *Forging A World of Liberty under Law: U.S. National Security in the 21st Century.* Princeton, NJ: Princeton Project for National Security.

Isaac, Jeffrey. 2015. "For a More *Public* Political Science." *Perspectives on Politics* 13 (June): 269–283.

Iyengar, Shanto, Gaurav Sood, and Yphtach Lelkes. 2012. "Affect, not Ideology: A Social Identity Perspective on Polarization." *Public Opinion Quarterly* 76 (Fall): 405–431.

Iyengar Shanto, and Sean Westwood. 2015. "Fear and Loathing across Party Lines: New Evidence on Group Polarization." *American Journal of Political Science* 59 (July 2015): 690–707.

Jackson, Patrick Thaddeus, and Stuart J. Kaufman. 2007. "Security Scholars for a Sensible Foreign Policy: A Study in Weberian Activism." *Perspectives on Politics* 5 (March 2007): 95–103.

Jacoby, Russell. 1987. *The Last Intellectuals: American Culture in the Age of Academe.* New York: Basic Books.

Jacoby, Susan. 2008. *The Age of American Unreason.* New York: Vintage Books.

Jacobs, Lawrence, and Benjamin Page. 2005. "Who Influences U.S. Foreign Policy?" *American Political Science Review* 99 (February): 107–123.

James, Aaron. 2012. *Assholes: A Theory.* New York: Anchor Books.

Jentleson, Bruce W., and Ely Ratner. 2011. "Bridging the Beltway–Ivory Tower Gap." *International Studies Review* 13 (March): 6–11.

Jervis. Robert. 2004. "Security Studies: Ideas, Policy, and Politics," in Edward Mansfield and Richard Sisson, eds. *The Evolution of Political Knowledge: Democracy, Autonomy and Conflict in Comparative and International Politics.* Columbus: Ohio State University Press.

Jervis, Robert. 2008. "Bridges, Barriers, and Gaps: Research and Policy." *Political Psychology* 29 (Summer): 571–592.

Johnson, Paul. 1989. *Intellectuals.* New York: Harper and Row.

Jones, Bruce. 2014. *Still Ours to Lead: America, the Rising Powers, and the Myths of the Coming Disorder.* Washington, DC: Brookings Institution Press.

Kagan, Robert. 2002. "Power and Weakness." *Policy Review* 113 (June/July): 3–28.

Kaplan, Fred. 1983. *The Wizards of Armageddon.* New York: Simon and Schuster.

Kaplan, Fred. *The Insurgents: David Petraeus and the Plot to Change the American Way of War.* New York: Simon and Schuster.

Karger, Howard Jacob, and Marie Theresa Hernández. 2004. "The Decline of the Public Intellectual in Social Work." *Journal of Sociology and Social Welfare* 31 (September): 51–68.

Kaufmann, Chaim. 2004. "Threat Inflation and the Failure of the Marketplace of Ideas: The Selling of the Iraq War." *International Security* 29 (Summer): 5–48.

Kelley, Judith, and Beth Simmons. 2015. "Politics by Number: Indicators as Social Pressure in International Relations." *American Journal of Political Science* 59 (January): 55–70.

Khanna, Parag. 2008. *The Second World.* New York: Random House.

Khanna, Parag. 2016. *Connectivity.* New York: Random House.

Kiechel, Walter. 2010. *The Lords of Strategy: The Secret Intellectual History of the New Corporate World.* Cambridge, MA: Harvard Business Press.

King, Andrew, and Christopher Tucci. 2002. "Incumbent Entry into New Market Niches: The Role of Experience and Managerial Choice in the Creation of Dynamic Capabilities." *Management Science* 48 (February): 171–186.

King, Andrew, and Baljir Baatartogtokh. 2015. "How Useful Is the Theory of Disruptive Innovation?" *MIT Sloan Management Review* 57 (Fall): 77–90.

King, Charles. 2015. "The Decline of International Studies." *Foreign Affairs* 94 (July/August): 88–99.

Klein, Daniel B., and Charlotta Stern. 2005. "Professors and Their Politics: The Policy Views of Social Scientists," *Critical Review* 17 (March): 257–303.

Klein, Daniel B., and Charlotta Stern. 2006. "Economists' Policy Views and Voting." *Public Choice* 126 (March): 331–342.

Krauthammer, Charles. 1990/91. "The Unipolar Moment." *Foreign Affairs* 70 (Winter): 23–33.

Krebs, Ronald. 2015. *Narrative and the Making of US National Security.* New York: Cambridge University Press.

Kuklick, Bruce. 2006. *Blind Oracles: Intellectuals and War from Kennan to Kissinger.* Princeton, NJ: Princeton University Press.

Kull, Stephen, and I. M. Destler. 1999. *Misreading the Public.* Washington, DC: Brookings Institution.

Kuo, Dido, and Nolan McCarty. 2015. "Democracy in America, 2015." *Global Policy* 6 (June): 49–55.

Kupchan, Charles A., and Peter L. Trubowitz. 2007. "Dead Center: The Demise of Liberal Internationalism in the United States." *International Security* 32 (Fall): 7–44.

Lake, David A. 2011. "Why "isms" Are Evil: Theory, Epistemology, and Academic Sects as Impediments to Understanding and Progress." *International Studies Quarterly* 55 (June): 465–480.

Lamarche, Gara. 2014. "Democracy and the Donor Class." *Democracy* 34 (Fall): 48–59.

Lapsley, Irvine, and Rosie Oldfield. 2001. "Transforming the Public Sector: Management Consultants as Agents of Change," *European Accounting Review* 10 (October): 523–543.

Lilla, Mark. 2001. *The Reckless Mind: Intellectuals in Politics.* New York: New York Review Books.

Lippmann, Walter. 1955. *The Public Philosophy.* Boston: Little, Brown.

Lipset, Seymour Martin, and Richard Dobson. 1972. "The Intellectual as Critic and Rebel: With Special Reference to the United States and the Soviet Union." *Daedalus* 101 (Summer): 137–198.

Lott, Eric. 2006. *The Disappearing Liberal Intellectual.* New York: Basic Books.

Lowen, Rebecca. 1997. *Creating the Cold War University.* Los Angeles: University of California Press.

Lucas, Robert E. 2003. "Macroeconomic Priorities." *American Economic Review* 93 (March): 1–14.

Lynch, Marc. 2016. "Political Science in Real Time: Engaging the Middle East Policy Public." *Perspectives on Politics* 14 (March): 121–131.

Lynd, Robert S. 1939. *Knowledge for What: The Place of Social Science in American Culture.* Princeton, NJ: Princeton University Press.

Mahnken, Thomas. 2010. "Bridging the Gap between the Worlds of Ideas and Action." *Orbis* 54 (Winter): 4–13.

Maliniak, Daniel, Amy Oakes, Susan Peterson, and Michael J. Tierney. 2011. "International Relations in the US Academy." *International Studies Quarterly* 55 (June): 437–464.

Mann, Thomas, and Norman Ornstein. 2012. *It's Even Worse Than It Looks: How the American Constitutional System Collided with the New Politics of Extremism.* New York: Basic Books.

Markides, Constantinos. 2006. "Disruptive Innovation: In Need of Better Theory.*" *Journal of Product Innovation Management* 23 (January): 19–25.

Martin, Chris. 2016. "How Ideology Has Hindered Sociological Insight." *The American Sociologist* 47 (March): 115–130.

Mason, Lilliana. 2015. "'I Disrespectfully Agree': The Differential Effects of Partisan Sorting on Social and Issue Polarization." *American Journal of Political Science* 59 (January): 128–145.

McCloskey, Dierdre. 2016. *Bourgeois Equality: How Ideas, Not Capital or Institutions, Enriched the World.* Chicago: University of Chicago Press.

McCubbins, Mathew, and Thomas Schwartz. 1984. "Congressional Oversight Overlooked: Police Patrols versus Fire Alarms." *American Journal of Political Science* 28 (February): 165–179.

McDermott, Rose. 2015. "Learning to Communicate Better with the Press and the Public." *PS: Political Science and Politics* 48 (September): 85–89.

McDonald, Duff. 2013. *The Firm: The Inside Story of McKinsey.* London: OneWorld.

McKenna, Christopher. 2006. *The World's Newest Profession: Management Consulting in the Twentieth Century.* New York: Cambridge University Press.

Mead, Lawrence. 2010. "Scholasticism in Political Science." *Perspectives on Politics* 8 (June): 453–464.

Mead, Walter Russell. 2001. *Special Providence: American Foreign Policy and How It Changed the World.* New York: Knopf.

Mearsheimer, John. 1990. "Back to the Future: Instability in Europe after the Cold War." *International Security* 15 (Summer): 5–56.

Mearsheimer, John. 2011. "Imperial by Design." *The National Interest* 111 (January/February): 16–34.

Mearsheimer, John, and Stephen Walt. 2006. "The Israel Lobby." *London Review of Books* 28 (March): 3–12.

Medvetz, Tom. 2012. *Think Tanks in America.* Chicago: University of Chicago Press.

Menand, Louis. 2001. *The Metaphysical Club: A Story of Ideas in America.* New York: Farrar Straus Giroux.

Menand, Louis. 2010. *The Marketplace of Ideas.* New York: W. W. Norton.

Merry, Robert. 1996. *Taking on the World: Joseph and Stewart Alsop, Guardians of the American Century.* New York: Viking.

Mills, C. Wright. 1958. *The Power Elite.* New York: Oxford University Press.

Milne, David. 2010. "America's 'Intellectual' Diplomacy." *International Affairs* 86 (January): 49–68.

Milner, Helen V., and Dustin H. Tingley. 2011. "Who Supports Global Economic Engagement? The Sources of Preferences in American Foreign Economic Policy." *International Organization* 65 (January): 37–68.

Milner, Helen V., and Dustin Tingley. 2016. *Sailing the Water's Edge: The Domestic Politics of American Foreign Policy.* Princeton, NJ: Princeton University Press.

Momani, Bessma. 2013. "Management Consultants and the United States' Public Sector," *Business and Politics* 15 (October): 381–399.

Morozov, Evgeny. 2013. *To Save Everything, Click Here.* New York: PublicAffairs.

Mower, Joseph L., and Clayton Christensen. 1995. "Disruptive Technologies: Catching the Wave." *Harvard Business Review* 73 (January/February): 43–53.

Mukunda, Gautum. 2014. "The Price of Wall Street's Power." *Harvard Business Review* 92 (June): 3–10.

Muller, Jan-Werner. 2016. *What is Populism?* Philadelphia, PA: University of Pennsylvania Press.

Munk, Nina. 2013. *The Idealist: Jeffrey Sachs and the Quest to End Poverty.* New York: Signal.

Nye, Joseph. 1990. *Bound to Lead: The Changing Nature of American Power.* New York: Basic Books.

Nye, Joseph. 1990. "Soft Power." *Foreign Policy* 80 (Autumn): 153–171.

Nye, Joseph. 2004. "The Decline of America's Soft Power." *Foreign Affairs* 83 (May/June): 16–21.

Nyhan, Brendan, and Jason Reifler. 2010. "When Corrections Fail: The Persistence of Political Misperceptions." *Political Behavior* 32 (June): 303–330.

Obama, Barack. 2007. "Renewing American Leadership." *Foreign Affairs* 86 (July/August): 2–16.

O'Mahoney, Joe, and Andrew Sturdy. 2016. "Power and the Diffusion of Management Ideas: The Case of McKinsey & Co." *Management Learning* 47 (July): 247–265.

Orwell, George. 1984. "Politics and the English Language." In *Why I Write.* New York: Penguin Books.

Page, Benjamin, with Marshall Bouton. 2006. *The Foreign Policy Disconnect.* Chicago: University of Chicago Press.

Page, Benjamin, Larry M. Bartels, and Jason Seawright. 2013. "Democracy and the Policy Preferences of Wealthy Americans." *Perspectives on Politics* 11 (March): 51–73.

Page, Benjamin, Jason Seawright, and Matthew LaCombe. 2015. "Stealth Politics by U.S. Billionaires." Paper presented at the annual meeting at the American Political Science Association, San Francisco, CA.

Pepinsky, Tom. 2012. "The Global Economic Crisis and the Politics of Non-Transitions," *Government and Opposition* 47 (April): 135–161.

Piketty, Thomas. 2014. *Capital in the Twenty-First Century.* Cambridge, MA: Belknap Press.

Polanyi, Michael. 1966. *The Tacit Dimension.* Chicago: University of Chicago Press.

Porter, Patrick. 2011. "Beyond the American Century: Walter Lippmann and American Grand Strategy, 1943–1950," *Diplomacy and Statecraft* 22 (July): 557–577.

Posner, Richard. 2001. *Public Intellectuals: A Study of Decline.* Cambridge, MA: Harvard University Press.

Poundstone, William. 1992. *Prisoner's Dilemma.* New York: Doubleday.

Putnam, Robert. 203. "The Public Role of Political Science." *Perspective on Politics* 1 (June): 249–255.

Quiggin, John. 2012. *Zombie Economics.* Princeton, NJ: Princeton University Press.

Ramdas, Kavida. 2011. "Philanthrocapitalism: Reflecions on Politics and Policy Making," *Society* 48 (September): 393–396.

Rathbun, Brian. 2012. "Politics and Paradigm Preferences: The Implicit Ideology of International Relations Scholars." *International Studies Quarterly* 56 (September): 607–622.

Raynor, Michael. 2011. "Disruption Theory as a Predictor of Innovation Success/Failure." *Strategy and Leadership* 39 (July): 27–30.

Rich, Andrew. 2004. *Think Tanks, Public Policy, and the Politics of Expertise.* Cambridge: Cambridge University Press.

Rielly, John E., ed. 1999. *American Public Opinion and U.S. Foreign Policy 1999.* Chicago: Chicago Council on Foreign Relations.

Rodgers, Daniel T. 2011. *Age of Fracture.* Cambridge, MA: Belknap.

Rodrik, Dani. 2014. "When Ideas Trump Interests: Preferences, Worldviews, and Policy Innovations." *Journal of Economic Perspectives* 28 (January): 189–208.

Rodrik, Dani. 2015. *Economics Rules: The Rights and Wrongs of the Dismal Science.* New York: W. W. Norton.

Rogers, Rubin. 2011. "Why Philanthro-Policymaking Matters." *Society* 48 (September): 376–381.

Rogowski, Ronald. 2013. "Shooting (or Ignoring) the Messenger." *Political Studies* 11 (May): 216–21.

Romer, Paul. 2015. "Mathiness in the Theory of Economic Growth." *American Economic Review* 105 (May): 89–93.

Ronson, Jon. 2015. *So You've Been Publicly Shamed.* New York: Riverfront Books.

Rosen, Sherwin. 1981. "The Economics of Superstars." *American Economic Review* 71 (December): 845–858.

Rothkopf, David. 2008. *Superclass.* New York: Farrar Strauss Giroux.

Rothkopf, David. 2014. *National Insecurity: American Leadership in an Age of Fear.* New York: PublicAffairs.

Russett, Bruce. 2005. "Bushwhacking the Democratic Peace." *International Studies Perspectives* 6 (September): 395–408.

Sachs, Jeffrey. 2005. *The End of Poverty: Economic Possibilities for Our Time.* New York: Penguin.

Schmidt, Brian C., and Michael C. Williams. 2008. "The Bush Doctrine and the Iraq War: Neoconservatives Versus Realists." *Security Studies* 17 (June): 191–220.

Schulz, Kathryn. 2010. *Being Wrong: Adventures in the Margin of Error.* New York: HarperCollins.

Seabrooke, Leonard. 2014. "Epistemic Arbitrage: Transnational Professional Knowledge in Action." *Journal of Professions and Organization* 1 (January): 49–64.

Selee, Andrew. 2013. *What Should Think Tanks Do? A Strategic Guide to Policy Impact.* Stanford: Stanford University Press.

Shaw, Daron. 2012. "If Everyone Votes Their Party, Why Do Presidential Election Outcomes Vary So Much?" *The Forum* 10 (October).

Shils, Edward. 1972. "Intellectuals, Tradition, and the Traditions of Intellectuals: Some Preliminary Considerations." *Daedalus* 101 (Spring): 21–34.

Sides, John. 2011. "The Political Scientist as a Blogger," *PS: Political Science and Politics* 44 (April): 267–271.

Silver, Nate. 2012. *The Signal and the Noise.* New York: Penguin.

Skidmore, David. 2005. "Understanding the Unilateralist Turn in US Foreign Policy." *Foreign Policy Analysis* 1 (July): 207–228.

Skocpol, Teda. 2014. "How the Scholars Strategy Network Helps Academics Gain Public Influence." *Perspectives on Politics* 12 (September): 695–703.

Smeltz, Dina, and Ivo Daalder. 2014. *Foreign Policy in the Age of Retrenchment.* Chicago: Chicago Council on Global Affairs.

Smeltz, Dina, Ivo Daalder, Karl Friedhoff, and Craig Kafura. 2015. *America Divided: Political Partisanship and US Foreign Policy.* Chicago: Chicago Council on Global Affairs.

Smith, James A. 1991. *The Idea Brokers.* New York: Free Press.

Smith, Rogers. 2015. "Political Science and the Public Sphere Today." *Perspectives on Politics* 13 (June): 366–376.

Snyder, Jack. 2003. "Imperial Temptations," *The National Interest* 71 (Spring): 29–40.

Sowell, Thomas. 2009. *Intellectuals and Society.* New York: Basic Books.

Steel, Ronald. 1980. *Walter Lippmann and the American Century.* Boston: Little, Brown.

Sunstein, Cass. 2009. *Republic.com 2.0.* Princeton, NJ: Princeton University Press.

Tai, Zixue, and Tsan-Kuo Chanfe. 2002. "The Global News and the Pictures in their Heads." *Gazette: The International Journal For Communications Studies* 64 (June): 251–265.

Teles, Stephen. 2008. *The Rise of the Conservative Legal Movement.* Princeton, NJ: Princeton University Press.

Teles, Stephen. 2016. "Foundations, Organizational Maintenance, and Partisan Asymmetry." *PS: Political Science and Politics* 49 (July): 455–460.

Teles, Stephen, Heather Hurlburt, and Mark Schmitt. 2014. "Philanthropy in a Time of Polarization." *Stanford Social Innovation Review* 12 (Summer).

Tetlock, Philip. 2009. "Reading Tarot on K Street." *The National Interest* 103 (September/October): 57–67.

Tetlock, Philip, and Dan Gardner. 2015. *Superforecasters: The Art and Science of Prediction.* New York: Crown Books.

Thaler, Richard H. 2015. *Misbehaving: The Making of Behavioral Economics.* New York: W. W. Norton.

Timberg, Craig. 2015. *Culture Crash: The Killing of the Creative Class.* New Haven, CT: Yale University Press.

Troy, Tevi. 2012. "Devaluing the Think Tank." *National Affairs* 10 (Winter): 75–90.

Vavreck, Lynn, and Steve Friess. 2015. "An Interview with Lynn Vavreck." *PS: Political Science and Politics* 48 (September): 43–46.

Walt, Stephen M. 2005. "The Relationship between Theory and Policy in International Relations." *Annual Review of Political Science* 8: 23–48.

Walt, Stephen M. 2012. "Theory and Policy in International Relations: Some Personal Reflections." *Yale Journal of International Affairs* 7 (September): 33–43.

Waltz, Kenneth. 1979. *Theory of International Politics.* New York: McGraw Hill.

West, Darrell. 2014. *Billionaires: Reflections on the Upper Crust.* Washington, DC: Brookings Institution Press.

Wilson, Ernest J. 2007. "Is There Really a Scholar-Practitioner Gap? An Institutional Analysis." *PS: Political Science and Politics* 40 (January): 147–151.

Yarhi-Milo, Keren. 2014. *Knowing the Adversary: Leaders, Intelligence, and Assessment of Intentions in International Relations.* Princeton, NJ: Princeton University Press.

Zakaria, Fareed. 1997. "The Rise of Illiberal Democracy." *Foreign Affairs* 76 (November/December): 22–43.

Zakaria, Fareed. 2003. The Future of Freedom: *Illiberal Democracy at Home and Abroad.* New York: W.W. Norton.

INDEX

———❖———